THE HUMAN JOURNEY

The Human Journey

Reginald Paget

DAVIS-POYNTER

London

TO MY WIFE

First published in 1979 by
Davis-Poynter Limited
20 Garrick Street WC2E 9BJ

Copyright © 1979 by Reginald Paget

ISBN 0 7067 0231 X

Printed in Great Britain by
Clarke, Doble & Brendon Ltd
Plymouth and London

CONTENTS

AUTHOR'S NOTE

The idea of this book came on a sailing weekend with John Strachey, Kenneth Younger and Harold Lever, during which we discussed the role of instinct in political economy. I drafted a note on our theme and put it aside for some years, until Peter Jay came across it, said 'You must make this into a book', and introduced me to Peter Grose of Curtis Brown. I had decided to retire from the House of Commons and after a little prodding became absorbed.

I soon came to wish that I had been born in a more leisurely age, when a book could run to a dozen volumes. Mine had to make do with chapters. Even then it proved to be far too long—about 220,000 words, not counting a volume of notes and a bibliography in which I had referred to 173 books. Then came the painful process of pruning. The notes and the bibliography went. The text was stripped of fascinating information which I had come upon in my researches, but which was not strictly relevant to my theme. During my long political life the one speech I never heard was the speech that was too short. The same may well be true of books. My book, for all its surgery, is probably still too long, but should it prove popular I retain the hope of a later expanded edition.

I would like to thank my friends Professors David Balm and Robert Nield, Tony Halsbury, Julian Amery and my brother John Paget who over a period of four years have read and annotated these chapters as they came along and Professors Carleton Coon, Eysenck and Biesheuvel who with great kindness advised me as to certain chapters. All were patient.

I

ORIGINS

What my book is about

IN THIS BOOK I have sought to illustrate a theme. It is that man is a social animal and that he cannot be human in isolation. His evolution has been social as well as biological. His social needs go back hundreds of thousands of years. He looks to society as he looked to the pack, for identity, for stimulation, for security and for love. Moral philosophy has ignored these animal needs of social man. Society is not a rational arrangement come to by reasonable beings; it never has been and it never will be. Society is a hit-and-miss association that has grown as man has multiplied; its purpose is both to satisfy and to control instincts deeply rooted in heredity and emotions that are largely irrational. Control or, if you prefer it, repression grows as society grows. No two societies are ever the same, for each is based on its own experience and on balances between contending pressures, claims and compliances for which time has won acceptance. Rationalist philosophers from Plato onwards have sought rational solutions for difficulties that were essentially irrational, and in the process have done much mischief, for they have in the name of reason, upset established balances. I shall argue that many of our present troubles have resulted from a failure to recognise man's animal needs, and to respect the compromises that he has ground out of his social history.

The basic units of human society have been two: the family and the hunting party. The family was the domain of the woman, she brought up the children and looked after the camp; the hunting party was male and rarely if ever numbered more than eleven. These units sufficed for about 95 per cent of man's existence as a fully evolved *homo sapiens* and probably for some million years before that. It is only in the last 10,000 years that, with the coming of agriculture, man has tried to fit himself into larger units.

Tribal society came first. It started as a loose association of families and bands for occasional cooperation. It was not concerned with government. The units assembled for dancing, for ceremonial or for a hunt. The limit was about 500, which is probably about as many people as a man can know personally. With the emergence of the Chief, the tribe became an entity; the city and the nation followed. These larger entities were not natural to man. They were concerned with government and with change.

The families and the hunting groups had evolved as natural units and required little more in the way of coercion than a beehive or an anthill. Coherence was instinctive. Links were personal and public opinion sufficed. The enlarged societies needed new and stronger bonds. They were bound by fear and force and faith. I have sought to look through world history for examples of how the links of the greater societies evolved, worked and decayed. Fear came first. Tribes united because they were afraid. The Hebrews chose a King because they feared the Philistines. War has been a great uniter. Force followed. Public opinion governed the tribe. The Chief and the King, the city and the state needed force, criminal law and police power. Faith became ever more necessary. It had always been important. The safety of the baboon tribe depends on the willingness of its strongest males to turn and die that the tribe may live. The larger the unit the greater the faith that men must have in that which holds them together, be it a flag, an idol, an anthem, a god, a king, a prophet or an ideal. Above all, societies to survive must have faith in their own virtue. It matters little how irrational that faith may be, with it cities, states and nations are alive, creative and potent; without it they decay and are conquered.

Nations are complicated and difficult societies. They do not come ready made. They emerge from the struggles of disparate interests; they are hammered together by their foes and linked by their fears. A state, any state, is a great and precious achievement for it sires faith. The healthy state is a deity. Britannia, *La France*, The Star-Spangled Banner, Mother Russia, The Fatherland, have all been gods, for they have received devotion and given faith; but as is the way with gods, they retain their divinity only so long as they retain the faith of their worshippers.

The bricks that go to the building of a state are the families and the hunting bands. If the bricks disintegrate the building falls. The family depends on the woman, for home is where Mum is. I have looked in vain in world history for a society that has survived woman's emancipation from the home. The hunting band is the all-male group that sets out to provide. Hunting has become work, the forest and the savannah have become the factory and the office, but we are finding more and more that a society is in trouble when it fails to provide men with the opportunity to go out and work in their natural groupings.

Religions and political faiths are sometimes uniting, and within the definitions I have used, social, and sometimes disruptive or anti-social. Sometimes they are a bit of both.

The social importance of religion has depended not at all upon the credibility of its dogma, little on the validity of its ethic, a great deal upon its capacity to unite emotions behind the group interest of the day and age. Any religion can be equipped with any ethic. Christianity inspired the rapacity of the Conquistadores, the martial fury of the Puritans, the sadistic racialism of the Inquisition, the acquisitive greed of the mill owners and the total service of a Mother Theresa. Quietist Buddhism has been drafted into the lethal struggles of South-East Asia. Political faiths are not very different. 'Liberty, Equality and Fraternity', 'Free Trade', 'Liberalism', 'Socialism', 'Communism'—all lost their meanings long before they could be put into practice, but this is not to deny their importance, for each in its turn generated faith and through faith, will and power. Conflict is the stuff of creation, and the ideals of the contestants are involved in each new balance that forms a deceptively stable looking step in the eternally dynamic life of an evolving society. In retrospect political ideals have proved more effective in upsetting old balances than in guiding new ones.

I have tried to follow some of the faiths that have moved mankind.

The faith that led man from the static security of the tribe into the dynamic society of the city was the worship of a god-king. This happened in all the five original societies: Sumeria, Egypt, China, Central America and Southern America. All had a tradition that the god-king came from a far off land. Within these states men had faith in a divine, centralised revelation, a certainty that was their guide. Authority and revelation became implanted in their social evolution. The god-king empires of China and Russia accept the Communist revelation and Marx is their prophet. The Middle East accepts the revelation of Mohammed. All need centralised total authority. I have tried to show that the transition from divine to Communist autocracy in China and Russia came naturally and logically. I have contrasted them with India where no uniting faith emerged until a British orientated middle class adopted nationalism.

In Greece and Japan man moved out of tribalism by a different route. Theirs were essentially mongrel civilisations. Invaders married and ruled indigenous populations. There was no single authority. Rights and duties were divided. Law rather than authority became the basis of society; liberty rather than adoration became the fashionable emotion. A system of balanced rights and obligations which we call feudalism, emerged and this through a variety of stages developed into some sort of social democracy. A different social evolution had resulted in a different kind of people with different social needs.

I have tried to trace the faiths that built up the city states of Greece and the republican empire of Rome to the point where Rome split. Byzantium was the successor of the empires of Sumeria, Akkad, Babylon, Persia and Macedonia. Her people had evolved within the idea of divine kingship and a central authority that provided all the answers. The west was far more complicated. The republican ideas of Greece and Rome were not quite dead. The invaders were the same people who as Dorians had founded the city states of Greece. Christianity, which in the East had proved a social force and had been converted into a department of state proved in the West, on balance, to be an anti-social force in conflict with the development of Western society.

In a later chapter on 'The Catholic West' I have tried to describe this dichotomy. Neither the civilisation of Greece and Rome nor the tribalism of Germany had conditioned man to accept the idea of a single, supreme revelation, to which the Church was dedicated. The result was a conflict between the states that Romanised German conquerors tried to build on Roman foundations and a Church, essentially Eastern, that strove for supreme authority. A stalemate which we call the Dark and Middle Ages, or sometimes the Age of Faith followed. This faith was not of this world. It was a faith in dying rather than in living. It could on occasions, as in the Crusades, inspire feats of sterile heroism that strain credulity, but it could not inspire social advance for it rejected the virtue of human society. For a thousand years it held Western civilisation in a trance. Then came the break. In the section in Chapter 11 on 'Renaissance, Reformation and Counter Reformation' I have described both the astonishing violence that resulted from the rejection of an established ethic and the bounding creativity which that conflict released before religion was replaced by reason as the relevant ethic that guided the West.

Reason released the tension, but it failed to provide the dynamism which Western man demanded. There emerged a new dichotomy. The cult of the individual and the cult of the nation. This found expression in the Age of Revolution, and in the nineteenth and twentieth centuries the rise of the nation states and of the colonial empires.

I have looked at societies where no idea or faith emerged that was strong enough to lift man out of his tribal niche. Africa is an example. Colonialism presented Africa with the framework of a Western society, but her social evolution had not provided her people with the qualities necessary for that form of society. Her new states seem to be breaking down and her reversion to tribalism can probably only be checked by a new colonialism, which will probably be Russian.

I have looked at the artificial states, states that have not grown but have been created by external authorities, the ex-provinces of empires, Austrian, Turkish, British, French and Belgian. They have not in general proved to be very satisfactory states. A successful state achieves its own balances and invents its own faith. Successor states have seldom had this opportunity. It is very rare indeed for one state to be able to take over ready-made institutions from another. I have looked at the supra-national institutions that have not grown but have been superimposed on the groupings that man has evolved, and I have looked with sadness, for I find that such institutions serve only to subtract from the real authority that human groupings must possess. Authority is the business of the state and must be strong enough to contain the state's internal antagonisms. Liberal ideas are luxuries in which only strong and established states can indulge, and they will do so in moderation if they wish to survive. States that become ungovernable fall apart. Statecraft involves the subordination of rights, privileges and liberties to an overriding duty of service. The state needs the faith of the citizen. Neither loyalty nor sovereignty can be satifactorily shared.

All this the West has forgotten. The cult of the individual has destroyed the extended family and sapped the mystique of the nation. Public service is neglected and denigrated. Politicians are rated as lazy rogues. Parliaments have lost respect. Authority, whether it be of God, of parents, of employers, of trade unions, of morals, or of law, has been rejected. The Liberal Age has found its contradiction and looks like being destroyed, for men cannot hold together at the level of disunity that the West is displaying.

Our hope lies in finding a new synthesis and a new faith. I have tried to express this need, not very hopefully, before it is too late.

Human Origins

Today we know as plainly as we can know anything that we we are descended from apes. We still do not know just how or when we became human; but at some time the primates divided, some to become man and some to become apes. That division occurred not less than eighteen million years ago.

This we know because the bones of a hominid, as we call the man-becoming branch of the primates, has been found in a strata that can be so dated. Some two million years ago these hominids were making crude stone tools and wielding bone weapons. *Australopithecus afrikanus*, the man ape from whom we may have descended, was a hunter, killing beasts far larger and stronger than himself. He could not have done this without organisation and means of communication. He continued for some millions of years. About 250,000 years ago *homo sapiens*, the big brained creature, began to appear. We do not know how or when he got his brain and with it the physical capacity to be a human being. We do know that for hundreds of thousands of years he made very little use of his big brain and that he lived and behaved in much the same way as the small brained hominids had done before him. Some 25,000 years ago, this creature, *homo sapiens*, started activities which no animal would indulge in. He painted his caves; he developed an art form that achieved great brilliance, as is shown in the caves of Lascaux; his pictures evidenced religious and ritualistic activities; his hunting became a large-scale communal activity. But some 15,000 years had still to elapse before somewhere in ancient Sumeria or maybe at Jericho, he achieved his first civilisation, and by civilisation I mean a balanced and stratified urban society. Why, when man's potential is so ancient, has his advance been so slow? The answer would seem to be that biological evolution is not enough. Man had to evolve socially before he became human.

Kipling invented Mowgli, the boy who was brought up by the wolves and grew to splendid manhood. In the 1930's two children were found in India who had actually been fostered from babyhood by wolves. They were not at all like Mowgli; they ran on all fours, they snarled and they howled; they were wolves. By our standards they proved incurably insane and did not long survive life in human conditions. They had lacked the society necessary to make them human. So, too, for some hundreds of thousands of years, did the creatures with human potential, whose bones we have discovered. Thomas Jefferson when drafting the American Declaration of Independence declared: 'We hold these truths to be self-evident that all men are created equal, that they are endowed by their creator with certain inalienable rights, that among these are life, liberty and the pursuit of happiness.' Nothing could be less true. Man, the risen ape, is born without obligations, rights, or knowledge of good or evil. He becomes human only as he enters a human society. He never can be free for he is involved in a pattern of social obligations. His rights can never be individual, they arise out of the social system within which he lives. He is human only as a unit of society, his virtues are social virtues, his vices are social vices and his personality is a social adjustment. Independent existence is available only to the psychopath. Society is not merely a conglomeration of individuals, it is a condition of humanity without which none can be human.

Society is no human monopoly. It exists often in a far more perfect state among insects, birds and animals. The problems of human society arise from the wider play of individual and collective choice. In insect society choice plays very little part. Eugene Marais described the termitary of the white ants as a sort of anchored animal in which the workers and the soldiers performed the role of the red and white corpuscles of the blood, the fungus gardens served as a stomach and the queen as the brain. Each ant in the community has the same sort of independence as my finger, just occasionally it may twitch, but otherwise it moves as the centre directs.

In 1956 I went on a Parliamentary visit to Kenya and asked to see the Nairobi Museum. I was received at about 9.30 in the morning by Dr L. S. B. Leakey; we parted at five o'clock next morning. Ever since that wonderful day I have been fascinated by origins. Amongst the things he showed me was an insect flower. It was shaped like a lupin, the tip was green and passing through a gradation of yellow, the body of the flower was a pinkish apricot colour. Each petal was the wing of a very small butterfly. When this colony settled on a twig they always sorted themselves into this order. How did they know? There is no natural flower to suggest this camouflage. Dr Leakey watched the hatching. Did the greens perhaps hatch first and so assume the leadership in settling? No. The proportion of green, yellow and pink was constant but the order of hatching, quite random. Nor did there seem to be any order in the settling. The flower was not formed from the tip downwards nor from the base upwards, each fly took its place in random order. How did they know? Camouflage is a common insect device. The stick-bug imitates a stick. The leaf-moth has the veins of a leaf. A caterpillar has markings resembling a savage face. This, one can understand. The bugs that were mistaken for something less edible tended to survive and passed on their disguise, but the origins of the group flower camouflage of the flattid bug are harder to imagine.

A swarm of bees settles. Scouts fly out in all directions to find new foraging grounds. Each returns and makes his report. He does so by a dance. That dance indicates the distance, the direction, and, by the measure of its enthusiasm, an assessment of desirability. This is a marvellous thing to happen. No animal save man and, just possibly, the dolphin can use language in this manner to make a report and a proposal. The baboon scout screams as he sees, the watchdog barks; neither can come and tell what he has seen. What happens next is even more marvellous. The swarm sees the reports and recommendations and it chooses; it chooses as a body and the whole swarm flies off to the chosen place. To each bee the choice, as is the case with all his choices, is resolved by an inevitable and certain answer, but how is the choice made? The religion of an insect society is totally acceptable. There are no heretics, every bee and every ant has inherited all the answers and knows all the responses; there is nothing to question; each is driven to social virtue by inner compulsion, and frustration induces a nervous breakdown that soon proves fatal. The insect has little to learn for he is born knowing almost everything he will ever have to know. His society is 300 million years older than ours.

When we come to birds education begins to play a part, though only sometimes. The weaver bird is a tiny African finch that weaves grass into a coconut shaped nest and hangs it on a twig in a harness of hair tied with special and characteristic knots. Marais hatched weaver birds under canaries and denied them access to their building material for five generations, but the great-great-grandchildren of the last weaver to make a nest made the same nest and tied it with the same knots as those used by his ancestors. Nest-making and knot-tying was knowledge built into his genes and required no education. For some birds song is instinctive. They may be hatched out under foster-parents, they may be brought up in soundproof boxes, but they still sing as their natural parents sang. With some other species song has to be learnt. When separated from their natural parents they sing an imitation of their foster-parents' song. Some birds sing a mixture of their natural song and their foster-parents' song; some learn by imitation; you cannot breed a parrot to say 'pretty polly'. Jackdaws, and indeed most social birds, have a lot to learn. Konrad Lorenz studied a colony of jackdaws. He found that the jackdaw chicks had no instinctive recognition of their enemies. They showed no fear of an approaching cat or of the shadow of a hawk. They had to be told and they were told by the danger cry of the older birds. Each generation passed on its experience of new dangers, and this experience gave better protection than any individual instinct. The fly never learns about the flypaper, but the baby jackdaw chick learns about creatures carrying dead jackdaws. When Lorenz carried black bathing drawers he was set upon by his own colony and would have lost all the confidence he had built had he not promptly thrown away the offensive garment. The summons to attack a creature taking dead jackdaws is quite different from the warning cry to get away from a man carrying a gun. Each needs learning. Jackdaw social order also has to be learned. It is a hierarchy. As in the Conservative Party of old, a leader emerges and so does a No 2 and a No 3 right down until everyone knows his place, the hens taking the precedence of their husbands. It is an order that must be learned, but one in which individual decision has a very limited role. Couples pair for life, and the order once established is very rarely challenged, but just occasionally there is a scandal. Somebody commits adultery or goes off and joins another group. This involves a break with instinct and nascent free will.

Sex is assumed to be instinctive but this is not always so. My wife brought up a pheasant chick that hatched on the shelf over our Aga stove. He grew into a very fine cock bird but he would pay no attention to hens. His courtship ritual was reserved for females of the human species. To women he displayed and dropped his wing and he savaged women's legs.

He treated men as pals. He was wholly unafraid and was always ready to come for a walk when invited. We only saw him fly once when startled by a dog, otherwise he regarded flying as an undignified means of progress. He thought of himself as a person and he walked as a person. Konrad Lorenz had a similar experience with a jackdaw that was brought up by hand. On the other hand Otto Koehler reports that rats brought up by hand, who have never seen their own species, upon being introduced to a female rat in season behaved just as any other rat would, although they paid no attention to the females of any other species.

In animal society the role of choice becomes wider. All young animals require education. They are born with far more built-in knowledge than human babies, but they still need to learn. Instinct plays a great, indeed a dominant, part in their nature but they need a parent to show them how. Animal society is less automatic and more variable. It includes an element of uncertain muddle. Indeed there is much in the societies of the higher primates that is reminiscent of our own. Marais' account of the baboon pack with which he lived for three years reminded me greatly of the Leicestershire of my youth. There, the 'pack' was run by three elderly male baboons who between themselves recognised an order in terms of courtesy rather than force and who never quarrelled. They had a high sense of social responsibility. They were neither bossy nor interfering, but they intervened when family quarrels looked like getting out of hand. They saw to it that the young were not bullied and that the old and sick were cared for. Our three top baboons were Sir Arthur Hazlerigg, Colonel Martin and Mr Pochin. Between them they held the chairmanships and vice-chairmanships of the County Council, the Quarter Sessions and the Cricket Club. When I joined the Labour Party there was a great family row. My father declared, rather publicly, that he would never speak to me again. Then, at his house arrived a landaulet car driven by a chauffeur who had plainly once been a coachman. It contained Sir Arthur Hazlerigg. He explained to my father that family rows over politics were bad for the County; that young men must be allowed their own political ideas; with more experience they would settle down. The top baboon had spoken and my father, as a lesser baboon, accepted it. Peace was restored in our family. In the end, I suppose, I settled down.

Social animals are certainly capable of altruism. Marais records an incident where two baboons attacked a leopard, thereby sacrificing their lives in order to save the pack. There are many accounts of baboons carrying away a wounded member at great risk to themselves. There are accounts, too, of similar conduct by elephants and dolphins, perhaps the cleverest of all the mammals save man.

In human society, choice plays an ever-increasing role. It is this fact that has made possible over the last 10,000 years man's astonishing acceleration in social achievement, but it is still a choice limited by man's nature. Our trouble may be that our choice has lost touch with our nature and that ethical and political adventurousness has led us to build societies that are in conflict with our emotions. Animal societies do not have this difficulty. Rules, or maybe we should call it the religion of the pack, are accepted without question: each member knows what is right and what is wrong, each accepts his duty and his niche without question; there is no occasion for change in this order.

Man's early tribal society was not very different. We do not know how it arose, we may have been tribal before we were men. The small brained hominid, who may be our ancestor, was almost certainly a co-operative hunter, and since he was neither fast nor strong he could hardly have survived save as a pack animal. Our direct knowledge of early man is limited to his bones, his chipped stone tools and the ashes of his fires, but to this we can add our knowledge of tribes in many parts of the world whose cultures seem to have altered little if at all, since they became men, and of those other primates, the baboon, the gorilla and the monkey, whose instincts, passions, ways of living and tribal customs have been watched in the wild by devoted zoologists. We know quite a bit about heredity and how the characteristics of living things are settled at conception, and we know something of brain surgery, how physical injury can change a man's whole character and personality, in short, can turn a good man into a bad one.

This new knowledge in a range of new fields combines to

impose certain conclusions: man is an animal; his society has evolved as his body has evolved; he is special only in the sense that every other species is special; he lives while he lives and dies when he dies; he is lumbered with a nature which you may call a parcel of instincts and desires or, if you prefer it, a soul, and with this he must live. This nature is far wider than the sex drive analysed by Freud, for the primates, of which man is one, have many natural desires other than sex. Some of these instinctive desires may be listed—we shall probably in some degree recognise them in ourselves.

1. *The desire for primacy*
This would appear to be both the strongest and most universal of primate instincts. Each individual feels a compulsion to establish and maintain a status and to win recognition for his identity.

2. *The pack interest*
The need to love and hate as a group – the partisan passion.

3. *The hunting instinct*
The desire to pursue, capture and kill. Few who have taken part in a hunt have escaped the wild excitement which surges through man as a hound opens in covert or as a rat bolts from his hole. I was once at a meeting of the Kipsigis tribe in Kenya. They had been up to no good and the District Commissioner was giving them a dressing down and threatening fines when a little Duiker gazelle jumped up. The whole tribe leapt up and was off in pursuit leaving the DC and myself alone at our table. After catching the Duiker they returned in ones and twos, looking very sheepish. The instinct to hunt had been too strong for their manners.

4. *The feeling for arms*
Arms gave man and probably pre-man his power, strength and authority. It is no accident that the US constitution guarantees the right to keep and bear arms or that the effort or expense devoted to develop ever more ingenious weapons produces such pride and pleasure.

5. *Territory*
Not all primates are territorial and the evidence that our ancestors were a territorial branch of the primates is shaky. Indeed the best evidence that he was territorial is probably the intensity of our own feelings for a house or a bit of land we own. One of the great problems which municipal authorities have met turns on just this. An owner-occupier will go to the

greatest trouble and expense to improve his house and garden. A tenant, however secure and advantageous his tenancy may be, will not.

6. *Aggression*
Instinctive antipathy to any not of our pack or race or nation or football club.

2

TRIBES

WE DO NOT KNOW when or how society started. Neither among the insects, nor the birds, nor the fish, nor the animals nor among men have we seen a society start. By the time we meet societies each has achieved its own peculiar complicated balance—the equilibrium that enables it to continue. Social evolution has one notable advantage over biological evolution. Acquired characteristics are heritable for the culture, the skills and the learning of one generation pass on to another. It has a built in acceleration for the more that has been learned, the more there is to pass on.

Human society has been evolving for hundreds of thousands of years. It has comprised men at different levels of biological evolution. It has followed many paths. It contains a constellation of customs. It has achieved an acceleration that may well be getting out of control.

We are descended from a small running hunting ape. How was his pack organised? When he started to make tools and use weapons, did the new technology change the order of his pack? Was there any deviation in function? Did the males hunt and the females gather and care for the young? Were there family units that coalesced to form the pack?

We shall never know. No living ape has learned to make tools or has reached that stage in social organisation at which functions are divided. It is clear, however, that at some point between ape and man a new kind of society became necessary.

The change was gradual. The running ape first appeared in Southern Africa. New discoveries of old bones keep putting the date further back. Gradually he spread to China, Java, India and Europe; gradually he evolved to become *homo erectus*, the pre-man with the small brain. Pre-man divided into sub-species or races, Mongoloid, Caucasoid, Australoid probably Capoid (Bushman and Hottentot) and possibly Congoid, and within each race the new cranial form and enlarged brain continued to evolve independently. The threshold between *erectus* and *sapiens* is arbitrary. The process of change was gradual and in some of the more primitive tribes is probably still incomplete.

By the beginning of the Pleistocene age, perhaps one and a half million years ago, the man-becoming ape had spread from his African home to occupy most of the old world and in the process had become more and more like man. Some very early fossil men were found in 1937 some thirty miles south of Peking in a cave at Choukoutien. They had been a meal. Père Teilhard de Chardin worked in these caves for ten years on these early men whom Weidenreich had named *Sinanthropus pekinensis*. The publication of his work created difficulties with mother church and his efforts to reconcile his scientific findings with Catholic orthodoxy contained astonishing subtleties that were to prove more acceptable to him than to his spiritual masters, but the bones spoke for themselves.

They were the remains of some forty individuals. The skulls were broken at the bottom to extract brains and the bones were cracked to get the marrow, and they were 360,000 years old. They had been killed and eaten by their own kind. With the bones were found crude stone tools, the remains of many other animals, charcoal from fires and cherry stones. This tool-using, fire-using creature was getting near to being a man, and what is more to be a chinaman for his bones already showed the characteristics of the Mongoloid race. The volume of his brain cavity lay between 915 and 1,225 cc. We classify him as *homo erectus*. His brain had to grow by about 300 cc before he became *homo sapiens*. This took 100,000 years or perhaps a little more. We have a sequence of fossil bones that lead to the first Mongoloid *homo sapiens* who lived about a quarter of a million years ago. The Mongoloids spread over China and Japan, and some 20,000 years ago they entered and occupied the Americas. They mixed with Australoids in Indonesia and with Caucasoids from India and Burma.

Pithecanthropus, the ancestor of the old Australians, is earlier than *Sinanthropus*. He was found in Java and is, perhaps, half a million years old. His evolution, which we can trace in Java through Solo man (about 150,000 years old) and Wadjak man (about 50,000 years old) was much slower than *Sinanthropus* and the first Australoid *homo sapiens* is only 38,000 years old.

China's *Sinanthropus* was physically more evolved than Java's Solo man who was 200,000 years the younger, and to judge by his tools and by his use of fire his technology was also more advanced. This illustrates the different rate of evolution in mankind to be found in different surroundings and among different races.

We whites, or to express it more accurately, Caucasoids, since our race covers the whole range of colour from white to very nearly black, have yet to identify our earliest *erectus* ancestor. In Europe the candidates include the possessor of the Heidelburg jaw, the occipital bone from Vertesszollos in Hungary, the Arago face in south-western France and two skulls (the cranial capacity of which can be measured) one from Souard in south-western France (1,063 cc) and the other from Petralona in Greece (1,220 cc). All these were probably contemporaries of *Sinanthropus*.

We then jump some 150,000 years to Swanscombe man found in the Thames just below London, and Steinham man found in Germany; both are undoubtedly *sapiens*. This branch of *homo sapiens* inhabited Europe until the last Ice Age, 75,000 years ago.

Evolution then seemed to take a step backwards for there appeared the more brutal-looking Neanderthal man. This impression results in part from the fact that Marcellin Boule, who described a nearly complete Neanderthal, unearthed at La Chapelle-aux-Saints in the Dordogne country, as a shambling ape-man with bent knees and hands that trailed the ground, had failed to observe that the poor chap had been crippled and bent by arthritis. Neanderthal man, who appeared both in Europe and in the Middle East, walked as straight as we do, he had short legs and arms, a long thick body, a very large nose, protruding jaw and heavy brow ridges. His shape was probably the result of adaptation to the Ice Age cold in close breeding communities. We know that he looked after the old arthritic of La Chapelle-aux-Saints long after he was incapable of looking after himself, and we know that the Neanderthals were capable of surgery, for in the Shanidar Cave in Iraq we have found one whose withered arm had been amputated above the elbow years before his death. The Neanderthals disappeared between 40,000 and 30,000 years ago when, during a warm intermission, they probably shed their Ice Age specialisation within the wider breeding groups that became available as their world became more open and less hostile. They were certainly *homo sapiens* and probably occupied a place in our family tree.

The ancestors of the Bushman and Hottentots lived in Northern Africa. They were then a full-sized people. In about 12,000 BC they were driven south by Caucasoid invaders, the ancestors of the modern Berbers. They moved down the eastern highlands where the Hottentot branch acquired cattle and perhaps some intermixture of genes from the Hamitic Caucasians who drove them on. They arrived in their present South African home about 7,000 years ago. We do not know when the Capoids became *homo sapiens* and we have not identified any *homo erectus* ancestor.

This brings us to the Congoids, or Negroids. They are the late-comers. We know of no evolved Negro skull that can be firmly dated before 13,000 BC. Dr Leakey has found in Olduvai Gorge in Tanganyika bones of an *erectus* that lived something like 400,000 years ago. Rhodesian man, whose nearly complete skeleton was found in a mine shaft, was still in the erectus stage of evolution, a mere 40,000 years ago. He was a strong heavy creature standing about 5 foot 10 inches, with legs and sacrum that could be mistaken for those of a modern Negro, but his skull was very ape-like indeed, the brow ridges were huge, the forehead nearly horizontal, the eye-sockets big and square-rimmed, and the face very long and flat.

Rhodesian man possessed some Negro features but we have no fossil link between him and the modern Negro. Professor

Carlton Coon believes that he sired the Pygmies. A change of weather made the high veldt much colder, and that the negro is a cross between Pygmy and Caucasian. Cold may have driven Rhodesian man to the warmer north. There he found the forests which, in those days, stretched from Liberia to Ruanda. Dwarf stature had great survival advantages. M. Gusinde in his work on the Pygmies, has shown how perfectly adapted they are to the dark damp sour-smelling selva where they live in constant warm humidity. The European and the Negro have difficulty in getting through the forest, but the little men glide through, jumping and running, sometimes on the ground and sometimes in the branches. Before the dawn of history the Pygmies were the sole inhabitants of the rain forests. Some 10,000 or 12,000 years ago Pygmies must have met parties of African Caucasoids moving south, and these parties perhaps as a result of desert formation, may have been cut off as the Caucasoid Ainus were cut off in Japan. Isolated parties took Pygmy women, as the Negroes living on the edge of the forests do today. This results in a one-way flow of genes as Pygmy women move into the relative comfort of Negro villages, but no Negro women move into the forests where they could not survive. These isolated bands would have formed tight breeding units, ideal for fixing a cross.

Herodotus (450 BC) tells us of the circumnavigation of Africa (600 BC). South of the Equator the navigators said they met only Pygmies. Herodotus disbelieved them for they also said they had seen the sun in the north, and this he deemed a traveller's tale! Earlier still, a Pharaoh of the Old Kingdom (*circa* 2,400 BC) instructed the leader of an expedition to the far south to bring him a Pygmy dancer. This is long before our first account of a Negro, for the Negro is not depicted in Egypt before the New Kingdom (1,550 BC).

When I met Dr Leakey he told me that the Negroes had only arrived in Africa some 5,000 or 6,000 years ago, and that they had come from India by canoe and had travelled up the African rivers. I think it is perhaps more likely that Indonesians who came up the rivers brought to the Negroes, who were then evolving in the Congo Basin, Asiatic seeds and the knowledge of how to smelt iron, and that the consequent increase in food supply resulted in a population explosion that brought the Negro bursting out of the forest glades into the pages of history.

This theory—and it is no more than a theory which may be overturned at any time by the discovery of fossil Negro bones—is supported by the following facts:

The Negro shares with the Pygmy the sickle blood cell that guards against malaria, and it is from the Pygmy that he almost certainly obtained it. Pygmies and Negroes alone suffer from a skin hernia in which both the intestine and the lining of the abdominal wall protrudes outwards making the con- dition harmless. In all measurable and observable character- istics save size the Negro is intermediate between the Pygmy and the African Caucasoid. The Negro is loose-jointed com- pared with the European, the Pygmy more so; the Negro exudes a characteristic body smell, the Pygmy exudes the same odour but much stronger; the Negro has the blood groups of the Pygmy plus some others of his own; Negroes have a slower heartbeat than Europeans, Pygmies have an even slower heartbeat.

Caucasoid, Mongoloid, Negroid, Australoid and Capoid are all sub-species of the species *homo sapiens*.

Racialism has become such a bad word that it banishes rational discussion; and one scarcely dare suggest that races differ in more than pigmentation They have evolved on differ- ent time scales in different climates with different needs and in environments that make different qualities into positive and negative survival factors. If in these circumstances the genetic basis to the intellectual and nervous capacity of the differently evolved groups proved to be identical, I would believe in God, for I would be in the presence of a miracle that defied all scientific explanation.

It is silly to claim superiority but absurd to deny difference. We should instead study the differences. We are inhibited from doing so by a reversion to mediævalism. Once again we are faced with the conflict between the truth of observation and the truth of revelation. The truth of revelation tells us that all men are created equal, the truth of observation tells us they obviously are not.

An objective or scientific approach to the question of race

has not been encouraged by the leaders of liberal culture. Professor Shrockley, a holder of a Nobel Prize for Physics, has been deprived of his honorary degree by Leeds University as a punishment for racial heresy, and Professor Eysenck has been assaulted by the students of the London School of Economics behaving like Coptic monks who had viewed a stoic philosopher, but for my part I shall stick to the truth of observation and state the evidence to the best of my ability.

Firstly as to genetic, heritable differences. Races do not differ only as to the colours of their skins. Races have different skull shapes and different skeletons. It does not take many bones to enable Scotland Yard to identify the race to which the deceased belonged.

Races smell different. The smells of the Caucasoids, the Negroids, the Australoids and the Pygmies are different and offensive to each other and all are offensive to the Mongoloids, who scarcely smell at all.

Races differ in their aptitudes and capacities, for these qualities are heritable just as the sheep-dog's aptitude for herding, the pointer's aptitude for setting game and the hound's aptitude for working a line, are heritable.

Men differ in intelligence, in judgement, in application and in moral qualities, kindness and cruelty, generosity and meanness, loving warmth and coldness, courage and cowardice, self control and licentiousness, honesty and criminality. These are all qualities that we can recognise, even if we find them hard to measure. They all depend in part on environment and training and in part on heredity. It would be odd indeed if they were identically distributed amongst races that had evolved so differently, or if the social organisations that suited one race were to suit another race equally well. Man's genius does not lie in his equality but in his variety.

The unit that is common to all societies is the family, founded upon what Desmond Morris calls the pair bond. Man is the most sexual of all creatures. He does not have to wait for his partner to be on heat. She can always receive him and she can enjoy orgasm. Why has this happened?

Morris believes it developed as man became a hunter. The sex life of a vegetarian primate is quite different, copulation is confined to a short period of ovulation, and is over in a matter of seconds without any apparent sexual satisfaction to the female. The dominant male attends to all the females of the group and the young males are driven away. But hunting required a different system, for the male hunting group had to trust each other. They could not afford much in the way of sexual jealousy. They depended on brain and the big brain took longer and longer to mature. The female had to stay at home. She not only had to suckle but she had to bring up the children. The single dominant male did not fit into this evolving group: the woman needed a husband and the husband needed a wife. Evolution is a slow process.

Pair bonding has involved physical changes that have taken many thousands of years and are unique amongst primates. Human courtship is prolonged. The hymen protects the immature female in child play until courtship has reached the point at which pain is acceptable. She can receive her lover when she is not ovulating and when she is pregnant, when in fact copulation has no evolutionary function other than to cement the pair bond. As the *News of the World* tells us every week this pair bond is by no means perfect or complete, but it still remains true that amongst humans promiscuity is the aberration and that natural sex involves an emotional link special to lovers and a deeply shared enjoyment.

The woman looked after the camp, gathered roots and berries, and ruled the children. When the hunter came home he not only resumed the pair bond but he got to know the children. They did not have to be driven away because so long as the pair bond was functioning, they were not sexual objects. The woman trained the girls because she would need help in the camp and the men taught the boys the hunter's skill so that eventually they might join the band. It is not necessary to invent incest taboos, the children were protected by the pair bond. Many died young and the new entry could generally be absorbed. The family gave the children identity, stimulus and security. Children learned the social rules and obligations of their particular group and grew up as social beings tightly integrated into their culture. They learned how to hunt and to gather, and they learned above all that their lives depended on those with whom they lived.

The most primitive people that we have known have been

the Tasmanians, now extinct, and the Tiwi of Melville and Bathurst Islands. The Tiwi are still evolving. Professor Carleton Coon says of them (*The Origin of Races*, p. 98):

Tiwi society is undeniably archaic. The Tiwi lie on the fringe of a marginal continent; they are the most marginal of marginals. They have never had spear throwers, stone-tipped spears, boomerangs, circumcision, or other elements of advanced Australian aboriginal culture. I think physically they are also archaic, full-sized human beings with a plethora of heavy brow ridges, big teeth and brains of only moderate size. They have had the fortune to be preserved in a geographical paradise in which . . . an agreeable form of human life can be led by healthy people without too much effort and they have the sophistication of participants in a culture that has long since arrived.

The Tiwi have never had anything that could even loosely be called government. The 3,000 square miles of their islands were divided into recognised areas where groups of one or more families hunted and gathered. They were naked. They built no houses. Their shelters were of the flimsiest. Their tools were clam shells and chopping stones. The women gathered fruit and roots; slow game and shellfish belonged to both sexes; only the men hunted and fished. Selection operated through the males. The boy who wanted a woman had to get himself accepted by a hunting group, for only thus could he supply a wife with meat. On his skill and prestige in the hunting group depended the number of wives he could feed. This is how a pack selects, though among the Tiwi it was not quite so simple. Marginal as they were, providing was not their only value. They had language, they sang songs, they decorated funeral posts, they rewarded their artists, and the artist who was not too good as a hunter could still have a family. The general result was that the males whom Tiwi society selected for their desirable qualities sired the next generation. They had evolved to a level which the Caucasoids and Mongoloids left behind them a quarter of a million years ago; judged by both their bones and by their tools they are more primitive than the Neanderthals.

Of all the hunter-gatherers that we have found the Tiwi were the most relaxed. They were not under pressure from man, beast or the elements. No neighbours raided them and only an occasional crocodile disturbed the island peace; the rains came regularly and bush burned fiercely to clear the hunting grounds. Tiwi society was in balance within itself and within nature. Alone of surviving hunter-gatherers nobody had pushed them into an inhospitable corner. They belong to the dawn of mankind, and they serve as an example of how man lived at the point where *erectus* was becoming *sapiens*. From them we learn that even at this the most primitive stage of marginally human society, there was an awareness of death, of a time before and of a time afterwards. The Tiwi believed in divine beings from whom they were descended and in the spirits of their ancestors, which had to be propitiated lest they disturb the living. These beliefs formed a part of the society into which every Tiwi was born and they conditioned his life.

At the other end of the hunter-gatherer societies are the Bushmen of the Kalahari. When Tiwi society was being born, Bushman society was dying. The Bushmen were once full sized people inhabiting Northern Africa. Today their dwarfed remnants, no longer the talented artists of the caves, face extinction in the Kalahari desert for they are nomads hunting for existence and persecuted by game wardens who do not seem to realise that though game be protected, little people must eat.

Laurens van der Post has written of them most movingly, of the life of their imagination and of their strange Gods, the Praying Mantis, his wife the Cape Rabbit, their son Young Mantis who was killed in the war with the baboons, and their daughter the Rainbow.

Like the Tiwi, but far more elaborately for they are an old people, they believe in a magical origin and in the surviving spirits of their dead.

We know of some hundreds of hunting peoples but in one way or another all have been affected by encroaching civilisation. The Negritoes, and Pygmies exchange goods with neighbouring agriculturists. The goods they receive in exchange for forest products have put their own archaic tool-making industries out of business. The Eskimos are in the fur trade and have modern weapons; the Alakalufu, Yaghan and Ona down by Cape Horn are crippled by the white man's diseases.

Hunting and gathering as a whole and independent way of living no longer exists.

The customs of the hunters varied greatly but there are certain constants that we can extract.

The basic unit was the male hunting group which rarely numbered more than eleven; it was almost certainly pre-human in its origins; it needed no captain. Its cohesion depended neither upon the force of internal authority nor the pressure of external danger; it was and is the group that comes naturally to man. The wisest hunter may lead but he is only followed after debate for man is a chattering animal. In early times the group linked families together in what we may call bands or tribes that had yet to evolve government.

At certain times of the year bands came together for ceremonial or hunting purposes. On these occasions most of the hunting people of whom we have first hand knowledge, seem to have entrusted the arrangements to a committee of elders, who advised on the customs. Bands that joined up shared a common language, common religious ideas and in general common descent from a divine ancestor. Hunting is seasonal and the movements of game and of food supplies directed the coming together and the parting. Bands that spent most of their time together were on the way to becoming tribes. Even if they had no name for themselves, others with whom they came in contact found a collective name for them.

There was always some form of incest taboo. We do not know when man or pre-man so chose to limit his sexual choice. For my own part, I think these taboos derived from the hunting group whose coherence was its prime survival factor. The group members would normally be related, fathers, sons, brothers and cousins. Sexual competition within the group would be disruptive; there would be less trouble in groups where the individual imported his woman from outside, for it would be clear from the start to whom she belonged. Groups that adopted this custom would avoid over close inbreeding and so breed better replacements. Exchanging women could form valuable inter-group alliances. In a hunting community without means of food preservation, survival may depend on being able to turn for help to a neighbouring group when one's own has a run of bad hunting luck. All these considerations indicate that the incest taboo had a survival value for the groups that adopted it.

There was always a division of function. The men hunted and the women gathered. It was often the women who provided the greater part of the food but this did not alter the inferiority of their status. There is very little evidence for the primitive matriarchies imagined by Sir James Fraser in *The Golden Bough* and if any existed they were very rare.

The hunters were all concerned with a past and a future. All had creation stories, the Garden of Eden being but one such story in thousands. The spirits of the dead lived on and must be appeased lest they disturb the living. The beasts they hunted also had spirits, and they too required conciliation. The world of the hunter was full of spirits and full of fear. He was not like the buck that grazes happily by the lion's kill. He was too clever for that. He knew that every rock could crush him; that every stream could drown him; that the very air could build the lightnings that killed. He was always afraid.

The hunters had little sense of property. Kills were divided by custom each being entitled to his particular cut. Few if any of the hunters whose customs have been studied, have evidenced that territorial possessiveness which we find amongst birds and monkeys. They may object to poaching but seldom to transit. Women would seem to have been the first objects of private property and the first subjects for conflict.

Fighting amongst hunters operating at a subsistence level is rare. Rows in the group, and the subject is generally women, result normally in a mutual denunciation before the group and loss of face by the party whom the group judge to be in the wrong. Occasionally, and very rarely, when an individual continuously made trouble, he was driven out or even killed. Injury to a member of another group was something for which the offender's whole group was responsible and customary compensation was nearly always paid. The methods for claiming and assessing varied hugely but they all seemed to work. I know of no hunting society that practised cannibalism. This is odd because most of the remains found of pre-man seem to show that he did so.

Violence came when the hunters passed into surplus. This

happened on the west coasts of Canada and northern California. Different species of fish returned from the sea at different times of the year and the Indians had a series of rich harvests. Once they learned to dry, smoke and pack their fish they found themselves with a huge surplus. We do not know when they so learned or why they solved the more difficult problems of fish preservation when the Plains Indians failed in the easier task of preserving bison meat. We do not know the intermediate steps in social development that took place between the era of bands wandering between fish, berry and ground game and that of highly organised tribes.

By the time the white man came, a number of tribes coming from different regions and different language groups on this fish coast had each developed chiefdoms that worked on broadly similar lines. None of them seemed to have been very old, that is to say that their age was measured by centuries rather than millennia. The chief was a semi-divine figure; his was the personality of the tribe; his illness was the tribe's illness; lack of respect for the chief was an insult to the tribe. The chief held the property of the tribe and received the stored surplus, which he re-distributed. This permitted some degree of economic specialisation but curiously it did not result in political specialisation. The chief had no army, no police and no servitors. His authority depended upon persuasion and status. Every member of the tribe had and knew his place in the pecking order, everyone save the last of all had an interest in supporting the status system that put him above somebody.

The great social event in these societies was the Potlach or 'show-off' feast at which the chief acted as host. Canoes were broken up, decorative copper shields were smashed, piles of blankets were burned to display the chief's indifference to wealth in much the same way as the *nouveaux riches* have been known to light their cigars with fivers. The feasts served also to announce status. The order and the size of the gifts distributed to guests were noted in the same way as the position of Russian officials on the saluting rostrum are noted at the May Day Parade. From year to year favour moved up and down. With surplus came property, leisure and war, each the consequence of the other.

Bands do not go to war either to destroy each other or to seize territory. Hostility is normally confined to stylised gestures of aggression that result in the retreat of the trespasser. The inhibition against killing one's own kind observed by Konrad Lorenz in the pack animals, seems to apply. War is an occupation of governments and must await the arrival of governments. It came with the chiefs. Savage and most cruel, wars were fought to destroy rival tribes and to capture their territories. Chiefdoms grew by conquest and sometimes by voluntary accession, but lacking both police forces and civil services they broke up nearly as quickly as they formed. The system was in continuous and violent flux. It was too unstable to have a long history.

We do not know whether a surplus has always been a condition precedent to the formation of a tribe at chiefdom level of social evolution. It may well have been. At the hunter level surplus was a rarity.

During the first few hundred thousand years of their human existence our ancestors saw very little change. Both pack and tribe are profoundly conservative organisations. The search was for a stable balance that gave to each a place and a status. All change was to be avoided. Even if there were no other objection, who could be sure that anything new might not upset the spirits? The Committee of Elders was not a decision-making body, it was a decision-avoiding body. Its job was to look backwards and say what the custom had always been. The word legislate can be translated into no tribal language. Not even the most advanced of tribal societies make any provision for change. If custom does not provide the answer the tribesman must look to magic.

The Shaman was the first specialist. In the earliest societies he was neither priest nor doctor, but simply someone who talked to spirits. He went into trances, and had dreams and visions. He tended to be a neurotic. He was often epileptic, and the holiness of epilepsy endured in classical times. He was conditioned by a society which conceived of itself as being surrounded by spirits, and he believed in his role.

Everything unusual was the work of spirits. This did not include all illness. The Tasmanians had a purge for constipation; the Mbuti Pygmies used an enema; the Ahoa Pygmies used at least twenty-one plants for medicinal purposes; Neanderthal man used surgery to sever a crushed arm and staunched the blood with herbs, but any unusual illness and in particular a wasting illness was the work of spirits. It was for the Shaman to identify the spirit and either to appease it or to drive it away. The weather too was the concern of spirits. If the rains did not come the Shaman called them. The game too had spirits that had to be appeased or they would become scarce and go. The Shaman's task was wide and he soon started to add to his psychic and hysterical repertory conjuring, regurgitation and fraud, but for all this his contribution to primitive society was a real one. He could often substitute a faith that healed for a despair that killed.

Further specialisation and all that derives from specialisation, government, religion, slaves, cities and war had to await agriculture.

The turn from hunting to herding and from gathering to sowing was the greatest revolution in all man's economic history. We do not know how it happened. The first trace we have found was at Mount Carmel in Palestine. Wild wheat and barley grew in this area. This grain may have been gathered and used for hundreds and thousands of years. By somewhere between 8,000 and 9,000 BC some cave dwellers with Mediterranean characteristics whom we call the Natufians were reaping these grains with sickles made of mounted flints that still bear the traces of silicone deposited on them in the process of cutting the grain-bearing grasses. We do not know if the Natufians sowed, but soon afterwards people in this area were not only sowing but selecting the seed grain to improve the stock. Domesticated wheat and barley had arrived, and with them a settled society. The domestication of animals is even harder to date. The dog associated with man, the hunter towards the end of the Old Stone Age. We do not know when this association first amounted to domestication but it had certainly done so by the opening of the New Stone Age. It is uncertain too when some men began to herd useful animals as well as to hunt them. The change was gradual and unimportant. The domestication of animals became important when this became a part of the living of settled communities.

Sheep came first. Selective breeding improved the wild, hairy long-horned sheep of the mountains and developed the 'golden' fleece that came to Europe from the Caucasus around 8,500 BC. Goats and pigs came later, about 6,500 BC and cattle about 5,000 BC. The draught animals, first the onega or wild ass and then the horse came later between 4,000 and 3,000 BC and with them came the wheel. In the new world agriculture arrived quite independently several thousand years later with the tilling and breeding of quite different crops, maize, beans, tomatoes, squash, manioc and potatoes. There was little stock farming and, apart from llamas in the Andes, the draught animals came only with the Spaniards, while the wheel was used only for toys.

Farmers did not always acquire governments. Some lived in isolated family homesteads, some in hamlets, some divided their time between growing crops and seasonal migrations in quest of pasture. Families were linked by marriage and by language and religion that survived from hunting times. They met at shrines. Many did not even reach a tribal level of government, but by 6,000 BC civilisation, which means the state way of living, had begun. The first city may have been Jericho III. Contemporaneously or maybe a little later similar cities started to appear in the valleys of the Euphrates, the Nile and the Indus and it was in these valleys that the first states were organised. In the rest of the world the hunting bands were still becoming tribes, and a tribe is very different to a state.

In the hunting band there is no government and the Shaman is only an occasional specialist. The groups are small and assemble only occasionally for special ceremonies or hunts. With settlement the task of living together becomes more difficult. People have to learn their place. Rules become necessary as liberals who try to run 'free' nurseries and schools re-discover. Tribal rules are strict. Every man, woman and child must know his or her place and accept his or her duty or communal life becomes impossible. This is branded into the young on reaching adult status. The initiation ceremonies are both cruel and terrifying. They include such things as circumcision, knocking out teeth and penis splitting. Female initiation sometimes has an added purpose, for female circumcision deprives a woman of sexual pleasure and reduces an inclination to stray that might otherwise disturb the tribe.

Tribal life by rule and custom satisfies man's nature and there are tribes that have continued virtually unchanged for thousands of years, but at some point change comes and the tribe is not equipped to meet it.

The new pressure on the tribe may come from man or from nature. If from man defence imposes war leadership on someone who acquires a new authority; if from nature then the spirits are responsible and new authority comes to the Shaman who talks to spirits. Sometimes the war leader is the Shaman and the tribe finds that it has a priest king. This happened quite often. The most primitive people we have known, the Tasmanians, had a Shaman chief. The West Coast Indian chiefs combined religious and war leadership. The American civilisations Maya, Inca and Aztec all had priest kings but they had passed from tribalism to statehood. So had Egypt under its dynasties of Gods. Other tribes kept leadership and religion separate. This was so with the Plains Indians, with the Zulu and with the Lotzi, but for all these differences the tribe is always designed to frustrate change. Each tribesman has his role according to his age within the tribal custom that altereth not. Creative or sceptic intelligence is a negative survival factor in so conformist a society.

The tribe was egalitarian. Slaves were an embarrassment. The West Coast Indians gave them away at Potlachs, tortured them for entertainment, bound them and used them as rollers for guests' canoes or adopted them as members of the family. In an undivided society there was nothing else to do with them. Africa had no use for slaves until the Arab and the European provided a market. David Livingstone who fought the trade, wrote approvingly of African domestic slavery and quotes a fellow missionary as saying that slaves brought in as a result of a foray assumed the name and received the treatment of children in the captor's household. He commented.

Neither the punctuality, quickness, thoroughness nor amount of exertion is required by the Africans as by the European Master. In Europe the difficulty is want of time; in Africa what is to be done with it.

The alternative to adoption was killing. Chaka, the great king of the Zulus, who came a bit late for the slave trade killed his captives by the thousand. In the tribe there was but one living role and it was the same for all.

Mr Ardrey in his fascinating trilogy has reduced human demands to three—identity with its opposite anonymity, stimulation with its opposite boredom, and security with its opposite of anxiety. To these I would add a fourth, love in its asexual sense; the emotion that holds the family, the group, and perhaps the tribe together. This applies amongst herd and pack animals as it does among men. It works as a substitute for government amongst small groups that perhaps descend from the hunting group. Eleven seems to be about the top limit. It is the basis of successful military organisation, the section; the section commanders plus the platoon sergeant and platoon commander; the platoon commander, company commander and second in command; the battalion commander, second in command, adjutant and company commander, each group working upon a basis of considerable affection and mutual loyalty and with a controlled but noticeable antipathy to other sections, platoons, companies, battalions, etc. The phenomenon was particularly strong in RAF bomber crews and squadrons. Recent research in industrial relations has brought out the drop in production and morale that results from breaking up established groups.

Tribal society satisfies these demands. The tribe provides each member with an identity and an established niche. Age groups operate on the small group basis without a leader. Everybody knows his destiny and his rights. Taboos and female circumcision eliminate sexual competition as far as possible.

Stimulation comes from hunting, dancing and war.

Security comes from extreme conservatism. Organisation and customs of tribe must have evolved at some time perhaps hundreds of thousands of years ago, from trial and error but are now ascribed to a mythical ancestor. The whole organisation of the tribe is a conspiracy against change. It is a society dedicated to doing what father did.

Affection is satisfied by the small unisex group.

I shall now look at the Societies that have succeeded the

tribe and see if they have in their turn been successful in satisfying man's basic demands.

NOTE

Where the experts differ (and they differ quite a lot) I have in general followed Professor Carleton Coon. He eschews the prejudices of ideology and sticks to the facts of observation and the deductions of logic. I would like to mention his *History of Man, Origin of Races, Living Races* and *The Hunting Peoples*. Robert Ardrey's four books are stimulating— *African Genesis, Territorial Imperative, Social Contract* and *The Hunting Hypothesis*. He sets out to prove that man descends from a carnivorous hunting ape (I agree), and concludes from this that man has inherited a blood-thirsty aggressive nature (I disagree). The birds that fight to the death are not the birds of prey. They are territorial worm-eaters like the robin. The songs of challenge that greet the dawn do not come from hawks. The elephant, the rhinoceros, and the water buffalo are far more dangerous than the lion. The hunting peoples who we know are peaceful people. Aggression comes with farming, and war with government.

Origins involve race and for those who want to go more deeply into the subject I recommend *Race* by J. R. Baker; *Race, Intelligence and Education* and *The Inequality of Man* by Professor Eysenck; *Testing Negro Intelligence* by Professor A. M. Shuey, and *Study of African Ability* by Professor Biesheuve.

The books of Eugene Marais, Conrad Lorenz and Heinz Friedrick deal with animal society. *The Wolf Children of Midnapore* by the Reverend J. A. L. Singh is interesting but doubt has been cast on his evidence. With regard to human tribes *Politics, Law and Ritual in Tribal Society* by Max Gluckman is a must. Good books on the sociology of particular tribes can be numbered by the score.

3

THE CITY AND THE STATE

THE MOVE FROM BAND and tribe to city and state involved the first great revolution in man's social history.

It was a move from a static to a dynamic society. The tribe was concerned with custom. The state with authority. The tribe was linked by family and clan, the state by habitat and subordination. When decision could no longer be avoided the tribe turned to omens and sought to shift responsibility on to the spirits. The state had to learn to take decisions for itself on problems as they arose. The tribe conspired to avoid change but the state was a living organisation that had to change, grow or die. The tribe was a broadly egalitarian society. The state was a mixed society.

Civilisation came when slaves could be used to create a surplus. If you could use slaves to dig your land, to reap your crops and to build your houses then you could be a full-time soldier or priest. This was the primary division but it was soon followed by new divisions, both amongst slave and citizen. Guilds of free craftsmen grew up, men farmed not for mere subsistence but to supply the town, and slaves rewarded by freedom became free craftsmen and traders.

Property took on a new significance. The tribesman has no use for property. There is but a single way of living. Chaka slept on the same earth in the same traditional hut as his subjects and ate the same traditional stew from the same traditional pot. The only property he could enjoy separately was women and without a specialised seraglio service he was a long way behind Solomon. His wealth was measured by cattle as articles of display.

It is only when ways of living are divided in a specialised society that wealth can be used. The Pharoah's way of living did not resemble that of his subjects. He lived in a palace and in a temple. His cooks numbered scores, his attendants hundreds, his priests thousands, and many more thousands spent their whole lives building his tomb. He also had a professional army, a civil service and a nobility, all of whom had to live on the property created by slave and serf. Of course, not all property holding was as top heavy as this. Where civil and religious authority was not too closely linked property was more widely spread, as in the city states of Greece, but it was always based on a slave foundation from which the surplus derived. The function of law changes too. Primitive law or custom is concerned with status. There is no law enforcement authority other than tribal opinion. The chief when he arrives may be the judge, but he is rarely the policeman. There is no theft because there is nothing to steal. Killing is a family matter, for which compensation must be paid—it matters not how accidental the slaying may be. Adultery is the main tribal trouble. The judge is primarily a conciliator. The common interest is the peace of the tribe, it's capacity to live together as a unit. When property comes then law concerns property. Offences become the concern of the state and the need to hold the state together demands force in contrast to the consent of the tribe.

Man's first permanent buildings had been shrines The old Stone Age hunters painted in caves and no living artist would be capable of seeing and remembering animal movement as they recorded it. In parts of France and Spain they achieved great art. It is unlikely that they intended art. They worked beyond light sometimes as much as half a mile from the surface. Their roof painting required scaffolding. Their lighting was by pine torch. They did not live in these caves for there is no debris on the floor. The caves were shrines where hunters assembled for a sacred purpose. Some 9,000 years ago hunters built a shrine at the lowest level of Jericho. Stonehenge and Avebury ring were shrines and one is astonished that an unsettled community could build so hugely and with such skill. The Indians of North America built shrines for the assembly of their hunting bands and the Tiwi met at shrines to bury their dead. The shrine seems to have been the first link between the bands that were to become tribes.

The shrine was for the nomad. Where the surplus was big the shrine might be magnificent, but it was visited only occasionally. The city was different for it was occupied all the time. It was the storehouse, the refuge and the fortress of a settled society. It marked a new way of living, for it could not stand still. Militarily and economically competitive development was the condition of its survival.

The city followed settlement and agriculture but not automatically. Many agricultural societies have remained tribal. The negroes never built a city, although as victims of the slave raider, they certainly needed cities. The city involved not only a new way of living, but a revolution in man's nature. Jericho III was built in about 7,000 BC on top of two previous layers of habitation. Its wall was of dry stone over 6 feet thick and contained an area of some 10 acres. It had at least one round tower with a staircase in it and its population was probably about 2,000, housed in round, partially sunken huts within the wall. It was a Stone Age town. Pottery had yet to be invented.

What caused this first city? The answer must surely be war. The farmers were raided by the nomads and pressure mounted to a point at which they joined together in common defence and built a stone fortification, the first that the world had ever seen. It was a remarkable response, made possible by a number of factors additional to the raiders' pressure. Pastoralists require a big range. Fertile land was filling up and there was nowhere else to go. The farmers had been nomads themselves. They had experienced pressures while still on the move. For some generations they had assembled at the shrine that lies below Jericho. They had built temporary accommodation. Their crops had increased. The neolithic city of Jericho had no writing so we do not know what happened, but the tribes almost certainly had a sacred king as their leader in war and religion. The two roles had to be combined, for only magic and the spirits could meet a new situation in a new way. All the early cities had divine kings. There were still divine kings in those neolithic societies that survived till historical times.

The same kind of people that built Jericho spread along North Africa. Some were marooned in the Canary Islands. They had arrived by boat bearing with them the same neolithic crops, wheat, barley and beans, and the same dogs, goats, pigs and sheep as we find at Jericho. Professor Carleton Coon believes that they were marooned because the islands lacked stone that could be polished into axes and that this prevented them from repairing their boats or building new ones. I do not myself believe that Stone Age people could build boats with keels and ribs. Neolithic boats were skin coracles, dugout canoes, and reed boats built of faggots lashed together. I think that lack of suitable reeds on the islands was a more likely reason than lack of stone. These Canary Islanders called Guanchies were found by the Spaniards in the fifteenth century. Their clothes were goatskin, their needles bone, their houses dry stone, windowless and single-storied, their weapons bone-pointed spears, slings and Homeric skin shields. The population was divided into commoners who worked, and nobles who fought. Nobles formed an elite disciplined force which successfully resisted the Spaniards for some years. Each island was divided into kingdoms and had at least two priest kings. There were pilgrim shrines, colleges of sacred women, oracles and sanctuaries, but no cities. The kingdoms remained small because the rocky islands had no roads and aggressors could rarely concentrate in superior force.

On the other side of the world in Hawaii, Captain Cook found another Neolithic society. It was richer and more elaborate than that of the Canaries, but the organisation was very similar. It was class-divided into nobles and commoners with a further class of slaves. Specialisation went further. There were four classes of priest attached to each of the four great gods, there were courtiers, soldiers, farmers, fishermen, axe-makers, carpenters, shipwrights and the pounders of tapa bark cloth. Each craft was hereditary. At the top was the sacred person of the king, divine and untouchable. The kingdoms remained small, for transport, communication and war were not efficient enough to enable a king to administer anything larger than a Welsh county. Polynesian customs included abortion, human sacrifice and, on many islands, cannibalism, all of which operated as population controls.

When, a hundred years ago my grandfather was appointed governor of Fiji, according to family tradition he received from the Colonial Office a letter in the following terms:

> King Thakanbau of Fiji has requested the protection of Her Majesty and this Her Majesty has been graciously pleased to grant. You will proceed to Fiji as Governor. Your staff will consist of a Secretary and a Naval Attaché. The islands are said to number some 200. The extent of the king's authority is unknown. The inhabitants are said to be cannibals and I have to inform you that if you get yourself eaten Her Majesty will be gravely displeased.

My grandfather records that the king, a man of great wisdom and integrity, had participated in at least 1,000 cannibal feasts. His dignity was punctured only once. At Government House he partook of a marvellous new delicacy called 'iced cream' and shovelled a spoonful into his hollow tooth.

Society in Fiji was simpler, but very similar to that which Captain Cook had met in Hawaii 100 years before.

The survival of these neolithic societies demonstrates man's distaste for change, for his nature is not radical. The king of Jericho had change thrust upon him. He needed a wall. He probably had slaves to build it.

In the wars of hunters and pastoralists, prisoners were seldom taken. The way was left open for the trespasser to run away, but as the population built up, bands grew and retreat was cut off. Substantial captures must have taken place. In other societies they might have been sacrificed but Caucasoids and their gods have never had much taste for human flesh. The king who thought of a wall may well have had to find something for his captives to do.

The city required government that differed from that which had sufficed the tribe. The tribal chief used force but he had no monopoly of force. Bands went off to raid independently. Clan, family and individual enforced compensation for wrong. In the city and in the state government could tolerate no force save it's own. Within the tribe the chief had a customary role. Within the city the kings had to do new things. The wall itself was a new thing. It imposed division of function. Stones had to be collected, plans made, building directed and improvised, guards trained.

The state followed the city. It came into being when a city acquired control over an area which might or might not include other cities. Its subjects were both urban and rural, its population was more stratified, its production was more specialised. Man had moved from a static to a dynamic society. When the ice melted, thirty or forty thousand years ago, it is unlikely that there were a million human beings. Twenty or thirty thousand years later when the first cities were built there may have been five million. To-day, some ten thousand years further on, there are over four thousand million. Five civilisations have arisen spontaneously, Sumer, Egypt, China, and, in the New World, in Central America and in South America. The Indus, Mycenae and Crete may possibly be added. The rest were either imitative or derivative.

Sumer came first, and irrigation probably had something to do with this. From the middle of the sixth millenium mixed farming villages were being formed in the hills above the valleys of the Tigris and Euphrates. Population was increasing. The valley soil was either too wet or too dry, but when drained or irrigated it was amazingly fertile. By 5,000 BC farmers were beginning to build simple dykes and canals. If drainage and irrigation was to open up the new land down to the head of the Persian Gulf, the job needed to be on a large scale. It was a much bigger enterprise than the building of a city wall. Eridu, Ur, Uruk, Nippur and Girsu, the cities of the plain, appeared and each was served by an irrigation area. We do not know who founded these cities in the days before history. We know only from their bones that they were a Caucasoid people of the long headed Mediterranean type. Some time before 3,500 BC they were conquered by a new and most talented people of similar racial type, whom we call the Sumerians. According to Sumerian tradition they came from a hill country in the east and they brought with them bronze. As far as we know it was the first bronze and we have no idea where or how smelting and the blending of copper and tin was invented. In Mesopotamia there was no tin so Sumeria reverted to copper for about 1,000 years till bronze came again from the north.

The Sumerians founded the world's first state. They came as a military aristocracy, bringing with them a new language. In each city they seem to have established a priest-king dedicated to the god which that city chose especially to honour. On the cylinder seals that pressed their pictures we see the king, superhuman in size and dignity, leading the festivals, the lion hunts and the armies. The society they established was stratified. At the top the soldiers and the priests, then the commoners, some independent, some retainers of the temples and of the aristocracy, and finally the slaves. Primacy passed from city to city, but the system remained stable for a time perhaps as long as that which separates us from the Romans.

During the third millennium Sumerians invented writing. Within a state records had to be kept. Year by year that which was due to the king at his temple treasury increased. Grain, vegetables, cattle, hides, smoked fish and all the rest came to the temple and had to be recorded. The signs used for this most necessary recording became the first form of writing. Wedges pressed into clay. Before very long signs that had represented things represented sounds. By 2,800 BC the script was adequate and history began.

Between the two rivers and in their delta the Sumerians dug a system of navigable canals and ditches so well-planned that the current ambition of the Iraqi government is to restore these to their former excellence. In the cities, temple building was on a huge scale. By the second half of the third millennium in Erida and Uruk there were temples capping terraced pyramids over 200 yards square. They built in baked brick for this delta had no stone.

In Sumeria we find the first code of law. The code of the King Ur Nammu was written about 2,000 BC. We have it only in fragmentary form on clay tablets. The code of Hammurabi, 200 years later, which we have complete, is on the same lines although the penalties have become more severe. It is a civilised code for an urban society. The values are our values, the purpose moderate and liberal, the abuses familiar. Apart from sex and violence, they include every form of cheating, fiddling, commercial chicanery and criminal neglect with which our courts are familiar. The penalties are ferocious. The laws are those of a society concerned with property. Sumeria lay between the Elamites in the hills of Persia and the Semites of the Arabian hinterland. From very early times Semites were infiltrating into Sumeria. In Akkad a Semitic state modelled on Sumeria had come into being by about 2,500 BC and it was from here that Sargon founded the first empire. He conquered the cities of Sumeria, then turned east and defeated the Elamites and, moving north-west, occupied Subartu, a district that included what subsequently became Assyria and which we call Iraq; he reached the Mediterranean and took the cedar forests of Lebanon; he entered Anatolia and in the south he founded ports on the Persian Gulf. It was an astonishing performance that illustrates the effectiveness of riverine communications. From his day, and he is said to have reigned for fifty-six years, Akkadian became the language of Sumeria, while Sumerian survived only in liturgy, like medieval Latin.

Egypt was the next civilisation. The Nile, from its delta to the First Cataract, was the most navigable of rivers. The current flowed north and the wind blew south, so boats could drift downstream and sail back up. The Nile flooded every summer and deposited fertile mud over the valley and the delta. In the area from the delta, north to the Cataract lay Upper Egypt, stretching some ten miles on each side of the river; Lower Egypt comprised some 7,000 square miles of delta soil through which the river fanned to its many mouths. In prehistoric times it was occupied by a neolithic community that hunted and fished and did a little mixed farming. Racially Capoids were giving way to Caucasoids. Upper Egypt may have been united under some sort of rule. There were some largish villages and one big cemetery but nothing that looks like a royal tomb, and no signs of the gods Osiris and Horus. Then, rather suddenly, a little before 3,000 BC came civilisation and the gods. According to the myths Osiris brought agriculture, animal husbandry and the arts and crafts to Egypt. After his death he returned to his original home, there to receive the souls of those dead Egyptians who had memorised the Book of the Dead.

This home from which Osiris came was in the north. The

land was foggy and bordered by high mountains. Beneath the mountains lay a huge lake. On the mountain side of the lake was a forest and on the other a desert. The trees were conifers sacred to Osiris. This description resembles nowhere in Egypt or anywhere known to the Egyptians. It is quite a good description of the Amu Darya region by the Caspian Sea which was the seat of an early neolithic culture, dated about 5,400 BC, and it may well have been the heartland of the Caucasoids. It certainly seems quite likely that in Egypt as in Sumeria, civilisation was sparked off by the arrival of Bronze Age invaders. The legendary founder of the First Dynasty is Menes, who united Upper and Lower Egypt: from this point Egypt became a class-divided community owing allegiance to a god-king who was the incarnation of Horus and Osiris. Egyptian rule was more centralised than Sumerian.

Chinese civilisation arrived rather mysteriously with the Shang dynasty about 1,700 BC, that is some 2,000 years after Sumeria. I class it as original because it lacked wheat and barley. Had it derived from the west it surely must have had these two basic crops. It arrived equipped with character writing and an advanced bronze-casting technology. Where it got these from we have no idea.

A neolithic cutlure of earlier but uncertain date raised both dogs and the scarfa variety of pigs for meat in North-Eastern China. They made grey pottery. At much the same time a similar cutlure in the West made painted pottery and kept sheep and goats. They were followed by a late Stone Age people who had horses and cattle, made black shiny pottery and may have been concerned in the building of the Shang city of An Yang. This city cannot be dated precisely but it is not older than 1,700 BC. It's people foretold the future by means of the shoulder-blades of animals, a process still followed in Albania. The blade was heated and destiny read from the cracks. In the nineteenth century, peasants ploughing at An Yang in Northern Honan province turned up many of these old yellow bones. They sold them in the towns as dragon bones for medicine. About one in ten bore inscribed character-writing which the city pharmacists carefully scraped off, realising that dragons could hardly be literate. It was not till 1899 that the first unscraped bones reached Chinese scholars who found on them an archaic record of the supposedly mythical Shang dynasty. Over 100,000 of these inscriptions have been discovered. Question and answer were simple, sincere and to the point.

They tell us the sort of things ordinary citizens wanted to know and the sort of answers they got. Few of them would be out of place in an astrology column today. In 1928, Harvard-trained Dr Li Chi dug. He found An Yang, the capital of the Shang kingdom. The palace was 92 feet long. There were royal workshops for bronze workers, stone-masons and arrowsmiths working in bone. There were bronze vessels rated by experts as amongst the best ever produced. Some, taken by tomb robbers, have realised over $100,000 at auction. There were bronze weapons and chariot fittings. There were chariots buried in clay. The wood had gone but its space had been filled by a different earth so that the chariot could be precisely reproduced. The bronze was smelted at An Yang but we do not know where the tin came from. Indeed we do not know of tin within 1,000 miles. Most of the cutting tools were of stone and included a leather-worker's knife of a kind unknown in the West. Animal bones included species from both west and south: horse, ox, sheep and scarfa pigs from the west; Water buffalo, chickens and vittales pigs from the south. There were also elephant and whale bones. A character indicating a man's hand on an elephant's trunk, would seem to indicate that the elephant was domesticated.

Most interesting of all were the royal tombs. The kings and queens were not lonely in their graves. They were buried in their regalia and were accompanied by a band of courtiers, servants and guards. Their funeral retinue included sixteen war chariots complete with horses, charioteers and warriors. Only gods could have been buried in this style and with this exuberance of seemingly willing human sacrifice.

In the Americas, two civilisations started independently of the Old World and, so far as we can see, independently of each other. There may have been prehistoric contacts between the old world and the new. Native Americans were Mongoloid and their chins grew little hair but all had folk stories of white bearded men who had come from across the sea. An African gourd and an Egyptian hybridised cotton have been found on prehistoric American sites and in the case of the cotton at any rate, it is hard to imagine any means of transit other than man, but there is no evidence that such contacts influenced the American civilisations.

In Central America during the third millennium, the now barren plain of central Mexico was wooded and fertile, and it is here that we have found the first settled villages. Crops were gradually ousting hunting and gathering as the principle means of living. By 1,500 BC, maize, beans, squash, peppers and other vegetables and fruits were being grown. The technique was slash and burn and the tools, digging-sticks and hoe. There were no domesticated animals.

Then in the late thirteenth century BC on the coast of Mexico, between the Rivers Panuco and the Grijalva the first American culture appeared. We call it Olmec and it lasted a thousand years spreading right across to the Pacific coast. As moulded by their artists the Olmecs appear to have been a jolly plump, thick-featured Mongoloid people but their figurines included some with beards and thin Caucasian features very like the Guanchies from the Canary Islands and this they may well have been. If you throw a bottle into the sea off the Canaries it will arrive in the Gulf of Mexico four or five months later carried by the Canary current. These Gaunchies, if such they were, probably came by accident for they did not bring with them the crops, sheep and cattle which they had taken to the Canary Islands. Some of them seem to have crossed the Isthmus and travelled down another current to the Peruvian Desert where four hundred mummies draped in beautifully-woven hybrid Egyptian cotton sheets and dating from 1,200 BC have been found in a cave. Some of these mummies are white-skinned and have soft, blond or red beards clearly Caucasian.

Diffusionists acclaim the presence of these strangers as proof that the civilisations of the new world were imported from the old. This is nonsense. The thirteenth century BC Berbers of North Africa and the Guanchies of the Canaries had no civilisation to bring with them. When the Spaniards found them two and a half thousand years later, they were still Neolithic tribesmen. They may have carried across the Atlantic a new technology of embalming and of weaving but this is a long way from bringing civilisation. Thor Heyerdal has suggested that these hirsute blonds may have been Phoenicians acquainted with the ancient civilisations of the two Rivers. Apart from the fact that it is hard to imagine Phoenicians founding civilisations that lacked items wherein lay their principal trading interests—weights, measures and money— the dates do not fit. The Phoenicians of the thirteenth century were Canaanite farmers. They did not take to the sea until after the incursions of the Peoples of the Sea in the twelfth century. Carthage was founded in 814 BC and archaeology finds no evidence of Phoenician presence in the Western Mediterranean before the tenth century other than a single thirteenth century bronze figure found in a wreck off Cadiz. The evidential value of this find must depend on how old the figure was when it was lost! Diffusionist theories are attractive but in general the more people know about ancient civilisations the less do they incline to diffusionist solutions. Civilisations tend to move in similar directions, but they do so in such different ways.

The Olmec's god was a jaguar and they played a ritual ballgame after which somebody's head was cut off. It is not clear whether this was the referee or the losing captain. They were excellent craftsmen in jade, quartz and diorite. They appear to have been at the judge-shaman level of tribal organisation, although there is evidence that towards the end the shamans were becoming a priesthood and society was stratifying into peasant, craftsmen and trader. They do not seem to have been occupied with war. Archaeology has revealed many of their shrines, built of earth and wood with some stone altars. Then, around 200 BC, they disappeared as mysteriously as they had arrived.

Later in what is now Guatemala, villages of temporary buildings followed the forest clearing and shrines began to appear, with platform mounds and some sort of temple. About AD 300 this became what we call classic Maya. The list of Mayan achievements is as surprising as the list of their omissions. In astronomy they made the best calendar in the contemporary world, in mathematics they invented the zero and the system whereby the value of the figure depends on its position in a series, and they did it before the Hindu, the

Arab or the European. This may seem simple to us but it did not occur to mathematicians of the stature of Archimedes. They built temples comparable to those of Sumer and Egypt and cities as great and as populous. They invented a glyphic script form of writing which unfortunately we cannot read, but they had no weights and measures, no metal tools, no wheels (save, oddly enough, a few on children's toys), no ploughs and an agricultural system that never passed beyond slash and burn. Their religion involved much human sacrifice and they ate the victims.

The Mayan civilisation only lasted about 600 years. It then for some unexplained reason started to disperse in the direction of Yucatan and had collapsed by the time the Spaniards came. They were succeeded by the Toltecs of Tula in Mexico, a civilisation that built similar stepped pyramids. At Chichen Itza in Yucatan they built a replica of their own capital in Mexico and it is from this that we know what Tula looked like before the conquistadors destroyed it. The Toltecs and their successors the Colhua were crushed by the Aztecs, who towards the end of the thirteenth century arrived as wanderers with a fierce intolerant tribal god whom they called Huityilopochtli. They obtained employment as mercenaries of the Colhua in the civil wars that split the Toltec realm. They multiplied as they stole wives from their neighbours. They demanded, and received a Toltec princess as a bride for their chief. In 1323 they sacrificed her in the hope that she would become a war goddess. In the resulting unpleasantness they were sacked by the Colhua and wandered again, but by this time they had learned much. They founded a city, in accordance with a prophecy, on an island where they saw an eagle sitting on a cactus eating a snake. That island became Mexico City. By 1486 Huityilopochtli, who had started life as the little tribal god, 'Humming-bird on the left', had become the great and jealous god of the sun that tolerated no other gods; Mexico, from the gulf to the Pacific, had been conquered; the island city had become a great capital larger than contemporary London, and their chief was a divine emperor, but they had succeeded too fast. They had not learned tolerance and they had failed to incorporate the conquered into a civil system. They ruled like the Assyrians, by terror and when the Spaniards came they collapsed for every hand was turned against them.

Mexican technology was on a level with that of the kings of Sumer and of the First Dynasty of Egypt. Metal was profusely used for ornaments, but swords were of wood set with obsidian.

We know very little about the early civilisations of South America. We do not even know their names because it flattered the Incas to think that they had invented civilisation and, like the people in Orwell's *1984*, they dis-remembered all the history that preceded them.

Carbon tests show that agriculture and weaving appeared on the Pacific coast as early as 3,000 BC. The first identifiable culture we call Chavin. It appeared on the Andes about 1,100 BC and involved a savage-looking cat-god. It became a city civilisation with walls of well-cut stone, decorated with human and animal heads. The Marchicoes (we have no idea what they called themselves) were a caste-divided nation in North Peru and they left a temple built of 130 million baked bricks, gold work and painted pottery. They flourished between AD 400 and 1,000. In the south sometime before AD 900 at Ica-Narea, a culture that worshipped an odd weeping god, cut huge figures on the hills, as did our ancestors in the vale of the White Horse. They were destroyed by a people dominant in Bolivia and Peru between AD 1,000 and 1,300 who built a great shrine at Tichuanoco in Bolivia. Stones are fitted together with insets and tenons and large blocks are bound in copper. It is work that could only have been done by people with a long technical tradition, but we know nothing of them for they were 'dis-remembered' by order of the Inca. When in 1549 Pedro de Ciena de Leon asked the oldest Indian then living about the ruins, all he could say was that they were built before the Incas ruled but that he knew nothing of them. Another people, the Chimus, were defeated only shortly before the Spanish came and we know something of them because Inca methods of historical relativity had lacked time. The Chimus had built, near modern Trujillo, a city of 8 square miles containing huge step pyramids, irrigated gardens and stone-lined reservoirs. They ruled some 600 miles of coast from Lima to Equador, and had developed roads adequate for the administration of their state. They domesticated the Llama and the Alpaca, two members of the camel family that served for wool and transport, and they grew potatoes and quinoa grain, unknown in Mexico. They bred guinea pigs for food.

I have mentioned but a few of the cultures developed in Peru before the Incas, like the Romans, came to build on their foundations and to unite the coastal desert, the high mountains and the rain jungle that lie in three strips 3,000 miles long.

The Incas were a hill tribe living on the 9,000 feet high tableland in the very centre of Peru. In about AD 1,100 they founded their capital of Cuzco and established themselves as a ruling aristocracy on the high sierra. From there they set out on their career of conquest and organisation that was to unite the whole of their known world. They built two great trunk roads 24 feet wide, one running the length of the coast and the other the length of the mountains, and joined them by lateral roads, linking the mountains to the coast. They built or reconstructed hundreds of stone cities to a common plan, without walls but equipped with a fortress to which the garrison could retire in case of trouble from within or without. They established a system of couriers, who jogged their memories with knotted strings (an elaborate form of our 'tie a knot in your handkerchief'); they had official historians called rememberers; they established the safe exchange of goods between forest, mountain plateau and coastal desert; their weaving, pottery, metal work and masonry were of the highest quality. In their towns were textile factories with looms set in rows. Astonishingly they had no writing save the knotted string, no wheels, no weights and measures, and no coinage. Their god and their dictator was the Sapa Inca. All that lay under the sun was his. He was descended from the sun, the creator god, and everything, the land the people, gold ('sweat of the sun'), silver ('tears of the moon') belonged to him. He was absolute. He was God. His authority was not theoretical, it was real. His queen was his sister. His administrators were the sons of the 500 lesser wives and concubines kept by himself, his father, and his grandfather. These lesser wives included some promoted from the people on account of their exceptional beauty and talent. Occasionally a commoner could rise to the rank of honorary Inca, but in general it was a rigidly stratified society. The Sapa Inca, the sons of the Sapa Inca, the Inca clan, the subject peoples maintaining within themselves their ranks from Mayor downwards, free craftsmen, farmers and, at the bottom, slaves. Politically they reached the stage of empire. The Aztecs conquered and enslaved their neighbours, carrying thousands to sacrifice on their high altar. The Incas conquered, taxed and tolerated. Alien subjects spoke their own languages and worshipped their own gods.

In his book, *Race*, John R. Baker would deny civilisation to the American societies because their religions were superstitions without morality and because they both sacrificed men and ate their flesh. I disagree. The temple and the sacrifice shows that they were possessed of the kind of faith that can override man's nature and make his progress possible.

In each of the five self-made civilisations we find this common factor. There has been a superstition, a delusion, or a faith—whichever word you choose to use—so powerful that it has persuaded man to abandon his niche in the tribe and launch himself on the fearsome waters of change.

This mood has been expressed by an acceptance of divine rule so complete that it transcended the fear of death. Sacrificial victims were not all unwilling. The courtiers who joined the kings in their tombs chose the road to paradise with their god. In the Toltec city state of Chichen Itza we have an account of children dancing and playing bells as they went to die. Teeny-boppers in high hysteria at a pop festival would as joyously follow their idol over a cliff if he so commanded, and it was the fashion.

All the great achievements of human society have been acts of faith and so long as man believes with sufficient intensity it matters little what he believes, for it is from the common believing that power comes to man's society.

In Egypt, China and Peru there was a single god, the lone supreme ruler. In Sumer and Central America, cities had their divine kings, and a supreme ruler only came after conquerors had won control of the city states.

How did it start? All five had a tradition that the divine founder came from a distant land. It is generally accepted that the Sumerians arrived after the cities of the plain had been founded at least as large villages and that they came with bronze. In Egypt the Osiris-Horus tradition is supported by a change in the proportion of round-headed to long-headed people in upper-class graves which is consistent with the arrival of a new ruling class; in China, the Shang were a conquering bronze-age clan that imposed themselves on a neolithic society.

In America the white bearded Gods who were said to have come from beyond the sea did not bring civilisation but they may well have broken tribal rigidity and founded the Faith that made advance possible.

That divine monarchy came through aliens, equipped with new technology who imposed themselves on a settled population seems probable. It is easier to understand people accepting the divinity of one whom they had not known as a boy. In an age when magic and the spirits explained the unusual, the arrival of a new man equipped with new weapons demanded a supernatural explanation.

But what was the quality of the belief that had such great results? Did the king believe in his own divinity? We do not know. Does the Pope sometimes wonder whether God really has endowed him with infallibility? Probably not. I know men who accept their own infallibility on less authority. Does the Aga Khan, when he is carried through the adoring mob of his worshippers, wonder whether perhaps after all they are right? Does the politician, as he feels a great crowd rise to him, sometimes sense within himself a something divine? Did that effeminately beautiful king whom we call Tutankhamun, really feel a god? Probably—it is not too difficult to accept a general opinion that flatters. But whatever the king may have thought, there can be no doubt that the people believed with an intensity that united them in a compelling destiny. They lived in a world of fear. The rain, the sun, the crops, life itself were ruled by spirits, and the god-king ruled spirits. If he did not actually fire the lightning he was a very good friend of the fellow who did, and could persuade him to mitigate his wrath.

Chaucer tells us that the farm-yard believed that the sun rose because he was summoned by the cock, until one day the cock had a sore throat and the sun still rose. The subjects of a divine king risked no such disillusionments. The whole structure of the state saw to it that no king omitted to fertilise the seeds, to summon the fish or to call the rain, which eventually always came. The acceptance of a shared religious experience was the seed from which these civilisations sprang, but germination depended on the soil being right. The problems that tribal society could not solve were generally pressing when the king emerged.

Nomads raided newly settled farmers. A wall and the new kind of social organisation that came from living behind a wall, became necessary to the development of this new settled pattern of life. Generally the miracle did not happen. The wall was not built and agriculture remained a furtive scratching in the bush. A population, living on alluvial soil, increased, and their future depended on planned and controlled irrigation. The miracle generally did not happen, but occasionally, as in Sumer and Egypt, it did, and a god came to manage the river. In Egypt the problem was irrigation, in Sumer irrigation and raiders, in China probably raiders, in Peru the need for a secure communications system between the mountains and the coast and in the Maya's land we have no idea. The cities built in the Mayan jungle do not seem to have been built for defence, or for any obvious economic purpose.

A stratified society was also necessary. Egalitarianism is for the tribe, in civilisation it just will not do. The achievements of all the self-made civilisations were based on slavery. That slavery generally, and perhaps always, originated in conquest by an invading aristocracy. At the bottom were the slaves, then the indigenous population serfs, peasants and craftsmen, then the nobles, administrators, soldiers and priests. At the apex was the divine king. In Sumer the invaders were a bronze-age tribe that found a settled population with villages that had become, or were near to becoming, cities. The conquered were probably culturally in advance of the conquerors, who took the cities with their bronze weapons and adopted the city way of life. They appreciated the irrigational needs of their new properties and they had the authority to compel the necessary labour.

Initially they were probably a divine aristocracy rather than subjects of a single god-king. Nobility was hereditary and so may have been the offices of state, but the religious idea was there. The surplus energy of the cities was turned to temple building. As the giant ziggurats grew so did the divinity of the king. In the temple of Ur the king was attended in death by scores of richly dressed ladies, soldiers, courtiers, servitors, and grooms, who seem to have died with their god readily, peacefully and in accordance with custom. The king of Ur was divine, but he was a city deity rather than a state deity, a local divinity in which the city aristocracy had some sort of share.

In Egypt the class divisions were similar save that the aristocracy existed by favour or merit rather than by heredity. There were no living gods but Pharaoh. In life he was Horus, and in death Osiris, and he presided over gods and man. All the land of Egypt was his. He made great grants to temples, but then he was supreme pontiff of all the temples. Land granted to servants or generals could always be resumed and was heritable only by special favour. The great officers of state were generally relations of the Pharaoh, though slaves and eunuchs could rise to the highest office. Joseph may have been an example. When the old kingdom became decadent the office of viceroy or nomarch, became hereditary, but with the new kingdom the nomarchs were suppressed and the land reverted to the Pharaoh.

Jacquetta Hawkes in *The First Great Civilisations* quotes the vizier Reckhmire of the Eighteenth Dynasty: 'What is the king of Upper and Lower Egypt? He is the god by whose dealings we live, the father and mother of all men, alone, by himself, without an equal.'

In China the Shang were a clan mysteriously equipped with bronze weapons, writing and a calendar. Their subjects were of the Stone Age, accustomed to thinking of gods as enlarged humans who, on occasion visited the earth. One rarely met them but one sometimes found their footsteps. The Shang king made no decisions. All decisions, religious, military and agricultural, were made by Shang-ti the ancestral god. The Shang did not invent writing in order to list stores. They wrote to communicate with Shang-ti and the priest king read the answers. The calendar helped divinity. It told the Shang king when the seasons would change, and when the seed should be sown. The peasant had observed that the seasons changed, but, poor ignorant fellow, he had not known why. Now he knew. It was Shang-ti who did it. In China the Shang rule was a tight theocracy under a priest-king who danced the rain dance, offered the sacrifices and read the dreams. The aristocracy was by favour and merit within the Shang clan. The Shang expanded as neighbours submitted to the god. Wars were slave raids, generally in the direction of Tibet, and the slaves tended to become a racially distinct minority. All the land belonged to the king. A Bronze Age aristocracy presided over and owned highly skilled craftsmen in the towns and Stone Age husbandmen in the country. There were no metal agricultural implements.

Central America like Sumeria, had a city state civilisation and each state had its own divine king. Aristocracy was hereditary with the Toltecs and the Maya. Many of the royal temple cities lacked defences. The Toltecs appear to have gathered the Mayan cities under a single divinity but any movement towards feudalism was checked by the Aztecs, who achieved empire before they had sloughed off the remnants of tribalism. They made their chief, a divine emperor, but left in being a council of the elders of the tribe, that delayed royal decision in a manner that proved fatal in the Spanish war. They retained tribal intolerance and an Amalenkite complex that equated massacre with godliness.

In four of these five spontaneous civilisations, the Maya being the exception, we find the need for a large organisation to cope with a common task, in all five we find a pyramidal society, class divided, based on slavery and crowned with a divine leader. The tribesman had lived in fear. In the god king he found a saviour who fought his human enemies, appeased the spirits and conciliated the elements.

Three of these five civilisations were annihilated by their enemies, Egypt by Persia and the Americas by Spain. They have left little by way of heritage. Evolution, natural and social, is a wasteful process. China, octopus-like, gripped her Mongol and Hunnish conquerors in the tentacles of her culture and squeezed them till they became Chinese. In the land of the two rivers Sumer, Akkad, Babylon, Assyria, Medea, Persia, Macedon, Byzantium, Moscow, Arabia and Turkey were each absorbed by the social structure of their predecessors and each in its turn became a class-divided hierarchical society centred on a divine autocrat who ruled as god's regent and to whom certainty was revealed.

Later in this book I hope to show how the successors of the Shang dynasty of China and of the god kings of the two rivers have maintained this autocratic form of society and are guided by a divine revelation which it is both treason and sacrilege to challenge, even unto this day.

4

GREECE

EUROPEAN CIVILISATON came later: it sprang from the
marriage of two races, the small, dark, long-headed Mediterraneans whom the Greeks called Pelasgians and the tall,
brown haired, round-headed people who spoke languages of
the Aryan group and came from somewhere in central or
south-eastern Europe.

At a time when urban civilisation was well established in
the Middle East, Europe had not reached even the tribal level
of social organisation. In Greece and the Aegean neolithic
farmers and fishermen had settled, but the area was thinly
peopled and villages rarely added up to a dozen huts. Further
north the Aryan speakers were still mainly nomadic, although
they did cultivate some grain. Judging both from the finds of
archaeology and our experience of other peoples at this stage
of development, man was a peaceful animal. The cannibalism
in which very early man indulged had disappeared, at any
rate in Europe, and war had to await government. In the
fourth millennium we find little or nothing in the way of
fortification or weapons.

In clan society we often find a code of hospitality to
strangers and something of this sort probably applied in
Europe and made travelling possible, if unusual. Goods certainly got about. Baltic amber reached pre-dynastic Egypt,
and Irish gold arrived there at some time around 2,400 BC,
but this does not signify anything like trade. Prestige gifts

passed from hand to hand. The journeys of amber and gold south and of daggers and seals north to Wessex graves, may have taken generations. Unlike many early historians I do not believe that neolithic man was an aggressive seafarer. His boats were not suitable, for he was confined by his technology to rafts, coracles and dugout canoes. Boats with keels and frames need nails. Pegs and thongs do not provide the necessary rigidity especially when the holes have to be made with stone drills or pokers. Coracles linked the Aegean Islands from very early times but I do not think that the planked Homeric long ship appeared until late in the second millenium.

Thucydides, writing in the fifth century, says: 'Because of the wide prevalence of piracy, the ancient cities, both on the islands and on the mainland, were built at some distance from the sea and still remain to this day in their original position. For pirates would rob everyone who lived on the coasts.' I think the long ships came with the pirates and that we can date them from the time when we begin to find towns sited and fortified for protection against an attack from the sea. Save for one or two instances on the Troad coast this does not seem to have happened before twelfth century BC.

From about 2,600 BC people were arriving on the islands with artefacts and skills from the established civilisations. It was infiltration rather than an invasion. The shipping of Phoenicia, Egypt and possibly part of Anatolia had passed the coracle stage. Pharaoh Snofru (2,800 BC) imported cedars from Lebanon to build boats. These boats were frame built without a keel, river boats not sea boats. Nile transports were generally built of reed bundles. The method was to lash the bundles together and to build them into a spoon shaped vessel with high pointed bows and sterns. When Egyptian shipwrights came to use boards they used them in the same way as they had used faggots. Herodotus described the process that still continued in his day, 2,000 years later: 'They cut short planks, about three feet long, and the method of construction is to lay them together like bricks and through-fasten them with long spikes set close together, and then, when the hull is complete, to lay the deck-beams across on top. The boats have no ribs.' These boats were river boats with very little grip on the water. There is a carving of

2,450 BC depicting the return of some of them from Syria. The bow and stern posts were joined by an overhead cable. A lever thrust between the strands of the cable and functioning as a tourniquet enabled the crew to twist up and tighten the cable when the ship looked like breaking her back, and nets were wrapped round the hull to hold it together. The fact that Pharaoh got his fleet back shows that he was lucky with his weather. After this we have no record for 1,000 years of these river boats being sent to sea. Such sea-going shipping as existed lacked compasses and other navigational instruments, and was strictly for coasting. So far as we can find they had no anchors.

A ship that lost sight of shore was in trouble. Doubtless it happened. The Eastern Mediterranean can be squally. Ships were blown away and either wrecked or beached on islands. This probably accounts for the gradual spread of culture into the islands. Newcomers with new skills, hospitably received, stimulated the inhabitants. In the development of the islands one can see the influence of the nearest civilisation, in Cyprus Canaanite, in the Cyclades Anatolian and in Crete Egyptian. Crete and perhaps Thera led the way. As early as 1,900 BC the so-called 'Palace Civilisation' began to appear in Crete. The name is unfortunate. A palace involves a king and civilisation a city. I do not think Crete had either. Kings are warlords and kingship is an office made by war. I do not think Crete had got as far as war, indeed the most remarkable thing about the 'Palace Civilisation' is the absence of all defences.

It has been argued that the Palaces of Crete were unfortified because the Cretan navy commanded the sea. Navies do not stay at sea all the time and they do not live long if they have no well secured base to return to. I believe that the Palaces were unfortified for the simple reason that fortification was unnecessary. The sea-going warship had yet to come and villages were peaceful. It is wrong to assume in all societies that war has always been there. In some war has been quite a late comer. I believe this was so in the Aegean.

It sometimes happened in the south seas that an Englishman or a Dutchman or a *Bounty* mutineer landed up on an island and was hospitably received. He married and got the natives to build him a bungalow and showed them how. He taught them new crafts and improved their fishing gear. Something like this may have happened in the Aegean, but the break with the newcomers' homeland was probably more complete and the process went on for centuries. The end products in Crete and Thera were 'Palaces' of great refinement. Excavations at Thera, an Aegean Pompeii buried in lava some time in the fifteenth century BC are still progressing. The Cretan palace at Knossos has been restored to what Sir Arthur Evans, the English archaeologist, thought it once looked like. His enthusiasm has tended to out-run his evidence, particularly in the case of some highly imaginative reconstructions of frescoes. Knossos is some miles inland. Malia, Gournia and Kato Zakros are near the north-east coast. Phaestos is on a flat topped hill in the Messara Plain, close to the south coast. All were originally built in the nineteenth century BC and rebuilt on a larger scale in the sixteenth, probably because they had suffered from an earthquake. All were destroyed in the fifteenth century. Malia, Gournia and Kato Zakros may have been submerged by a tidal wave that resulted from the volcanic explosion that destroyed Thera. Knossos and Phaestos were burned, probably as a result of earthquake but it may have been by invaders. Only Knossos was rebuilt.

Malia is much the same size as Knossos and benefits, for me at any rate, by not having been restored. Gournia is the smallest palace but the largest 'town'. A charming custodian told me that 20,000 people had once lived there. He added that they were very small people. They would have needed to be. There are less than fifty excavated rooms. There may be added a few yet to be excavated and some on first or even second floors, but I think that accommodation for 200 would be putting it high. Gournia was a very small village. Kato Zakros is the only palace that could be described as having been built on a harbour. It stood about half a mile back from a sandy cove on the eastern tip of the island. Phaestos on the southern side of the central mass of mountains, was connected by a paved path two miles long with another palace or villa, Aghia Triada which stood below it on the river. I find Phaestos the most impressive as well as the most beautiful of the palaces.

The palaces give me the impression of large English country

houses that started quite small and sprouted new wings and offices as family and prosperity increased. Only Phaestos has the coherence of a single plan. All contain store rooms, wine cellars, work shops, stores and offices. The main buildings have bathrooms and, at Knossos certainly, what appears to be a flushing wc. This is the more surprising because the water supply was singularly inadequate. At Phaestos there is no well at all and rain can have been the only source. When the Romans built their capital they chose a site further up the valley where there was a spring.

The Palaces are all open fronted and designed to catch and enjoy every breeze. None are fortified. There are no temples but each Palace contained shrines in which were found little clay images of mother goddess and of her snakes. Similar shrines to household gods are found in Roman villas. The throne room at Knossos, so called because a chair is built into one wall, is probably such a shrine. Crete had bull games found nowhere else, in which athletes vaulted over bulls. There is no evidence one way or the other as to whether these games had any religious significance. They may have taken place in the palace courtyards.

The Cretan economy was rural and the palaces had store-houses for wine, grain, honey and oil, and a market. There were shops and workshops for craftsmen, carpenters, metal workers, jewellers and potters who may or may not have been free. At Phaestos there was a bronze foundry, about 10 feet by 12 feet in size. Accounts were kept on clay tablets, first in Linear 'A', a script we cannot read but which seems to be related to Akkadian, and later in Linear 'B' which, when deciphered by Michael Ventris, was found to be earliest Greek. Cretan potters developed charming and original flower and sea patterns and Cretan painters showed an impressionist enjoyment of nature. It does not feel like a slave economy. Still less does it feel like a theocracy.

There is no evidence of shipping and very little of foreign trade. In the bay by Malia we have found Minoan fishing gear but nowhere have we found the copper or bronze fastenings or equipment that one would expect to form part of Bronze Age sea-going ships. We find no quays or breakwaters and no warehouses. Malia, Gournia and Zakros, which were sealed in destruction have disclosed nothing like an import export merchants' stocks. Some exchange of goods certainly took place. Two tusks were found at Zakros, and some Minoan pottery has come from Egypt and Canaan, but not enough to evidence regular trade as playing any substantial role in the economy. The links with Egypt are plain throughout the Minoan period but my impression is that these links were occasional rather than regular.

I was brought up in a Grade 2 stately home, Sulby Hall. It was much the same size as Phaistos. Before 1914 Sulby was a community of about 100 people, indoor staff, stables, chauffeurs, gardeners, game keepers, estate woodmen, carpenter, builder and forester. Larger houses may have employed double. I think that the inhabitants of the palace complexes fell within these limits, and that the farming community that used the palaces lived in timber or wattle huts on their land. If I am right it was not the kind of society that required much in the way of government. The palaces were not labour intensive projects like the pyramids or Stonehenge. They made no excessive demand on a rural surplus. It was a pacific society. We find no weapons other than the all-purpose bronze knife or dagger, with which Cretan males were buried, until the fifteenth century or later, when the more warlike Achaeans may have taken over. There is no evidence that Crete was ever a single political unit or that one palace ruled over another. The palace owner may have been some sort of a chief and may have had some religious functions, but no more. We do not know when the Mycenaeans came but it must have been at some point before the change to Linear 'B'; it may have been a long time before or a short time. There is fierce controversy as to the dating of Linear 'B' finds, but be the date what it may, we find no signs of resistance or discontinuity in the palace culture. One squire takes over from another. On other Aegean islands the same kind of thing was happening, but on a smaller and slower scale.

Thucydides writes: 'Minos, according to tradition, was the first person to organise a navy. He controlled the greater part of what is now called the Hellenic sea; he ruled over the Cyclades, in most of which he founded the first colonies putting his sons in as governors after having driven out the

Carians. And it is reasonable to suppose that he did his best to put down piracy in order to secure his own revenues.'

Thucydides was writing of a myth a 1,000 years old in his day. Archaeology can find no evidence of Cretan colonisation in the Cyclades or anywhere else and Minos, who according to myth became a judge of the underworld is as real as his friends Heracles and Jason. There is no evidence of slipways or of quays or of ship building. We have no remains of early Aegean ships and no reliable pictures. From the third millennium we have a terracotta 'frying pan' from Skyros including in its decoration what may be a flat boat or dugout canoe with a high prow and a fringe which could be oars or paddles; a fragment from Phylakopi in Melos showing the stern oar of a river boat; a few very crude graffiti, and clay and lead models of very small boats. From Crete we have a sarcophagus dated before 1,500 BC and a number of seals. On the sarcophagus is a crude sketch that looks like a substantial ship with sails set. It could be a merchant but it could also be a ship of the dead, models of which we find in Egyptian graves. The seals do little to identify the boats they represent. There is nothing to show that they were Cretan boats. Many Cretan seals show exotic symbols, mainly Egyptian. There is nothing to show that the seal carvers had seen the ships they drew; they are the sort of drawings that a child could do from descriptions. Cretan decoration draws much on marine themes It is astonishing that ships were not drawn if they existed and were familiar sights upon the sea, for ships are so decorative. The real ship pictures we have from the Aegean before about 1300 are those recently excavated by Professor Marinatos at Thera. Here in the Aegean Pompeii, buried in lava since about 1,500 BC, he has found a fresco that depicts in great detail a fleet against a background of coastal or riverine towns which the professor identifies as Libyan. He believes that this is an Aegean or Minoan battle fleet. I do not agree. I think that they are Egyptian or possibly Libyan river boats that could not survive on an open sea-way. They are not rowed but paddled canoe-fashion by black snub nosed men facing the bow. The have the high overhanging bows and sterns derived from the reed boat. They have no keels and no rigidity. I can see no sign of warriors. The passengers seem to recline under awnings and are lighter skinned than the paddlers. The silhouette is too top-heavy for a sea way. It may be that an Egyptian or Libyan Canaletto was painting a scene from his homeland. I do not know either the Persian Gulf or the Southern Red Sea. It may be that the river boats could serve in these waters but I am sure that they would not live long in the squally Aegean.

The first picture we have of warships is that which depicts the Egyptian battle with 'the people of the sea' in 1,190 BC. Here for the first time we see Egyptian ships that look as if they could go to sea, open long boats propelled by oars and the people of the sea in galleys very similar to those described by Homer. Even then the ram had not been developed and the fight was by boarding.

In the north from about 1,900 BC a new people had been entering mainland Greece. They were Aryans. This is a word that has gone out of fashion because it was misused by the Nazis in their romantic racialist cult. Aryan is not a racial word. It denotes an Indo-European language group. It is the right word for its purpose and Hitler is not going to inhibit me. The people from whose language Hittite, Greek, Latin, German, Hindustani and English are derived can be placed by the words that are still common to all these tongues and must therefore go back to the common source. They include trees (birch, beech, oak, willow), animals (wolf, bear, goose), fish (salmon, pike), honey, domesticated animals (cattle, pigs, sheep, horse but not goat), transport (copper, wheel, axle, hub, yoke, but not spokes). They have no word for sea. This vocabulary indicates a copper using, pastoral people with knowledge of horse and cart that inhabited an area somewhere in central and south-eastern Europe, in the late third millennium.

A common language source does not necessarily mean a common descent, for the conquered often take the language of the conquerors and sometimes conquerors take that of the conquered. The Jamaican negro is an Aryan. It does mean a common tradition. When you take a language you take the stories which that language tells and the method of thinking from which that language derives. Aryan traditions differed from the divine king ideology of the civilisations. The Aryan gods were men, and all too human men at that. Aryan tradition was resistant to civilisation. It was heroic and anarchic. In about 2,200 BC an Aryan tribe, the Glutians, came out of the Zagros Mountains in Persia, and burst into the Empire of Sumer Akhad. In 1,700 BC another Aryan tribe smashed the civilisation of the Indus. Early in the second millennium they appeared in Anatolia as the Hittites and in 1,595 BC they raided Babylon and ended the dynasty of Hammurabi. After the Hittites another tribe, the Kassites, led by a chariot-driving Aryan aristocracy, won the Babylonian empire and about 1,500 BC the Hurrians, again led by an Aryan aristocracy, formed the Mittani state that extended from the Zagros Mountains to the Mediterranean and that received tribute from the Assyrians. We know of these exploits because they impinged on civilisation and were recorded in the histories of their victims or at least in writing they had captured. We know almost nothing of what was happening in their homeland and of their arrival in Greece we know only that they came early in the second millennium as Bronze Age warriors with a metal industry as sophisticated as anything in the civilisations. They found a neolithic mixed farm culture. The newcomers came gradually in quite small parties or clans. Some may have been led by warriors whose fame had attracted a following of braves. Their faith was loyalty to the hero. If he went into exile they went with him. If he was killed they recovered his body or died, for to abandon a leader was shame worse than death. Tacitus described this process of band formation as it operated amongst the Germans many centuries later. Fealty held the group together and the values, prejudices and quirks of the leader became the aspirations of the followers. Others may have been family groups but the whole picture looks much more like male bands who found women locally.

The indigenous population was no match for the invaders who set up petty principalities. These seem to have consisted in general of a castle in fairly substantial stone where the chief and his warriors lived as a military aristocracy and a farming community who fed them. Wealth was arms. Bronze was never cheap. The hero, helmeted, armoured with a shield, a long sword, a short sword, and several javelins was borne by a chariot into the thick of the fray, where he was a match for a great many ordinary men. Within the Bronze Age economy very few could be so equipped. War was a battle of the tanks. At some time, I think in the thirteenth century BC, they learned how to build the long boats that could take warriors to sea. Gradually over the centuries the newcomers, whom we know as Achaeans took over the islands, and absorbed the cultures they found there. They married their gods to the local Earth Mother Goddess. Zeus, the father of the Gods married Argive Hera. The qualities of the Goddess were hived off to provide wives for Zeus' sons—Athene was her wisdom, Artemis her care for the hunter and, oddly, the woman in child-birth, and Aphrodite her passion. It all fitted. Peter Farb *(Man's Rise to Civilisation)* quotes an aborigine as saying 'we do not believe. We fear'. The Greeks did little fearing. They had no devils, just gods and fate that ruled even the gods. The Greeks prayed standing up. In Crete they found writing and adapted to their own language. Unfortunately they only used it for accounts. In about 1,230 BC they landed on the mainland and at Troy faced a civilised city.

We have no contemporary account of the Greece of the second millennium because no one there could write, but we have two epic poems composed some centuries later from a tradition then still living. If you ever visit the stately home of the chieftain of the Colquhouns at Rossdhu on Loch Lomond you should buy a brochure that tells the clan story. Divine descent is claimed from the Fair Maid of Luss, hereditary high priestess of the Celts. Sir Humphrey, a contemporary of John Donne and Sir Walter Raleigh, made love to the wife of the chieftain of the Macfarlanes. He was pursued, slain, and castrated, and his grilled testicles were served on a chafing dish to Lady Macfarlane. Sir John the necromancer married one sister of the great Montrose and eloped with another. Sir Ian, DSO and Bar, who commanded the Scots Guards at Ypres kept a fairly tame lion in the forward trenches. He was court martialled and condemned to death for fraternising with the enemy on Christmas Day 1915 but was pardoned by King George V; he celebrated his return by killing five Bavarians with a club. He met the colonel of a Prussian regiment in single combat; they fired simultaneously, the Prussian fell dead but his bullet hit the drum of Sir Ian's revolver; his hand lost all feeling; he thought it had gone but, fortunately, found that it was still there when he required it later in the battle to kill some more Germans. A bullet hit the hilt of his drawn sword and passed through his thigh; his clansmen plastered the wound with green cow-pat, a custom that may have anticipated penicillin. On exhibition you will see the sword with the twisted hilt, the club (with five notches) and the revolver with one chamber discharged and five irretrievably jammed. If you went along to the Macfarlanes I have no doubt they would show you the chafing dish. In the halls of just such chiefly mansions in Ithaca, in Pylos, in Sparta and in Mycenae, tales such as these were told and trophies such as these were shown to a wandering bard called Homer and he, or perhaps, he and others, made of them the greatest of epic poems. From it we learn what the heroic Age of Bronze felt like, and the traditions it left behind.

I do not think the Achaeans achieved civilisation. They did learn to write but only used it for accounts, and those accounts are the accounts of a manor not of a state. They built castles but they did not build cities. They lacked that talent for subordination that is the price of statehood. The Clans could combine for an idea as the Greeks did under Agamemnon and the Scottish Highlanders under Montrose and Bonnie Prince Charlie, but they could not stay together, they could not go on obeying.

> It is a heroic society, with all the barbarity and insecurity that such a condition involves, the antithesis of the corporate civic life which out of Oriental seed was now striking roots in the Aegean, but it is one in which the craftsmen and the artist have their valued place and though unlettered may nevertheless foster a great tradition in poetry. It is something which was peculiarly European, and was to perpetuate its simple pattern for centuries beyond the confines of the City States and Empires. We are the heirs of the one way of life as much as we are of the others. [Clark and Piggott *Ancient Societies*, p. 304.]

The Aegean story of the second millennium up to about 1,200 BC concerns the very gradual infiltration of a pacific, politically underdeveloped Pelasgian culture by small warrior groups which could be absorbed without much disturbance of the cultural pattern. The faith that gave the Achaean bands their cohesion was faith in themselves expressed in devotion to a hero who was a man as they were. They did not build a civilisation but they did lay the foundation upon which humans could build without the need to prostrate themselves. A dark age followed their overthrow by a new wave of savage Dorian Greeks, but their sagas inspired a new and greater civilisation. They offered man an alternative destination. The god-led empires in time moved from divine to communist autocracy, the Greek tradition from heroic confusion to democratic confusion.

The Dorians were Greek-speaking Aryans from the north. The Achaeans had infiltrated as Bronze Age warrior bands; the Dorians came as a migration driven perhaps by some folk movement further north and destroying what they found in their path. They came with iron. The chieftains were driven from Mycenae, from Crete and from the islands and became part of 'the peoples of the sea' who overturned the Hittite empire, fought Rameses III in Egypt, founded the Philistine state that left its name to Palestine and the Ionian cities on the Anatolian coast. On the mainland only the Arcadians in the highlands of the Peloponnese and the Athenians in their Attic peninsula survived the invasion.

The Dorians brought with them war, Iron Age war, something very different from Bronze Age heroics in which small groups of warriors feasted and champions met in single combat. In the Iron Age fighting was not left to the hero in his chariot. Walls had ceased to be inviolate. The long ships provided military mobility. The mainland smoked and piracy depopulated the islands. For some 400 years darkness enveloped the Greek world, and from that darkness emerged, in a whole variety of forms, the city state.

How did it happen? In India and Sumeria the Aryan wreckers had in due course become subjects absorbed by empire. Only in Greece did they choose freedom. How did it happen? We can only guess.

We must look for the constants. All city states seem to have had a tradition that there was once a king. Migrating tribes normally have a chieftain who assumes authority when the tribe is under stress either through war or because it is on the march. It is in this sense that we must understand the word king.

Amongst the Dorians' chieftaincy seems to have been hereditray in the sense that it was confined to members of a single family. In more settled times authority, in so far as it existed, was exercised by a council of elders or heads of families. In the city states we find an aristocratic class descended from these families. We also find a lower class with different privileges who would seem to be descended from the indigenous population absorbed by the invader. The extent to which slavery existed in the dark age is uncertain.

Each city state, (or 'polis' as it may more conveniently be called, since it included more than a single city and can perhaps best be visualised as a sovereign county), had a traditional law giver, sometimes mythical, sometimes historical and sometimes a bit of both. The laws always seem to record a balance achieved as a result of class conflict and external threat. The Greek laws were plainly forged in conflict.

Finally they had a common religion and a very good one too. In the days of the Achaeans the marriage of the Man-Shaped Gods of the North to the Mother Goddess of the Mediterranean had been consummated and all the little gods and sprites of field and river and hearth legitimised as their offspring. The Dorians accepted the marriage. Greek religion was concerned with humans. Gods were humans on a bigger scale. They were not concerned with morals. Man has and doubtless will suffer much from religion's concern with morals. At its best religion debases morals by applying to them a system of rewards and penalties, and at its worst it divides mankind into the armies of the saints (us) and the armies of the devil (them). Few emotions have proved more lethal than competitive righteousness. The Greeks were pugnacious but they fought for better causes than religion and were more moderate in victory than Jehovah would have permitted. Religion brought the Aryan invaders and the indigenous people into the same temples. The Greeks were not burdened by a professional priesthood. Humanism is self worship. It is respect for oneself; the perfection of oneself, one's whole self, body and mind, without fear and without thought of reward in the hereafter. This is what the Greeks meant by the whole man.

Specialisation was not respectable, it involved neglect of other parts. Specialisation was for slaves. The whole man was a politician who played his part in the government of the polis, a soldier who fought in the army and might well command it, a seaman who navigated the ships, a farmer who ploughed a straight furrow, an athlete, a poet and musician. As Aristotle put it, he should play the flute but not too well. He should live only so long as life was a fulfilment. To die was more honourable than to decay. But for all his search for glory man must remember that he is not a God and that he must not presume too far. 'Hubris' was excess. It could be wilful pride, ambition, wealth, or natural beauty or talent, but if it were taken too far the gods became jealous. 'Sophrosyne', or moderation implying self-control and caution concerning the consequence of one's act, was the admired antidote. The Greeks asked their gods for favours, but they asked standing up.

Here then were the ingredients of civilisation. They are strangely the same as those upon which were built the older civilisations. A vigorous aggressor invaded a more advanced culture; a clan structure resulted in which a conquering aristocracy learned from the conquered; the confusions of the time imposed the discipline of walls; a religious idea was acceptable to both races; slaves were available, some of more advanced culture, to provide services and specialist trades.

Freedom was the variant. If one had asked a Greek why he was superior to the barbarian he would have answered that it was because he was free. This does not mean that he was a democrat. Authority within the polis might be entrusted to a tyrant, an oligarchy or to the whole body of the citizens. It meant that at some level he participated. It meant that the polis belonged not to the tyrant nor to the aristocracy, but to him. It meant that his voice was heard, and that he spoke standing up. It is in this that the polis differed from the older, god-ruled civilisations. All this happened in the dark age, and the polis emerged differing as the balance struck between the classes differed.

The polis was not an association of individuals, it was an association of families. Public life belonged to the men, private life to the women. Later, in Rome (and Rome was a polis), stern old Cato said, 'We Romans rule the world but our wives rule us'. The wife ruled the home and brought up the children. She was not emancipated and took no part in public life. Emancipation of women involves the breakdown of, at any rate, the enlarged family and woman exchanges the role in which she is supreme for a subordinate role in a male society. Greek women avoided this fate.

The polis was the club and men went to the public places to associate with men. It was also the church. The Greek religion had no doctrine. In so far as it had a bible it was Homer; the *Iliad* sorted out the relationship of the gods and established the Twelve Gods of Olympus. It stated the humanist ideal. It was better to die young and glorious as Achilles or, later, Alexander, than to outlive glory, but it stated no doctrine. The polis instructed citizens in their social duties and in the 'laws'. The polis was the idea that not only moved mountains but, more difficult still, moved man from the static security of the tribe to the dynamic stresses of civilisation.

Sparta took this to the extreme. She was admired for her 'Eunomy', her state of being well lawed and well administered, the near total dedication of her citizens. She was laughed at. An Athenian who dined at her military mess said that after eating Spartan food he could understand their willingness to die, but she was still admired. In stress Spartan leadership was accepted. Spartans were the puritans of the faith. Their constitution was extraordinary. They had two kings, each drawn from a family who commanded in war but held no other authority. In peace they were ruled by five ephors or magistrates drawn from the five Dorian tribes that united in Sparta. Originally the state had developed like any other polis. When they felt the stress of mounting population, they had, like any other polis, sent their surplus to form a colony. Then, about 750 BC, they took a fatal decision. Instead of forming another colony, they determined to take their neighbour's land. They conquered Messenia and enslaved the inhabitants. Messenia rebelled and Sparta was nearly destroyed. She accepted the lesson and accepted too permanent mobilisation, lasting 300 years. This was the law of Lycurgus. We do not know who Lycurgus was. J. B. Burns, a rationalist, remarked of him, 'He was not a man, only a God'. His laws were the means whereby a minority of 10 per cent ruled 90 per cent.

Dedication to the polis was total. Male babies were vetted and those that failed were exposed and left to die. At seven the Spartan was taken from his mother and handed over to the state. He passed into a company led by an elder youth. There is no brutality to equal that of boy to boy. He had no home. Distinction within his group was his only satisfaction. At twelve he was permitted a single garment. No Spartan wore shoes. At eighteen he became a soldier and lived in barracks until he was thirty. The girls, too, were trained to be the mothers of warriors. The Council were men of sixty and the assembly of the Spartans were males of over thirty. No speeches were made and no votes taken. Decisions depended on who shouted loudest; but for all this the Spartans were admired for their dedication to what all Greece recognised as the supreme value, the polis. Greece did not consider even this level of discipline inconsistent with liberty when it was in service of the polis. Plutarch tells the story of an old man who wandered round Olympia looking for a place. When he reached the Spartans all the young men got up. The old man accepted and said, 'All Greeks know what is right, but only the Spartans do it'. The memorial to the Spartans who died to a man at Thermopylae reads 'Go tell the Spartans, you who now pass by, that here obedient to her laws we lie'.

Another story is told of the Spartan exile who had led Persians in their outflanking march. The Greeks saw no baseness in service by an exile against the polis which had rejected him. To do so had a certain heroic quality, the avenging of a wrong, though it did not expunge the longing to return. Xerxes asked this man:

'What do the Spartans?'

'Great king, they comb their hair.'

'Why do they so?'

'Great king, because they are about to die and by all the Gods, and for all thy favour I would that I stood with them now.'

Yet Sparta was not typical of the polis. She took things to extreme. She had a fate imposed upon her by the conquest of Messenia and the helot population she condemned herself to hold down.

On reading this passage, a friend remarked they were

fascists. This is only partly true. They were fascists without a dictator. They were fascists without bombast or show-off. They had a kind of boorish dignity. Herodotus tells the story that when the Samians asked Sparta for help, they made a long speech. The Spartans answered the speech by saying that they had forgotten the beginning of it and could not understand the end, so the Samians had better try again. On the next day, the Samians brought a bag and merely remarked that the bag needed flour, to which the Spartans replied that the word bag was superfluous but, that they should still have their aid. In the war with Athens, which lasted for thirty years and became steadily more brutal, the Athenians destroyed Melos and sold her inhabitants into slavery. Not long afterwards Sparta destroyed Athens's last fleet, and the city lay at their mercy. It was in that hour, Thucydides tells us, that the people of Athens remembered Melos, but Sparta, in spite of the advice of her allies, chose to spare Athens. This is not a decision which would have been taken by Hitler or by Mussolini, or even by General Franco.

Corinth, also Dorian and also in the Peloponnese, formed an extreme contrast. Corinth chose trade. When the light rose over Corinth in the second half of the eighth century BC, it revealed her as a fortified port on the gulf that bears her name controlled by a Dorian class, the Bacchiadae. Her population was growing. She had already thrown off the colony of Corcyra (Corfu) and more were to follow. A new and prosperous class arose to challenge the Bacchiadae. The response was a reforming tyrant. This was not an unusual event in the history of the polis. 'The laws' were generally expressed to be unalterable. When they ceased to conform with the power relations in the state, it required a popular dictator to overthrow them and establish a new settlement. Tyrant was not then a word of abuse. It meant a single ruler, but one who ruled only so long as his rule expressed the will of the polis. He could call on no divine authority. He must be sensitive to the will of the polis. He rarely lasted more than a single generation.

Tribal authority in the form of the heads of the original families had a way of surviving after the tribe had become a polis, and a tyrant was sometimes the means of getting rid

of them. This was the case with the Bacchiadae in Corinth.
A Dorian clan had become an anachronism in a commercial
port. In 657 BC Cypselus expelled the Bacchiadae. He was so
popular that he required no bodyguard. He threw all public
offices open to the citizens and published his laws. By destroying the ruling class he eliminated a loyalty that had competed
with the loyalty due to the polis. Destruction of the tribal
clan system was nearly always a step in the making of the
polis. For thirty years Corinth prospered. Cypselus was succeeded by his son Periander, who was less popular. This was
partly for personal reasons but mainly because times had
changed. The interests which Cypselus had emancipated
wanted power, and the colonies, many of which he had
founded along the Adriatic, wanted independence. Tyranny
was succeeded by an oligarchy of rich merchants very similiar
to that which was to rule Venice. Corinth differed from the
other Greek cities in that she had little hinterland and was
almost exclusively a trading port. Trade was the common
interest that the corporation fostered. Corinth lacked a citizen
army and navy, preferring to hire mercenaries.

Athens was Ionian. The Acropolis had successfully resisted
the Dorians, but Athens had remained a backwater long after
Sparta was a military and Corinth a commercial power. Attica
is said once to have been a kingdom and Theseus, the slayer
of the Minotaur, her most famous king. This is mythology.
Achaean war lords were settled amongst the Pelasgian aborigines. The Acropolis of Athens was the strongest point in
Attica and had been a fortress by tradition even in Pelasgian
times. Visitors are still shown the Pelasgian walls although it
is doubtful whether these are older than the Achaean invasion.
The Acropolis may have served as a place of refuge to the
whole district and this may have given the local chieftain a
certain primacy, but there is no evidence of an organised
kingdom. When history begins to dawn, in the late eighth
century before Christ, it reveals a tribal type of heads of
family government under pressure from new interests and
probably new arrivals. This aristocratic council, which became
known as the Areopagus and which elected magistrates, survived but lost its power. In 632 Cylon, a young Athenian,
who had married the daughter of the tyrant of Megara, tried

to establish a tyranny but failed. In reaction the aristocracy published a code of laws drawn up by a magistrate called Draco, who has given his name to arbitrary and brutal laws. That is all we know about him. His code provided death for all theft and enslavement for debt. Pressure continued and somewhere about 590 both sides agreed that a man called Solon should settle their differences. Solon is certainly a historical character, although much that is mythical has been attached to his name. Unhappily this includes his famous advice to Croesus, 'Call no man happy until he dies, he is at best but fortunate'. The dates do not fit. Solon appears to have been an Athenian aristocrat, a traveller, a merchant and a poet. The poetry ascribed to him is full of earthy good sense. He is said to have been elected Archon (then chief magistrate) in 593.

Solon said that he was aware that the poor man saw the rich man as hoarding what he did not need, and that the rich man saw the poor man as coveting what he did not deserve, and that it was for him to satisfy both points of view. He came near to doing so. He started by freeing all debt slaves, and cancelling rural debts. He established a new coinage. He saw the value of Attic clay and invited potters to settle. He opened public office to men who had proved their ability by getting rich. All men were admitted to some level of participation in government, but the extent was weighted in accordance with wealth. Solon's system was to substitute for aristocracy, a graded plutocracy. He provided a compromise that was an alternative to revolution and the probable destruction of the nascent polis.

Solon's laws worked no better than one would expect. The conflict continued. On two occasions government broke down and anarchy in its literal sense—no archons—existed for none could be elected. Peisistratus took over. He established himself at the head of the reform party. He had the backing of those citizens whom Solon had enfranchised, and of the poor who hoped to be citizens. He recognised that Solon's hope of government under law was premature. Having faked wounds, the citizens granted him a bodyguard with which he seized the Acropolis. The conservatives fought back and succeeded in exiling him. He returned by a stratagem. Herodotus tells the story:

The Greeks have never been simpletons; for centuries past they have been distinguished from other nations by superior wits; and of all Greeks the Athenians are allowed to be the most intelligent: yet it was at the Athenians' expense that this ridiculous trick was played. In the village of Paeania there was a handsome woman called Phye, nearly six feet tall, whom they fitted out in a suit of armour and mounted in a chariot; then, after getting her to pose in the most striking attitude, they drove into Athens, where messengers who had preceded them were already, according to their instructions, talking to the people and urging them to welcome Peisistratus back, because the goddess Athene herself had shown him extraordinary honour and was bringing him home to her own Acropolis. They spread this nonsense all over the town, and it was not long before rumour reached the outlying villages that Athene was bringing Peisistratus back, and both villagers and towns-folk, convinced that the woman Phye was indeed the goddess, offered her their prayers and received Peisistratus with open arms.

The return proved a great success. Peisistratus was an excellent ruler. Power in the state passed to the new commercial and shipping interests, but the conservatives were not driven to desperation, for they were left with their farms and became the 'squirearchy' of the polis. A model tyrant, he used his power only in so far as was necessary to sustain his programme. He never put himself above the state in any personal sense and he lived no ostentatious life. He held no office, though he saw to it that his men were always elected. He worked for the glory and the beauty of Athens and in this he expressed himself.

Aristotle is often quoted as having said that man is a political animal. This might be better translated as 'man is an animal whose fulfilment is to live in a polis'. The Greeks inherited both the Olympian individualism of the clansman hero and that collectivist sense of congregational security that belonged to the worshippers of the Mother Goddess. The result was that the polis became their means of self-expression political, artistic, heroic and religious. Peisistratus was not alone in devoting his power and wealth to the beauty of Athens, to the festivals of her special goddess and to the theatre, a truly Greek invention that grew with the polis. All had a part in the city. To skip forward 100 years when it came to building the Parthenon, that loveliest of man's works, the job was sub-contracted. A master mason employing two journeymen and five slaves had the job of fluting a section of the third pillar and just curving all straight lines so as to give the optical illusion of greater straightness. So parcelled out was the great task. All Athens contributed in skill and money. One of the charges against Alcibiades was that he employed an artist to decorate his private house. That sort of thing belonged to the polis.

Solon the law-giver and Peisistratus the tyrant converted the Attic backwater into the education of Greece.

The sons of Peisistratus lacked both their father's tact and his magnanimity. In 515 BC the tyranny fell and, after an attempted intervention by Sparta had failed, Cleisthenes established a democracy. Democracy worked, after a fashion, till the end of the Peloponnesian War. It nurtured the greatest flowering of the human mind that the world has ever seen. In sculpture, in architecture, in thought and in living Athens set a standard that still endures and has yet to be surpassed.

In Sparta, Corinth and Athens I have taken three examples of the polis with very different institutions, but overriding similarities. Scores of such states dominated the shores of Italy, Sicily, the Adriatic and Black Seas. Their citizens shared common ideals, customs, beliefs and language and owed loyalty to a polis that expressed themselves and was their true god. The bedrock of the polis was sovereignty. It was its own supreme authority. It chose, it altered and it rejected its laws, its constitution and its gods. It was not based on a social contract or upon fundamental laws but upon a social balance which determined how and by what means the supreme power of the polis should be exercised. Government was responsible. In Sophocles' *Antigone* Creon, the tyrant quarrels with Heamon his son. 'What,' he cries, 'Is anyone but me to rule in this land?' And Heamon replies 'It is no polis that is ruled by one man only.'

The variety was great but the differences trivial when compared with the oriental state where the monarch was god.

It has often been said that Greece failed because she could not unite. This is nonsense. The great majority of the Greek polis did combine in free alliance to beat the Persians. The trouble came when Athens tried to convert this alliance into an Athenian empire, for no polis could accept an overriding authority, imperial or federal. The supreme power to decide for themselves was what the Greeks meant by freedom; without it the polis lost the faith that bound it together, lost its will and lost its power. Athens forgot that the Greek whose polis was not sovereign, was not free and that freedom was as precious to other Greeks as it was to her. As a result all Greece was torn over the next thirty years by the Peloponnesian war. Eventually Philip of Macedon did what Pericles had failed to do. He united Greece and so united Greece conquered the world, but she ceased to be Greece.

When Alexander's Greek empire split the essential nature of the parts did not change. Persia and Egypt were conditioned to divine rule and Alexander became their god. His successors Seleucus and Ptolemy, Macedonian generals, also became gods and founded divine dynasties. In Greece Alexander had been Captain-General of the Greeks and King of Macedon. His successors as rulers of Greece did not become gods for it was not in the nature of the Greeks to worship a ruler.

Under Macedonian rule Greek civilisation declined. The polis lost their sovereignty and with it their political, intellectual and artistic fertility. It was left to Rome to be the first city state to convert itself into a successful nation.

So far I have shown two very different kinds of society that have come with the change from nomadic tribal living to sedentary urban civilisation. Initially, in both types, settled indigenous agricultural people who have participated in their society through simple ritual and religious rites have been conquered by less advanced warring people whose allegiance has been to their chiefs, heroes and leaders. There the similarities end. In the ancient civilisations the invaders came to dominate, to centralise control under themselves and to create a hierarchy at the top of which stood the personification of the leader in a god-king figure. Authority was vested in him: it was above and without the people. He gave orders and these percolated down to the people through the hierarchies.

In Greece the invaders integrated with the indigenous farmers and authority passed to the people, who came to participate in all aspects of their society which they controlled through laws they themselves helped to make.

These have been the two mainstreams along which the human race has flowed as it advanced from tribalism to nationhood, but before following their courses through the civilisations of Asia and Europe, there is one maverick example that should not be overlooked, for it concerns a tribe that has been struggling to reach nationhood for over 3,000 years: Israel.

5

ISRAEL

THE STORY OF ISRAEL concerns the impact of monotheism upon a polytheist society.

Our main source is the Old Testament. Its purpose was
religious rather than historical. It was written by priests who
wished to establish the validity of the covenant which Moses
had made with Jehovah. They wrote after the return from
Babylon some 600 or 700 years after the conquest of Canaan.
They were selective and imaginative. The facts they state
require the corroboration of archaeology, which is not always
forthcoming. A recent dig, for instance, proved that Bosrah,
Heshbon and Ammon, towns in Trans-Jordan which, according to the Bible, were captured by Moses, did not exist until
about 700 BC; that is 500 years after the date attributed to
Moses. The authors had simply assumed that the geography
of their day was the same as it had been in Moses' times.

Canaan was an old civilisation dating back to 3,200 BC. It
comprised a group of cities that never joined together to form
a state. Their gods were nature gods. Astarte was the Mother
Goddess. Baal the Redeemer was the dying god who rose in
the spring and dispersed the ranks of death; in Assyria he
was Adonis; in Egypt Osiris.

For a thousand years the Canaanite cities seem to have been
in balance. Egypt and the empires on the Tigris and Euphrates
remained within their frontiers. Donkey caravans passed un-
molested and sea-borne traffic followed the coast. There is

very little evidence of destruction that can be dated before 2,200 BC, but then the picture changes. The empire of Sargon had fallen and the old kingdom of Egypt was in disarray. Pastoral nomads came in from the desert and down from the hills. The cities of Canaan were destroyed and sheep grazed their crops. After about 100 years Egypt recovered under the Middle Kingdom; the empire of Babylon was established; the cities of Canaan were rebuilt and the shepherds were pushed back into the hills.

In about 1,700 BC the Hyksos, a Semitic aristocracy, came through Canaan to conquer Egypt and to establish the dynasty of the Shepherd Kings. A number of tribes followed in their wake. These may have included the Patriarchs, and it may have been that under a Semitic Pharaoh, Joseph rose to power. The historicity of the Patriarchs is, however, doubtful. In 1550 the Hyksos fell and there followed a period of confusion before they were succeeded by the Middle Kingdom.

According to the Bible, the Jews spent the next 300 years as slaves in Egypt where they multiplied till they constituted a major immigrant problem. There is no Egyptian evidence of any such captivity and I do not believe it ever happened. Archaeology tells us that the Hebrews who subsequently broke into the Canaanite civilisations were primitives lacking those skills which they must have acquired if they had served the high civilisation of Egypt for several generations. The Egyptian monuments were built by the forced labour of peasants who had nothing to do during the Nile floods. The Hebrews were nomadic shepherds. Their flocks always needed tending. They had only to slope off when the recruiting officer came. To be useful, slaves must have reached the level of settled farmers. This we found in Africa, where the Masai herdsmen were never bothered by slavers. They were not worth catching. When we built the Nairobi railway through Masai country we had to import Indian labour. The native labour was useless. The Indian population of East Africa descends from these coolies.

Hebrews were at this time Bedouin shepherds living on the marginal lands of the Nile Delta, in Sinai and in parts of Canaan.

The Jewish story has to be fitted into the general history of the region. Towards the end of the thirteenth century BC, the Dorians moved into Greece and the Phrygians, another Aryan tribe, entered Anatolia. It was a time of great folk movements. The Achaeans gave before the Dorians and took to the sea. The Hittite empire in Anatolia was overthrown. The peoples of the sea who included Sardinians, Lydians and other Aryan peoples on the move, invaded Egypt by land and water. In 1192 they were met by Rameses III and stopped in a great land/sea battle, but this was Egypt's last major effort. Some of these sea people, whom we call Philistines, settled on the southern coast of Canaan.

The Canaanites, who had been in possession for 2,000 years were under pressure from three sides, the Philistines on the southern coast, nomadic Hebrews in Sinai and Ammonite tribes from beyond Jordan. Hebrew infiltration had been going on for a long time. Manasseh had probably occupied the land round Shekem since the days of the Hyksos. Some clay tablets dug up at Amarna in the last century came from the archives of the foreign office of Akhnaton (1375–1358 BC). Many concerned the state of Canaan which was then subject to Egyptian suzerainty.

Local governors were asserting their loyalty and impugning that of their colleagues; bandits called Hapiru ('dusty ones') were making trade impossible and had closed the two great caravan routes, the King's Highway and the Way of the Sea. These Hapiru have been identified with the Hebrews and there were doubtless Hebrews among them. Shekem had entered into agreement with the Hapiru and a Hapiru chief named Labaya had operated from Shekem and fought the Egyptian Governor. The towns were Canaanite but the Hebrews seem to have occupied the hills and grazing lands peacefully for many generations, and their early villages have been found in the hills. At about this time, a second group, which included Ephraim, occupied the northern and higher part of the southern hill country. This neighbourhood was not of much interest to the Canaanites who were farmers and city dwellers. The few cities they had in these hills were destroyed in the late fourteenth century BC, and rude huts were built on the sites.

In the thirteenth century the Hebrews were under pressure

from Egypt and were being pushed out of the Delta grazing lands both by Egyptians and the Peoples of the Sea. They pressed on the Sinai tribes, who in turn pressed on Trans-Jordan and Canaan. This third group included Judah and Benjamin.

Canaanite civilisation was gradually destroyed over a period of 200 years, mainly by Hebrew-speaking tribes which, although often at war with each other, did have some sort of religious link. Shrines and high places, of which the principal was Shiloh, a sort of Palestinian equivalent to Delphi, were maintained and there was a system of truces that enabled fertility rites to be celebrated. The shrines where the Hebrews met for worship were certainly not confined to one god. It is difficult to date and place the Hebrew conquests, for they brought nothing with them. They built nothing. The simplest wall was aparently beyond them. They had no pottery of their own and no distinctive metallurgy. They did not even have tombs. Their signature was ash and rubble.

Religion does not at this time seem to have been a problem. When Hebrews took to farming they worshipped the local fertility gods. It was no use sowing if one did not make a proper sacrifice to the god who had made the corn grow. The libation then did the job of a spray in our scientific age. Novice farmers had to do the right thing. In many places Israelite and Canaanite lived in peace: 'And the children of Israel dwelt among the Canaanites, Hittites and Amorites and Perizzites and Hivites and Jebusites, and they took their daughters to be their wives and gave their daughters to their sons and served their gods.' (*Judges* iii, 5 and 6)

During their first century, the Israelites were no match for the Canaanite chariots on the plains. The position is stated in *Judges* i, 19; 'And the Lord was with Judah and he drove out the inhabitants of the mountains; but he could not drive out the inhabitants of the valley, because they had chariots of iron.'

Deborah and Barach seem to have caught a chariot squadron under Sisera in what may have been boggy conditions. It is a strange story as I know of no other record of a priestess among the strongly patriarchal Semitic tribes.

There were some cities destroyed at this time, but we have

no means of knowing whether they were destroyed by Israelites or by Pharaoh Menepta, who raided in 1,220 BC. His victory stele records for the first time Israelites among his victims. The fiercest fighting was reserved for tribes pressing on them from the desert and for each other. Gideon fought the Midianite invaders and routed them in a night attack. Gideon's father Joash (a pure Hebrew name) had an altar to Baal with a grove beside it, and after the battle Gideon made a golden ephod from the spoils 'and all Israel went thither whoring after it.'

The Ammonites came out of the desert and were driven back by Jephthah, who then sacrificed his daughter. If the Bible is right in saying that this was a sacrifice to Yahweh, one can only say that it does not fit in with anything else we know about Yahweh worship.

There were Hebrew tribal wars between the men of Ephraim and the men of Gilead who seized a crossing of Jordan and killed all whose pronunciation of Shibboleth betrayed an Ephraimite accent, and between Israel and the Benjamites over the rape of a Levite's concubine. This was followed by a woman-catching raid on Jabesh Gilead, apparently to replace the Benjamite women slaughtered by Israel.

The general picture is one of primitive pastoral tribes infiltrating into a civilisation, whose customs and religions they were adopting and of the masters of the country accepting them as second-class citizens.

The Hebrews had been moving from Egyptian territory under pressure. Somewhere at the back was a tribe who had acquired a new god whom the authorised version calls Jehovah, but whose name is more accurately rendered as Yahweh. The name 'Yahweh' is the pronunciation generally given to the 'sacred tetragrammaton' (Greek τετρα γραμματμου, 'four letters') JHVH (or YHWH), which in the Old Testament was the symbol for the name of God and sometimes a title for the deity. Due to rigid interpretation of passages in the Old Testament, the name was regarded as ineffable, and the Jews were instructed to substitute 'Adonai' ('adhōnāy) meaning 'Lord' in its place. The Masoretes, or group of Hebrew scholars who contributed to the *Masora* or *Masoreth*, the body of traditional information relating to the Hebrew bible, pointed the sacred tetragram-

maton in the Old Testament with the vowels of Adonai—
ē (=a), ō, ā—as a reminder to the reader to make the sub-
stitution. Students of Hebrew at the Revival of Letters saw,
therefore, the name of God written thus—JᵉHōVᵃH—and
made a natural mistake. 'Yahweh' or one of its variants is the
true sacred name. 'Adonai' meant 'Lord' though now, through
usage it means 'Supreme Being', as does 'Jehovah', originally
a meaningless transliterator's error. The pronunciation, deriva-
tion and meaning of 'Yahweh' is a matter over which scholars
still wrangle. According to the good book this tribe wandered
for some forty years in the desert and in Trans-Jordan, and
they probably entered Canaan in the late twelfth century BC.
This Yahweh was not the god of Abraham, nor of the tribes
that first came to Canaan. Their gods had been family gods
common to all Bedouin and they had also worshipped the local
gods whom they found on their travels. When they took to
agriculture, they had sacrificed to the gods who made the seed
grow. If Joseph served Pharaoh he had worshipped Pharaoh; it
went with the job, but he had still, as did all the Egyptians,
paid proper tribute to his private, domestic gods.

Moses was the author of the Yahweh cult. He was an
Egyptian of 'uncircumcised lips' (Exodus vi, 12) and the bearer
of an Egyptian name. He was on the run. He is said to have
slain an Egyptian, and it is just possible that he was a prince
in trouble as a follower of Aknaton's monophysite heresy. He
went to live with the Priest of Midian whose daughter he
married. Now the Priest of Midian was a Kenite, a wandering
tinker with the Hittite secret of smelting iron. The god of the
Kenites was the god of the thunder, of the forge and the
blown fire, the unnamed that the Bible calls Jehovah. Moses
was a religious genius. He had two tremendous ideas. The
first was that God was directly and very personally concerned
with the tribe he had chosen and with whom, through Moses,
he had made a two-way covenant. The tribe promised ex-
clusive obedience and God promised Canaan, the land of milk
and honey that lay beyond the desert and the mountains.
This was the covenant. The second great idea was monotheism.
There must be but one god. The God of Moses was no mere
desert storm god. He was the god that for good or ill, would
rewrite the history of the world.

Somehow Moses became the brother of Aaron, and Aaron's family, the sons of Levi became the priests of Yahweh. They formed a unit in a pastoral tribe under pressure in a no-man's-land contested by the Egyptians and the Sea People. Moses led a mixed group of refugees. Aaron acted as his spokesman, possibly because Moses could not speak Hebrew (Exodus iv, 14). Mutiny was not long delayed. Moses had climbed a mountain to commune with Yahweh and when he came back he found that his followers had made a golden calf and were celebrating in the orgiastic manner appropriate to the worship of fertility gods. They were saying, 'As for this Moses, the man who brought us up out of the of the land of Egypt, we know not what has become of him' (Exodus xxxii, 1). Moses dealt with this trouble by arming Aaron's family and sending them into the camp to 'slay every man his brother and every man his companion and every man his neighbour'. 'And the children of Levi did according to the word of Moses and there fell of the people that day about three thousand' (Exodus xxxii, 27 and 28).

The story is a strange one. We can ignore the figures, but this is surely not something that happens in an established tribe; it is the sort of thing that may happen in a mixed group of refugees. The Book of Numbers tells us that those that remained with Moses were 603,000 fighting men of twenty or over. That would mean a total of something over two million people or about the present population of Israel. It would have taken more than manna and quails to support that kind of population in a desert. The tribe that got pushed out of the Delta and wandered for a generation in Sinai can only have been small.

The account of Joshua's victories does not fit the archaeological record. Excavations show that the last Jericho was destroyed before 1,400 BC, that is some 200 years before Moses' time, and that Ai, Joshua's second victory was destroyed before 2,000 BC. Ai means ruin. Jericho and Ai were ruins long before the coming of the Hebrew tribes and their destruction was adopted to adorn a tale. Canaan was not taken in a single campaign.

I think that the tribe which Moses and Joshua led came too late to have had much to do with the conquest of Canaan.

When they arrived the good land had gone and they were left with the desert and hill country behind Jerusalem. Their power lay in their fierce commitment to a new intolerant god. The old gods had been happy to live together and share their altars, but Yahweh would suffer no rivals. He went to war with foreign ways and would admit no compromise. His followers proved difficult to live with.

By the end of the twelfth century BC the Canaanites had retreated to the coastal cities of the north and the Israelites were left to face Philistia. They were in no shape to do so. They were scattered tribes led by judges or shamans of whom Samuel is an example. Their link was the Shrine at Shiloh. Apparently the tribes took it in turns of a month each to maintain and staff this holy place.

As a result of the battle of Eben-ezer, early in the eleventh century BC, Shiloh was taken and destroyed by the Philistines and Gibean-Elohim, a high place served by Samuel, was occupied by a Philistine governor. In an effort to deny their subjects iron the Philistines decreed that smiths should work only in Philistia and that Israel should bring their tools for sharpening.

If Israel was to avoid absorption she needed a king.

Canaan had by now been in confusion for some centuries and bands of warriors plied their trade as mercenaries or bandits. Saul the Benjamite led one. By religion he was pagan. At least three of his children were given names honouring Baal. He was chosen king because he was the best available warrior. He did his best to unite the tribes under his authority. This did not please the shamans, who till then had led the tribes. Saul apparently killed a good many of them, but not enough, for tribal authority remained in being and challenged royal authority. He failed to get rid of Samuel, who apparently forced him to murder the Amalekites in primitive tribal manner instead of using them within his realm after the manner of a king.

I can find no reason for believing that either Saul or Samuel served the Yahweh cult. Saul's favourite god was Baal, while Samuel served a 'high place'. High places were pagan shrines which were destroyed whenever the Yahweh followers gained power.

The Philistines seem to have brought a Homeric spirit with them, that changed the simple bloodiness of tribal conflict. Battles were decided by champions. Goliath challenged and was taken by David. Jonathan and his armour-bearer went to the Philistine camp and had their challenge accepted. David's mighty three broke through the Philistine army to get water from the well of Bethlehem; and David's exploits and conflict with Saul would fit into the *Iliad*.

Saul was not strong enough to beat the Philistines, but he did defeat a number of other nomad tribes that were pressing behind the Hebrews. David, from the tribe of Judah, was another mercenary captain, who first took service with Saul and then with the Philistines. 2 Samuel, xxiii, gives a list of thirty mighty men who led David's private army. They included Uriah the Hittite, and many had foreign names. It was this private army that took Jerusalem from the Jebusites and established David's city. On Saul's death David was elected King of Judah and Saul's son Ishbaal ('man of Baal') succeeded as King of Israel. War followed and David won. He proved to be one of the world's great conquerors. He crushed the Philistines, took Damascus and won an empire extending from the Euphrates to Egypt. The Canaanite cities of the coast were his humble allies. His troubles were at home. The tribal system that he inherited was far too primitive to give him a secure power base. Tribal custom remained in being and shaman judges exercised tribal authority. There were shifting inter-tribal feuds of which the most constant was that which divided Judah and part of Benjamin from the rest. The law of Moses had acquired many Canaanite additions necessary for a settled people, but it was still essentially tribal law. Property was primarily the property of the clan, and it was from the clan that authority derived. As a system of law it is said to derive from Hammurabi but it is far more primitive than the Babylonian code that preceded it by about 700 years.

During David's reign the cult of Yahweh gained strength, particularly in the tribe of Judah. Men are potent when they believe, and the Yahwehites believed. Their hereditary priests preached to the tribes. They stood for the puritan ways of the desert against the more permissive ways of civilisation. They probably helped David defeat Ishbaal, but later they proved to be an embarrassment to royal government. In some measure they formed a state within a state. Whenever anything went wrong there were always zealots from hill and desert who prophesied and made things a lot worse. David did what he could. He collected the Ark of the Covenant from Shiloh and brought it into his own personal domain of Jerusalem. He tried to centralise, but tribalism proved too strong. Twice, under Absalom and under Sheba, Israel rose against Judah and David had to fight to restore his authority.

David is the hero of the Old Testament, the man who walked in the ways of Yahweh, but they were sometimes odd ways. There was a three-year famine. David enquired of the Lord (we do not know how) and the Lord answered 'It is for Saul because he slew the Gibeonites'. The Gibeonites were Amorites to whom safety had been sworn. Seven descendants of Saul, none of whom had committed any fault, were handed to the Gibeonites and hanged by them 'and they were put to death in the days of the harvest, in the first days, in the beginning of the barley harvest' (2 Samuel xxi, 9). This sounds like a fertility blood sacrifice and does not fit into Yahweh worship. David provided the victims. The Gibeonites were not Jews.

Egypt and Mesopotamia were in decline and Solomon, the son of Bathsheba who had been the wife of Uriah the Hittite, inherited the leading empire of the world. He did his utmost to escape from tribal bonds. He built himself a palace fit for a monarch who was the equal of Pharaoh and of the King of Babylon. He married Pharaoh's daughter. Nomadic Yahweh, who till then had lived in a tent, was provided with a temple designed on the same plan and with the same magnificence as that provided for the gods of Egypt and of Syria. The Hebrews could not build palaces and temples. Hiram, King of Tyre, was persuaded to undertake the job and he sent architects, craftsmen and cedars from Lebanon. The Palace had a large seraglio and the temple provided accommodation for the gods of the royal wives. Solomon controlled the caravan routes between the Euphrates and the Nile, traded from Aden to Cyprus and maintained a professional army which included 1,400 chariots housed in chariot cities. He was setting out to govern an empire and he had no truck with a particularist or jealous god. All the gods of the empire must be honoured. In the temple was the great 'molten sea', a huge bowl carried by twelve life-size brazen bulls. Baal was the god who confined the waters and the bulls were his fertility symbols.

'Solomon loved the Lord, walking in the statutes of David his father; only he sacrificed and burnt incense in high places, and he went to Gibeon to sacrifice there; for that was the great high place. A thousand offerings did Solomon offer on that altar' (1 Kings iii, 3–4).

Solomon probably tried to assume divine kingship on the Egyptian model (Psalms 2 and 110 appear to attribute divine qualities to the king), but by the end of his reign he was on the retreat and Syria was lost. He had sought to make bricks without the straw of a uniting faith. Yahweh was tribal. He had made his bargain with a tribe. There was no accession clause. He could not tolerate the open-ended, inclusive faith that cements a state. The worship of the god-king and the overriding love of the polis were equally unacceptable to the jealous god. Solomon had done his best, but tribal instincts and a nomadic priesthood had proved too strong. On his death the nation split. His son ruled only Judah, while Israel seceded under Jeraboam and Ahijah the priest of Shiloh. In 940 Pharaoh Sheshonk invaded Judah and sacked palace and temple.

Judah never worked. The tribal area led by sectarian bigots was in continual conflict with cosmopolitan Jerusalem.

Israel became an important empire. She had a mixture of people worshipping a variety of gods. The quality of respect due to other people's gods is illustrated by some stories from this period. When Naaman, the Syrian general, had suspected leprosy, he travelled to a Yahweh prophet for a cure. When Hadadad, King of Syria was in trouble he too sent for a prophet, who travelled to him. Most remarkable is the story of Mesha, King of Moab. Israel, Judah and Edom, in temporary alliance attacked Moab. Mesha was defeated and bottled up in his capital. He tried to break out through the Edomites but was driven back. Mesha then took his son, the crown prince up on the wall and sacrificed him to Chemosh, the God of Moab, with the result that the armies of Israel and

Judah bolted. They can only have thought that Yahweh would be no match for a Chemosh fed on that sort of royal jelly. We have both versions of the story, 2 Kings iii, 4–27, and the Moabite Stone, a stele on which Mesha celebrated Chemosh's victory over Yahweh. These stories are tribal and concern gods that were both private and tribal property and generally credible—kings had to keep such gods in balance.

Israel threw up two such king-emperors. Omri stopped petty tribal bickering with Judah, formed an alliance with Phoenicia and built the first major Hebrew city, Samaria. To do so he still had to use Tyrian skill. His son Ahab married Jezebel, a Tyrian princess. One of his chariot barracks, with stabling for 700 horses, has recently been excavated. He regained Moab and Edom that had formed part of David's empire. He defeated and captured Hadadad, King of Syria. As Ahab was not a king who 'walked in the way of the Lord', he did not slaughter his prisoner as the prophets demanded, but released him on generous terms. This enabled Ahab a few years later to form the Aramaic league with Hadadad when they both faced the terrible threat of Assyria. In 853 BC they met Shalmonesar II and the might of Assyria at Qar Qar on the Orontes, in what may have been the greatest battle that had then been fought in the Middle East. The priestly authors of Kings do not mention this fight, for it brought Ahab much glory, but according to Shalmoneser he met Hadadad of Damascus with 1,200 chariots and 20,000 foot, Irhulen of Hamath with 700 chariots, 700 mounted cavalry (I think the first recorded in action) and 10,000 foot, and Ahab of Israel with 2,000 chariots and 10,000 foot. It appears to have been a drawn battle, but the Assyrians were stopped and did not return for ten years. Ahab was then dead and Elisha the prophet had conspired against his son Joram with a chariot officer called Jehu. There was a war with Syria. Joram was recovering from wounds. Jehu murdered his wounded master, his master's ally, King Anaziah of Judah, Jezebel the Queen Mother, the Judean ambassador and his entire suite, seventy sons of Ahab and most of his civil servants and then conducted a most treacherous sectarian massacre of his Canaanite subjects after inviting them to meet him (2 Kings, chapters ix and x).

'And the Lord said unto Jehu thou has done well in executing that which is right in mine eyes' (2 Kings, ii, 30). The
Assyrians returned. Israel was crippled and her allies lost. We
have a picture of Jehu on his hands and knees before Shalmoneser III. Unfortunately we have no picture of Ahab
the Israelite standing before Shalmoneser II at the head of
2,000 chariots and 10,000 foot. The hill mullahs had triumphed
and the greatness of Israel was over.

Transference of populations was a practice of both the
Assyrians and of the Babylonians who followed. When new
territory was captured, those males who were spared were
marched off for hundreds of miles and resettled, their women
and their homes having been allotted to the conquerors. The
transferred population often became loyal subjects. I think
the idea was not unlike one which I found in operation in
the US Marine training depot. The recruits were bullied,
humiliated and exhausted for six weeks by which time they
were blubbering wrecks. Then they were picked up, rehabilitated and given a new personality as marines. The process is
sometimes called brain washing. We see Assyrian prisoners
on monuments in bas-relief, marching shackled across the
empire. Those that arrived must have been shocked, terrified
and broken. They were then handed over by their escorts to
a local governor, who wanted them, and who found them
food, land, tools and women. If he was intelligent he could
make them devoted followers.

Transportation was the fate both of Israel and of Judah,
the former by Assyria and the latter by Babylon. The tribes
of Israel were lost, which is to say that they were successfully
absorbed. Yahweh worship in Israel was probably never more
than a minority cult and its devotees were either converted
or exterminated. Judah prospered in Babylon and the followers
of Yahweh gained strength. Their monotheism enabled them
to retain their identity and their self-respect. This was the time
when much of the Old Testament was written and it was
written to the glory of Yahweh. After about fifty years Babylon was defeated by Cyrus the Persian, and the Jews were
permitted to return to Jerusalem. Many had been assimilated
but according to contemporary records something like 40,000
did return accompanied by 7,000 slaves, which illustrates how

the transferred population had prospered. Those who returned were certainly the followers of Yahweh and I believe that it is from this time that the Jews became a people with a single religion, fanatically held. At first they were confined to Jerusalem and its immediate neighbourhood. Gradually they extended. Persia was succeeded by Macedonia. Eventually the Seleucid empire broke up and the Jews established an independent theocracy under the Maccabees or Hasmonaens. The religion that had served them so well in exile and servitude again proved disastrous in power. The new state set on its neighbours, destroying and forcibly converting. It turned on itself in bitter sectarian conflict. It's last dynasty, the Herods, came from the Edomites who had been forcibly converted a generation before. Israel became a Roman province, but when they rebelled, as Josephus tells us, rival sects tore the country to pieces. In the last act, as the army of Titus advanced on Jerusalem, the zealots demonstrated their faith in God by burning the corn stored by John of Gishala, the city's commander.

The story of Israel and Judah is a story often to be repeated, of tribes that failed to develop a collective loyalty powerful enough to bind them into a state. Civilisation is a psychological revolution. The whole personality of the tribesman must be overturned, by a single overpowering emotion. There is no room for division between church and nascent state. The king, if he be not god, must be *pontifex maximus*, god's mouthpiece to the nation, for the faith that founds a state cannot be divided.

Before the Babylonian captivity I do not think that Yahwehism, save possibly in the tribe of Judah, was ever more than a divisive minority cult. It was during exile that its unique quality emerged. The believers retained their identity, the rest dispersed. The Jews whom Cyrus the Great returned to Jerusalem were a congregation; they were also a people of the book, for the priests had written the history of their god. The saved who testify at a revivalist meeting tend to exaggerate the depths from which they have been lifted. Slavery in Egypt is, I think, such an exaggeration. 200 years of fighting are compressed into a single year of god-given victory, and all the later disasters are ascribed to back-slidings in faith, but the Jews who returned were not historical critics, they were believers and their special god gave them an identity.

There is much beauty in the Old Testament, but I cannot find anything that modifies in its essentials the bloodthirsty intolerance of monotheism. If this be morality, it confirms my belief that ethics are better left to reason. General Amin is, I am sure, as confident in his godliness as was the prophet Elijah.

I know many reasons for reverencing Jewry. I admire their lay state beyond measure. I hope that they will never let Yahweh interfere with it, because I believe that the brand of intolerance that we have learned from the Old Testament prophets has been the recurring curse of our civilisation. The story of ancient Israel should serve as a cautionary tale. Priests should be kept out of politics, for of all governments, priest-run governments have proved the worst. On the other hand, as a religion in captivity and exile, Judaism achieved greatly. For over 2,600 years of dispersion and catastrophe it has maintained a Jewish identity. To Eastern European Jewry the Mongolian Kassans were added by conversion in the twelfth century, but since that date the Jewish stud book has been closed, for their own rules against exogamy were re-inforced by the ghetto system that was imposed upon them. Many individual Jews, of course, became absorbed in neighbouring communities, but those who retained their Jewishness did so because of their faith. The ghettos became close in-breeding isolates. Their admired qualities were erudition and music. They were ruled by the wisest. The ghetto was a confined community. A surplus had to disperse. In the Europe of the ghetto period many did so, as travelling pedlars. The cleverest remained, and married the daughters of the cleverer ones of the preceding generation. The ghetto in-bred and line-bred for brains and music in much the same way as a pack of hounds is bred for its hunting qualities by keeping the best dogs and drafting the rest. The result has been astonishing. The Jews are far less than one per cent of humanity. Perhaps one-half of the best musicians, mathematicians and pure scientists have been Jews. It is hard to name a great violinist who was not a Jew. The Jewish contribution to literature has been out of all proportion to their numbers, and to cap it all, they have today built an army which man for man is far and away the best in the world. If they indeed be a Yahweh's fancy, he has every reason to be proud of his rosettes.

6

ROME

WE KNOW VERY LITTLE of the first inhabitants of Italy. An Aryan language-speaking tribe moved from Central Europe into Italy at much the same time as the Dorians were entering Greece—about 1,200 BC. Then, in about the ninth century BC, there arrived by sea from Asia Minor a new people, the Etruscans, who had achieved an urban level of culture. They occupied most of Central Italy. They were a mysterious people of high artistic achievement of whom we know little because we cannot read their language. A little later, probably in the seventh century, Greek colonies began to occupy Southern Italy.

In about 600 BC a band of Etruscan migrants established their authority over a group of Italian or Latin villages on seven hills beside the river Tiber, some fifteen miles from its mouth. They converted these hills into a city kingdom to which they gave the Etruscan name of Rome. They ruled for about a century (600–500 BC), and then the Latin tribes expelled the proud Tarquin, their king, and set up a republic. Magistrates were appointed in duplicate for one year only so that no-one should become established in power, and the ex-magistrates formed a senate. The state they created was essentially a family league. The *pater familias* ruled his family as a king. In Rome, unlike Greece, he retained authority over the adult and married children and in early times had the power of life and death.

It was not long before the republic was faced with an immigrant problem. Rome was strategically placed at the head of the Tiber navigation. Its suburbs contained a mixed population of mariners—Greek, Phoenician and Sardinian, indeed all the people of the sea who, for one reason or another, had taken shelter in the Tiber and settled. These people, who became known as the 'Plebs', gained nothing from the fall of the monarchy and they started to press for rights.

Now Rome needed the Plebs and the Plebs needed Rome. This the leaders of the Plebs, who became known as tribunes of the people, had the wit to recognise. When a military crisis loomed they staged a walk-out. The Patricians had to negotiate. The Plebs demanded that laws be published for all to see, applicable to Patrician and Plebeian alike. They had their way. The twelve tables, the foundation of the Roman legal system that still today regulates much of the civilised world, were caste in bronze and in the year 450 BC they were erected in the forum. All else followed. The Plebeians won full rights as citizens, and indeed they became privileged, for while they could, and often did, hold the old Patrician magistracies, only a Plebeian could be tribune and the tribunate wielded great power. When Julius Caesar wished to be tribune he had to get himself adopted by a Plebeian family.

The differences between the Roman polis and the Greek derived from origins. The Greeks descended from warrior bands, Achaean or Dorian, married into a native pre-tribal society. Authority did not come primarily from the resulting families; it already existed within the band, it was the authority of the heroic clansmen. The Greek polis was the whole manpower; the Roman was the Fathers. This did not cease to be so when the Plebeians won authority. All that happened was that the Fathers of the old families formed a coalition with the Fathers of the new families. It was quite a small group. Rome was never a democracy.

Greek ideals and Greek religion were essentially individualistic. The clan heroes sought personal glory and the gods were heroes writ large. The Roman ideal was corporate and patriotic.

Regulus, the consul who returned to die in Carthage after advising the Senate to refuse the treaty that would have given him liberty, was a Roman hero. Had the story been Greek it would have ended with Regulus outwitting the Carthaginians. Roman virtue was expressed in two words which we find it hard to translate, *pietas* and *gravitas*. *Pietas* involved the respect due to the father, to the state and to the gods together with a feeling for and acceptance of the traditions of the tribe; *gravitas* was the father's quality; weight, seriousness, calmness, self-control, steady nerves and justice—all were included in a single word. The Romans adopted the anthropomorphic gods of the Greeks and the Auguries of the Etruscans, but the gods they really minded about were household family gods, (*lares et penates*) and the great god that was Rome.

Roman law, too, was different. Greek laws tended to be generalised principles. Whatever form the government of the Greek polis took, the ruling authority acted arbitrarily claiming only to be guided by the general principles set out in the laws. In Rome the laws were the constitution, and the bronze tablets in the Forum were the ark of the covenant that bound Patrician and Plebeian alike. This reverence for law was important when Rome expanded.

Just as the laws had been the security of the Plebs, they became the security of the Latin cities. Those that surrendered were spared pillage and granted rights under the law, which in some cases amounted to full citizenship. They accepted duties and contributed their quotas to the Roman armies. Rome also set up colonies of farmer soldiers in Italy which did not become independent cities as Greek colonies had done but remained a part of the republic of Rome. There was a framework of law and administration within which this state could grow. When the crunch came and Hannibal invaded Italy most of the Italian cities stood by Rome. Carthage was defeated. Macedon followed shortly afterwards and the Mediterranean became a Roman sea bordered by her provinces.

Roman history may be divided into three periods, the Republic, the Principate and the Dominate. Each achieved great things but each dissolved in civil war. All lacked an effective means of transferring power. Faced with Empire, Republican institutions that had served to govern Rome and to create Roman Italy met new problems and failed.

Hannibal spent fifteen years in Italy. When he left, Southern Italy was destroyed and in a real sense has never recovered. The ruined countryside was taken over by 'hard-faced men who had done well out of the war', and their vast estates were run by slaves. The citizens became a rabble fed at public expense and entertained by ambitious politicians who bought their votes with circuses. These politicians, after holding Republican office, passed on to govern the new provinces. Their appointments were generally for a year, not a long time in which to get rich and recoup the expenses of a Roman political career. The conquered provinces were taxed rapaciously and the collection farmed out to private enterprise. Liberty and justice were for sale. 'Words cannot express', said Cicero, 'how bitterly we are hated among foreign peoples because of the outrageous conduct of the men who in recent years we have sent to govern them.'

When a lower level of civilisation defeats a higher, it often happens that the conquered culture conquers. In a measure this happened to Rome. Roman boys who before had been trained by their fathers passed into the hands of Greek tutors. Athens became Rome's university. Roman values shifted from group solidarity to individual happiness. The quest for wealth and power displaced *pietas*. The extended family crumbled as the young became rich and opiniated. We should know. Divorce became common, but the organs of the state remained group orientated. Tensions grew. Traditional religion which had served family and state, lost both its intellectual respectability and its coherence. The Senate legalised the importation of foreign cults. Aesculapius from Greece, Isis from Egypt and the Greco-Italian Bacchic-Orphic mysteries.

The Gracchi, grandsons of Scipio Africanus, the conqueror of Hannibal to whom Sir Basil Liddell Hart awarded his personal Oscar as the greatest general that ever lived, attempted reform. They were both murdered by the conservatives. Rome dissolved in anarchy. The frontiers began to crumble. In 122 BC Gaius Marius was consul and so, contrary to all precedent, he remained for seven years. He threw open the legions to volunteers, thus creating for the first time a professional army. Recruits were promised a grant of Italian land after sixteen years' service. Rome's enemies retired defeated but henceforward the loyalty of Rome's armies would be to their general. The power of the Senate had diminished. In 88 BC, danger reappeared in the form of Mithridates, King of Pontus. Eighty thousand Romans and Provincials were massacred in the province of Asia. The Senate sent Sulla. He beat Mithridates but by his brutality and greed ruined the province. Sulla returned to Rome and after a civil war against Marius made himself dictator for life. He raised his taxes by prescription. If you name was on the list you were killed. The price of keeping your name off grew higher and higher. About one-third of the Senate were killed. Then, in 79 BC, Sulla retired, and returned to his farm; but the system of rule by terror remained and as always violence answered violence. In 70 BC there occurred that which is always the ultimate terror in a slave owning society; the slaves under Spartacus the gladiator rebelled. Pompey saved the day. He was a fine soldier and succeeded in his military tasks, the slaves were crucified, the pirates destroyed and Mithridates was killed. Had Pompey been a revolutionary he might have played the role of Augustus. Instead he tried to restore the Republic, which by now meant the rule of a corrupt and greedy Senatorial aristocracy. Caesar led the radical forces and the time came when a clash was inevitable. Caesar won, but was murdered by the conservatives in a last rally for power. When his nephew and heir Augustus won the next civil war, the Republic was at an end and the Principate had begun. Augustus ruled the Roman World. In what was later called the Golden Age he solved all his problems save one—the succession.

Augustus did not take the title of king, which Rome hated. The title he chose was *princeps* or chief. The machinery of popular rule continued to function; Senate, magistrates and popular assemblies, but the Princeps exercised the functions. He was legislator, chief justice, high priest and commander-in-chief. He was not a god during his life, but after death his spirit was worshipped. This was in the tradition of Roman ancestor worship, but it did not create a royal family. The chief was appointed or elected.

Augustus created a professional civil service. Provincial Governors were appointed by him and held office at his pleasure. He ruled for forty years and the Pax Romana was his work. The provinces knew order and on the whole honest government. Everything depended on the right Emperor. He held office for life. His absolutism was limited only by assassination. If he became senile the empire fell into chaos as rival candidates played for the succession. Augustus kept his wits, but his heir did not. Tiberius became a recluse on Capri suffering from a persecution obsession, and the succession was contrived for his nephew, Caligula who became a raving lunatic within months of his accession. He was killed by his guards, who in panic proclaimed as Emperor his old uncle, Claudius, an elderly scholar who had played no part in public life. He proved an excellent ruler, but eventually he lost control of his family and his third wife contrived the succession for her seventeen-year-old son. To rule the world at seventeen would strain most characters. Nero did better than might have been expected. He chose two excellent ministers and supported them; but after a great fire had destroyed Rome the cost of his private indulgences and of the huge palace he designed to build on the ruins of Rome became more than the treasury could bear. The pay of the legions fell in arrears and Nero was doomed. The Augustan dynasty was at an end. Of the successors Tiberius alone had been a fit person to be appointed Princeps. No rules of inheritance, election or appointment had emerged, but the Augustan civil service was still working tolerably well.

The next Emperor came from the army. His name was Vespasian and he came from the Senatorial Flavian family. When the vacancy occurred he was commanding three legions in the Jewish war. He ruled in the Augustan manner with largely the same civil service that had served Nero. He was succeeded first by his son Titus and then by a second son, Domitian, who proved impossible. Succession within a family was rated a failure. In the second century AD a new principle was put into pratice. Each Emperor chose the man he felt most fitted to succeed him and adopted him as his son. This worked for a time. The so called 'Good Emperors' who followed Domitian —Nerva, Trajan, Hadrian, Antonius Pius and Marcus Aurelius maintained internal peace and guarded the frontiers.

Gibbon called this part of the second century 'the period in the history of the world during which the condition of the human race was most happy and prosperous', but this depended a little on which bit of the human race one belonged to.

Roman civilisation was urban. The Roman Empire was a conglomeration of cities. Not till the nineteenth century was the second century's level of urbanisation equalled. Rome itself was the extreme example, the eater of the profits of empire. This was the great period of public buildings, but the cost of works was trivial when compared with that of welfare. A population verging perhaps on two million lived on subsidised food and were appeased by entertainments of astonishing cost and brutality, for there was a strong sadistic streak in the Romans. The provincial cities were little Romes with the theatres, amphitheatres, baths, bridges and aqueducts, that were the constants of Roman urban planning. The civilisation of Rome rose and ebbed with the water supply. Britain's cities date from this second century. In Africa there were 500 Roman cities. The roads came too. By AD 150 Britain had 6,500 miles of paved roads.

The cities lived on the countryside. The physician Galen has left descriptions of rural starvation: 'The city dwellers as was their practice, collected and stored enough corn for all the coming year immediately after harvest. They carried off all the wheat, the barley, the beans and the lentils and left what remained to the country folk.'

Beyond the frontiers the Parthian empire was undefeated and the German tribes seethed.

Expenditure outran income. Military expenditure needed priority. The Augustan system still remained. Government was largely Roman, the Emperor's senior servants were drawn mainly from the Senate and his administrators mainly from the Equestrian order; but with the squeeze on civil administration, public service became less attractive. Rich men tended to return to their country estates and prefer personal culture to public service. In the provinces City Councils found themselves more and more becoming the tax collectors of central government. The rich began avoiding the cities and the cities to decay. New religions became the fashion. With the loss of self-confidence the Greek tradition or reliance on reason gave place to faith in divine forces and a search for personal salvation. Mystery, magic and astrology became all the rage. Of the new religions Mithraism and Christianity were the most successful.

The principate died with Marcus Aurelius. We know Marcus well. Michael Grant *(Climax of Rome)* says of him, 'Marcus Aurelius is the noblest of all the men who by sheer intelligence and force of character, have prized and achieved goodness for its own sake and not for any reward.' Throughout his active life he wrote his thoughts first in letters to his tutor Fronto and later in private notes which were not intended for publication but which have come down to us as the *Meditations of Marcus Aurelius.* They are indeed writings to himself.

> 'Never be flustered, never be apathetic, never be attitudinising.'
> ' "How unlucky I am that this should have happened to me!" by no means, Say "How lucky I am that it has left me with no bitterness . . ." The thing could have happened to anyone but not everyone could have emerged unembittered.'
> 'Resolve firmly, like a Roman and a man, to do what comes to hand with natural dignity and with humanity and justice . . . if you do the task before you, adhering to strict reason with zeal and energy and yet with humanity . . . if you hold steadily to this . . . seeking only in each passing action a conformity with nature and in each word a fearless truthfuness, then shall the good life be yours.'
> 'It is peculiar to man to love even those who do wrong.'
> 'My city and my country so far as I am Antoninus, is Rome, but so far as I am a man, it is the world.'
> Marcus described his ideal state: 'a polity in which there is the same law for all, a polity administered with regard to equal rights and equal freedom of speech and a kingly government, which respects most of all the freedom of the governed.'

The Christian ethic based on promised salvation did not earn Marcus's respect and he had little patience with Christian Martyrs. Life should be taken seriously, it was indeed men's highest responsibility and to throw it away on a mere matter of contumacy was not respectable.

Marcus had fifteen years of supreme power during which he made these writings the rules that governed his conduct. I can think of no Christian king who in the practice of power even distantly approached the standards of integrity which this Pagan set and to which he adhered, and this is the more remarkable when one realises that the task that destiny had placed before Marcus was impossible.

The people of the heart lands were moving. and the frontier peoples were driven on to Rome. This was the inevitability, Rome could never stabilise her frontiers because her neighbours both in the north and east were under pressure from folk movements in the backlands. The Parthians in the east, a nation of mounted archers pushed out of the steppes invaded Cappadosia where they defeated and killed the Roman Governor. Marcus sent his colleague Lucius Verus to deal with the situation. Then the Germans crossed the upper Danube, broke into the flat plain and turning east crossed the Austrian Alps, entered Italy and lay siege to Aquilea. Other Germans crossed lower down, plundered Eleusis and nearly reached Athens. The legions had to be recalled from the East. Marcus, who amongst his other qualities was a great general, deemed it his duty to take personal command. For the last fourteen years of his life he was engaged in war. Gradually he drove the Germans back. He found no triumph in war. Victory was the exultation of a robber or of the spider that has caught a fly. The imperial purple itself was but the gore of a fish. Marcus sought to admit the Germans, who came under pressure and to make them into Roman citizens. He sought to push forward his frontiers to the line of the Carpathians and the Sudetan mountains so as to secure the rear of the tribes he sought to Romanise. The trouble was that the Empire could not afford the war. Plague had hit the Roman world. The cities had drained the countryside and were now in the throes of inflation. They could no longer be squeezed for the pay of the army. Cities were falling into disrepair and were being abandoned. With the death of Marcus (AD 180) ended the rule of Roman men and of Greek civilisation. The titles of Augustus and Caesar were conferred by armies no longer Roman, sometimes on their generals and sometimes on those who offered them the most money. This was when the dark ages of the west really started.

7

BYZANTIUM AND
RUSSIA

WE NOW COME TO those civilisations that are god-given,
where the divine autocrat, if he be not god, is god's deputy,
he to whom the truth has been revealed; where religion and
politics are one and where opposition is both treason and
sacrilege. The contradictions that obstructed Israel are eliminated at a price.

Christianity found a place in this system. The Roman empire
had divided and Constantine (AD 312) was building a new
imperial capital at Byzantium. He chose christianity as the
new Imperial religion.

Why?

He was a soldier of Danubian descent and a politician
dedicated to power. He had won the empire as a Sun worship-
per, the creed of his ancestors and the favourite of his army.
After victory he had moved east to the urban civilisation
that must support the armies of the frontier. He had found a
great divide. The frontier provinces from which the army
was recruited were a world apart from the cities of the
Eastern Mediterranean. If the army was led to a city it was
to sack it. This happened when cities rioted and killed imperial
officials, but as a method of government sacking had its
limitations, Constantine wanted an instrument of urban administration that could operate between the governors and
the governed and serve as a political intelligence service. The
Christian Church fitted this purpose.

The Church had changed since the first century when Tacitus saw the Christians as haters of mankind who besought their god daily to destroy the human race. Christianity had turned respectable, and Christians had found that they could identify themselves with the culture, outlook and needs of an urban middle class. The learned Origen taught that Christ had existed from the beginning and had 'tended' the best in Greek culture, particularly in philosophy and ethics, in just the same way as he had revealed laws to the Jews; that his coming had been synchronised with the foundation of the Pax Romana by Augustus that any Christian who rejected Greek culture and Roman Empire was denying the divinely ordained progress of the human race.

Civilisation had come through a very rough century. The classical belief in the potency of reason had been broken. The world of the imagination was populated by demons. Demons were the germs of late antiquity, the unseen agents that carried disease and misfortune. Christianity had adopted from Zoroastrian Persia an acceptable antiseptic; there was an absolute division in the spirit world between good and evil, the angels and the devils; the devil was allotted great but limited powers; he was the source of all the evils that humans suffer but Christ had defeated him in heaven and on earth he could be held in check by Christ's human agents; it was a mopping up operation which the Church would surely win. Obey the Church and there was no need to fear the devil. Christ had entrusted the keys of heaven to his Church. The life of the slave might be hard but his patience would be rewarded a thousandfold in heaven where he would be allowed to witness the eternal torture of his pagan master.

Constantine felt that this was the right stuff for keeping cities obedient. Christianity was by far the best organised of the competitive religions and mysteries. It had organised to survive. In face of persecution it split into cells within which the leader or presbyter linked with the next cell higher up and so to the bishop. It was thus both cellular and hierarchic. It was a system that depended on discipline and obedience. Finally the Church was willing. Its best leaders were sent to court and convinced Constantine of the suitability of Christianity as a state religion. A Church trained to obedience accepted

the service of Caesar as a divinely commanded duty, and became the divine aspect of Imperial rule.

As a department of state its importance was to grow. For
a century the Empire had been ruled by soldiers and administered by military juntas. Constantine started the move
back to civilian rule. Within this process the founding of a
new capital, played a vital part. Military administration can
move with a camp, civilian rule needs a settled capital.

Gradually an administrative balance developed. At the
centre was the Emperor. The great offices of state were staffed
by a civil service of scholars drawn from the Greek gentry of
the provincial cities of what had once been the Empire of
Alexander; the Emperor was advised by court officials, many
of them eunuchs, and led by the Great Court Chamberlain
who was always a eunuch, while local government and welfare services outside of Constantinople itself came more and
more to be administered by the Church. Military influence was
squeezed out of politics. A very similar triple balance developed in China.

The story of the Arab conquests runs on much the same
lines. Arabia, south of the great empires of Rome and Persia
had been barbarian territory whose nomadic tribes were controlled by a system of alliances and subsidies. Mecca and
Medina were old trading cities ruled by oligarchies. Suddenly,
in the second half of the sixth century, the oligarchs became
merchant princes. The caravans of Mecca merchants visited
Jerusalem and the cities of Byzantium. Mohammed, one of
the less successful merchants had travelled with such caravans.
He had been impressed by Jewish monotheism. In 610, at the
age of forty he started to have visions which he recited in
verse. This became the Koran, and the modern Arab hatred
for the Jews is all the sadder when one remembers that they
owe to Judaism at least as much as we Christians.

The Bedouin tribal ideal had been extrovert; conduct was
guided by fear of losing face within the tribe and desire to
win admiration, to uphold superiority of ancestry by exhibi-
tionist performances in generosity and courage, and to exact
revenge. The blood feud was a way of life. It had its advantages. It put a high value on human life. Nobody wanted to be
stalked by the relations for the rest of his life. The Egyptians

found this in the 1960s when they intervened in the Yemen. There tribal war had continued for generations with a maximum expenditure of ammunition and a minimum casualty rate. When the Egyptians came the tribesman found he could shoot an Egyptian for free. Tribal marksmanship showed a spectacular improvement. The blood feud had its points but it was the creed of a static society. Mohammed was for progress. He attacked the communal tribe ideal. Man was an atom. At the last judgement he would stand alone before Allah, without tribe and without family. In his life man must rule himself not by 'face' within the tribe but by personal intimate fear of God, driven into his heart by the thought of God's last judgement. This was the fear and the only fear of Cromwell's Ironsides. Shame was no longer the fear of tribal opinion, it was the fear of God. Mohammed created a new tribe. Temporarily at any rate he killed the blood feud. Arabia knew peace. Her neighbours knew war. Arab armies seized the provinces of Byzantium and swept along North Africa and into Spain till they met Charles Martel beyond the Pyrenees. In the East they took and converted the empire of Persia. Only at the walls of Byzantium were they stopped.

They proved strangely tolerant conquerors. They were so confident of their own superiority that they did not need to assert it, and in this they were only equalled by the nineteenth century English. The 'Garden guarded by Arab spears', was encouraged to administer itself, and the tribute was moderate. Mohammedans did not prosyletise. The Prophet had said all Moslems were equal, and the Arabs were not looking for equals. The Christian bishops who had ruled the cities for Byzantium ruled them for the Caliph. This continued up to the fall of the Turkish Empire. A distinguished British Governor of Cyprus included in a despatch 'HMG must realise that in the middle East religion *is* nationality.' But the Arab aristocracy, aloof in its garrison cities, could not go on for ever. They found themselves in the same position as the Roman aristocracy had found itself in the third century, their certainty was swamped by the energetic patriotism of the provinces. The Umayyad dynasty of Damascus gave way to the Abbasid dynasty of Baghdad; but power was not moving to barbarians, it was moving to the advanced culture of

Persia. By the end of the eighth century the Arab Empire had become the Persian Empire once again. Haroun al Raschid (788–809) ruled a Moslem theocratic empire much as his contemporary Nicephorus ruled a Christian theocratic empire in Byzantium. Both were based on the Near Eastern tradition of divine rule.

Over the centuries new dynasties from the heartland of Asia won Baghdad and assumed the divine authority of the Moslem Caliphate. Eventually, in 1453, the Ottoman Turks who had succeeded to the Abbasid Caliphate stormed Byzantium; the Empire of Constantine that had endured for a thousand years came to an end. A Muslim sacred empire was substituted for a Christian, and lumbered on until Kemal Ataturk (1923) attempted the ruthless imposition of democracy. In the Arab provinces of the old Turkish Empire Britain and France were trying to do the same thing by milder methods.

The extent of their success will be discussed in another chapter; but we can say here that in this Middle Eastern area the idea that held society together, that controlled both family and tribe for 8,000 years from the days of Sumeria and of dynastic Egypt, was the need to submit totally to a divine authority in human form, and it has mattered little whether the god was pagan, Mohammedan or Christian.

Moscow became the heir of Byzantium; her ruler the Czar was the divine autocrat of all the Russias.

The conversion of the Russians is quite a story. St Vladimir (980–1015) became dissatisfied with his pagan god Peroun and threw him into the river. He was washed ashore and the Slavs rushed to meet him but Vladimir threw him back, and no more was seen of Peroun of the silver face and golden moustache. Then Vladimir looked about for a new religion. He sent a commission to report on Judaism (which had recently been adopted by his neighbours the Kazakhs), Mohammedanism and the two brands of Christianity. Judaism was rejected as it involved circumcision and this Vladimir did not fancy at his time of life; Mohammedanism was teetotal, and this he considered inappropriate for a cold climate; between the Christian sects he preferred the greater magnificence of the Eastern Church. A prince of his importance required an

Archbishop to baptise him. He was too great to ask a favour of Byzantium, so he decided to capture his archbishop. He attacked Kherson, an ancient city on the Black Sea coast which was a self-governing dependency of Byzantium, carried it by storm and grabbed his archbishop, who duly baptised him and married him to a Byzantine princess, several previous wives not withstanding. The Prince's followers took to the new religion with the enthusiasm with which troops will sometimes take to a battle song captured from the enemy. The Good Book tells us that there is but one way to enter the Kingdom of God. St Vladimir proved that there are at least two.

His methods were fantastic and his results profound. A people with a special talent for prostration and with strong masochistic predilections were saddled with a religion developed and geared for authoritarian rule. The result is still there. It is only the faith that has changed.

From the plains of Hungary through the Ukraine, across the Ural mountains, on through Siberia and into Mongolia runs a broad grassy highway. To the north lie the forest belts, first of deciduous trees and then of conifers, thick difficult marshy country where the only roads are rivers. The 'heart lands', as the areas from which conquering tribes emerged have been called, lay at either end of this Savannah highway. In the west, living roughly in central Europe, where we find their Paleolithic and Neolithic burial places, were the Arian speaking peoples. They were the first to move. In the third and second millenniums BC they went down the highway, rounded the Black Sea, crossed the Caucasus mountains, founded the Hittite Empire and the Mittanian State and passed on to overthrow the Indus civilisation. Behind them the Scythians moved into the steppes north of the Black Sea.

Somewhere about 800 BC the movement began to reverse as the people of the eastern heartland, speaking Turkish and Mongolian dialects, began to move west. It started when they learned to ride horses. Man has made three disastrous inventions, the first was how to smelt iron, the second how to ride a horse and the third (and probably final) how to split the atom. The foot soldier marched, married and settled down. The Arian charioteer was not too bad. He was a very expensive Bronze Age warrior with a large walking retinue, that became absorbed by and contributed to the advance of civilisation. Mounted invaders burned, massacred and went home as stupid as they arrived. A brother-in-law of mine always maintained that it was the ammonia from horse urine that rotted the brains of all concerned with horses. Be this as it may, the record of mounted invaders is appalling. The land of the two rivers and of the Persian Empire has never recovered from the extermination of its intelligentsia and the destruction of its irrigation systems by Mongol horsemen, and for nothing. The horsemen put nothing where they destroyed. One after another they came across Southern Russia, Sarmatians, Huns, Pechenegs, Khazars, and Polovtsy, destroyed and disappeared like dinosaurs who were too stupid to live.

The forests north of the steppes were undisturbed by these passers-by. The area from Novgorod in the north to Kiev was inhabited by a slavonic speaking people who had created a stable tribal society with well established villages, that depended mainly on organised hunting and fishing, that traded furs down the rivers and used their women to grow a few simple crops. The Slavs were not a race but a language group forming part of the larger Aryan group. The aboriginal foresty people had been Finns, primitives who may have been the Eastern people who according to Tacitus, 'solved the problems of human existence by having no requirements at all' and they had probably intermarried with Slavonic speakers moving into the forests from the adjoining heartland. Hidden and guarded by their environment this tribal society had enjoyed stability for a long time but at some point in the ninth century AD the tribal balance had become disturbed. An old chronicle says 'Family armed itself against family and there was no justice', and that the Varangians were invited in to restore order. This probably means that the losers in a village fight asked the help of the Norse river pirates, and the pirates stayed. At any rate, somewhere about AD 862 Rurik the Viking, accompanied by a warrior band, established himself at Ladoga and was worshipped by the Slavs. The blood of Rurik became sacred and the Slavs insisted for many centuries they would be ruled only by the sons of Rurik, to whom they gave abject obedience. Within a generation the house of Rurik had established themselves as the autocrats of the northern Slavs and were raiding to the walls of Byzantium. St Vladimir was Rurik's grandson, and the Church he had captured knew well who to obey.

The family of Rurik knew no rule of primogeniture and the next century was occupied with the wars of the contending princes. Then the Mongols came. They were the last and most powerful of the horse archers from Asia. They overran the principalities of Moscow, Kiev and Novgorod. At Liegnitz in Poland and Mohil in Hungary (1240), Batu Khan destroyed the feudal armies of Germany, and Europe lay open to the Golden Horde of the Mongols.

Then, as suddenly as they had come, the Mongols left Europe for their great Khan had died in distant Karakoram and his funeral was a must. They did not leave Russia. The Princes of Russia became their vassals and the Church accepted their authority and consecrated the bishops they nominated. Only the squabbles between the princes continued as before, and brother prayed the aid of the Mongol against brother.

After more than a century of Mongol power, the Golden Horde broke up. Byzantium fell to the Turk and Vasili the Darkened, who had been blinded by a cousin into whose hands he had fallen, succeeded in killing nearly all the surviving descendants of Rurik and leaving his son Ivan III of Moscow, Prince of all the Russias and master of Orthodox Christianity. Ivan, called the Great, was a gloomy, acquisitive man who hated taking risks. He avoided battle where possible as he pushed in all directions into the divisions and weaknesses that surrounded him. He enhanced his prestige by marrying the daughter and heiress of the last Emperor of Byzantium. The title he passed to his son Vasili (1505) was Czar and Autocrat of all the Russias.

The Russia Vasili inherited was a strange and barbarous place. Moscow was an Asiatic city. It was said to have forty times forty churches adorned with bulbs of gold, silver and blue. 'This city', reported the ambassador of The Holy Roman Empire, 'is broad and spacious and so very dirty that bridges over the filth have been constructed in the main highways'. The houses were made of wood and the ordinary Muscovites lived in wattle shacks. The whole was dominated by the

Kremlin fortress. The city itself was unfortified and was periodically burnt by Asiatic or Polish raiders. This was the only cleaning it got. Here, confined by dreary ceremonial and waited on by courtiers and servants whose robes came from Baghdad rather than Rome, the Czar dwelt apart, insulated from the outside world, able to judge by no standard but his own. He was autocrat of Church and State, the real object of his subjects' worship. How the sons of Rurik had earned this worship is hard to see. For over a century they had served the hated Mongol with cringing ferocity and were free only because the Mongol state had dissolved in internecine strife.

The last of the sons of Rurik, last because he murdered all the others including his own son, was Ivan the Terrible. Jealous, punishing, torturing, unpredictable and terrible, these are the qualities which most men have seen in their gods and Ivan had the lot. He succeeded at the age of three (1533). His mother, assisted by her lover, acted as regent until she died, probably from poison in 1538. Her lover was then murdered and the regency was fought for by two noble families, the Bielskis and the Shouyskis. In the struggle for power the young Ivan was neglected. He emerged as a force to be reckoned with suddenly at the age of fourteen. He had been out hunting and returned with his hounds. He strode into the Council Chamber and accused the ruling nobles of abuse of power. Many, he said, had been guilty but he would satisfy himself with one example. Calling his kennel men he bade them seize Count Andrei Shouyski, strip him and throw him to the hounds, an order no sooner given than executed. Prince Andrei was eaten in the reddening snow outside the Council Chamber in full view of his colleagues and relations, on the orders of a fourteen-year-old boy, and apart from that, nothing much happened. The rest of the Council went on governing (very badly) and the lad returned to his religious and other hobbies. The next group to win power in the Council were Ivan's mother's relations, the Glynskis. They ruled even worse and seem to have courted young Ivan's favour by encouraging his savagery. It was at this time that a party of arquebusiers, employed on contract, interrupted a hunting party to ask for their pay. Ivan ordered that they be tortured to death forthwith, and thoroughly enjoyed the spectacle. When another party of petitioners came from Pskov to complain of the Governor's conduct, he ordered burning spirits to be poured over their heads. They were disfigured, though none of them actually died.

When he was seventeen, Ivan had himself crowned Czar and married, but he still did not assume the burden of government. This was left to the Glinskis. That summer Moscow burned; 1,700 adults died, besides children who were not counted. The people accused the Glinskis whom they now saw as the source of all evil. Anna Glinski, the Czar's grandmother, had been seen sprinkling the streets with a decoction of boiled human hearts, which all agreed possessed inflammable qualities. Uncle Uric was torn to pieces in Church. The people came to the Czar craving more Glinskis. Then one Silvester, a monk of Novgorod, appeared. He announced that he had seen a vision and that the fire was the judgement of God. There was no further doubt for Ivan too saw the vision and put himself into the hands of Silvester, who got rid of Glinskis, Shouyskies and Belskies and brought his own men into the ministry, including an able layman called Adashev. The nobles were separated from power. This was the good period of Ivan's reign, a period that included the conquest of Kazan. Then, in 1533, the Czar fell gravely ill and was not expected to survive. He summoned the nobles and princes and ordered them to swear allegiance to his new-born son. They hesitated, for it would have meant a regency for the Romanov Czarina, and the rule of Czarinas had left bad memories. The Czar had an adult cousin who bore the sacred blood of Rurik. Silvester and Adashev hesitated too. Then the Czar got better. The old chronicles ascribe Ivan's bout of virtue to his meeting Silvester the Holyman of Novgorod, and his reversion to evil ways to a meeting with Vassian, the unholyman from Kolumna.

On his recovery, Ivan went on a shrine-visiting tour. H. H. Munro, better known as 'Saki', tells the tale:

Among the religious establishments visited was the Piesnoshkie monastery, wherein was caged an interesting prisoner. Vassian, Bishop of Kolumna in the reign of Vasili, had been deprived of his episcopal office during the time of the regencies on account of his evil life; now, in the decrepitude of age, he is represented as harbouring with unquenched passion the unholy frettings of a sin-warped mind. Ivan desired an interview with the hoary reprobate; perhaps after a course of devotions among a community of irreproachable saints, living and departed, he was attracted by the rare personality of a sometime bishop who was no better than he should be. The monk-with-a-past seized the grand opportunity to poison the monarch's mind against his boyarins, his relations, and his subjects, and Ivan drank in with greedy ears the vicious counsels of the unhallowed recluse. It is a fascinating picture, the aged priest who had eaten his heart out in helpless bitterness these many years, and chafed against the restraint of his prison-cell, given at last one deadly moment of revenge in which to work a superb evil against the society that had mishandled him. And as the Tsar went out from his presence a changed man, might not the ex-prelate have flung a crowning blasphemy at his heaven and chanted exultingly *nunc dimittis?*

Be this as it may, from the date of his illness Ivan's savagery ceased to be occasional and became routine. Not only did he torture and kill all who annoyed him; he slaughtered their entire families. Silvester was banished to the White Sea, where he starved. The entire family of Adashev were killed; his brother Daniel, a successful general, Daniel's young son, his wife's father and brothers and his cousin Ivan Sliskin with wife and child; all were executed. He appointed a special bodyguard which became known as the Opritchnics, first 1,000 strong and later raised to 6,000. They were guards, police and assassins answerable only to the Czar. In later history they became the Okhrana, the Cheka, the OGPU, the NKVD, the KGB.

Most of the Czar's time was now spent at Alexandrouski, half-fortress, and half-monastery, about 100 miles from Moscow where he diverted himself in chapel and torture chamber. A contemporary account describes him grovelling before the altar, then sliding out to superintend the torture of some poor wretch, and returning radiant and comforted.

The arrival of the Czar accompanied by his familiars, the Opritchnics, became an occasion of terror. In Novgorod some 2,770 were slaughtered 'besides women and common folk', because there was a report that the bishop had been in communication with the King of Poland. The Opritchnics rode black horses with a dog's head tied to the saddle to act as a warning to the enemies of the Czar, and seem to have sacked and burned villages indiscriminately in their line of march. On his return to Moscow, Ivan ordered the arrest of a number of nobles who had been among his favourites. Eighteen gibbets, a boiling cauldron and other instruments of torture were set up in what is now the Red Square. When the terrified citizens stayed at home the army was sent to round them up. The Czar wanted an audience. When the sad file entered the square he asked of the people if 'What he was going to do appeared just to them'. A servile 'Yes' circulated the square. The first victim led before the Czar was cut in pieces. The next was plunged alternately into boiling and cold water till he was dead. A third was impaled by the Czar himself; and so it went on till at last a son was compelled to kill his father, being then himself tortured to death. The Czar kept a list of his victims so that he could inform God of their arrival and intercede for their souls. This he did prostrating himself before the altar. A document in the Krillov records the Czar praying for the souls of 3,470 victims. Among the last of them was his son and heir, whom he killed in a moment of temper by striking him on the head with an iron tipped stick. Ivan was the monstrous climax of a line of Norse Princes of Moscow, within which the idea that Czar and God were one had built a megalomania so powerful that it had infected a whole nation. When he died (1584) peacefully in the middle of a game of chess, the nation was inconsolable.

He was succeeded by his only surviving son, a mental defective. The ruler was the new Czar's brother-in-law, Boris Godounov, and he ruled extremely well. Indiscriminate terror had demoralised both the army and the administration, central and local. This Boris repaired and he drove back the enemies that were impinging on the frontiers. When the half-wit died and the House of Rurik came to an end, the estates unanimously elected Boris Czar, but strength and ability were no substitute for divinity. The Russians craved the House of Rurik and supported a series of imposters claiming to be miraculously revived sons of Ivan. Boris maintained himself during life but on his death (1605) the people of Moscow murdered his wife and fifteen-year-old son and welcomed as Czar a man known to history as the False Dimitri.

Who this man was nobody knows. He proclaimed himself in Poland and raised an army of adventurers, had some minor successes and then, on the death of Boris, everybody started joining him. All he had to do was march for Moscow. Had he then slaughtered his enemies he might well have established a dynasty, but he failed to behave as a prince of the beloved House of Rurik and as a son of the lamented Ivan. He pardoned his enemies. He told his nobles that they needed education and sent them to school. He told his army that they lost battles because their battle drill was inadequate, and started to drill his army in person; when he went hunting he killed bears instead of watching others at a safe distance; he tolerated Catholics and Lutherans and enjoyed intelligent conversation; he liked music and was sometimes sober after dinner. This was no son of Ivan. After a reign of eight months the Muscovites rose and murdered him, together with most of the foreign guests who had come for his wedding. There followed a decade of chaos in which various pretenders fought Czars claiming to be elected, and the Poles profited from the confusion. Finally the people turned to a young Romanov, then aged nineteen, whose only claim was a relationship to the beloved first wife of the now even more beloved Ivan. A new dynasty had come and the Russians had found themselves a new line of autocrats, but they did not fall in love again until they found another monster. His name was Peter the Great.

Like Ivan, Peter (1682–1721) had a minority during which the families of his mother and stepmother fought for the regency. Each conspired with the Streltsy, a sort of Praetorian Guard quartered in Moscow and forming the professional element in the Russian feudal levy. Peter learned his lesson. When he was 17 he learned of a plot by his half sister Sophia, who was then acting as regent. He had by then grown into a giant of enormous energy. He had little formal education (his tutor was later promoted to court fool) but he was an inspired mechanic with a passion for war, and had trained and drilled a group of companions into a regiment. He fled to the Trinity Monastery and raised his standard. He sent summonses to the leading nobles and one after another they joined him. Then he summoned two regiments of the Streltsy. They hesitated but came. Sophia in Moscow was becoming isolated. Her minister went to negotiate. Under torture he confessed a plot. Then Peter summoned the rest of the Streltsy. Sophia was alone and when Peter entered Moscow he despatched her to a convent.

Peter had found an English boat that would sail to windward. This fascinated him. He determined to learn the skill of a shipwright and to build a navy. He did so and led a combined operation that was successful in taking Azov from the Turks. Then he determined to visit the West and learn her technology. He travelled anonymously as Peter Mihailoff, with a group of companions headed by an ambassador. At Zaandam he lived in a cottage and worked as common shipwright on the wharves. In England he was assigned quarters in Deptford, and John Evelyn's *Diary* describes the condition he left them in. Europe was fascinated by its savage visitor. He was interested in all things mechanical. In Paris he enquired about instruments of torture. He was shown the wheel on which victims were tied while their limbs were smashed one by one. According to a contemporary account he asked to have a demonstration and when he was told that nobody had been condemned he replied 'Take one of my people'. The story is probably untrue, but it conveys the impression he made in a civilised city. He certainly took the wheel back to Russia and made frequent use of it.

On his travels he not only informed himself but recruited technicians by the thousand. He willed that Russia's technology should be brought up to date. In Vienna he learned of a mutiny in the Streltsy. Some regiments ordered from Azov to the western frontier returned instead to their homes in Moscow where they got in touch with Sophia. Peter hurried home to find that the mutiny had been suppressed. He decided to make an example to all opponents of reform. To him beards were the badge of Conservatism. He shaved some boyars with his own hands and ordered that no one should enter his presence with a beard. Then he turned on the rebels. He killed the first five himself and compelled his principal lieutenants each to kill a specified number. The killing went on and on, sometimes hundreds in one day. He had plenty of opportunity to see how men died on the wheel.

Then, having played the vengeful God, he set about creating his war machine. Not since the days of Sparta had a state been so dedicated to war or burdened with so pervasive a totalitarianism as Peter's Russia; and never has any state had so high a proportion of slaves.

Peter had inherited a medieval levy without commissariat or medical services and with little artillery which was useless against European troops. The Streltsy were the only regular regiments and there was little left of these. Peter put the army on the rates. Each province had to conscript, clothe, quarter and pay for the units assigned to it. The army was quartered permanently on the population, and its roll call was trebled. Thousands of foreign officers were employed to train it. The burden was enormous. In effect the local commander ruled the province.

Nobility was abolished and meritocracy imposed. A table of ranks was drawn up with three columns Military, Civil and Court. The first eight grades became gentry. State service was compulsory for all. Education—reading, writing, geometry and fortification—was imposed on all gentry. It was fiercely resented. The children fled the schools, but Peter was inexorable. Gentry refusing education were outlawed and they could not marry without producing a certificate of education.

For military supply Peter set up *ad hoc* companies composed of men of all classes, Russians and foreigners, to whom he gave loans, taxation exemptions and free labour. This was done by making them masters of the peasants in a given area.

The Patriarchy was abolished and was replaced by a Synod including a layman to act as the Czar's eye. The Church became a department of the totalitarian state performing a police function.

The peasants had by now lost all the rights that once distinguished them from slaves; they could be bought and sold by their masters, their property was his on demand, their only court was his. If a master killed another's slave he was required to replace him, that was all. 30,000 of these peasant slaves were taken every year to make good the wastage in the Czar's armies, for in Peter's long reign there were less than two years of peace.

The Russians hated the tyranny and adored the tyrant. It was a kind of suffering they could not do without. Peter, like Ivan, had killed his heir, and when he died (1725) Russia felt lost. The years from 1725–1762 were really an interregnum very similar to that which followed the death of Ivan. Peter's second wife was chosen as a means of continuing Peter's reign without Peter. She was an ex-servant from Lithuania, had little ability, and only outlived him by two years. Then the throne started to change hands as a result of a series of sordid palace revolutions. The country, searching for its lost Peter, supported a series of impostors claiming to be his dead sons or grandsons. The last coup organised by the palace guards disposed of Peter III, a thoroughly nasty, mental defective. His wife had inspired the plot and succeeded to the throne (1762).

There followed a vaguely civilised aberration in Russian history. Catherine II was a German princess with no claim to the Russian throne other than the support of some rebel guards regiments. She survived on her wits, and they were very good wits indeed. She had intelligence and charm and proved a fine judge of both men and events. If politics be an art, Catherine was a master. She enjoyed writing letters and they are very good letters. Among her correspondents were Frederick the Great, Joseph II, Voltaire, D'Alembert and her particular friend Grimm, the encyclopaedist. She was not only a patron of the encyclopaedists but a contributing member of their company. She used her lovers as her ministers and generals, for they were her friends selected at least as much for their brains as for their beauty. Orlov and Potemkin are two of the greatest names in Russian history. It was only in her old age that she selected lovers as pets, but she was never foolish enough to imagine they were anything more. By sheer skill she won acceptance for Russia as a European power. Home affairs were more intractable. Peter's aristocracy of service had been rather grand state slaves compelled to train for and engage in state service. This was Peter's justification for granting them all power over their peasants. The gentry had since been freed from their obligations but the peasants remained their slaves. Many nobles were idle, some became absentee landlords, some became dilettantes despising Russia and speaking only French, some dabbled in Liberalism but rarely applied it to their own estates; they owned two-thirds of Russia and three-quarters of the Russians. Too many were drones. Catherine saw the problem but failed to find a remedy. At the end of her reign there were still more serfs, still more helpless than there had been at the beginning. It was really only the court that became more civilised.

Catherine tried to reform Russia but she did not succeed. She died in 1796, the year Napoleon appeared in Italy, and was succeeded by her son Paul III. Paul had been deprived of the throne he believed to have been his for thirty-four years and by the time his day came he was a deeply embittered man with a strong reactionary temperament and a belief in his divine right that bordered on insanity. Ladies in splendid gowns from the Paris of the Directoire had to get out of their sleighs and kneel in the snow when the Czar passed. By 1801 the Czar's arbitrary behaviour had become intolerable to his Praetorians. A plot was hatched to which his eldest son Alexander was privy. Only assassination can limit tyranny.

Alexander had been Catherine's favourite grandson. He was very good looking. She had had him educated in the principles of the French enlightenment. His tutor was Laharpe, a republican. He was a brilliant diplomat with the gift of being all things to all men; to Europe he was splendid Liberal; in Russia at the beginning of his reign he made Liberal noises, which were probably sincere though in practice they never amounted to much. Not one iota of his sovereign power was surrendered. Nothing was done to free his slave peasants. After the campaign of 1812 and the defeat of Napoleon he abandoned enlightenment and took to religion. He became a founding member of the Holy Alliance and the leader of European reaction. He was succeeded by his brother Nicholas (1825–1855) who made no pretence of Liberalism. His nephew Alexander II (1855–1874) lacked both the brilliance and the double talk of Alexander I. He was a solid Conservative who recognised sadly but firmly that times had changed and that the slaves must be freed. Resolutely and patiently he imposed reform. It was a slow process and the last slave was not freed till 1881, twenty-five years after the last black had been emancipated in the USA.

Alexander II, the Liberator, was murdered by a dedicated group of Liberals who had decided, quite logically, that assassination was the only answer to autocracy. The bombers were led by a beautiful, and by her lights, heroic girl, the daughter of the military governor of Moscow. The plot is brilliantly described in *Red Prelude*. The result was that a boneheaded reactionary was substituted for a sensible Conservative. Alexander III (1881–1904) was a giant of a man, with the good character and intellectual limitations of an ox. His policy was total repression, lay and ecclesiastical. All newspapers were censored; sermons had to be submitted in advance and parish priests were required to report on the political reliability of their parishioners. Dissenters and Jews were persecuted. Count Leo Tolstoy was excommunicated. The judges were brought under tight political control. It was strong government and there was little evidence of dissatisfaction. The Trans-Siberian Railway was built and Russian industry expanded. Nicholas II (1896–1918) was as reactionary as his father but lacked his strength. He allowed himself to be run by a very silly wife, and by a disreputable and illiterate monk called Rasputin. The empire disintegrated not only because it became involved in a long and disastrous war. It was the process which the Chinese describe as losing the mandate of heaven.

Liberals succeeded the Czar but Liberalism was not what Russia wanted. She split into half a dozen warring fragments. Eventually the Bolsheviks, much to their surprise and in defiance of their theories, won. Marx had said that Socialism must follow a capitalist industrial society, and must be founded on an industrial proletariat. In Russia less than 6 per cent of the people worked in industry. Lenin's highest hope was to light a spark in Russia, which would ignite the proletarian revolution in the industrial West. That Socialism could succeed in one country (and that a backward peasant country), was a proposition which Lenin would have rejected with derision. The Bolsheviks won because they were disciplined, because they were ruthless and because they understood terror's attraction for the Russian people, but their victory was not complete until they found their monster. Joseph Stalin proved to be the jealous, vengeful, all mighty and all seeing God whom the Russian people love to adore, and under him they survived the sufferings of the Hitler war and the almost-as-grim reconstruction in isolation, carrying the while the instruments of state power at a war-time level of mobilisation. It took the Russians a year or two to realise that Uncle Joe really was dead and to dare to criticise. Much the same thing happened after Ivan and Peter, the Russian giant relaxed. To-day she is ruled by old conservative men. It is when she finds her next young Czar that we can begin to fear.

8

CHINA AND

JAPAN

IF MAN BE NOT HUMAN until he joins a society, it follows
that the kind of human he becomes depends greatly on the
kind of society that he joins. This proposition is illustrated
by the story of the two great civilisations of China and Japan
that developed in relative isolation.

China is and always has been an autocracy centring on a
divine emperor. Japan too had a divine emperor but he did
not rule. Japan was a feudal state and power came upwards
from the feudal authorities.

The Chinese derive from the Shang state. As we have seen
the Shang were a clan that imposed their divinity upon a
backward but settled population. This involved three tiers. At
the top God, in the middle God's relations, at the bottom the
peasant mass divorced from all control and free from all
public responsibility. This has resulted in a kind of fatalism
that is uniquely Chinese, a feeling that everything outside the
family circle is directed by a fate which must be accepted
and that any attempt to influence, to turn, to avoid or indeed
to interfere with destiny is not only futile but in a sense
impious.

When in the last war Madame Chiang Kai-shek was asked
about Chinese casualties she replied: 'They do not matter.
When the Yellow River changes course a million die and
another million move in till the river shifts again. When a
junk containing pigs and men upsets the pigs are saved. They
are worth something.'

The Shang set the model. Every successor dynasty has built on a peasantry bred and trained to accept its fate.

The Shang was followed by the Chou who justified their usurpation by a new theory, 'The Mandate of Heaven'. The emperor was divine but only for so long as he enjoyed the mandate of Heaven. Personal misbehaviour and public misfortune indicated the withdrawal of the mandate, which then fell upon another dynasty. The change was total. A new God was in office. He might be, and on several occasions was, a foreigner, but so long as the mandate lasted he was entitled to universal obedience. The prize-fighting maxim 'they never come back' applied. The Chinaman is not a supporter of lost causes. When Lin Yutang wrote his charming book *The Importance of Living* he assigned to his people the highest mark for realism and the lowest mark for romanticism.

The Shang had occupied a relatively small area on the banks of the Yellow River. The Chou had been their vassals lying to the west, and they conquered more than their communications enabled them to govern. They delegated authority to vassals who recognised the mandate of the Chou emperor, but in practice heard little from him. The states under Chou suzerainty enjoyed effective autonomy. This was not a feudal system. It was closer to the system of local satraps that developed later in the Middle East. Feudal rights are legal rights, under a law that binds king and baron; each is subject to his obligations and to the law. The divine Emperor was subject only to the will of Heaven. The rulers of provinces within the Chou State, however independent they might be in practice, drew their authority from God, and as there was no legal limitation to their subordination so there was no legal limitation to the subordination of their subjects. Freedom under the law was a conception quite foreign to the Chinese system.

Western social order is a balancing act. It derives from families buying protection by granting limited powers to chiefs, and from chiefs according limited authority to kings. This idea of limited authority conferred by consent permeates our system. King, lords and commoners; church and state; capital and labour; industry and trade unions all have their balanced rights set out in the law and the job of government is to keep them balanced. Nothing balanced the authority of the divine Emperor. It was total. The controls were personal. The Emperor owed to God probity, loyalty, sincerity, benevolence, and a courtesy that recognised the dignity of the most humble of God's creatures; his subjects owed to him the same virtues right down to the family from which this conception derived. As the Emperor stood to God, the prince stood to the Emperor and the son stood to the father.

The man who put this idea into words was Confucius. He lived about 500 BC during the later Chou dynasty a little before the great Greek philosophers and a little after the major Hebrew prophets.

He was a civil servant. He recognised God and the spirits but he was not much concerned with them. When asked about death he replied 'Not yet understanding life, how can you understand death?' He was a conservative and a traditionalist. 'Let the ruler be a ruler and the subject a subject; let the father be a father and the son a son.' But for all that, his conception that good government was a matter of ethics, rather than of auguries and sacrifices may have been novel. His ideal was very like our concept of the gentleman. He must have virtue, integrity, respect for others and for their position, kindliness to all, but he must also have form, polish, education and manners. 'Uprightness uncontrolled by good manners becomes rudeness.'

Confucius believed that 'manners makyth man'; that if man follows a correct code of behaviour that code becomes part of his nature and human conduct becomes a sincere ritual. This he called 'Li', a word we cannot translate. It involves a sense of propriety and covers the relation of parent and child, teacher and pupil, sovereign and subject. It was the basis of his conception of harmony within the Chinese state.

The West has sought 'the good and the just' as absolutes. Confucius was a relativist. To him 'the good' and 'the just' were balances. He sought a golden mean.

A traditional text taught to Confucian scholars reads:

When the knowledge of things is gained, then understanding is reached: when understanding is reached then the will is sincere: when the will is sincere the heart is set right: when the heart is set right the personal life is cultivated: when the personal life is cultivated the home life is regulated: when the home life is regulated and the national life is orderly: and when the national life is orderly the world is at peace. From the Emperor down to the common man, the cultivation of the personal life is the foundation of all. It is impossible when the foundation is disorderly that the super structure can be orderly. There has never been a tree whose trunk is slender and whose branches are heavy and strong. There is a cause and sequence in things: and a beginning and end in human affairs. To know the order of precedence is to have the beginning of wisdom.

China had no religion and no priests. Neither Emperor nor prince deputy could any longer rule simply through a family or clan administration. They required a class of scholarly administrators responsible to and dependent on them. Confucianism provided an ideal ethic and grew as the administrative class grew.

By about 400 BC the Chou dynasty was losing its mandate. The centre had lost control of its local delegates. They acted independently and far from peacefully. It was not a happy time. Chinese history knows it as 'the time of the warring states'. The ideal remained. It was to get back to the real authority of a human god on whom Heaven could confer its mandate.

Ch'in won the war of the Satraps in 221 BC. The Ch'in ruler assumed the mandate of Heaven and the title of Universal and Everlasting Emperor. He confiscated all the arms of the other provinces and marched their hereditary aristocracies to his capital. He divided the empire into thirty-six commanderies without regard to previous state boundaries and applied to all his realm the same imperial laws and taxation. Having dealt with China he invaded the Barbarian states which had not acquired Chinese culture. He extended China's boundaries to include Northern Vietnam and all the southern coast of China, and in the north he drove back the Nomads and built the Great Wall, the only man-made feature visible from the moon. He laid out a radiating system of roads, unified weights and measures, standardised the coinage, the axle length for wagons and the written language. It took him eleven years and then he died. His everlasting dynasty survived him by only four years, but his system, with occasional breaks, lasted 2,000 years.

China now had a centralised communication system, a common language, and a professional civil service. These were the means by which centralised imperial government could become effective. The Ch'in dynasty broke because the only man who could run it died. The pieces were picked up by the Han. There were two Han dynasties that lasted from 202 BC to AD 220. In extent and authority they paralleled Rome.

Under the Han the form of imperial government took shape. At the centre was the court, the emperor, his relations and later his eunuchs; radiating into the provinces the mandarins, a professional and dedicated civil service governing and administering and in the provinces the armies, half military and half police, usually commanded by mandarins. The whole rested on the obedient peasant.

The civil service was a profession theoretically open to the talented but in practice confined to a land-owning class that alone could afford the time and the books necessary for the competitive examination system. The subject was Confucianism, or rather the officially approved commentaries on Confucius and hand writing. Chinese characters were a much prized art form. The examinations were also a test of stamina. The candidates were shut in a cubicle and told to write what they knew. The civil service became a corps of administrators and governors available to whosoever for the time being held the mandate of Heaven.

The Chinese civil service faced its moment of truth when the Mongols came. For 1,000 years from AD 400 the horsemen with the composite bow ruled the battle field. Genghis Khan in about AD 1190 organised the Mongol nomads into an irresistible horde. They destroyed Mesopotamia and exterminated its urban population. They sacked Moscow and Kiev. They reached the Adriatic. They conquered China too, but there they were then swallowed by the civil service and became just another dynasty. They collapsed when they failed to provide effective emperors and were replaced by the Ming (AD 1368–1662). This was the last wholly Chinese dynasty.

Appointments circulated and no official was given time to

establish a territorial base. As a conservative administration it worked well, but Confucianism was not geared for change or adjustment in a technologically advancing world. There was China and there was barbarism. It was not conceivable to the Chinese that barbarians could have any ambition higher than the acquisition of Chinese civilisation. China was the middle kingdom, the centre of the Confucian world. The Emperor could have foreign relations only with tributaries.

The Ming lost the mandate for traditional reasons, two incompetent emperors, a greedy blood-thirsty and over-mighty eunuch, population increase, inflation and eventually foreign invasion. The Manchu (1662–1911) were Mongolian invaders but they took over the system and received the obedience due to the mandatory of heaven.

The weakness of the system was and is a tendency to inertia. The administrators were thin on the ground. Local affairs were run by the local gentry. The magistrate shouldered the responsibility. He probably had an area of 300 square miles. His virtuous conduct was supposed to set an example, and he was to blame or praise for all that happened. It was a doctrine that tempted officials to cover troubles up. Looking forward to transfer every few years, they were more interested in avoiding immediate embarrassment than seeking long term advantage. To suppress disorder involved acknowledging that there was disorder. It was better to square bandits by enlisting them in the local militia. There was a bias to compromise, and to harmonise rather than to resolve. Chinese officials waited for things to happen and hoped they would not.

The government structure from the very top was designed to keep a steady course rather than to set a new one. The personal rule of the emperor was passive. He did not initiate. He received memorials. If the emperor approved, the memorial passed into the ministerial machine and returned as an edict. The volume of business was great. The emperor could only be a clearing house. Officials in the provinces could not innovate and the emperor was too busy to do so. Under the Manchu dynasty China stood still for three centuries while Europe galloped. In 1840 the inventors of gunpowder were still using bows and arrows. Power relations had changed. The middle kingdom could no longer treat the rest of the world as tributaries. China was confronted by another civilisation. This was a new experience. She had often met the barbarians; they had conquered her on occasion but she had always swallowed her conquerors. Now she met a civilisation that she could not swallow. In this confrontation she failed utterly.

There were many excuses. The Manchu dynasty was failing; its foreignness prejudiced resistance; the Europeans used force to open up trade. All this is true, but it applied equally to Japan where the Takagawa Shogunate was in decline; agrarian and urban disturbances were developing; and an American squadron had invaded her chosen seclusion with humiliating force, and yet the Japanese responded brilliantly. The truth of the matter is that Chinese and Japanese society had produced two different sorts of men. The Japanese could respond to the challenge of change, the Chinese could not.

Japanese history has been a lot shorter than China's. The Japanese are a Mongoloid people with some admixture from the Caucasoid Aboriginal 'Hairy Ainus'. They speak an Altaic language from North Asia which differs markedly from Chinese. Their ancestors seem to have come in two waves, as a paleolithic culture about 150,000 years ago and as a neolithic culture about 6,000 years ago. By about AD 200 an Iron Age culture had developed and is known to us by its tombs. It was aristocratic, led by armoured horsemen with long spears. In the fifth century AD Japanese history began. It was a tribal or clan society. Each clan had its chief and worshipped its own god, thought of as a tribal ancestor. By the fifth century the clans were forming groupings and had an order of precedence. The Yamatu clan, claiming descent from the sun, enjoyed a generally accepted primacy, and its authority was expanding. There was little distinction between the civil and sacred function of the clan chief; he was leader of the clan and maintainer of the cult of the clan god. These gods were worshipped with a variety of nature gods and the generalised religion became known as Shinto, or 'the way of the gods'.

By the sixth century Yamato had established a court, but it was not long before the function of the priest and ruler began to drift apart. The Yamato chief remained primate of the Shinto and this has endured till today. He is the symbol of Japan and her continuity, but he has never ruled. In this he differs from all the other divine emperors. The real ruler became a hereditary functionary of the divine court. His office was fought for in courtly power struggle and feudal war while the Emperor remained impotent and inviolate.

In the seventh and eighth centuries efforts were made by successful court rulers, later to be known as Shoguns, to adopt the Chinese Imperial system. The Sun Emperor was endowed with the absolute authority of the holder of the mandate of Heaven, but the power was exercised by the great court families. Indeed the ritual functions as primate of Shinto and mandatory of Heaven were so onerous that emperors generally abdicated young. Power was centralised but it was still exercised by hereditary feudal nobles at Court. There was no bureaucracy of merit, as in China. The provinces were ruled by governors sent from the court but they were generally local magnates in their own right, and the officials in district and village were local leaders.

The land did not just belong to the Emperor. It was subject to a variety of differing rights and to important tax exemptions. Aristocratic families were entitled to rent charges on the basis of offices that had become hereditary. Religious institutions were also the owners of rent charges. Reclaimed and newly cultivated land was often subject to special tax exemption and to charges in favour of a patron, normally a leading court official who had negotiated the exemption. These pieces of land often clustered together in great estates. Subject to these charges was the proprietor, usually a local aristocrat, and below local managers whose offices often became hereditary, and finally smallholders who did the farming and had legal rights to possession. The system was strikingly similar to European feudalism, and from Emperor downwards was subject to law and custom.

From 900 the movement towards centralisation went into reverse. The big estates acquired warrior bands to protect their rights and power passed to local lords. In about 1200 the office of Shogun or commander-in-chief was created in favour of the victor in a major feudal war. His authority depended much on his capacity to balance the local feudal leaders. This balancing act provided a form of collective leadership which has since been a Japanese preference and has been operated by them with great skill.

Loyalty was central to the whole structure. Effective feudal power depended on the loyalty of vassal to lord, a loyalty that transcended all competitive loyalties. The image became one who sacrificed all life, love and family to honour, and that honour he owed to his chief. In the same way as the Chinese was oriented to the family, the Japanese was oriented to his lord.

The century from 1467 to 1568 was a period of feudal war and the breakdown of central authority. The Shogunate lost control and Daimyos or local dukes became virtually independent. The dues paid by local estates to the court ceased.

With the rise of the Tokugawa Shogunate in 1603 this tendency was reversed. Power reverted to the centre but involved a centralisation rather than a destruction of local power. In the course of feudal war the Tokugawa had become much the most powerful duke, with feudal domains spread all over the country from which he received the duty owed to a feudal lord. To this was added his authority as the Emperor's commander-in-chief. Tokugawa linked the major noble families by marriage. Local peers were required to spend alternate years at Shogun's court. The system is reminiscent of Louis XIV's insistence on the French aristocracy's residence at Versailles.

The nobility or Daimyos were graded by origin, wealth and retainers into many levels stretching from territorial dukes to foot soldiers but each had a hereditary status, a hereditary job and a hereditary income. Below the Daimyo came the Samurai, hereditary retainers and warriors of the Daimyo, privileged to wear the long and the short sword. Next came the countrymen and the townsmen and merchants, theoretically at the bottom.

The countryside was divided into autonomous villages containing land owning families often of Samurai descent, peasant smallholders, and landless labourers. The land did the paying. Land taxes were 40 to 50 per cent of yield and supported not only the Shogun and the Daimyo but the entire Samurai class —about 6 per cent of the population.

Having fixed the social mould the Tokugawa closed the

country. Foreign enclaves, Portuguese, Dutch and Chinese were expelled and Christians, who then existed in fairly large numbers, were exterminated.

The result was the longest period of prosperous peace that any society has ever enjoyed. It endured from the suppression of the Christians in the Shinbara revolt of 1638 to the arrival of Commodore Perry in 1854.

With no wars to fight the Samurai class became clerks and administrators, but they still wore their two swords and trained in sword play and archery. Gunnery was ungentlemanly. Their image of loyal, brave honourable soldiers exercising total self control remained. It spelled self respect which of all things is the most important attribute of a civil service. Confucianism, which had been introduced by Zen Buddhist monks, became important. Much of it was inconsistent with the Japanese way. To Confucius all loyalty was due to the divine Emperor; in Japan primary loyalty was due to the immediate feudal lord; to Confucius government was the function of a meritocracy, in Japan it was hereditary both in principle and detail, but the Confucian idea of a moral basis to society, centralised and administered by an educated and honourable bureaucracy became engrafted on to the Shogunate structure.

Mixed feudal and Confucian values created in the Samurai a dogged determination to live up to all that society expected of them.

The contradiction in the Tokugawa state was that a rigid political system was locked on to a dynamic economy. The rule was feudal and aristocratic, based on the countryside. Agriculture expanded, but not as fast as the new urban economy. The nation as a whole prospered but the classes on which the government depended—noble, Samurai and farmer suffered a relative decline. Both central government and local lords became more and more indebted to the urban merchants. The division between rich farmer and poor peasant grew. The military role of the Samurai had largely disappeared and the administrative role contracted as government, local and national became impoverished. Educated, able, proud men were facing unemployment. When after 1830 foreigners began to batter at Japan's closed doors, the Shogunate system was under internal attack, and had to face serious rioting in some of the cities, and peasant rumblings in the countryside.

But for all this Japan was a successful nation. This is not something that is easy to define. It involves a sense of belonging and participating that is shared, albeit in different degree, by the great mass of the people and is expressed in a determination to defend a common national inheritance. The mutiny of the English Fleet at the Nore in 1792 illustrates this feeling. Our wooden walls were manned by pressed men, kidnapped in the ports; confined on their ships in appalling conditions often for years on end; never allowed on shore lest they desert; permitted to see their wives only when in home port when the women were allowed on board to share their men's hammocks on a communal deck; flogged unmercifully for any infringement of a savage discipline and finally discharged without pension or provision for the disablements they had suffered in their country's service. In 1792 they mutinied, and put their officers on shore. Their leaders suggested that they sail for America, with whom we were then at war, and join a free country. 'What' they said, 'and leave England to be invaded by the French?' The mutineers arrested their leaders and sailed the fleet back to duty. Such is the power of that feeling which we inadequately name patriotism, and which is the stuff of successful nationhood. It is something that can contain strong internal conflict, even on occasion civil war. In our civil war the Royalist cause was finished when the Parliament at Naseby captured and published the king's secret correspondence inviting the intervention of a French army. In France it survived the revolution and united the people to meet Austrian intervention. It is something recognisable but indefinable. It involves the conception of one's country as being something more than a geographic expression or a collection of individuals as being one's own. It existed in Japan. The villager was involved and concerned in the government of the village, the townsmen in their guilds, village and town were involved in the duchies and the duchies in the state. Japan was still feudal but a national spirit had developed.

In China things were different. There was consent, acceptance and subordination but no involvement or participation.

The peasant farmer acquiesced in his fate, the Confucian scholar was concerned with a personal virtue, even the role of the Emperor had become a passive acceptance. China was an empire which had enjoyed unique success. Her imperial history had out-lasted all other empires. Britain was a nation state performing an imperial role but she was never herself an empire. China was never anything else. Left to herself there was no reason why she should not, under a new dynasty, have resumed her imperial cycle. She was not left to herself. Confronted with an array of nation states she could neither continue her imperial isolation nor adjust herself to a national role. Her people were subjects, not citizens, and they could not change.

Foreign intervention in China started on the southern coast. It culminated in the Opium War of 1842. The Manchu government did not object to opium because it was bad for people but because it cost silver. China had a balance of payments problem. Tea and silk which had been exchanged for silver were now sold for opium. The British, in a war in which we have no occasion to take pride, forcibly opened up trade. It was a very small war. Britain employed about 2,000 troops and a few gun boats. China submitted. Further petty wars took place and China ceded ports and territory. The Chinese people were neutral, as willing to serve the invaders in coolie corps as to serve the home government. Inland rebellions broke out. They were not anti-foreign. They were anti-chaos and anti-starvation. The Mandarin administrators' search for a quiet life had brought them into corrupt collusion with the landlords and the peasants were not left a living. Banditry became the alternative to starvation.

Unlike nineteenth century Japan, China made no effort to study the invader's methods. She had seen this sort of thing before. The mandate of dynasties was not forever. She could only wait patiently for Heaven to act. It was not till 1900 that the scholar class began to study a world beyond the Middle Kingdom. Japan's constitutionalism defeated Czarist autocracy in 1905. China decided to try having a parliament. It made little difference. Manchu princes and scholarly mandarins kept the same jobs under new styles. In 1908 the old Empress Dowager died leaving an infant heir.

Meanwhile overseas Chinese, particularly in Japan were studying new and revolutionary ideas. The name of Sun Yat-sen began to be heard. Revolt started in the army, though little blood was shed. The court summoned the local military commander Yuan Shih k'ai. The Emperor abdicated and Yuan with the support of Sun became president in 1911. The presidency did not carry the divine prestige, and did not receive that consent which was due only to the son of Heaven. In 1915 Yuan tried to make himself Emperor and start a new dynasty, but it was too late. He was not accepted, and the vacuum at the top remained. 1916 to 1928 was the time of the war lords. Armies had been the reaction to foreigner and rebel. There was now no centre to control the armies. Local commanders proved incapable of creating government and simply lived off the country. The war lords had no roots. They and their armies moved from province to province like locusts.

The old system was broken and new ideas were available. During the First World War there came to Europe a Chinese Labour Corps of 140,000, not a big number by Chinese standards but the first Chinese peasants to learn that other civilisations and other ideas existed. An American-financed University of Western Learning was created. New writing with letters was introduced, but China could not use these new ideas. They got little further than discussion groups. War lord China had rival parliamentary governments at Pekin and Canton. Both were nominal. In Canton Sun Yat-sen tried to provide the local war lords with a political instrument, but had to fly to Shanghai under British Treaty protection. It was here that he reformed the Kuomintang or national party and entered into alliance with the Communists, who were then obedient to Russian leadership. Sun sent his future brother-in-law Chiang Kai-shek to Moscow to study Soviet methods. In China he accepted Borodin and reorganised the Kuomintang on the Leninist cell principle. Needless to say Sun and the Soviets were each busily engaged in trying to cheat the other. Chiang Kai-shek returned to found the Whampoa military academy and to train a party army. Chou En-lai, later China's prime minister, was deputy head of the political education department. Sun died in 1925 and promptly became the object of a revolutionary cult very similar to the ancestor worship accorded to dynastic founders.

A government was set up in Canton with Chiang as military commander. He and his Whampoa cadets defeated the local southern war lords. All was now set for war against the more powerful northern group. By the end of 1926, thirty-four war lord armies had been absorbed and Chiang had reached the Yangtze. The communists had failed to gain control over Chiang's new army. In April 1927, Chiang set up his own military dictatorship in Nanking and turned on the communists. Few escaped the massacre. One who did was Chairman-to-be Mao. He was a peasant and one of the few Chinese communist leaders who had never been to Russia.

Chiang's strong suit was not imagination. He looked for inspiration to the modern West and to the golden past, and found it in neither. Like nearly all nations that have been built on the ruins of ancient empires, China stuck in the middle. Chiang could not get back to the old tradition for it was dead, nor could he mould a people shaped by empire, into Western models. Chiang became just another war lord.

Kuomintang as a party had consisted of the old and corrupt official class and the young reformers. Most of the latter were massacred with the communists. The civilian side of the Kuomintang became simply the old mandarin class. Chiang developed separate but overlapping civil and military bureaucracies. He used the party in the old role of eunuch and censor to supervise both the army and the ministries and to report to him both openly and secretly. It was the old imperial tripod of power, without its prestige. Chiang's authority was insecure. An anti-Chiang wing of the Kuomintang centred on Canton. In Yunnam, Szechwon, Shensi, Sinkiang and some other provinces local military authorities paid no more than lip service to Nanking. The Communists in Kiangsi till 1934 and then in Shensi formed a regionally based rebel power. The Japanese controlled Manchuria in 1931 and later Jehol and part of Hopei. Chiang's army (and it became more and more just Chiang's army), was occupied with civil war.

Japan set up a puppet government in Manchuria under the last Manchu emperor, Pu-yi. With Japanese efficiency they industrialised the province. Chinese labour flowed in, for

Japanese rule was to be preferred to war lord rule. The Japanese moved into North China. They were not resisted. Some Nationalist feeling had developed in the old treaty ports where the Western powers had established themselves and in the cities where some industry had developed. The peasants remained passive.

For six years from 1931 Chiang avoided a show-down with the Japanese while he pursued a policy of 'unification before resistance'. This meant fighting native communists instead of Japanese invaders. By 1936 the Communists had achieved their long march and offered a new anti-Japanese coalition. Chiang was kidnapped while visiting a northern war lord. Chou En-lai negotiated his release and Chiang was forced to agree.

In 1937 Japan attacked and took the whole coast and Chiang retired to Chunking. Puppet Chinese regimes were set up in Peking and Nanking. There was no shortage of collaborators and the ordinary Chinese submitted to government; any government, as had always been their wont. The Kuomintang were still unwilling to mobilise the peasants, for to them order rested and always had rested and always must rest on peasant submission. Social change was worse than foreign rule.

When Japan surrendered in 1945, no level of American aid could prop up Chiang and the war lord regime he represented. The time had come for the Communists. As in Russia they fitted onto the ruins of divine Empire, for the Chinese, like the Russians, had been conditioned to autocracy. China needed industrial revolution. In an industrial world she could not continue as a peasant backwater. She had proved incapable of adopting a private enterprise system. Communism provided the means whereby autocracy can create an industrial society. It was the form which the new dynasty had to take.

In twenty-eight years of trial and error the Chinese Communist Party (CCP) had acquired the experience, vision and self-confidence to assume the mandate of Heaven. After their military victory, they left most of the local administrators in office and the Communist cadres created a feeling of festival as the Kuomintang were swept away. They called it a democratic coalition under Communist leadership. Mao's Prime Minister Chou En-lai, recognised the need to use the training and skill of the mandarin class and of the scholars who had returned from the West and had long been sickened by the Kuomintang. Like the latter, the CCP set up a tripod of power, the army, the administration and the Party. Agrarian reform swept away a class of useless and oppressive land lords. The Chinese army gave the Americans under Douglas McArthur a sound drubbing in North Korea. In the early 1950's it looked as though a great new dynasty had arrived like the Ming to sweep away foreign influence, to survey the land and people and to restore the power and greatness of the Empire. It was splendid and it was formidable. I remember a Turkish officer who had met the Chinese army in Korea saying to me, 'They are the best infantry I have ever seen. Do you realise that there are 600 million maybe soon 1,000 million, and between only the Russians, and there are not enough Russians'.

Then things began to go wrong. The trouble was Chairman Mao. Mao was the heroic peasant who had led the great, and now legendary, 'long march' of the Communists, Kiangsi to Shensi, a distance of 6,000 miles. He had led the guerrilla war against the Japanese and had expelled the Kuomintang. He was the divine figure whom the Chinese could worship. His thoughts became holy writ. So long as he was prepared to be a figurehead he was just right, but around 1958 he started to interfere. Mao was not a scientific Communist. His philosophy was nearer to Rousseau than Marx. He was a moralist rather than a materialist. He believed in the natural goodness of man and in the virtue of the masses which seems to be very much the same abstraction as that which Rousseau called the common will.

For China the road to industrialism had to be slow. China started from much further back than Russia. In 1900 Russia had a higher per capita industrial production, a better railway system, a bigger corps of educated and professional manpower and a more advanced educational system than China had in 1952. The Chinese peasant's concern was and always had been to keep alive. Government was not something to resist, it was something to avoid.

The process of industrialisation and of collectivisation had to be gradual. This was clear to Liu Shao-ch'i and the Moscow-trained scientific socialists who were then running the party, but Mao became impatient.

Mao believed that peasants must become citizens and that society must be remade by remaking the people. This meant persuading the Chinese people to change themselves; it involved a fusion of morality and politics, and a mistake became a crime. The idea that conflict was the stuff of creation was stressed: the conflict between Imperialism and Socialism, between individualism and collectivism and most important of all, the conflict in every breast between Socialist virtue and Bourgeois vice.

These ideas, optimistic and enthusiastic were in flat contradiction to the scientific Marxist concept that you change people by changing society not the other way about, but it prevailed. Mao had his way and the great leap forward was launched. The enthusiasm of the people would overcome the absence of planning, of trained personnel and of materials. There was frenzied activity from the party cadres. Volunteer brigades marched out of the villages to build dams and roads, to reclaim land and to create local industries. Smelters sprouted in village gardens. The result was disastrous. Activities underplanned and under-controlled did not produce a worthwhile product. Too often the dams leaked, the reclaimed land salted up and the iron was unusable. The people got tired. All nations have had trouble over the mobility of labour. Marching off workers in labour battalions just did not work. To top it all Mao quarrelled with Russia. Gross national product declined by perhaps a third in 1960 and malnutrition was widespread; the people were apathetic and exhausted.

In mid-1959 the Central Committee denounced Mao's romantic policies. He was still indispensable as the divine figurehead but he was removed from day to day administration of the party. Under Liu Shao-ch'i recovery started. The Chinese people had learned to live with the CCP as they had with autocracies in the past, but the initial enthusiasm of the revolution had been thrown away. Agriculture, squeezed to finance industrialisation for a decade, was given top priority. Private gardens were re-introduced. Control was decentralised. The CCP built great structures of administration. The administrators became bureaucrats. The privileged families with access to special schools re-appeared. Talented peasants competed for positions in the emergent elite. The army was an elite organisation, with a Prussian sense of rank and status, controlled from the top down. The Party had drifted from the people. Then Mao went to war with the Party.

In 1966 Mao moved against the party and destroyed it. He conspired with Lin Piao, the hero of Korea and army leader, and offered him the succession. Within the tripod it was the court and the army against the bureaucracy.

The conflict between Mao and Liu Shao-ch'i was expressed under several headings: *Leader v Commissar*—Mao the little father against Liu's disciplinarians. *The Mass line v Party building*—Mao stood for struggle and wanted the party to stir up the people and lead them against what they disliked in the spirit of the Mass line; Liu wished to subordinate struggle to Party unity and build an elite leadership. *Village v City*—Mao disdained the townsman. His ideal was the all-rounder, farmer craftsman and soldier. Liu wanted specialists. *Voluntarism v Planning*—Liu wanted the systematic growth of 5-year plans. Mao, more interested in politics than economics, backed local initiative. Finally, *Red v Expert*—the politically indoctrinated versus the professionally trained.

In 1966 Mao started a new revolution. Through the army he organised a new force. The youth, newly emancipated from the family, he turned into Red Guards and set them on the Party. The Party fought back. In some provinces they organised Red Guards of their own. In places it became a shooting war, but when this happened the army intervened. The attack on the party gave civil power to an increasing number of military men. The universities were closed and in the autumn of 1968 millions of student youths and Red Guards were sent down to work on the farms. The Ninth Party Congress in 1967 elected a preponderance of military men and named Lin Piao crown prince. Then Lin Piao was eliminated and Mao, old but with a young ambitious wife, was left in control without a named heir. It was a situation which one had been accustomed to find in old rather than new dynasties.

Gradually the universities re-opened; administrators, purged by Red Guards, returned; harvests were good and the age old system of court, bureaucracy and army reasserted itself.

With Mao's death, the struggle was on again. The court lost the first round. Mao's widow and her supporters fell and the bureaucracy assumed power. But at the time I am writing (1977) the army stands menacingly independent. Somewhere a new autocrat is waiting to take up the mandate of Heaven and to lead the most intelligent and industrious people on earth to their natural position as a great perhaps the great industrial power.

Japan's response to invasion by Western civilisation was the opposite to China's. The Japanese decided to learn the new tricks and beat the west at its own game. They did. They industrialised in about half the time that it had taken free enterprise America and was to take Socialist Russia. In both the industrial and agricultural fields the know-how of the West was garnered and applied.

Japan prospered. By 1910 she had beaten China and Russia in two wars and entered into alliance on equal terms with Great Britain. Japan had arrived among the great powers. She passed through the 1914–18 war with minimum participation as an ally of the winning side.

The 1920's were less successful. Japan suffered in the 1922 post-war slump. She became involved in China's chaos. The role of the military within her internal power balance became too strong. Communist Russia appeared as Japan's natural threat. Mongolia was part of her defence. She was satisfied to remain a protecting power until some of her junior officers provoked an incident and she annexed the province. The League of Nations was foolish enough to interfere. It was an imperial age. For the great satisfied empires to complain of a little annexation based on security considerations, struck Japan as outrageous hypocrisy. To Japan it seemed an attempt to thrust her back into the era of unequal treaties from which it had taken her eighty years to climb. The Japanese people were furious and the army's influence and power were strengthened. In due course, the Tripartite Pact of 1941 with Germany and Italy, the other anti-League of Nations powers, became natural.

Japan was and is without oil. It is a weakness which many powers now feel. The military felt that oil within her control was necessary to security. There were other things too. The more the military looked into it, the more raw materials did they find that were necessary to Japanese security. Other nations secured their needs by having empires, why should not Japan do the same or at least acquire a Co-prosperity Sphere? And then Roosevelt confirmed the military fears by threatening Japan's oil supplies as a sanction directed against their operations on the Chinese mainland. To the military it seemed now or never so they hit Pearl Harbour and seized their empire.

It did not come off. They suffered total defeat and submitted to occupation, but for the second time they were ready to learn. They learned so well that they are now, after America, the world's greatest industrial producer. It is the achievement of a very remarkable people.

In the span of time that separates Constantine from Stalin and Chairman Mao, I have highlighted a few incidents and a few men to illustrate a general theme.

Divine empire was a system that developed from the centre outwards. A ruler, almost always a foreigner, proved stronger than the certainties of the tribe. This was divinity. This was the central theme that moulded the society and society moulded the people. The tribe looked back. In the days beyond memory God, Allah, Jehovah, N'Gai, call him what you will, revealed 'the truth' to the first father. The god-king or prophet-king made himself the master of this ancient truth. He decided all things.

The people needed to be told. They wanted the decision that was beyond argument, indeed they still do. There was once a lady who visited a psychiatrist. 'Doctor, it's my job. I have to put the big oranges on one side and the small ones on the other and, Doctor, it's decisions, decisions all the time and it's driving me mad.' This is a story that will be recognised by all who have tried to deal with Russian bureaucracy.

The people needed fear. The life of the tribesman had been full of fear. He had been surrounded by the mysterious wounding powers of nature. 'Thou shalt fear the Lord thy God.' They needed a god who was awe inspiring, punishing, terrible, the fear that expelled all lesser fears. This was the attraction of Ivan and Peter and Joe. I believe that inadequate awfulness has been amongst the failures of modern Arab governments. No ruler has emerged who has been formidable enough to inspire the kind of dread which the Arabs need. Mustapha Kemal Ataturk was such a man. It is perhaps too early to say whether he succeeded in frightening the Turks into modernity, but he certainly came nearer to making a nation than have any of the Arab rulers. (Egypt is *not* an Arab nation.) He has been followed by the same kind of interregnum that succeeded Peter the Great.

The people need to believe. Faith is the source of collective power, the great social dynamic. It matters little what they believe for the validity of the belief seems unrelated to the power it creates. The Book of Mormon, a patent fraud by an immoral epileptic, inspired incredible feats of endurance, was responsible for the founding of the state of Utah and still directs a band of dedicated followers in a manner which is powerful. The belief that God dictated a book to Mohammed came near to conquering the known world, as did the racialist nonsense of the Nazis. The potency of a community at any given moment depends largely on the strength of its collective faith. The divine king satisfied this need to believe and harnessed faith to the service of the state. He was primarily a king, the master not the servant of his divinity. It is this that distinguishes divine autocracy from theocracy.

In those divine empires in which eternal and immutable faith has been codified it has mattered little whether it be in the Bible, the Koran or *Das Kapital*. It is for the emperor to interpret or to pronounce the line, and the emperor's ruling is correct. That is where the argument stops. Most sacred books have proved wordy enough to cover all the opportunist policies which required scriptural endorsement.

The authority of the emperor is not limited by law, but it is still limited. People will endure a lot from God, they certainly have to, but there comes a point where sectional oppression becomes so intolerable that the section ceases to feel part of the whole.

In the West competition looks after productivity and technological advance. Where all power and authority are centralised it is for government to provide the dynamic and to see that the empire does not lose the power to defend itself.

The Romanovs did not fall because their subjects objected to autocracy but because the balance of economic interest had been tilted intolerably against the peasant, and the technological leadership necessary to support the armies, had been lacking.

It seems to me that communism fulfils the needs of people who have evolved under centralised leadership. The people of Russia and China and of the Middle East have been conditioned from time immemorial to having their decisions taken for them. They crave certainty not choice. Both the capacity to choose and the desire to choose are lacking. Under communism the divine interpreter of the divine revelation settles all argument. All power is centralised. Authority moves downwards from the ruler, not upwards from the people. Within the Soviet system candidates are handed down from on top, not sent up from below as in democracies. The voter simply approves the choice that has been made for him. There may and always will be local grievances, but the structure is right and emerges logically from the past.

The problem with autocracy has always been how to find the right autocrat. Heredity, selection or adoption by the ruler and election by a senate or college, have all been tried. The Communists have invented a new method. The leader emerges as a result of a struggle in which he asserts his dominance in a committee, which at a certain point he dispenses with. This involves a sort of interregnum.

We have seen two great autocrats, Stalin and Mao. Stalin was succeeded by a commission. Khrushchev looked like re-establishing personal rule but did not quite bring it off, and there was a return to government by commission. Brezhnev is no more than *primus inter pares*. Historically autocracy in commission has never worked satisfactorily for long, and the heroic level of Russian achievement has certainly receded since Stalin's day.

Chairman Mao put China back a decade by his extraordinary second or 'Cultural' revolution, when he turned on the Communist Party.

I think that we shall find that the effectiveness of the Red Empires will depend on the periodic emergence of autocrats capable of generating the kind of faith that overcomes the inertia of a people conditioned to obedience, and that they will disintegrate if power is allowed to disperse.

All human societies have their problems, but for reasons which will emerge in the chapters to follow, the problems facing communism seem far more manageable than those facing democracy, primarily because their system is in tune with their history.

9

INDIA

THE THIRD GREAT ASIAN POWER, India, suffered from a historical misfortune. Her horses got worms and her men got malaria. New men on better horses came over the mountains conquered and decayed. She developed neither the divine autocracy of the Chinese empire nor the balance of rights regulated by known laws that was called feudalism in Japan and Europe. Her political history has been the story of her conquerors and her society a continuing adjustment to new masters.

In the third millennium the main Indian racial groups were the Australoids and the Mediterraneans, the long-headed little men who had initiated civilisation in Egypt, Sumeria and Crete. It was men of this type who created the Harrapa culture in the Indus Valley (2,300–1,700 BC). This was an urban civilisation and we are finding more and more of its cities. All were built on the same plan, unfortified inward-facing rectangles with a central fortress that may also have served as a temple. These fortresses were not like the Saxon keep and stockade, an area within which villagers could take refuge in the event of attack, for they appear to have been designed to dominate rather than to defend the cities. They were the refuge of rulers. Who were the rulers? They had an ideograph script which we cannot read or connect with the scripts of either Sumeria or Egypt. They were probably a theocracy. Their cities portray the dead order of a temple rather than the dynamic of a court. They had contact with the cities of Sumeria. Their civilisation was a considerable one and it disappeared as mysteriously as it came. Plague may have been the answer, or revolution by subjects held too low to use the civilisation of their masters, or possibly invasion, but of this we have found little sign. It may have been an original culture but more probably it derived from Sumer and Akkad. It left India no identifiable heritage.

The next comers were Aryans. They probably began to arrive in force about 1,500 BC after the Harappa civilisation had ended and at much the same time as they were entering Greece. They brought with them male anthropomorphic gods. The sky god was Dyaus, the Greek Zeus, the Latin Jupiter, the Norse Tyr and the Teutonic Ziu. Aryan gods were nature gods with very human habits. Indra had something of Apollo, the archer. He destroyed, and caroused with the joyous irresponsibility of a bomber squadron leader. Somewhere he destroyed an irrigation system. We do not know where or when (just possibly it was connected with the Harappa civilisation), but wherever it was Indra was very pleased with his prang.

The new gods did not find Indian brides. There was no Indian Hera, or Aphrodite, or Athene or Artemis. Had Harappa survived it might have been a different story, but the people whom the Aryans met were too primitive for their goddesses to be marriageable. At a later period we do find traces of indigenous gods being admitted to the Hindu pantheon, but there was no marriage of equals. As with the gods so it was with the men. Equal marriage of the races did not happen. Instead the caste system came into being. The word caste means colour in Sanskrit. There were originally four castes. The two highest, the priests and the warriors were supposed to be white or red complexioned. They were the children of Aryan wives. The third caste, merchants, land owners and clerks, were yellowish, but they were still twice born which is to say reborn into the Aryan society and admitted to the sacrifices. They were clearly the half-castes. The fourth caste, cultivators, were black. They were not twice born and were originally Dasa people, farmers whom the Aryan herdsmen had conquered. Below were the even more primitive people with no caste at all.

The Aryan period is prehistory for they had no writing, but they had a poetic tradition and a priestly discipline whereby their poetry was learned by heart and handed down from master to pupil. The Rig-veda consisting of 1,028 hymns to the gods is older, in parts much older than 1,000 BC. These are not narrative poems but they throw light on the nature of the Aryan tribes. The hymns to rivers indicate that the Aryans had not at this period got beyond the Punjab. The two great narrative poems come from the first half of the first millennium and tell of events in and around 700 BC, but their historical value is diluted by the fact that they were not reduced to writing till 1,000 years later. The Mahhabarata is the longest poem in the world, seven times as long as the combined *Iliad* and *Odyssey*. It tells of a tribal civil war between Kauravas and the Pandavas, during which all the Aryan tribes with their gods become involved in a great eighteen-day battle. Krishna drives the chariot of Arjuna the great Pandava warrior. Arjuna expresses squeamishness at the thought of slaying in civil war so many who were of his kith and kin and who were his friends. Krishna replies that Arjuna must do his duty as a warrior and goes on to say:

> Follow your destiny for action is better than inaction and you cannot support your honour with inaction . . . Your business is with action alone, not with results. Let not consequences be your motive. Do not dally with inaction.

There is something curiously Celtic about this passage. It is just the advice an IRA chief of staff would give to a bomber who was anxious about the results of a bomb in Harrods. There is something Irish too about the horse sacrifice: an Aryan chief bent on prestige loosed a horse. For a year the horse wandered followed by a warrior band. Where the horse went the chief fought to impose his rule. At the end of the year the horse was sacrificed. It is very like Paddy going to the fair with a chip on his shoulder, but then the Celts are an Aryan tribe.

It took the Aryans well over 1,000 years to occupy the sub-continent. They came as nomadic pastoralists riding their herds. Their tribes were organised into clans and the division between priest, warrior and servitor had probably already

taken place. They conquered primitive agricultural settlements and chased away even more primitive gatherers. The
tribes settled, grew crops, caught malaria, lost their horses
and their vigour, and were overrun by new tribes moving
south.

After tribalism came republics. Heads of families met in
public assembly summoned by an elected chief or *raja*.
Decision was taken by vote. The treasurer and the general
were assistants of the chief. Trial was by the elders. Land
was owned in common. In the sixth century BC republics
were established in the hill country and towns were being
founded both in the hills and on the plains. Aryan society
was becoming not only settled but urban.

Monarchy emerged on the Bengal plains. Land had begun
to be privately owned. Slaves or near slaves were tilling it.
The need for a stable and heritable system had become apparent. The chief and the priests got together. The priests
were given caste priority and the king divinity. He did not
become a god, but his office was consecrated. Bambisara
(493 BC) of Magadha, south of the Ganges, may have been
the first real king. Tradition says that he was a patricide and
that he was succeeded by five patricides in sequence. There
was then a period of confusion which ended with the Nanda
dynasty. The founder was said to be the son of a shoemaker
and a whore. The Nandas were at Delhi when Alexander
came and he longed to attack the low-born cobbler's son, but
his army wished to go home. In 321 BC the Nandas were displaced by the Mauryas whose rule modern Indians tend to
remember as a golden age. Chandra gupta Maurya moved into
the power vacuum created by Alexander and established his
authority over the Indus and Ganges valleys and north to
the Himalayas.

We know very little about the Maurya Empire. We have
no written document from India earlier than 250 BC but the
Asoka pillars and rock proclamations of about this date, to
which reference is made later (p. 158), indicate that a substantial number of people were expected to be able to read.
The bulk of our knowledge comes from Megasthenes, who
was sent by Seleucus Nikator as ambassador in about 300 BC.
His report has been lost but numerous extracts used by other

writers have survived. The Mauryan capital, if that be the right word, was Pataliputra on the junction of the Son and the Ganges rivers. It was eight miles long and one and a half miles wide. It was built in wood and defended by a mud wall. The standing army was said to number about 750,000. Greek numbers are always wildly exaggerated and one can probably knock off a nought. It was divided into infantry, cavalry, chariots and elephants. The infantry used the long bow. The emperor's bodyguard was a female division of all arms. This was but one of the many precautions against regicide. The army was administered by a board of thirty divided into sub-committees, which acted as a war office. Megasthenes also describes in detail the administration of Pataliputra but tells us almost nothing about the administration of the country. The provinces were ruled by governors and there was probably some administration similar to Pataliputra in the provincial capitals.

It was territorially a formidable empire by any standards, but was it really administered? Was it in any sense a state? Was there such a concept as citizen loyalty or a sense of belonging? I think the answer to all these questions is a probable no, and that with the break up of the tribes and the passing of the republics the Indians had ceased to be concerned with government. They suffered from debilitating diseases in a debilitating climate. Survival was their primary concern. The castes and, in the towns, the guilds that were rapidly becoming sub-castes, were where they belonged and where they found their identity and status. It was the caste authorities that settled disputes, the village authorities that ran the villages and the guilds that managed the growing towns.

The emperor did not administer. He was generally travelling and his court travelled with him. The capital was wherever he happened to be. The imperial officers were his. There was no professional civil service. The British ICS (Indian Civil Service) was the first mandarinate India ever saw.

The imperial government was that of an army of occupation. It was concerned with security, the supply of the forces, order in the capital and in the vice regal capitals, communications and gathering tribute. The rest was left to local caste authorities. The emperor though sacred was never an object of popular worship. There was no loyalty to the state. Loyalty to the emperor was personal and might or might not exist amongst officials and soldiers but it was no concern of the lower castes. Village life was concerned with survival, not government. The people of the great sub continent like rooted seaweed swayed but moved not as the tides of imperial struggle moved back and forth.

It was during these centuries that the Aryan religion took a very un-Aryan turn. The Aryan gods had been worldly. Living was for living. After death, man was but a phantom, retaining only the capacity to suffer. Jainism and Buddhism appeared in the sixth century. Both are 'Stop the world, I want to get off' philosophies. They are the products of a sick society. In part they were protestant and anti-clerical, a protest at the idle greed of the Brahman caste, but basically they were anti-living. Life was an unhappy experience from which the elect after many reincarnations might escape into nothingness, for this is what Nirvana means. The Jains were obsessed with non violence. One must not tread on an ant. Masks are worn lest a gnat be inhaled. The termination of any life may upset a cycle. Buddha preached the four noble truths: the world is full of suffering; suffering is caused by human desires; renunciation of desire is the path to salvation and salvation is possible through moderation but salvation is nothingness. Neither Jainism or Buddhism were concerned with gods. Sacrifice and ceremonial were worthless. Jainism lives mainly as an urban merchant cult. Buddhism after a great period when it was adopted by the Emperor Asoka left India for China,* but Hinduism took much from it, including the idea of reincarnation and the goal of ceasing to be.

Asoka (268–231 BC) was a Buddhist convert. He was the first Indian to leave a written memorial. He postered India from Southern Mysore to Afghanistan with inscribed pillars after the manner of Darius the Persian, whom he may have copied. They provide us with our first Indian letters. They

---

* In the twentieth century, Buddhism in Burma and Vietnam became a fighting nationalist creed, but this only illustrates that any creed can be turned to serve any cause, for power comes from collective belief and not from what is believed in. Christianity has, on many occasions, been reversed into a militant creed.

are in the local languages. In Kandahar it is Greek, in Peshawar it is the Aramaic used in Persia, elsewhere it is Brahmi. Curiously Sanskrit, the mother tongue of the Aryans had yet to be written.

Asoka's principal conquest was Kalinda, on the Bay of Bengal. According to his own account he deported 150,000 Kalindese to open up new lands. This movement of population is rare in the tale of Indian conquests. Later in life Asoka regretted the carnage and suffering he had caused. His proclamations fall into two parts. The smaller ones are the edicts of a lay Buddhist king to his fellow Buddhists and express a certain intolerance of dissidents. The larger ones on pillars and rocks in public places proclaim a new public morality, which he called Dhamma. The main tenets are tolerance, respect for all people and all religions, and non-violence. For a king he recognised that non-violence had its limitations. There were hill tribes to be controlled. There is no evidence that he cut his army estimates but he expressed the hope that his successors would refrain from wars of conquest.

With the death of Asoka the Mauryan dynasty began to disintegrate. The Aryans never had a law of primogeniture. Succession was seldom peaceful and often destructive. New people were pressing in from the north-west. Cyrus the Great (530 BC) had crossed the Hindu Kush and received tributes from the tribes north of the Indus. Herodotus (486–465 BC) includes Gandara (roughly the modern Punjab) as a Persian satrapy and Alexander entered India as a Persian emperor, claiming a Persian province. The Indians had not yet taken to writing so we still know of this time only through the writing of foreigners. When Alexander died his governors went home and pressures within the Greco-Persian Empire and from the steppes gave India a respite that lasted till 180 BC, when the Bactrian Greeks returned and set up kingdoms reaching from Delhi to the delta of the Indus. In 88 BC, they were overrun by Scythians, or Shokas as they were known in India. Then, in about AD 100 the Fuch-chi came over the mountains and established the Kushana dynasty with a capital at Peshawar and a kingdom reaching the rivers Narmada in the south and Banaras in the west. In the next century the Sassanians broke in from Persia and defeated the Kushanas. In Southern India

little local kings fought each other. One particularly successful warrior was a Jain who must have felt that the principle
of non-violence did not apply to kings. In the fourth century
the Sassanians weakened and a new Indian dynasty, the
Guptas, came and stayed for 150 years. In the plains the
former conquerors one after the other, seem to have been
absorbed into the caste system and save for some peripheral
hill principalities, to have disappeared as separate nationalities.

The next invaders, in AD 450, were the White Huns. They
established their kingdom in Northern and Central India and
in their turn decayed and became absorbed. They survived
only in the hill country of Rajastan where they formed a
warrior-caste, and became known as the Rajputs. In India
conquering proved easy but maintaining identity very difficult.

After the Huns there was a long interval while the people
of Bactria and Persia were engaged in their own power struggle
and India occupied itself with the interminable wars of local
kings.

Mahmoud of Ghazni (AD 1,000) in Afghanistan was the next
invader. He came on annual raids to fill his treasury while
he fought for Bactria. Mahmoud had stronger men and better
horses and he plundered at will. But it was not till 1182 that
his descendants came to stay. They took Sind and the Punjab,
and then turned towards the Ganges. They were checked by
the Rajputs, but sending for reinforcements renewed their
attack and conquered. From then till the coming of the
British the main parts of India were ruled by a small Moslem
minority. The new dynasty held because it had access to
reinforcements of horses and men from Central Asia and a
religion that resisted absorption into the Hindu caste society.
The Delhi Sultanate, as it came to be called, never made the
slightest effort to conciliate its Hindu subjects. It maintained
its vigour by importing Mongols, Afghans, Turks, Persians,
Arabs and even Abyssinians, and it was from these that the
Sultan promoted his highest officers.

Within this foreign group career was open to the talents.
The first dynasty was known as the slave dynasty because its
founder had been a slave of the Mohammed of Ghuri. According to the Koran all believers were equal but in the Delhi
Sultanate some were more equal than others. A Mohammedan

caste system emerged. The highest were the nobles of foreign descent, then came Hindu converts of high caste such as the Rajputs, and then, a long way down, the working castes divided into clean and unclean trades. These constituted the great majority of the Indian Moslems, for most of the converts came from the lowest caste Hindus who accepted the Moslem religion to escape from a caste system which rejected them. Their descendants became the citizens of Bangladesh.

There were Hindus in the Sultan's service but they did not rise very far. On the other hand it was the Hindus who controlled the economy. Some became very rich. Foreign trade was in Arab and Portuguese control. The Indians did not make sailors. Crossing the ocean involved loss of caste.

The Delhi Sultanate began to lose its vigour when the Mongols cut its communications with Asia. It could still import some horses by sea, but the main flow of strong immigrants stopped. Tamerlane raided in 1398 and sacked Delhi. His nominee in the Punjab became the next Sultan, but did not win his predecessor's authority. The foreign nobles set up independent principalities and when Baber Shah invaded in 1526, India was ruled by many dynasties of Afghan, Turkish and Hunnish descent whom the people accepted with indifference.

At Panipat, fifty miles from Delhi, Baber met the army of the Sultan Ibrahim. Baber was heavily outnumbered and he won largely because his cavalry were fitter men on better horses. Ibrahim was killed. There was no rally. No one owed loyalty to the Sultanate and personal loyalty to the Sultan died with him. All the Afghan nobles played for their own hands. The Hindus were unconcerned. They did not reckon that Baber would stay when the weather got hot. It was indeed a remarkable feat of leadership that enabled him to do so for neither he nor his army liked India. Here is his own description:

> Hindustan is a country that has few pleasures to recommend it. The people are not handsome. They have no idea of the charms of friendly society, of frankly mixing together, or of familiar intercourse. They have no genius, no comprehension of mind, no politeness of manner, no kindness or fellow-feeling, no ingenuity or mechanical invention in planning or executing

their handicraft works, no skill or knowledge in design or architecture; they have no horses, no good flesh, no grapes or musk melons, no good fruits, no ice or cold water, no good food or bread in their bazaars, no baths or colleges, no candles, no torches, not a candlestick.*

Baber's support was thin but his enemies were divided and lacked a rallying point. He was the best general and he had the best cavalry.

His grandson, Akbar, was the real founder of the Mogul Empire. He succeeded at the age of thirteen, and set out not only to conquer but to unite India.

First he ended the princely anarchy that had endured since the decline of the Delhi Sutanate. Then he turned on the other provinces: Rajastan 1568, Gujerat, Surat and the western coast 1572, Bengal 1574, Kashmir 1586, Orissa 1592, Sind 1595 and the Deccan kingdoms whose conquest was not completed until after his death.

But he was not only a conqueror. He set out to involve the ruled in the destiny of his house. He was a single-minded dynast, lacking both social and religious prejudice. The lower castes, Moslem and Hindu, did not count. Who governed was not and never had been their concern. No government depended on their support. Government interest was confined to enabling them to pay their taxes. It was with the nobility that Akbar was concerned. The Hindu nobles had been ignored during 250 years of Moslem rule. He brought them into his service on equal terms and promoted them to the highest office. He invented the office of *Mansabdar*, or 'holder of command'. Mansabdars ranged from the commander of ten to the commander of 5,000, who was a great officer of state. The Mansabdars were a pool available for employment in any role, civil or military. They were paid in cash and were not attached to particular localities. They were men whom Akbar had made and who were loyal to him.

Finally he looked for an idea that could hold a state together. He rejected the Moslem faith because within the Indian context, it was disruptive. This was no small thing to

* *Memoirs of Baber*, tr. J. Leyton and W. Erskine, quoted in Percival Spear, *A History of India*.

do. It lead to a formidable rebellion by the orthodox but this he suppressed with his usual ruthlessness; and with it he broke the power of the *Ulema*, as the college of Muslim theologians was called. He then set about inventing a new religion. It was based on Persian Zoroastrianism but its central theme was the divinity of the emperor not merely as god's elect or as the prophet of god, but as an aspect of the deity. He was portrayed with a halo and his subjects prostrated themselves before him. He saw a state religion centring on the dynasty as a necessary aspect of Indian identity. For the last twenty-four years of his reign obedience was a religious duty and disobedience sacrilege.

Akbar's idea was sound but it was not within the spirit of the age. Monotheism both in its Muslim and advanced Hindu forms had taken too strong a hold. It was too late to be the Pharaoh, the god incarnate. India lacked a faith to bind her into an Indian nation and it was too late for the worship of an emperor to serve as a substitute. Akbar's cult never spread beyond his immediate entourage, but it was not completely without effect. The Moguls did achieve an aura of sanctity that no other Indian dynasty enjoyed.

Akbar left strong successors but they lacked his imagination. The last, Aurangzeb, was a narrow Muslim puritan who reversed Akbar's principle of religious tolerance and reimposed the old Muslim tax on unbelievers. After him the dynasty decayed and the British came.

Before the British Raj India was never a state. Akbar came nearest to uniting the sub-continent, but he remained the only link that held his domains together. The people never became involved either as citizens of the state or as worshippers of its emperor. There was never in India the kind of emotion that was expressed by the words 'Holy Russia'. All through history there has been a sense of Chinese and of Japanese identity, but there has been no sense of Indian identity. Indians of the working and trading castes had no tradition of participation in state or national politics. The idea of an India that belonged to its people came with and through the British.

British India and the emergence of an Indian nation will be discussed in later chapters.

10

THE CATHOLIC WEST

IN THIS CHAPTER we return again to the West and pick up the thread where we left it at the end of Chapter VI with the death of Marcus Aurelius.

In modern terms the Roman principate was a republican empire within which presidential power had been stretched, but law still ruled. Provinces, cities and citizens had rights under law. They were not always rights that it was easy to enforce, but they were still there. The people of the West still found their identity within their cities and looked to Rome for their security.

With the death of Commodus, Marcus Aurelius' unworthy heir, the rule of law broke down, the army commands fought for the purple, and the next seventy years saw twenty emperors. They included a Berber, a Mauritanian, a Syrian sun priest, a Balkan peasant, two Africans and an Arab. A further sixty pretenders had assumed the purple in various provinces. The Emperor Dacian had been killed by the Goths and the Emperor Valerian was a prisoner of Shaper the Persian. The angle of land between the sources of the Rhine and the Danube had been lost and Zenobia of Palmyra was in control of Egypt and had proclaimed herself Augusta. The centre of empire had shifted from Italy to the Danubian provinces. The idea of Rome had changed, but it did not die. The armies of the frontier, now largely recruited locally, equated Rome with the security of their homelands. They were as passionately Roman as had been the Republicans that recovered from Cannae.

The Rhine provinces felt themselves neglected and the armies
of the west maintained, for a time, a separate emperor, but
he was still Roman. Even Zenobia of Palmyra claimed authority as a Roman defending a Roman frontier against the
Persians. So Rome recovered, but it was a different Rome. A
series of great soldier-emperors of Danubian peasant stock
restored the frontiers, reorganised the armies and created a
new, largely military civil service. They culminated in Diocletian. The frontier had been stabilised and fortified. New
mobile cavalry armies had been trained to support them.
Garrison troops were peace-time farmers and builders. A new
aristocracy of officers and officer civil servants had come into
being. Rome was still the symbol, but she had ceased to be
the capital. Diocletian governed from Nicomedia and the west
was ruled from Milan. Government was rigidly totalitarian.
The emperor ceased to be *princeps* (chief) and had become
dominus (lord). He had become an oriental despot and was
on his way to becoming a god, not a mere *divus* to whom
divine honours were granted after death, but a living god. He
lived no longer as Roman emperors had lived, accessible to
their Roman subjects. He and his colleagues lived in their four
capitals as oriental kings withdrawn from human contact; he
no longer received the Roman salute *(salutatio)* but prostration *(adoratio)*.

Diocletian divided the Empire because it was too big and
communications were too slow for tight and orderly government to be controlled from a single centre, but there may have
been a deeper reason. The East was God country or, if you
prefer it, totalitarian country; the West was not. There Republican ideas survived, and Greek ideas about freedom, and
to these must now be added the individualistic anarchic ideas
of the German tribes that were moving into the West. When
the Empire divided, civilisation divided. The East moved to
oriental despotism, and the West to a dark age within which
divided authority struggled for stable balance. The role of
Christianity within the two systems was opposite. In the East
the Church became a department of state that strengthened
and sanctioned imperial rule; in the West it turned away
from the state and after a time started to play an independent
role in the power game.

Historians have found many explanations for this forking of the stream of human destiny, but I believe that the real reason lay in the differing natures of the men who had evolved in East and West.

From the birth of civilisation the East had conceived of power as radiating from a single divine authority, and the Greeks of the East had become absorbed into imperial systems which had been adopted by Alexander and his successors; the West had been the heir to the polis and Western civilisation had grown from Republican roots.

The story of the Dark and Middle Ages falls into three parts. The first involved the break up of a colonial empire. It was a phase of creeping anarchy, as barbarian tribes sought to impose themselves on provincial civilisation. The order that Rome had maintained was remembered as a golden age.

Attempts to restore the unity that had been Rome followed. They failed, and for a very simple reason. You cannot have a colonial empire without a colonising power. Unitary empire is a very different political dispensation. Within it the subject sublimates his identity in surrender to a divine authority. The tribesman of the West was not that sort of person.

The third phase was building upwards. Feudal states emerged subject to a rule of law. King, noble and peasant all had their rights and their duties. Each has his niche within a regulated society. It was not an easy society to achieve or to maintain. Much depended on the strength of the king, for in practice it was for the king to see that duties were performed and rights were not exceeded. It was also a dynamic society in which rights and duties required constant adjustment. On the whole it fitted the nature of western man. He had a niche that was his, he had territory, he had a certain tribal security and when he went to the wars, he served with his fellow villagers in a formation that differed little from the traditional hunting group.

Gradually, towards the end of the Middle Ages the feudal state was becoming the national state and royal authority was upholding the law and keeping the peace.

Dissolution of empire in the West

Western man had not been conditioned to accept the new autocracy of the Dacian emperors. The senators who had served Marcus Aurelius as honoured colleagues did not feel at home in the courts where they were expected to get on their knees; Italy was not subject to immediate Barbarian pressure and the senators preferred private life on their great country estates and the leisured scholarship of a mature society. The army was away on the frontier and the great men defended and policed their localities, and advanced their friends. One Symmackus (AD 330–402) has left us his correspondence. This aristocratic way of life spread to the newer nobilities of Gaul and Spain. The Church too turned in on itself and separated from the world. Monasticism became the fashion.

When the Goths under Alaric cracked the imperial shell the inside was soft and divided. It was a curious situation; the Goths who sacked Rome (AD 410) were still overawed by Roman fame. In the Balkans they had been absorbed by the imperial system and their kings had become Byzantine proconsuls and generals. In the West they met a society that had neither the will to fight them nor the stomach to digest them. They did not destroy this society; even a century later their king was to say 'An able Goth wants to be like a Roman; only a poor Roman wants to be like a Goth', but they were never accepted by it. Goths in Italy, Vandals in Gaul and Spain, Burgundians in the Rhône Valley became the socially unacceptable rulers of a Roman civilisation; to the senatorial landowners they were barbarians and to the Church they were Arian heretics, so they remained a tight-knit warrior caste held at arms' length by their subjects. The Franks were the only exception. They came late, nearly a century after the Goths; they came to Northern France which was rather less snobbish than senatorial Italy and Spain and above all they adopted the Catholic revelation. At the Merovingian court, Roman and Frank murdered and married each other without discrimination, and Roman bishops hailed Clovis as the new Constantine.

Blame for the deterioration of European society during the

fifth and sixth centuries must rest primarily on the Church. The German tribes were never more than a small minority that had been partially Romanised before they crossed the Roman frontiers. They wanted to be Romans. In the East they became 'New' Romans and a valued addition to the Empire of Byzantium. Northern China was far more thoroughly occupied by far more primitive barbarians, and within two or three generations they were a part of the Chinese civilisation offering their sacrifices to the Chinese gods. In the West, the new rulers met only the intolerant sectarian hatred of the Christians. The result was an unhealthy and deteriorating society. Rude warrior groups perched insecurely on civilisations that rendered them contempt, hatred and minimal obedience. People felt insecure, for they had no leaders with whom they could identify and no overall pattern into which they could fit. Roman society was not destroyed, it just became anti-social; the great landowners became isolated barons; the roads were not repaired; the cities fell into ruin; the spirit that holds a society together had gone.

The Roman landowners went to the Barbarian courts but they remained outsiders; they intrigued; they tended to back the kings against their new rich nobility, for kings were easier to manipulate; Sidonius Apollinaris (431–89) backed his petitions by loosing at backgammon when he visited the king Theodoric; illiterate rulers required clerks and the clerks were Romans. Gradually too the Romans began to recognise that the devil you could handle was better than the one who knew you not. The refugees from Britain brought tales of what had happened when the backward Saxons came. The difference can be read in place names. The vilages of Garonne and Auvergne bear the names of Roman families who owned them in the fifth century, but no English village bears such a name.

Italy had a real chance of becoming a nation. Romulus Augustus, the last Emperor of the West, was removed in 476 and the Byzantine Emperor Zeno commissioned the Gothic King Theodoric, whom he had accepted within the empire as a vassal, to restore order in Italy. Theodoric (493–526) regarded himself not only as a Gothic king but as an imperial official; he accepted the Roman laws; he honoured Roman institutions and he restored the public buildings. For thirty-six years he kept the peace and extended the frontiers and prestige of Italy. He leaned over backwards to conciliate the Senatorial aristocracy and the Catholic Church. He was unsuccessful. The trouble with the Church was bigotry. The Visi Goths had accepted Christianity in its Arian form. Arius was an Alexandrian contemporary of Constantine who had been brought up in Origen's doctrine of the singleness of God and, like the Unitarians of later times, believed that Christ was distinct from God and, although created before all time, had nonetheless been created. This, the Catholics thought, put Christ in a position inferior to and posterior to God. It was a theological point for which civilisations were to be overturned and for which countless men were to die.

The trouble with the aristocracy was superiority. The senatorial families, and the huge basilicas that were theirs, dominated Rome, as did their vast estates the countryside. They formed a cultural aristocratic society and were prepared to live behind the Gothic armies, but not to be of their society. Boethius (480–524) was their detached ideal. His *Consolation of Philosophy* was amongst the admired books of the Middle Ages. In it, firm Christian though he was, he reaches back for comfort in the face of death to the wisdom of the ancients. He treated the Goths with condescension. It is to Theodoric's credit that it was only right at the end of his reign, that he felt he had had enough of Boethius. No nation grew, for the sections never joined in mutual reliance.

The senators learned their mistake when the liberators of Justinian arrived. In 534 Belisarius entered a divided Italy at the head of the army of an Eastern autocrat. Italy was destroyed in thirty years of war. The troops of Justinian were more alien than the Goths. The senators had survived barbarian rule but they were soon destroyed by the tax-gathering bureaucracy of the emperor. Only the Church was pleased. Blinkered by its intolerance, it welcomed the orthodox conquerors before finding that the Caesarian Church of Byzantium was much more difficult to live with than the Arian heretics had been.

In France things had gone differently. The Franks were Romanised Germans and when they entered France they became a part of a deep-rooted Roman civilisation. The cities were numerous and large, the Church was rich and influential and the land was controlled by a Gallo-Roman aristocracy. The Frankish masters were accepted, absorbed and taught Latin. Clovis the Frank was persuaded by Romans to head the coalition that beat the Huns.

In contrast to France and even to Germany, Great Britain owed little to Rome. Britain had been a colony in the sense in which we now use the word; the Roman army was stationed on the frontiers; a dozen or so towns were Roman; great private estates did not exist; villas or Roman country houses and farms were few and small; tribal areas were cantons where traditional tribal administration continued under the supervision of a district commissioner or count. So long as they paid their taxes the Britons had been left to look after themselves. Archaeologists find their farms and hamlets. The occupation, which lasted about 350 years, did very little to change either the tools or the culture or probably the religion of the natives.

Britain's written history starts with the landing of Caesar, but British government is a lot older. Beginning sometime before 1,900 BC and finishing about 1,600 BC someone built Stonehenge. Stonehenge is not a Zimbabwe, a pile of stones within the capacity of any primitive, but is a major engineering and scientific achievement. The eighty-two blue stones weighing about 5 tons each are amongst the earliest. They were quarried near Milford Haven in Wales, shipped across the Bristol Channel, up the Avon, then dragged or rolled across country to the River Wylye, shipped again and then manhandled up the downs to Stonehenge. The great trilithons weighing up to fifty tons were brought from Marlborough, a distance of twenty miles. They were erected with astonishing accuracy, tenon fitting into mortise. They were cut and dressed, and were set accurately to the rising sun. Avebury Ring is another astonishing achievement, as is Silbury Hill. These are examples of capital creation, available only to an organised society producing a considerable surplus. What happened to this empire we do not know. The people who met Caesar were the builders of the great Iron Age forts, of which Maiden Castle is an example, and were equipped with chariots and iron weapons involving a fairly sophisticated technology. Britain was a far more advanced tribal society than that of the Saxons who came 400 years later; and when the Roman peace was established Britain had a life of its own to develop. A few Britons became detribalised and lived in the cities. (The Portuguese called natives who made this move *assimilados*.) There were not many. Some of the chiefs doubtless made friends with the counts, just as native chiefs became friends of the district commissioner and acquired a smattering of his culture, but in general probably no more Roman culture rubbed off on to the natives here than English culture rubbed off on to the colonial Africans.

Christianity was a Roman religion. In the Middle East it had come upwards from slave, labouring and lower middle classes. It was a townsman's religion. In Britain it could only move downwards from Roman society and it does not seem to have done so. Even among the rulers it was a small minority cult. Christian remains are surprisingly few, only a fraction of the remains of Mithraic worship.

The Romans did not leave suddenly, and they were not driven out. The first big movement out of Britain came in 383 when Maximus led the legions from Britain to Gaul in his bid for the purple. Kipling in *Puck of Pook's Hill* tells the story of how Parnesius held the wall till the legions returned. It is a splendid tale and may well recapture the atmosphere of the wall and of the polyglot legions that manned it, but his 'Winged Hats' are 300 years early and the legions did not return.

We have no evidence that the defences of Britain were tested during the next fifty years, but we do know that in 410 the Emperor Honorius wrote to the counts of the civilian administrative districts in Britain urging them to look to their own defences. This letter is generally taken as marking the end of Roman rule in Britain.

The search for a new empire

The West's final break with the Eastern Empire came when the Byzantine Emperor, Leo the Isaurian, accepted a puritan revolt against the worship of images and ordered their destruction throughout the Empire. It was an epoch making decision. The Roman Church had always adopted those beliefs and customs which it could not get rid of. It had accepted the polytheism of Mediterranean man; the pagan genius had become the Christian angel; Isis the Madonna; the godlets saints and the festival of the reborn sun, the birthday of Christ. Man's craving for heavenly mediators was accommodated and canonised in the worship of relics and in pilgrimages to shrines. Image worship was the basis of a substantial part of the Church's income. There had been trouble between the Churches of East and West over the questions of the Single Nature, the Single Will and the Primacy of Rome, and to all this was added the claim of a Greek tyrant to deprive the Italian people of their beloved images. The Pope looked for a new emperor. He might have chosen the Lombard king. The Lombards had repudiated Arianism and accepted the Roman language and culture, but they were too near. The Pope had no wish to be a Lombard bishop. He offered the empire to Charles Martel, ruler of France, and consigned Europe to war.

To Charles' son Pepin he sent an invitation to come and fight the Lombards. Pepin beat the Lombards and transferred to the Pope those cities which the papacy claimed upon the basis of a forged donation of Constantine's. So started the Papal States that frustrated Italian nationhood for 1,100 years.

Charlemagne followed. In his first campaign he destroyed the Lombards and assumed their crown. He visited Rome. He saw a phial of the blood and water from the Saviour's side and the cradle in which he had lain when he was adored by the Magi. He saw the portrait of Jesus painted by the divine brush of God Almighty. He was impressed. He determined to convert the Germans and over the next twenty years, tribe by tribe, he drove them at the point of the sword into the fold of the Good Shepherd. This was something that Rome had never accomplished.

Meanwhile the Pope had got into trouble. He stood accused of simony, adultery and perjury; he had been severely beaten by the mob. Who was to judge the Vicar of Christ? Not the Greek lady on the throne of Byzantium. There was neither a valid pope nor a valid emperor. In 800 Charlemagne marched on Rome, acquitted the Pope and was crowned Holy Roman Emperor. He was neither holy, nor Roman, nor an emperor. He was a German chieftain, a first among equals. He had neither the habits nor the instincts of an autocrat. His court was no congregation of worshippers, it was a shifting group of companions who travelled, worked and dined with their king. His subjects were unused to kneeling, they were free tribesmen perched a little uncertainly on the remnants of a republican empire. He lacked not only the training, but the apparatus of empire.

Civilisation had regressed a long way since the days of the Antonines and of Diocletian. Charlemagne was, for most of his life, illiterate. He had no professional army, no police force and no settled revenues. For civil servants he had to make do with clerics. He lacked the tools to enforce his laws and to control his vassals. Only his great name linked his vast dominions. It was the name of a hero, not of a god. His achievements were remarkable: he re-introduced learning after the Dark Ages largely through the instrumentality of Alcuin of York and other scholars of the Celtic church who became his friends and companions: he moved the frontiers of Western culture from the Rhine to the Elbe, but he did not leave an empire, a state or a civilisation. On his death his estate was, according to Frankish custom, divided amongst his sons. This had to be so for Charlemagne was subject to the laws of his tribe. His so-called empire soon fragmented into independent fiefs, for there was no faith strong enough to hold it together.

Otto I was the next candidate for universal empire. After defeating the Magyars in 962 he marched on Rome and was crowned Emperor of the West by Pope John XII. He and his successors regarded the papacy as their property. In Rome they hanged thirteen nobles for insubordination. Unworthy popes they removed. Otto I's grandson Otto III appointed two popes while he was still in his teens. Henry III deposed two and appointed four, but the Emperor of the West lacked two things long established in the East, an imperial city and an imperial dynasty. Otto and his successors were wanderers, their capitals wherever they happened to be. Government trailed round after the Emperor. Worse still, his throne was electoral. Bargains had to be made by each new incumbent, and unlike their contemporaries in the East they did not become holy. Otto endowed the Church with lavish grants of land and expected entertainment for the court, subsidies for the exchequer and a complement of men-at-arms when he went to war. As pillars of the state fighting bishops were to be preferred to tribal chiefs and hereditary vassals. As literate men bishops were generally of more use to the administration. All this was fine so long as the Emperor kept control of the Church, but when the Church started to resist the Emperor found that he had competition.

The four popes appointed by Henry III restored the repute of the papacy but they brought from the Abbey of Cluny, where they had been trained, a dangerous idea. It was that the Church should prefer the service of God to the service of Caesar, and some went a little further in claiming that it was for the Pope to say how God was best served and for Caesar to obey. Leo IX was a Cluniac and by temperament an autocrat, a cosmopolitan and a reformer. Rome was not to him a local emolument but the throne of the Church Universal. His legates travelled throughout Europe on disciplinary missions, he appointed cardinals in all the national churches and held Synods in France, Germany and Sicily. He and his successors denounced lay patronage. In 1073, Gregory VII staked his claim to universal empire. All Christendom, he proclaimed, was subject to God's viceroy omnipotent and infallible, and earthly princes were vassals of the Church who could be driven from their thrones, denied the sacraments and severed from the allegiance of their subjects. The Church was to retain all the vast wealth that it had been given in Germany that it might serve the Emperor, but it was to serve him no longer. It was to be an independent power within the empire answerable only to the Pope. As the soul was nobler than the body, as the sun outshone the moon, so was the spiritual superior to the temporal power. The right of lay princes to appoint prelates was denounced.

These were fighting words. The Emperor responded. An anti-Pope and an anti-Emperor were appointed. Rome was beseiged. The Pope sent for aid to the Sicilian Normans and the Saracen levies of their duke sacked Rome. The Pope died in exile, but the conflict went on.

In 1216 Pope Innocent III was still pressing the full theo-cratic claim and demanding of the kings, homage for their kingdoms. He first excommunicated King John and then when John paid homage revoked Magna Carta and excommunicated the barons; he fomented a particularly horrible civil war in Germany; he exterminated the Albigensian heresy and de-stroyed Provence in the process; and he preached the Fourth Crusade that sacked Constantinople and imposed the Roman Church on Byzantium; but the Europe which he sought to unite became more divided than ever.

The Church in its bid for universal empire deliberately promoted disorder since strong governments challenged the papal right to govern national churches. Crusades were preached to distract princes from the building of national states. The Crusaders were barbarian aggressors who broke into civilisation. We have no single Greek manuscript that was brought to the West by the conquerors of Byzantium, of Athens, of Corinth or of Thebes.

The Middle Ages have been called 'the age of faith', and faith was the Church's stock in trade. Her claim was huge. All mankind was condemned to suffer eternal torture for the sin committed by our father Adam; salvation belonged to the Church; Christ the Saviour had entrusted the keys of heaven to the Bishop of Rome; the punishment for sin was eternal; only the church had the power to remit. We can still see the Church's propaganda, for much of it is in stone. At Moissac on the pilgrim route to Compostella the damned are carved in attitudes of agony to encourage the pilgrims; the morbid German imagination displayed and painted the horrors await-ing; and Dante had a three-headed devil eternally chewing Judas, Brutus and Cassius (for Dante was a Gibelline and killing the Caesar ranked with killing God). Travellers told tales of volcanoes where the flames of hell could actually be seen, but how much did people really believe? If they did believe, our forefathers were a race of heroes for they certainly went on sinning.

The armies of the princes did not flinch from anathema as they made war on the Pope. The chronicles do not tell of an age in which sin was out of fashion and yet in a way they did believe as they went on their pilgrimages to Walsingham, to Compostella and to Jerusalem, long and terrible journeys. They believed much, as we believe the doctors who tell us the consequences of smoking, but we go on smoking except occasionally when we get a shock. I think they feared too when all was darkening. Man has done much fearing in his long story, fearing the unknown. The Church exploited this fear. For all the pagan jollifications it was a sad time in which to live. Life was a vale of tears. The end of the world was nigh. This was a promise not a threat. It was expected in the year 1,000 but 1,000 from when? Our Lord's birth? His death? His ascension? Nobody quite knew, but all agreed that it was coming and that both the saved and the damned would soon be relieved from the burden of living. The Renaissance came when man found that life was worth living.

Perhaps the gravest charge against the medieval church is that it stockaded the human mind, and that it converted dogma into a system of clots that blocked the veins of human thought.

Classical education had covered the seven liberal arts: grammar, rhetoric, dialectic, arithmetic, geometry, astronomy and music, and two languages, Greek and Latin. Christian education was based on one language and one subject; the revealed truths of the sacred text.

The medieval philosopher was faced with two aspects of truth, the higher truth of revelation and the lower truth of observation or reason. His art was to hammer the truth of reason into conformity with the truth of revelation.

St Thomas Aquinas (1225–1274) was the leading performer in this school and is the philosopher of the Roman Church by the special appointment of Pope Leo XIII (1879). To disagree with Aquinas is heresy. In 1941 I spent six months swinging round a buoy in the harbour of Freetown, Sierra Leone. I had been in command of some landing craft, intended to carry the great Charles de Gaulle triumphantly to Dakar. Our failure was such that nobody cared to raise the subject and so for six months we were forgotten. It was the only really idle interlude in my life and I enjoyed it hugely. I spent much of my time walking in the hills, which are very beautiful, and talking with African farmers who were always ready to match my leisure with theirs. I also found a book on the philosophy of St Thomas. It delighted me. It seemed to provide me with a key to the thinking of all my African friends; no event predicated a cause; the idea of consequence was absent; things happened by God's will or, in Sierra Leone, by the will of the white man who shared God's directive function. It never occurred to my black farmer friends that the white man might have reason for closing a well. It was just something that happened and was accepted as a hail storm is accepted. To Aquinas, all seemed as acceptable and as undemanding of explanation. When I returned to St Thomas for the purpose of writing this chapter I must confess to some disappointment. To Aquinas Aristotle is the philosopher and the fount of reason. Now Aristotle believed that time was everlasting; that mind was uncreated and that a divine intelligence works in man. The contention that these beliefs were consistent with divine revelation as set out in Genesis involved dialectical gymnastics rather than analysis. Aquinas believed that the truth of revelation might transcend reason but could not contradict reason since both came from God. The task of the philosopher was therefore to make reason conform to revelation. Revelation comprised all that the Church held to be orthodox, whether or not it was to be found in the Holy Writ. The doctrine of transubstantiation, of purgatory, of eternal damnation, of the rejoicing of the saints at the torture of the damned as they contemplate divine justice and their own good fortune at having escaped it, all were acceptable to the reason of the angelic doctor. A Scottish revivalist's sermon is said to have contained the following: 'When y'are a-burning in the eternal fire that knows no quenching ye will cry across the Great Divide to the Lord and to His saints, "Lord! Lord! Ah didna ken", and the Lord, in His infinite mercy will answer "Well, ye ken the noo".' Aquinas would have used many, many more words for the same lesson. Only the baptised and absolved would be saved (and by a properly consecrated priest at that) for all others a fiery eternity.

The search to make reason conform with revelation involved with all seriousness conundrums such as this; What hap-

pens on the Day of Judgement to the cannibal who throughout his life (and his parents' too) ate nothing but human
flesh? Are his meals to be deprived of their bodies (which
would be a bit unfair) or is he to get away with having no
body to be condemned? No, says St Thomas, the body is
subject to perpetual change, at the resurrection the meals
(if they qualify) will go to heaven and the cannibal will be
provided with a body for burning even if it is not of the
same substance as he imbibed during life. There are also
the angels who have form but no matter and can therefore
all be in the same place at once. There are pages and pages
about angels, all total nonsense of a sort that would have
been inconceivable in classic philosophy, and yet in spite of
their absurdities the thirty odd volumes of Thomas Aquinas
are a prodigious achievement. I think, however, that Bertrand
Russell has the last word: 'The finding of arguments for a
conclusion given in advance is not philosophy but special
pleading.'

Revelation blocked science. Since the Bible said that the
sun travelled round the earth it was heresy to consider
whether things might be otherwise. The facts of nature were
revealed and she might not be cross examined. Aristotlelean
philosophers refused to look through Galileo's telescope for
fear of what they might see. When Roger Bacon (1220–1292)
pleaded for experiment and suggested that a knowledge of
chemistry would be of use to a physician; he was jailed for
ten years.

The Lay State

In the battle between Pope and Emperor, emotion, tradition
and instinct had clashed. The Church was Eastern, universal
and authoritarian, the Empire German, tribal and anarchic.
The Christian ethic was meek, submissive and essentially
feminine. It has been described as a religion for slaves. It was
certainly a religion for subjects. The German ethic was mascu-
line. Its moral values were heroic. It was not suited to empire,
for absolute power whether wielded by God or man was (as
yet) an alien conception.

Secular power throughout the West was German, and

178

authority was dispersed amongst an aristocracy that derived from conquering German tribes. Feudal society was roistering and romantic. The duel, trial by battle, the tournament and courtly love flourished despite Christian condemnation. War was man's proper occupation.

The besetting sin of the German is, and always has been, excess. Tacitus advanced the theory that the Germans were a pure race and supported it with the argument that Germany was such a nasty place that no one would have gone there who was not there already. His theory is now unfashionable but it may well be that the German genetic pattern lacks the variety necessary to civilised man. As an outcross, German blood has proved excellent but the history of the unadulterated Germans has been a tale of astonishing immoderation.

German excess resulted in the paradox that the Germans who ruled Europe could not rule themselves. When it came to making a German nation they fell back to near last in the queue. The lead was taken by Britain, whose development in the main had been separated from Europe.

Like Achaean Greece, Britain was infiltrated rather than invaded by her German conquerors. Some in Essex had settled before the Romans left. Hengist and Horsa arrived in Kent about 450, probably as mercenaries hired by a British count, and rebelled sometime after 455. On Hengist's death in 488 Kent was a Saxon kingdom and remained so. His dynasty was still ruling in 597 when Augustine arrived. Further along the coast in Sussex, and about a generation later, the south Saxons established themselves. The 'ings' are all early Saxon place names. The British under Aurelianus, whom we know as King Arthur, defeated a Saxon force at Mount Badonicus (probably Bradbury Rings near Wimborne) in about 500 and pursued them as far as Newmarket, but infiltration continued. Throughout the sixth century we find more and more Saxon cemeteries in Yorkshire and along the whole of the east coast south of the Tweed. In about 600 a British coalition fought the Saxons at Catterick and were badly beaten. Thenceforth Northumbria was Saxon and became the leading Saxon kingdom. In the south the Saxons crossed the Severn in about 550 and during the next twenty-five years drove the British kings into Wales and Cornwall.

The Saxons were pagans from East Germany who had not been in contact with Roman civilisation. Tacitus described the Germans in the first century AD. They seem to have changed little in the 1300 years that separated their arrival in Greece as Dorians and coming to Britain as Saxons. They were primarily pastoralists living on meat and milk. Their agriculture was of the slash and burn type, and field work was for women. The villages moved as the fields were exhausted. All land was communal; wealth was cattle, arms and bangles; man's occupation was war. Government was minimal. Tacitus tells us that they chose their kings for their noble birth and their commanders for their valour. The king, if this be the right word, was probably in the main a religious figure presiding at tribal festivals. The commanders were heroes who attracted followers not always from their own tribes. This was the special characteristic of the Germans. The commander relied on example rather than authority; he led from in front and his followers were shamed if they did not equal his valour; to leave the field after the leader had fallen meant lifelong infamy. The follower owed total fealty to the chief, to him belonged all achievements and to him alone were they ascribed. The chief owed generosity. It was for him to make the fortune of his followers His fame depended on the numbers he attracted and on the quality of their arms and horses. The chief provided the living of his adherents from the common booty or from mercenary pay. These warrior groups consisted for the most part of young unmarried men. Their loyalty was to the Chief and if he were exiled they went with him. Such exiled groups became the nucleus of a new tribe.

The Germans were a patriarchal society. The head of the family had complete power so long as the family remained together but the sons were free to attach themselves to a chief. According to Tacitus punishment outside the family could be awarded only by the priests. He does not say whether the priests and kings were the same people but, in general, I think they were. The public crime was witchcraft with which, for some curious reason, sodomy may have been equated. Men guilty of such a disgraceful crime were pressed face down under a wattle hurdle into the bog. The bog has preservative qualities and we have a number of men so killed, marvellously preserved, some with their last meal still in their stomachs. Tacitus tells us that the assembly of a tribe was competent to hear criminal charges, particularly those involving capital punishment. This I doubt. It is not corroborated elsewhere and it seems inconsistent with his previous statement that the award of punishment was confined to the priests. Law at tribal level knows offences against the gods and against the father. The offence against society comes later. Tacitus is ascribing to the tribe a concept of criminal law which it took them another thousand years to reach. Crime in the tribe was a family matter. It was for the family to avenge the wrongs of its members, but they were bound to accept the customary compensation, or *wergild*. There was a scale. So much for a lord, so much for a freeman, so much for a slave, so much for a hand and so much for an eye. Killing was excused if it were in defence of a man's lord or of his servant against an unlawful attack. This is where the judgement of the assembly may have come in, for it was for the tribe to decide whether blood feud was justified and if so whether the compensation should be accepted.

The Saxons who came to Britain were mainly war bands coming by invitation of British kings. They were not migrating tribes. They probably brought some women but most found their wives here. They came as a warrior aristocracy. The British were farmers, long settled on their homesteads. The Saxons neither owned nor worked land. The Saxon chiefs rewarded their companions with the booty of the Roman towns and villas which they sacked and with the British, who became bondsmen. The fiefs granted by the chiefs were originally gifts of men rather than of land. Vassals did not pay rent or taxes for their fiefs, they paid in service as warriors. Vassals acquired followers whom they established in their fiefs and who in turn owed them service. Only the bondsmen at the bottom paid taxes and these took the form of crop sharing. The king drew his income from his private demesnes. Montesquieu records the complaints of Louis the Debonair, the son whom Charlemagne had appointed to govern France, that he had no money because all the kingdom had been granted to vassals.

By AD 600 England had become a number of Saxon, or as we may now call them, English kingdoms. These kingdoms were beginning to be states; there was a division of function and a mutual dependence; coinage which had gone out with the Romans was reappearing; new towns, crude places when compared with the Roman cities, were growing from the needs of the kingdoms and they were no longer foreign towns. There was the beginning of a will to stand together. The Roman cantons had consisted of Romans and natives, the Saxon kingdoms even at this date had begun to feel English.

Christianity returned in the seventh century. It came from Rome and it spoke to kings. Augustine landed in Kent in 597, converted the King of Kent, and founded Canterbury Cathedral. In 625 Bishop Paulinus converted King Edwin of Northumbria. The new Christianity did much to build the English states and eventually the English nation. It provided the kings and the great vassals with a literate bureaucracy. It accepted its role within the government of the state. Only for a brief period under Henry II and John did the Church of England press its claim for exemption from the laws of England, and after a set-back resulting from the murder of Becket, the English kings successfully resisted this claim.

The Danish invasion hammered the English kingdoms into the English nation. Unlike the Saxons, the Danes came by nobody's invitation. They erupted from Norway and Denmark in the ninth century. They were pagan pirates. They travelled in long boats of Scandinavian oak carrying up to fifty men, primarily rowing boats but with square sails that could use a following wind. They were great navigators. They came down the rivers of Russia and attacked Byzantium. They swept round the British coast sacked Lindisfarne and Iona and destroyed the civilisation of Ireland. They founded kingdoms in Orkney, in the Western Isles and in Man. They drove through the Channel, established themselves in the Seine Valley, went on round Spain to raid the coasts of Africa and the Mediterranean, and to become kings of Sicily. They colonised Iceland and Greenland, and reached America, calling it Vinland. Like foxes, they killed for fun. Their tactic was to slip up an estuary, land at a sheltered spot, seize the local farm horses and set off to kill and burn and then back to the boats and away before resistance could be organised. They terrorised the coasts of Europe for a century. Chichester and Poole harbours knew them well. In 866 the Danish raids became an invasion. The English kingdoms of the north and east fell, but the West Saxons threw up a great dynasty. Alfred the Great beat the Danes and his son Edward reconquered the provinces where the Danes had ruled. England from the Clyde to the Channel was a kingdom and the Danes accepted Christianity and light rule. For all their savagery they were a legal people. Law is a Danish word. The English Common Law that today rules a third of the world developed from their amalgam of Danish and Saxon law. This legalism meant that the state that grew was ruled by law, and that all from the king downwards had to submit to laws. Alfred's dynasty lasted seventy-seven years, and then a Dane, King Canute, succeeded. This did not mean that the Danes had taken England, it meant that England had taken Canute, and we never had a more English king than this Danish emperor. The final code of Anglo-Saxon law was Canute's law. He was succeeded by Edward the Confessor, a Norman-educated Saxon, and he by Harold Godwynson, who was elected by the Council of the Realm. His throne was contested by Harold Hardrarda, the famous warrior king of Norway, and by William, Duke of Normandy. Harold was a military genius with every quality save luck. He raised an army and the vassals of England rallied to him. Hardrarda, by far his most formidable enemy, landed in Yorkshire. Harold marched north with a speed that surprised the Norseman, who did not believe that he could have reached York. He caught the Norse army at Stamford Bridge as it was crossing the river and destroyed it. Then he marched south.

William, probably intending little more than a Norse raid, had landed near Hastings on what was then a peninsula. Harold had directed a concentration of the Saxon fleet and William found his communications cut. He waited in the hopes that weather would drive off the Saxon ships and restore his communications. Then to his horror he found that Harold, of whom he was awaiting news from Yorkshire, was on him and that the famous Saxon Housecarls were entrenched and stockaded across the neck of the peninsula. William was beseiged on his battlefield. That night the Normans dined, as the officers of the *Bismarck* were to dine 900 years later, and toasted death in the morning. Tailfer the minstrel prayed of the Duke the honour of being the first to die. This was granted and he availed himself of his privilege. All day the Normans battled in vain against the Saxon line. Then Harold looked up at the wrong moment and an arrow entered his eye. Now, as the French found in 1940, any linear defence depends on a well-handled reserve. Harold commanded the reserve. When Norman knights had succeeded in forcing a way through the Saxon axemen and through the stakes and over the ditch, they had been met by a detachment of the reserve and destroyed. When Harold died the reserve panicked. They crowded round the dying king. Nobody stemmed a breakthrough. The Saxon line was broken. Harold's brother and vassals were unwilling to surrender their honour by abandoning their chief, and were killed to a man. William could not believe his luck, and his advance to London was slow and hesitant, but in truth England was decapitated. She was not destroyed, but it was for William to provide new heads.

The Normans were the same people as the Danes, but they had been in France for a couple of generations and had acquired French culture and language. That which England owes to Rome came with the Normans. William claimed as the heir of Edward the Confessor and as England's lawful king. His Normans numbered perhaps 10,000, the English perhaps a million and a half. He acquired the demesnes of those who had fought with Harold and regranted them to Normans taking care to so distribute them that none should have a local power that might challenge the crown. All this was done without doing violence to the laws and customs by which the state was governed.

It took England two centuries to absorb its new French speaking aristocracy. There was trouble with the Church under Becket and with the nobles under Simon de Montfort, but when Edward I beat the army of the nobility at Evesham England was English speaking and her Church English ruled. Her people were subject to a common law enforced in the king's court; her peers, her knights of the shire and her burgesses of the cities had the habit of meeting in parliament and of paying the taxes which parliament granted and all had the habit of public service whether it was as tenants called to serve in the wars, or as citizens to pursue malefactors, or as jurors to assess taxes, to judge criminals and settle disputes. England was a state.

What were the ingredients of this so marvellously destined realm; that was to provide half the world with a first or second language and a third of the world with laws; that was to win all its wars and, for a time, to rule the greatest of all the empires?

She had emerged from struggle. She was hammered into statehood by Saxon, Dane and Norman and in the process she had absorbed each in turn. The skein of continuity that ran through the Dark Ages was the village and the farm. Roman civilisation disappeared but the farms and hamlets continued. They were burned by Viking raiders but they were rebuilt; they survived the wars; a language evolved, in the main Germanic but containing many British-Celtic words. Norman French was for a time the language of the nobles. Those who ate spoke of beef and mutton and those who produced spoke of ox and sheep, but long before the time of Chaucer there was a common tongue.

There was a class society. Maybe one day an advanced egalitarian society may emerge, but we have not seen one yet. Civilisation has so far depended on class division, and on separation of function directed by an elite. The English peculiarity was an open class. Only the eldest son inherited. Nobility was not a caste.

The unit was the village and from the village the manor emerged, sometimes by force and sometimes by 'commendation' or submission to a protector. The village owed fealty to the lord of the manor and the lord of the manor owed fealty to an earl or a baron, for whom he had to fight or provide a substitute. He was entitled to his keep from the manor, a charge regulated by custom. Custom settled the rights of the lord and of the villager and disputes were settled in the manorial court.

In early times there were many slaves. Domesday Book mentions 25,000, but in a subsistence economy slaves soon become tenants. The villeins paid for their land by work. At one time they may have been bound to the land but this custom soon disappeared. Work was compounded for rent. Tenancies became marketable. The villages tended to produce more men than they had land for and the pressure was on these young men to find their fortunes elsewhere. Some went as apprentices into the growing towns, some became free rural craftsmen, some became servants, soldiers and priests. The path was not easy, but there was a way for men of ability. Common soldiers sometimes, not often but sometimes, won promotion and even became nobles; some apprentices became rich and powerful burghers; priests of the humblest origins became great officers of state. On the way up they met the sons of nobles on the way down, and before long all were of mixed descent from kings, nobles and peasants. There is certainly no native Englishman today who is not descended from William the conqueror, who, let us remember, was the bastard son of a washerwoman.

The feudal system was a pyramid. At the top was the king who, in theory, owned the land, then there were the tenants in chief, nobles who paid homage to the king, then there were the tenants of the tenants in chief, lesser nobles and lords of the manors, who in turn did homage to their lord, and then there were the heads of families whose loyalty was owed to the lord of the manor and the families whose duty was primarily to their head. Each authority was responsible for the protection and for the behaviour of his subordinates.

The medieval towns did not belong to the feudal state, for by their charters they contracted out. They compounded for their taxes, made their own bye-laws, were free of feudal servitude, tried civil suits in their own courts and selected their own officers. Serfs within their walls became free. Something more than five-eighths of their income was spent on their defences. The English king ruled at Westminster, but for him to enter London uninvited infringed London's charter. Great trading cities like Venice and Genoa became sovereign states. The Hanseatic towns recognised no prince. Ghent, Bruges, Cologne and Hamburg enjoyed virtual independence. The cities of medieval Europe functioned because they enjoyed extra territorial status in so far as the feudal authorities were concerned.

The English boroughs were the first to be integrated by being brought into a parliamentary system. Through the burgesses they sent to parliament they consented to taxation and to participation in the common business of the state. Their defence became a national rather than a municipal responsibility. In Germany and Italy the central authority was weak and the cities formed leagues as independent sovereigns, made war on the Emperor and not infrequently beat him. Venice and Genoa became empires in their own right. The Hanseatic League defeated the King of Denmark and, as Easterlings, founded factories in London and left us a currency which we now call 'sterling'. The government of France, after the House of Capet had established a strong monarchy, brought the cities into the state, but the process was slower than it had been in England.

The Church was English and the king appointed the bishops. This right was not easily won. The Church owned land, but for its land it paid homage to the king. The bishoprics and the abbeys never escaped from the common law, although after the murder of Becket it was, as the great Duke said of Waterloo, a near run thing. The Church provided the civil service, for they had the monopoly of education. Only churchmen could read and write, for letters formed no part of a noble education. It was essential therefore that they should be king's men. They were the eunuchs of the system for they, officially at any rate, had no sons to provide for.

The state that was formed under Edward I had much to learn. It was well served by its wars. From England's point of view the Hundred Years' War was a good thing. We exported the pugnacity of our aristocracy; we opened up Flanders to our wool trade and we bought the wine of Aquitaine. We acquired the habit of paying taxes which our prosperity could afford; we got rid of the feudal levy which was unsuitable for foreign service and we evolved a Royal army. Cavalry was no longer the sole arm that mattered and there appeared that steady infantry that was to rule the battlefields of Europe for 500 years. Above all was born a common enthusiasm, a certainty that one good Englishman could lick a dozen Frenchies. It was from this myth that nationalism was born.

The Wars of the Roses were good, too. They killed off our nobility who were unemployed after the French wars and pro-

vided our counties and cities with the challenge to look to
themselves for their order and safety. They cleared the way
for the Tudor nation state. We were Christian more or less,
so we did not build temples to the god England, but we
worshipped her just the same. We knew that God was an
Englishman and we were irresistible in our faith. Our story
is strangely similar to Rome's. A sedentary farming population
absorbs a nomadic conqueror; they resist pirates with varying
fortune; a nobility is forced to accept 'the plebs' as equals
and sometimes masters; peace depends on the acceptance of
a common law; the union is symbolised by the national ideal.

England was a nation under Edward I (1272–1307) but she
did not become a centralised state until her nobility had
rubbed each other out in the Wars of the Roses. Her great
King was Henry VII, a nasty, mean, cowardly man of occasional well judged cruelty. He left to his son an England
with a secure revenue, a humbled aristocracy, a confident
middle class and an obedient church. Louis XI (1461–1483)
was the maker of France. In Shaw's St Joan when the maid
appeals to Charles the Dauphin to think of his son he replies,
'My son, a horrid boy!' Few could cavil at this description
of Louis XI. A bad son, a bad father, shabby, mean, treacherous, cowardly and superstitious. But as Philip de Commines,
a Burgundian who knew him well, tells us; a great king, a
listener, a learner, one who sacrified all even his grudges to
his advantage. Louis reduced Burgundy and the other great
fiefs to obedience and established royal authority in the French
cities and in the French church. In one respect only he failed.
Neither he nor any of his successors have induced the French
to pay their taxes.

Henry and Louis illustrate an idea on which Machiavelli
was to enlarge. Mankind prospers under cynics and suffers
under romantics. Government demands a dedication that cannot accept the distractions of virtue. Lord Acton observed correctly that great men are bad men. Switzerland became the
first democracy. Hers was the first people who, without regard to race, creed or language, chose liberty. Their Emperor
Maximilian of Hapsburg, himself a Swiss described them:
'An ill conditioned rough and bad peasant folk in whom there
is to be found no virtue, no noble blood and no moderation;

but only disloyalty and hatred towards the German nation.' They fought the feudal armies and beat them. They won their nationhood. They provided little in the way of art or literature. It has been said that to the glorious heritage of Europe they contributed a cuckoo clock. I think they contributed also a lesson in statecraft, the importance of being Swiss, the determination of a people to be itself, neither taking nor accepting. The Swiss have a law that their Foreign Minister may not leave their country. It is an excellent law which we should all adopt. Nine times out of ten statesmen meet for mischief. The Dutch too won their statehood. They rebelled against a Spanish oppression and demonstrated Spanish vulnerability to sea power. The culminating act of oppression was a sales tax of 10 per cent. All historians have agreed that the imposition of such a tax was an act of madness that must have spelt ruin to a trading nation. Now Brussels and the Common Market have done it to the lot of us.

Spain had emerged from the union of Castile and Aragon and Moorish civilisation in Europe had been destroyed. In the north the Swedes and the Poles built nation states. In Germany and Italy many states came into being, but no nation. The Middle Ages ended at different times in different places and the variety of polities that appeared was great, but all had a common Western character. None had a divine ruler. There were many tyrannies but they were secular tyrannies. In the Papal States the Pope was a very secular prince indeed. Everywhere, even with tyrannies, the states contained a balance of interests and of power and all had a system of law. All had been formed in struggle.

II

EUROPE'S AGE OF
TROUBLES

Renaissance, Reformation and Counter-reformation

THE SECOND HALF of Western European social evolution
involves the supercession of an ecclesiastical ethic by a lay
ethic. Lay loyalties become impersonalised. Love of country
replaces love of God as the emotion for which men die
willingly. States count their martyrs by the million. Evil is
redefined as anti-social. Reason replaces revelation. Churches
become national churces. Successful nations identify themselves with the deity.

Neither the breakdown of the Christian ethic nor the
emergence of the national ethic occurred evenly. The conflict
between Renaissance, Reformation and Counter-Reformation
swayed backwards and forwards. By the end of the seventeenth century Britain had become a nation state with
which most of her citizens felt involved. Prussia, America and
France, by different methods, emerged in the eighteenth
century; Germany, and doubtfully, Italy in the nineteenth.
A host of new states of questionable validity arrived in the
twentieth. Spain never made the transition at all. In the Age
of Faith, ethics had been settled by revelation. Good was that
which the Church decreed good, and evil that which the
Church decreed evil.

'A Chinaman of the period, had he been in a position to survey
the turbulent European scene during the sixteenth and seventeenth centuries, might well have asked himself whether the art

of living was not better understood by a people with no religious quarrels because they had no religion but only an ethical code of deportment . . . and whether an attitude of mind towards the ultimate mysteries less aspiring, less heroic and less confident than that which prevailed among Western Christians was not in effect more conducive to human comfort'.*

As Bertrand Russell put it, 'to understand an age or a nation we must understand its philosophy'. It is not for me to judge between ethical beliefs for I am concerned with ideas only in so far as they have affected the development of human societies.

Philosophers have sought to identify 'the good', 'the true' and 'the just' with the same assiduity with which they have sought the philosopher's stone and the elixir of eternal life, but with equal lack of success.

Is there any standard of good and bad other than the seekers desire? Can the one logically exist without the other? In a famous dialogue with Socrates, Thrasymachus maintained that 'Justice is nothing else than the interest of the stronger', and it has always seemed to me that he had the better of the argument. There are few modern philosophers who agree with Plato that there is an abstract 'good' whose nature can be ascertained. Religion's simple answer that God decides and that the good man is he who is in harmony with God founders on the problem of interpretation. Who speaks for God? Who interprets Holy Writ?

Ethical disputes cannot be resolved by scientific experiment, or by looking through telescopes, or by more profound historical research; ultimately they can only be resolved by force, and when war comes both sides ask God to bless their banners with equal conviction.

The consequences of leaving good and bad to private conscience may be even worse, for this involves the arrogant certainty that that which has baffled the philosophers is uniquely revealed to oneself by a quiet inner voice. Conscience is essentially anarchic. Mankind has suffered under idealists—Philip II, Ignatius Loyola, Ferdinand II, Calvin, Cromwell, Charles I, Lenin and Hitler were idealists who

---

* H. A. L. Fisher, *A History of Europe*, p. 447.

obeyed their consciences. All were dedicated to the good as it was revealed to them, different 'goods' equally sure and equally intolerant. Man is not born with a conscience. Conscience is a part of man's culture, something that he takes from society. As a guide to personal conduct within a given society conscience is good so long as you have been well brought up. There is nothing particularly human about it. A dog brought up in human society has an acute sense of right and wrong within the context of the society into which he has been introduced. But conscience as a guide to public conduct, particularly as to conduct effecting groups other than one's own, needs to be tempered by much diffidence. The man who relies on his conscience appoints himself judge in his own cause.

As a general rule, I do not think that any act can be judged to be right or wrong by itself; it must always be judged by the circumstances that surround it and by the nature of the society within which it takes place. It depends upon the needs of the age. When I was a young man abortion was a felony near to murder. Today it is promoted by state subsidy.

It depends on custom. When Sir Afori Atta, Knight of the British Empire and a paramount chief of the Gold Coast, died, he left in his will that the usual sacrifices should be made. His sons preferred filial piety to the white man's law. The great chief was not sent lonely to join his ancestors. The sons were tried for murder, and eight were condemned to death. A group in Parliament led by Leslie Hale, MP fought for their lives. As the twelfth hour was striking Hale appealed dramatically to the British House of Commons. He was joined by Sir Winston Churchill then, leader of the Opposition. The Colonial Secretary Creach Jones quailed. 'Go,' said Winston, pointing his formidable double digit, 'telephone the Governor,' and the Minister scuttled off to do so. When he got through three had already been hanged, but the others were saved and in Ghana are probably held in high honour. At great risk to themselves they had done what they and their people believed to be right.

Ethical decisions have never been easy.

The millennium of Catholic revelation had not been a success story. Since the fifth century the population of Christendom had fallen; its civilisation had deteriorated; its cities had become fewer and more generally of wood and wattle; the amenities of the bath and sanitation had been forgotten; education had been restricted; the quality of thought had diminished; communications and public order had decayed. There had been some improvement during the later Middle Ages but taken as a whole the Age of Faith had left civilisation a long way behind the point at which it had taken over from paganism; the Church Triumphant had in fact presided over civilised man's longest regression.

It is true that the Church had converted the barbarians and had preserved such remnants of classical learning as survived the Dark Ages, but then barbarians are generally modified and often captured by the higher civilisations they conquer. The more relevant question is did the Church civilise the Germans as quickly or as effectively as the Confucians civilised and absorbed their far more primitive Mongolian conquerors, or as the Persian civilised the Arabs?

If Diocletian had succeeded in extirpating Christianity and the Germans had met Pagan gods with whom they could identify their own, and an ethic more concerned with this world than the hereafter, would they have integrated more smoothly and more quickly into western civilisation?

The real trouble had been that the Catholic ethic did not fit the nature of Western man. The Church was Eastern, authoritarian and universal. Western man had evolved through the tribal war party, the polis and the republic, his loyalties were personal and local, his subordination was conditional, he was assertive and legalistic. The faith that he accepted from his church was at war with his instincts. It was a dichotomy that had frustrated progress.

When the break came the immediate causes were two. The Church had lost its moral authority and classical learning, rediscovered, had challenged Catholic dogma.

Disorders in Rome had forced the Papacy to move to Avignon. In 1378 a return was made to Rome. There rival Popes were elected and the great schism followed. The issue between Clement and Urban had nothing to do with religion. Clement represented the French interest and Urban the Italian—it was as simple as that. The national Churches picked sides according to their interests. France, Scotland and Spain were Clementine, England, Germany and Portugal were Urbanite. The Council of Basle (1417) assembled to reform the Church and elect a single Pope. It elected Odo Colonna, a leading Roman bandit well armed to establish papal authority in Rome and in the Papal States. He took the name of Martin V. Reform was postponed. As Fisher* puts it, Martin placed the Papacy before the Church, Italy before Europe and the Colonna clan before everybody. He restored order in Rome, suppressed the other brigands of the Campagna and recalled the Church to obedience. He started a line of pagan Popes who were primarily Italian princes and to whom the Church was a useful pecuniary asset. Rome, long accustomed to anarchy, did not submit easily. Papal repression was savage. The Pope's mercenary captains slew, tortured and burned. Eugenius IV turned on the Colonnas and burned Palestrina, their home; Caesar Borgia, the hero of Machiavelli's *The Prince*, was the son of Pope Alexander VI. As a boy he had been a cardinal but he abandoned Holy Orders to become a prince. Pope Julius II who commanded the papal armies in person, seldom took prisoners. Men who were close to these events could not go on believing that on questions of damnation God was guided by one of these faction leaders, to whom he had entrusted the keys of Heaven. Worshippers further off did continue to believe, at least to the extent that they still thought papal remissions from Hell-fire, or 'indulgences' as they were called, were worth paying for; but then at a distance mankind is capable of believing almost anything almost indefinitely. A recent survey of the readership of the popular press showed that the column which was most often read first was the astrology column. To our Christian superstitions we add many that are older still. Some Greek peasants are still buried with a coin between their teeth in order to pay Charon for ferrying them across the Styx, just in case.

It was in Italy too that the new learning first became available. This began when the scholars of Byzantium were driven westward by the Turks. Greek literature had in the main been known only from Arab translations re-translated into Latin.

---

* *A History of Europe.*

Now the originals of Plato and of Aristotle and of a host of other classical authors became available and the Church's monopoly of learning was broken. The conception of wisdom changed. To Aquinas and the school men wisdom meant, as it was to mean to Luther and Calvin, the knowledge of God. To the humanists of the Italian Renaissance it meant 'know thyself'. The windows were opened to free enquiry and science was reborn; nature was cross-examined and her secrets extracted; painters and sculptors explored the human frame and gloried in their discoveries. Religious subjects still prevailed, for the Church was a great patron of the artist, but the style was humanist. The Renaissance Madonna is a lusty wench with a rollicking boy; Michaelangelo's criticism of Flemish painting expresses the change:

> Flemish painting pleases all the devout better than Italian. The latter evokes no tears, the former makes them weep copiously. This is not a result of the merits of this art; the only cause is the extreme sensibility of the devout spectators. The Flemish pictures please women, especially the old and very young ones, and also monks and nuns, and lastly men of the world who are not capable of understanding true harmony. In Flanders they paint, before all things, to render exactly and deceptively the outward appearance of things. The painters choose, by preference, subjects provoking transports of piety, like the figures of saints or of prophets.

The Italian aristocrat was no longer an illiterate warrior, he aimed to be a scholar, a poet and a philosopher. Society was no longer divided between lay and cleric, it was divided between rich and poor. Like fifth century BC Greece, which it so much resembled, its ideal was the whole man. Michaelangelo was painter, musician, sculptor, strategic architect and, at the age of seventy, turned poet. Leonardo da Vinci was painter, scientist and inventor. Benvenuto Cellini was a cutthroat. His many crimes were forgiven for his art. In his autobiography he depicts a society of appalling violence, both on a public scale as between the city states, and on a private one between family and family. The towers of San Giminagno, each a private fortress, are memorials of the interfamily wars within one small town. The feuds of Montague and Capulet were no exaggeration. Within this feuding the popes and their relations played a prominent part.

The attempt of Sixtus IV (1471–1484) to assassinate the Medici brothers in Florence will serve as an example. Lorenzo di Medici, called 'the Magnificent', had helped the Count of Imola to resist an attack by Papal troops. The Pope had been very cross and had resolved to murder Lorenzo and his bother Guiliano. He chose as his assassins his son, Cardinal Riario, Archbishop Salviati of Pisa and various other clerical gentlemen. They were hospitably received in Florence. Then these vicars of the Vicar of Christ chose the celebration of the Mass for their purpose and selected the raising of the host as their action signal. Guiliano died under their daggers. but Lorenzo and his friends fought back. Florence rose and the conspirators were seized. That night they were hanged from the balconies of the Signoria. The Archbishop of Pisa was so incensed with the bungler who had missed Lorenzo that he fixed his teeth in him as they both hanged together and did not let go even in death. Only Riario was saved. He had climbed on to the altar and embraced the cross as he cried for mercy. The altar cloth was wet with his urine. Lorenzo spared him: a hostage was needed. The Pope laid Florence under interdict as a punishment for executing his assassins.

Loss of faith in sacred values goes at least some way towards accounting for violence. It is less easy to explain the astonishing vigour. The city states of Greece provide the only comparable outpouring of creative energy. In both cases the city units were of comparable size and were under continuous stress resulting from fiercely contending factions at home, controlled, at least in time of high emergency, by an external challenge. This external threat to each separate city may be the key, for dynamic individualism operating at so high a level and without moral restraint would have burst any society that was not bonded by the constant pressure of enemies as vigorous as itself.

Niccolo Machiavelli (1469–1527) was a diplomat in the service of Florence. He did not invent the ethic of post-Christian Italy; he described it. Bacon says of him 'He set forth openly and sincerely what men are wont to do, and not what they ought to do.' His book *The Prince* is a manual in which he

examines political success and failure with extreme realism
and advises on the methods a prince should adopt if he aims
to survive. That advice may be summarised in a single phrase:
'If you will the end you must will the means. If you get
squeamish about your means you are in the wrong business.'
Anthony Jay, in his brilliant *Management and Machiavelli*,
has pointed the parallel between the great international and
national corporations and the city states and has advised
chairmen to consider the advice of Machiavelli with care.
The Prince is a book of pragmatic counsel. Italy had been invaded by the French. Machiavelli was an Italian patriot. He
saw the need for unity. He considered the case histories both
from his own times and from the classics and concluded that
unity meant the establishment of the authority of a single
prince. He had hoped Caesar Borgia might do the job and was
deeply disappointed by his failure. Then he set his hopes on
Guilliano de Medici (not the one who was murdered), and
addressed to him his advice.

If you feel a combine is necessary how do you set about
your takeovers? When should you do it by consent and when
by force? How do you bring them under your control? When
should you destroy the existing management and when should
you take it over? How do you assure loyalty? Is it better to
be loved or feared? If you have rough things to do, do them
all at once and at the beginning; your victims will not be
there to hurt you and the survivors will be grateful when you
are strong enough to relax a little. The methods which experience shows to work are not necessarily those which a
moralist would select.

I think Machiavelli accurately described the ethic that
guided the Italian Renaissance.

Robert Ardrey defined a noyau as a society of individuals
held together by mutual animosity, which could not survive
if there were no friends to hate; it is a gull island where gulls
assemble in their thousands for no discernible purpose other
than to quarrel with each other. A noyau is a noisy place, a
place full of threats and bravado but it is not really a dangerous place, for every would-be aggressor is distracted by the
need to look over his shoulder. Machiavelli's ethic is the ethic
of a noyau, the ethic of men who want no friends. Ardrey

describes Italy as a noyau. Italy, he says, is a collection of families that dislike each other and dislike Italy. Indeed they dislike rule in a general way. If a foreign driver (save possibly a German) collides with an Italian the crowd is all for the foreigner. Italians are very brave. They proved it with the Italian battalion of the International Brigade during the Spanish Civil War, but in Italy's wars they just have not been on Italy's side. Any escaped prisoner could be sure of the most gallant protection from the Italian peasant. Their own government was the real enemy. Successful societies do not work on this basis. There has to be desire for compromise and for cooperation. The ruthless competitiveness of the Machiavellian ethic will not do for long. Italy, was too distrustful to defend herself, and became a battlefield for others. In 1527 an imperial army of unpaid German mercenaries commanded by the Constable of Bourbon sacked Rome, burned the churches and raped the nuns. Two years later Florence fell and Italy, save for Venice, became a Spanish province. Popes chosen by Spain, the Jesuits, the Index and the Inquisition put the djinn that had been the Renaissance back in the bottle.

That which happened in Italy had already happened in the great age of Greece. Moral restraints disappeared because they were associated with discredited superstition, energy was unbound, genius flowered, great works of art were created. But the loss of a generally accepted ethic resulted in collective impotence. Both Greece and Italy lost their liberties to less civilised people who possessed a stronger social cohesion.

Reformation

In Italy the break with the Catholic ethic had been renaissance, clear, violent and pagan. In Germany it was reformation, muddled, passionate and in the end even more bloody. Wyclif in England and Huss in Bohemia had protested at papal corruption, but it was only with Luther that real rebellion came. It was rebellion against the paganism of Rome.

When one sees St Peter's, when one sees the Moses, when one sees the Sistine Chapel, it is hard to condemn a pagan papacy, that spent the tribute of Christendom with such taste; but the manner in which that tribute was raised is a different matter. The popes put God's mercy up for sale.

It was a sales promotion drive by the banker Medici Pope Leo X that drove Luther to rebellion. John Tetzel, the Pope's travelling salesman, adopted the methods of a cheapjack at a county fair. He assured his audience that if they bought 'in-dulgences' their mountains would turn to silver and that as their coins rang in the bowl, so would the souls on whose behalf they were paid leave Purgatory. Luther nailed his pro-test upon the door of the church at Wittenburg (1517) and the dogs of war were slipped.

Luther was German to the marrow and moderation had no part in him. He believed in salvation by faith alone, man was free to do anything save think, priests might marry, the monk's vows were worthless, divorce was lawful, Rome was Babylon and the pope was anti-Christ. Wisdom meant know-ing God. Human wisdom was a trap of the devil. Most im-portant of all, he believed that Church and subject should obey their ruler. When the wretched peasants rebelled he urged on their slaughterers. He served the German princes and they served him two years later (1519), when he was summoned to the Diet of Worms. It was a very different diet to that to which Huss had been summoned at Constance, and at which he had been burned without regard to his safe conduct. Luther had support. The Emperor Charles V sum-moned him to retract. He replied that he would withdraw nothing unless it was disproved by Scripture. He left Charles' presence repeating the words, 'I have passed! I have passed!' They were words of triumph. Pope and Emperor agreed to grab him, but the princes spirited him away. The outlawry of the Diet was a dead letter from the start. Frederick of Saxony took charge of him and saw to it that the Lutheran Church took proper care of the princely interest. Lutheranism became a state religion. All might have been well had the Lutheran states been left in peace to go their own way, but this was not to be. The League of Catholic States was formed at Ratisbon in 1524, and that of Protestant States at Torgau in 1526. They moved from confrontation to war. Catholic France, particularly under her Cardinal Minister, Richelieu, supported the Protestant cause so as to weaken the Empire. The war lasted, off and on, for 120 years and wrecked Germany. At last it was resolved by the Treaty of Westphalia (1648) upon the basis of 'Cujus regio ejus religio', that is that all subjects were expected to have their prince's religion. The decision had been taken that religion was no longer worth fighting about and a German nation had become possible.

England and France

The nation is the people; the state is the organisation of the people; the nation state is a people of common culture living within defined boundaries and ruled by a sovereign government. To be sovereign that government must, so long as religion is a political force, be the effective head of a national church. By the time the papacy lost its moral authority, England and France were on the way to becoming nation states and the English and French reformations took place within national churches.

Calvin, who led the French reformation, was Luther's opposite. Luther was the passionate peasant revolutionary who mellowed to conservatism. Calvin was the intelligent intellectual whose extremism grew with his power.

Calvin won fame as a scholar and writer at a very young age. Having made Paris too hot to hold him he moved to Geneva in 1536, and from there maintained a correspondence with all the groups in France who were rebelling against the paganism of Rome. H. A. L. Fisher* quotes a despatch from the Venetian ambassador to the Doge:

> Your Serenity will hardly believe the influence and the power which the principal minister of Geneva, by name Calvin, a Frenchman and a native of Picardy, possesses in this kingdom. He is a man of extraordinary authority, who by his mode of life, his doctrines, and his writing rises superior to all the rest.

Renan ascribes his influence simply to the fact that he was the most Christian man of his time.

---

* A History of Europe.

The young Calvin is an attractive figure. He had studied the Stoics and had written a learned commentary on Seneca's *De Clementia*. He accepted that virtue should be its own reward and rejected the stick and carrot principle as ignoble. He wrote beautifully. He had a quality of apparent modesty which is to be found in all the best French intellectual writing; his courage was as certain as his manners were good. The old Calvin was a monster. It was something he grew into.

He became dictator of Geneva. In form Geneva remained a democracy, but it was a democracy that always voted the Calvin ticket and if not, why not? The why was fire.

He rediscovered the Augustinian doctrine of predestination. Humanity was divided between those destined for eternal life and those destined for eternal punishment. It is an oversimplification to say that he taught that it was the duty of the predestined saints to exterminate the predestined damned, but it was the way in which he was often understood.

Calvin discovered that during the first three centuries of the Christian era, the unworthy were excluded from the communion table. This became the key to his rule. The private life of every citizen must be supervised. Pastors and laymen alike were subject to rigid control. All were enjoined to inform. The strong arm of the magistrate enforced the Church's sentence. A mixed council, lay and clerical, enforced morality. Adultery, blasphemy and heresy were punished by death. Pleasure became identified with sin. Nothing was good unless it was nasty. Geneva became a theocracy whose horrid influence spread not only to much of France, but to Scotland where it inspired the Covenant, to New England where it hunted the witches of Salem, and to the puritan army of Cromwell. At one point it is estimated that one third of France was Huguenot.

The French war of religion was a civil war rather than a series of regional wars. It was fought with spasmodic savagery, but without the tenacious brutality displayed by the Germans. On St Bartholomew's Day 1572, the Huguenot leaders were murdered in Paris. Their followers in the provinces fought back and Henry of Navarre emerged as their leader. At Coutras he beat the army of the Catholic League. On the death of Henry III he became the King of France by hereditary right, but he still had to fight for his throne. Paris was the price of his conversion to Catholicism. The Edict of Nantes, temporarily at any rate, closed the war. The Protestants were granted religious toleration and the right to garrison a hundred towns. This was a state within a state, and it could not last. In the next reign Richelieu compelled the Huguenots to submit to the state. The Catholic church in France had already become Gallican and was ruled by the royal government.

In England a pagan renaissance mingled with a puritan reformation. Learning did not burst in on us suddenly. The Earl of Worcester, one of Edward IV's (1461–1483) most hated ministers, had been educated at Oxford where he learned excellent Latin, had visited Italy and been astonished by the level of civilisation; had stocked a library from the bookshops of Florence and had learned the pagan ethic. Amongst the illiterate nobility of York and Lancaster, he cut a strange and frightening figure. Over the next century some hundreds of young nobles followed in his footsteps. They were known collectively as the 'devils incarnate'. Education became the fashion. Henry VII had his children most carefully educated. Henry VIII took the process even further. Elizabeth I knew Greek, Latin, French, Italian, Spanish and Flemish; and had studied mathematics, geography, astronomy and architecture. We had great visitors. Holbein came to paint. Erasmus, the charming and immensely influential Dutch scholar, came and spent much time with his friend Sir (later Saint) Thomas More, but the bonds of Christian and National Christian censorship were still pretty tight. It took the Marian burnings to melt them. The Elizabethan Renaissance was essentially pagan. Shakespeare is a pagan poet. To him destiny had the pagan meaning; it is the *Ananke* of Homer, an order of things that even the gods cannot overturn. The great Elizabethans feared much the displeasure of the Queen, but they feared the displeasure of God very little indeed. The deity tended to become a state convenience.

Henry VII, whom Bacon described as 'that most politic of princes', had given us strong central government; his son had reformed and disciplined the church, but it was only after the Marian reaction that with the accession of Elizabeth, England had experienced that marvellous burst of human energy that came from the freeing of the mind. It came in commerce, in adventure and invention, but most of all in literature. We produced no sculptor of note and no painter to compare with the imported Holbein. Some admire Elizabethan architecture, but to me it is like Elizabethan dress, the ostentation of the *nouveau riche*. The great names of the English Renaissance are Shakespeare, Jonson, Marlowe, Bacon, Spenser, Sidney, Raleigh and many others who gave to England an instrument of expression without equal.

The reading of Elizabethan and Jacobean parliamentary speeches, court judgements and private letters, establishes that this fair use of English was widespread and sadly, that it is lost. But we still have a heritage. One has only to attend international conferences to be grateful that one's language is English rather than those others which on the simultaneous translation take so much longer to say the same thing.

The English war of religion was as much social as it was religious. The puritan movement fell into two main groups. East Anglia had received the Flemish refugees from the Spanish Inquisition, solid respectable folk whose skills started a weaving industry. Their ideas, some Lutheran, some Calvinistic, were influential. Outside East Anglia, Puritanism was urban and middle class; it was the faith of those whose wealth and importance had grown with the prosperity of commerce and the dissolution of the monasteries. To these may be added a number of disgruntled nobles. For a time the swelling state was held together by the Spanish menace, but when our danger sank with the Armada, England was bursting and the process that led to the Long Parliament and the puritan reaction was under way.

In the Netherlands the wars of religion became an anti-colonial war against Spanish tyranny.

Spain never had a renaissance and is still essentially medieval. Her great art came with decadence. It was during the miserable reign of Philip IV that Velasquez painted and Cervantes wrote. And then there was Greco, to me the greatest painter of all time; but Greco was not Spanish, his subjects were Spanish, marvellously Spanish, but he himself was a one-man Byzantine Renaissance taking the serious, sacred, elongated art of Byzantium and giving to it a flowing spirituality that no other religious painter has ever approached. If I had to choose a single picture in all the world I would be torn between Greco's 'Saint Louis' in the Louvre and Rembrandt's 'Warrior in the Golden Helmet', in Berlin. Both are warriors, and both express the weariness and tragedy of war. Graham Sutherland's Winston Churchill did the same until it was so frivolously destroyed.

Renaissance, reformation and counter-reformation had filled an age of troubles between the breakdown of the old totalitarian ethic of the church and the building of a new ethic based on reason, legalism and nationalism.

In Italy the revolution had been violent, creative, amoral and pagan; in Germany it had been passionate, romantic and brutal; in France it had in the main been controlled; in England it had been a good deal rougher than we care to think, but it had also been creative. Everywhere reaction had come. In Italy it had been a Spanish army, in Germany imperialism and the counter-reformation; in France regal authoritarianism and a Gallican church; in England Puritanism and Cromwell's army, but nowhere was the Church's monopoly of morals and learning restored.

12

THE AGE OF

REASON

THE CHURCH OF ROME had stood for spiritual order. Ethics were excluded from the province of reason, for they belonged to revelation and revelation belonged to the Church. Revelation was not confined to the scriptures for God revealed his will from day to day through the mouth of his Church. Protestantism had rejected the Church's authority and looked only to the scriptures. When men differed as to their meaning nobody possessed divine authority to settle the dispute. In practice the State usurped the Church's authority but it did so without the consent of the Puritans who denied any intermediary between the soul and God. Renaissance, Reformation, Counter-Reformation had proved a shattering experience. There was no longer one Pope and one Emperor, but a bevy of heretical kings and princes; no longer one Church but a multiplicity of sects; no longer one scholasticism but as many philosophies as there were philosophers; the movement was towards individualism; anarchy in politics and mysticism in religion.

The wars of religion had resulted and had sickened Europe. By the opening of the eighteenth century the European states (Ireland always excepted) had concluded that religion was no longer worth fighting about. Theological questions had ceased to be socially decisive. They were not settled. They were abandoned. The people of Europe sought a new philosophy and a new faith.

This does not mean that Europe ceased to be Christian (even today the majority of Western Europeans would probably describe themselves as Christians) it was the intensity that changed. Religion ceased to be something which men wished to impose on others and they began to accept that good men might belong to another sect or even to another faith. They were still comforted by the promise of Heaven, but were a little less worried by hellfire. Religion was becoming a private matter and tolerance the fashion. Religions were only objectionable if like Communism, they involved loyalty to a hostile nation. This change did not happen all at once, but by 1700 it had become generally true of Europe's governing classes. Samuel Butler satirised the dichotomy in *Erewhon*. There he visited Musical Banks housed in splendid buildings with stained-glass windows, who dealt in money that was of no practical use. If one wanted real money one had to go elsewhere. He met too the gods that were worshipped and the other god, Ydgrun, who was obeyed. Ydgrun was conformity. Ydgrun saw to it that nobody wore a bowler at Ascot. The children of the upper classes were trained in the cult of Ydgrun at the Colleges of Unreason. Lord Melbourne, Queen Victoria's first Prime Minister, was heard to observe that things had come to a pretty pass when religion presumed to interfere with private life. He would have been even more shocked by any suggestion that religion should interfere with public life.

The Church lost her self-confidence and eventually submitted. In the days of her greatness she had threatened us with the end of the world and with eternal fire for all who lacked the credentials she alone could supply. Now that a fiery end has become a real prospect she assures us that we shall all saints and sinners, Christians and heathens, meet in Heaven at the end, a prospect of really liberal optimism, but the Church's adaptation was then a long way off, and in the meanwhile Europe looked for an alternative, for she still needed faith.

Man is a family animal before he is a social animal; his basic instincts are individualist and he needs must be yoked into society; his social cohesion is secured by his emotions, by faith and by ideals that seem to trascend reason, for the rational part of his nature has never of itself proved strong enough to keep him social.

It is for this reason that from the earliest times the philosophers of order have been chary of reason. Their sympathy has been with the irrational side of human nature. They have rejected happiness, at any rate in this world, as 'the good' and have preferred nobility, heroism and sacrifice. They have looked to revelation and have decried science since revelation as not susceptible to scientific proof. The Libertarians, on the other hand, have been all for reason and have been suspicious of passion and of the religions of revelation. They have in general given inadequate consideration to the emotional bonds that hold society together.

Philosophy has tended to rationalise the needs of the time and to express the spirit of the age and of the society in which it was written. Greek philosophy was the creed of man the citizen, rational, self-confident and social. Even Aristotle, the tutor of Alexander, had not thought beyond the city state. Then had come the sadness as Rome decayed and philosophy became subjective. The Stoic, with resigned dignity, looked inwards to the integrity of his own soul. Then came defeat, the destruction of civilisation and Christianity. Europe longed for the order it had lost. During the Dark Ages she was occupied in the atavistic task of escaping, backwards, into the security of the tribe. Society was dominated by the conservatism of the destitute. Attempts to change God's order defied God. It was a passive society. Reason had submitted to revelation. Life was something to escape from. The world was a mistake which would soon be rectified by a beneficent God and the sooner the better. The object of life was death. Any private questing for truth was almost certainly heretical since truth had been confided to the Church by God. Aquinas and the schoolmen had expressed the spirit of this age.

Seventeenth century philosophy was a reaction from this dismal tradition. Life was good and life belonged to the individual. Descartes (1596–1650) founded his system upon a single certainty, *Cogito ergo sum*, I think therefore I exist. From this all else could be inferred. Descartes' philosophy is subjective and individualistic. Since all knowledge derives from the individual's thoughts it may differ for different individuals. Descartes himself claimed to believe in God and adduced proofs as to his existence. They were borrowed from the schoolmen whose other reasoning he despised, but even those who believed in God began to find him insufficient. They began to look for systems of knowledge, of ethics and of social origins that were based on reason.

Now it seemed that if authority were not by divine appointment (and therefore irreformable) then it must result from contract. Feudal society had accustomed Europe to divided authority and to the legalism that goes with it. Feudalism was, in part at any rate, based on social contract. The German hero received service from his followers in exchange for a share in his earnings. When he became a Duke or King, there were reciprocal obligations between king and vassal. Lower down there were obligations between the vassals and the lords of the manor and even at the bottom of the scale many villagers had sought protection and negotiated terms; but this was not the Social Contract that the philosophers were looking for. It established the rights of the nobility and in the Protestant countries at any rate, the nobility was on the way out and a new professional and commercial middle class had arisen. It was the class from which the philosophers came. The social contracts they propounded were mythical. They assumed that man had once been free and had lived in primitive anarchy and that men had then agreed together to appoint rulers or governments and to grant them authority. They differed as to what primeval liberty had been like and as to the limits on the authority conferred, but it was clear that this social authority fell short of the divinity that once did hedge a king. It is true that Hobbes (1588–1679) put authority pretty high. According to him, primitive freedom was a war of every one against everyone and life was 'Solitary, poor, nasty, brutish, and short'. The contract was between the individuals. Man was not a bee. He did not agree naturally. Society had to confer authority on one man or one assembly by artificial covenant, for otherwise their agreement cannot be enforced. 'Covenants without the sword are but words.' When men have chosen their rulers their authority ends. Liberty consists of the right to obey the law. The state so formed was

Leviathan, a mortal God, but philosophies of authority, such as that of Hobbes and of the Catholics who still spoke of the divine right of kings, failed to win intellectual respectability since they seemed tainted with medieval superstition. The spirit of the age looked for an enlarged individual who had retained at least some rights.

The English, as was their habit, looked for compromise and John Locke (1632–1704) was their prophet.

Locke's state of nature differed from Hobbes'. He defines it as 'men living together according to reason, without a common superior on earth'. Later he says that the state men are naturally in is 'a state of perfect freedom to order their actions and dispose of their possessions and persons as they think fit, within the bounds of the law of nature; without asking leave or depending on the will of any other man . . . The state of nature has a law of nature to govern it, which obliges everyone; and reason which is that law teaches all mankind, who will but consult it, that being equal and independent no one ought to harm another in his life, liberty or possessions.'

According to Locke the state of nature was terminated by a social contract to make a government. Hobbes thought that this was a contract between the citizens whereby all abandoned their rights to the ruler, but Locke believed that it was a contract between each individual and his government involving mutual rights and obligations and that it was lawful to resist a government that exceeded its rights.

So far so good, but the difficulties started when Locke came to define the natural laws of reason and the natural rights with which men were endowed. In some places he appears to shuffle the responsibility on to God and to say that natural laws are God's laws but he has a feeling that in a sceptical age this is perhaps not enough and that there must be a rational basis. That basis he finds is property. Property is Locke's Ydgrun, the God who is obeyed.

'The great and chief end of man uniting into commonwealths and putting themselves under government is the preservation of their property.'

According to Locke the law of nature entitles a man to punish even by death any one who attacks his property. He makes no qualification. The storekeeper has a natural right to shoot the shop-lifter.

'Political power I take to be the right of making laws, with penalty of death and consequently all lesser penalties for regulating and preserving of property.'

The power of government could never extend beyond the common good but he omits to say who should decide the common good. On one point he is clear, 'The supreme power cannot take from any man part of his property without his own consent.' Military commanders, he says, have power of life and death over their soldiers but must not fine them. Taxation must be by consent but does the consent of the majority bind the minority? He is not clear on this. Elsewhere he warns against the tyranny of majorities. His definition of property was at times distinctly Socialistic for he held than man has, or ought to have, a property right in the product of his own labour. In this he anticipated the Labour Theory of Value generally attributed to Ricardo and Marx. It was an idea that made more sense in pre-industrial days, when work was generally parcelled out to cottagers, than it does now.

As a theory it usually served to get at somebody. Locke took it from Aquinas, who used it against usurers, mostly Jews. Value lay in the work of the craftsman and of the merchant who transported the goods. The middle man who took his gain without service was guilty of the sin of usury. Ricardo used it against landowners; Marx against capitalists.

Locke also held that every man should have a property right in the land he could till. In his day most labourers had some common rights, but the odd thing about Locke is that he writes as though he assumed that the state of affairs that he advocated actually existed, at any rate in England.

Premises could hardly have been more mistaken than those on which Locke founded his system. The process by which states are created is neither consensual nor rational; man does not combine naturally or willingly into groups more numerous than the hunting eleven; larger societies have to be held together by bonds strong enough to contain man's natural antipathy to other men; these bonds take the form of force and fear; of these fear is the more stable. The state comes into being when someone, probably always a foreigner gains such authority that he becomes a god and provides his society with a faith that transcends reason. Even in the later stages of civilisation when some states adopt constitutions that are contractual in form, they have to be imposed on at least a minority of unwilling citizens. But this did not really matter. Philosophies and religions are almost always based on false premises and are not less potent for that. They create faith. Locke provided an acceptable intellectual basis for limited government, property based ethics and religious tolerance. It was the faith his 'times' was looking for. Cromwell's major-generals had sickened the English people of theocracy. Locke provided the English balance with the ideas it needed at that point in its development and from the assurance he provided there grew a massive self confidence. The new balance was based on wealth and the creators of wealth moved to power.

James II's Catholicism was objectionable less on religious grounds than because it was a key to French subsidies that made the king independent of Parliament; commercial interests were powerful in the Commons only so long as the king needed the taxes they alone could grant.

The Glorious (and bloodless) Revolution of 1688 was a coup d'état by the Whig nobility to whom the new enlightenment had revealed that they were as great as the king and rather wiser than the Church. With the Hanoverian dynasty cabinet government was established and the Prime Minister became responsible to Parliament. Property ruled and England prospered.

Voltaire was amongst our visitors and fell in love with our institutions. In his *Lettres sur les Anglais*, published in 1733, he told of a surprising society without torture or arbitrary imprisonment (flogging and the press gang apparently did not count), where the press was free and religious secretaries left to their own devices. 'An Englishman,' he writes, 'goes to Heaven by the road he pleases. There are no arbitrary taxes. Nobleman and priest are not exempt. The peasant eats white bread and is not afraid of adding to his hoard for fear that his taxes may be raised.' Montesquieu described us as the freest country in the world, no republic excepted, since the sovereign could inflict no harm on anyone. I do not think that either of these great Frenchmen saw our urban poor or that they would have been interested to do so. To the eighteenth century intellectual the poor existed only as picturesque peasants; but to all those above the poverty line, England seemed to enjoy an assured and enviable inner peace. Nobody was aware of social problems. No large reforms were envisaged. Legislation concerned itself with petty local problems. In the words of H. A. L. Fisher, 'a society so stable and harmonious, so little superstitious or emotional, so sure of itself and apparently so well protected from the ruinous folly of the zealot that its like had not been seen in Europe since the days of the Antonines'. But the English age of enlightenment had something which the Antonines had lacked—hope. Stoicism is the philosophy that enables men to live with dignity but without hope. The English philosophy was empirical, rational and optimistic. It harboured the idea of progress.

Eighteenth century England contained the factors that go to make a successful society. Her people were inspired by a formidable faith that we may call patriotism. Britain was no collection of individuals, she was her people's God, and they served her with a heroism that went far beyond the call of duty. There was a general sense of participation that fulfilled man's need for identity. The Whig nobility generally controlled the Parliament as their proprietary boroughs enabled them to maintain a majority in the House of Commons, but Parliament did not rule. England was ruled locally by unpaid magistrates, in the countryside mostly Tory squires. The cities were under-represented, but their members were influential and their elections engaged the whole population, voters and non-voters alike. There was little absentee landlordism, the English nobility and squirearchy lived for most of the year on their land. There was a class of free and proud yeoman farmers. Villagers still had common rights to supplement their wages. All participated in the sports of the countryside. Those who could afford a horse rode, those who could not ran. There was a rough, coarse comradeship of sportsmen that crossed the barriers of class. It was an open society in two senses. Men of exceptional ability could rise, not perhaps all the way in one generation, but still a long way. The famous Dr Johnson was a man of the humblest origins. So were a good many lawyers, writers and teachers. There was no noble class. It was said that the trip from the plough to the coronet took three generations, and so did the trip back. In another sense the American colonies provided England with a frontier. Irreconcilable non-conformists could emigrate, the Puritans to New England and the Catholics to Maryland. It was a property-owning society. The urban poor lived degrading lives in degrading conditions, but even they felt that they owned their slums. It was a growing society whose surplus manned our Army and Navy, and there acquired a new pack loyalty that made them unconquerable. It was a society that catered for most of man's primal nature, his desire for primacy and identity, his need for a pack, his hunting and aggressive feelings, his feeling for arms and territory and his hatred for the foreigner.

It was also a society that contained the seeds of its own dissolution. Men multiplied faster than property. Throughout the eighteenth century enclosure acts deprived villagers of their common rights. Fair compensation was paid but this was soon spent, and with it went independence. The efficiency of agriculture improved and its labour force diminished. The displaced labourers swelled an urban proletariat. Scotland as a state ceased to exist. She was sold by her aristocracy. The consent of her commissioners to the Act of Union was bought by massive bribes. As always happens wealth and population moved to the centre and Scotland became an impoverished province with an emigrating population. But, for all its faults, no European country in the nineteenth century came near to equalling Britain's statecraft.

France

The French wars of religion had been more divisive than the British. Henry VIII was strong enough to impose an Anglican Church. His French contemporaries lacked this authority. When Henry II died in 1559 he left a widow and four sons; the first was invalid, the second was mad, the third was homosexual and the fourth died. The widow, Catherine de Medici, ruled. She was fat, agreeable and industrious. She had been educated in the ideas of Machiavelli. She bears responsibility for the Massacre of St Bartholomew. The Catholic Guises and the Huguenot Bourbons fought for power and the Queen played for balance. All the sons died childless and the Huguenot leader Henry of Navarre, became the heir. He was tough, humorous, shrewd and provincial. He reminds one of Sir Harold Wilson. He cared for the common people. His mind was pragmatic. He was not bothered by principles. He turned Catholic for the throne. He never looked beyond the immediate problem. It was said of him that not even for a quarter of an hour was he capable of fixing his mind on the future. His religious settlement was not one that could last. He sought to appease the Catholics by recalling the Jesuits (who had been banished by Catherine) and the Huguenots by the Edict of Nantes, under which he not only granted them religious freedom but also the right to garrison a hundred fortified towns at public expense. Financially he lived from hand to mouth, mostly on borrowed money. In 1601 he was murdered and after a period of anarchy under his widow, Maria de Medici, whose ludicrous quality is marvellously caricatured by Rubens in the Louvre, the government of France passed to two great unbelieving cardinals, Richelieu and Mazarin. Both saw that only the bonds of autocracy could hold France together. Richelieu corrected the political errors of the Edict of Nantes. He defeated the military power of the Huguenots but left them their religious freedom. Their incomparable soldiers joined his armies. In Germany he was the paymaster of the Protestants and maintained this cruellest of wars in order to reduce the power of the Catholic Empire. He executed the Duke de Montmorency, the greatest noble in France, but it was left to Mazarin his pupil and successor to finish off the aristocratic power. He did so. The two Fronde aristocratic rebellions collapsed. There are more ways of killing a cat than by choking it with cream, but this is sometimes the best way. The French aristocracy were commanded to court where their sovereign required their advice. They were diverted, feasted, involved in pageant and intrigue and kept from government. They were separated from their territorial bases. They were politically castrated. When Louis XIV, the Sun King, assumed authority in 1664 he was an autocrat, but France was not a nation. There was no English social unity. Church and nobility retained their ultimately intolerable exemption from taxation. Both were idle burdens on society. The mounting cost of royal government was extracted from peasant and townsman.

Louis was a very professional king. Rule down to the smallest detail was personal. He was a hard and conscientious worker. He was a good man to serve for he stood by his ministers. His presence was impressive, his will was formidable and his intelligence was Beta minus. His policy was the aggrandisement of his kingdom. The North German states, ruined by the Thirty Years' War, were his humble clients. He maintained a large professional army which he employed almost continuously in war. He would not have known what else to do with it.

The ideas of Grotius as to laws of war that protected civilian populations had taken hold, and wars had become the sport of kings. This came as a rather pleasant interlude between the wars of religion and the wars of nations. When Louis XIV's army burned some towns in the Palatinate, Europe, including the French court, was profoundly shocked. Eighteenth century armies did not live off the country for they were provisioned by elaborate commissariats; they were professional, disciplined and hibernating; battle was the king's gambit, often offered but rarely accepted, since casualties in an age of firearms were inevitably heavy and armies were valuable property. In general commanders manœuvred ponderously and responded in accordance with generally recognised rules. Marlborough was a brilliant exception. Fortresses defended themselves for a recognised time and then, if unrelieved, capitulated with the honours of war. There was no respect for the commander who held on too long and caused suffering. War was a game that involved rather less ill-feeling than most other international sports. The common people did not feel involved. This kind of war did not raise the emotions that make a nation. The Royal Government of France never took root in the governed, and when the revolution came only some pious peasants in the Vendeé were prepared to fight for their king.

In England the ideology of a new age had inspired a governing class; in France it became the plaything of an irresponsible intelligentsia frivolling on the periphery of a court. The philosophies took a different turn. In England the ideas of Locke were empirical, fitting people who were responsible for real problems. Voltaire carried this sort of thinking to France and society smiled as he mocked Church and establishment, but it was not Voltaire, it was Rousseau, the romantic, who inspired the revolution when it came. Locke's liberalism was not emotionally or ethically self-assertive. It had emerged from civil and religious war. It reacted from the consequences of uncontrolled passion and of unreasonable certainty. It was wary of zeal. Prudence was wisdom, intellect a shield against fanaticism, manners the expression of self-control. Lord Chesterfield wrote to his son that a gentleman may smile but must not laugh. Society, modelling itself on Newton's planets, moved in its regular orbits.

Under Louis XV the glory of the Sun King had receded. The pre-eminence of France had gone. Wars had begun to concern trade and colonies and France had been worsted. The Court at Versailles had become a society of brilliant unemployed in search of stimulation. It was bored with safety and craved excitement.

Rousseau said, 'To hell with tradition, to hell with reason, do what your heart tells you.' This was the essence of the Romantic movement.

Rousseau held that man is naturally good and that only by institutions is he made bad. This contradicted the Church's theory of original sin and of redemption by grace. His state of nature was inhabited by noble uncorrupted savages. They were governed by a natural law which they found in their own hearts, an idyllic state that was ruined by private property.

Rousseau's political theory is set forth in his *Le Contrat Social* (1762). His goal is equality rather than liberty. He believed that there came a time when men could no longer maintain themselves in primitive independence and it became necessary to their preservation that they should unite to form a society and that the contract they made consisted in 'the total surrender of each individual to the community as a whole, without any reservation of individual rights. Each citizen puts his body and his mind under the supreme direction of the Common Will'. The Common Will is an interesting

conception. According to Rousseau, we all have two wills,
the one directed to our individual interests and the other to
the common interest. The common will is the residue after
all the individual wills have been subtracted. It is not the
will of the majority for that is but a majority of individual
wills. It is that part of the wills of all that will the public
good, and are therefore at one. But who does the subtraction?
Who identifies the virtuous residue? In practice the dictator
who arrogates the revelation to himself. Rousseau admired
Sparta and deplored Athens. His state is the fascist state. His
ideas are still with us. During the autumn of 1975 there was
trouble in Kenya. A leading opposition figure had been murdered. A parliamentary committee had found that the police
were the murderers. Parliament had criticised the government.
President Kenyatta had ordered the arrest of the deputy
speaker and of another government critic. He descended on
the house and told members that criticism of his government
would not be tolerated. 'Know', he said, 'that there is a hawk
watching over the chickens'. That hawk was Rousseau's 'public
will'. Robespierre was the first Rousseauite to win power.
Robespierre's hawk was the guillotine. We should not under-
rate this idea of an abstract public will that one man can
know. It is the creed of almost the whole of the new world.

Spain

Spain never became a nation. When Philip II died in 1598,
the receipts from America had begun to fall off. Under
Spanish administration, and as a result of European diseases,
the population of Mexico had declined from about eleven
million at the time of the conquest in 1519 to two million
at the end of the century. There just was not enough labour
to produce and handle the treasure, nor was there a market
for the Spanish goods. Spain could no longer protect her
monopolies and the Dutch and English were moving in. In
1606 the Spanish government suspended payment of its debts.
Spain became a battlefield of other people's armies.

When her wretched dynasty petered out in 1700, the War
of Spanish Succession was fought between France on one

side and England, Holland and Austria on the other. Castile was for the French candidate. The crown of Aragon was for the Austrian and the Basques had a third candidate of their own. When Napoleon came, Spain was still divided and medieval, with a fierce pious peasantry looking for leadership to their illiterate priests. She was far too backward to be touched by the ideas of the French Revolution.

Gradually Spain's colonial empire left her. She remained much as Napoleon had found her. She was too backward to reap the enormous profit of neutrality in two world wars. Gonzales de Cellorigo (quoted by J. H. Elliott in *Imperial Spain*), writing in the reign of Philip III, saw the trouble. The greatness of a state depends not on its possession but on the constant and harmonious balance between the different classes. Spain was all contrast and no balance. The contrast between rich and poor was extreme. There were no people of the middling sort 'whom neither wealth nor poverty prevent from pursuing the rightful kind of business'.

Germany

Germany, who had supplied all Western Europe with its ruling classes, had never created a state of its own. Austria was the duchy of the Emperor, and the Empire a group of duchies, counties and bishoprics, the property of their rulers, over whom the Emperor exercised no effective authority. Prussia was to be the first German nation and she achieved her statehood the hard way.

In the Thirty Years' War, Prussia had been a victim rather than a participant. The Hohenzollerns had ruled without any particular distinction since 1417. After the Treaty of Westphalia (1648) they found their man of distinction in Frederick William, the Great Elector. His inheritance was divided and unpromising. In the centre lay East Prussia, Wend country forcibly converted by the Teutonic knights, further east across the Polish corridor was Ducal Prussia, and in the west by the Rhine the states of Brandenburg. Frederick William treated his subjects as he treated his cattle. He moved them around as his state planning required. Populations were marched to new homes. He reformed and he organised. He laid the foundations of a modern state, army, civil service, postal service, treasury, budget, graduated income tax, and efficient police. His son won from the Emperor the right to be crowned King of Prussia and he crowned himself. His rule was ascetic, economical, efficient and brutal. He was very Prussian. He had the mind of a drill sergeant, the manners of a German and the savagery of a Zulu. He left a large well-trained army, the best educational system in Europe and a full treasury. He also left a son of genius who just survived his father's brutality. That son became Frederick the Great.

To the fury of his father, Frederick was a disciple of the new enlightenment, the friend (for a time) of Voltaire and an amateur of the flute, but when in 1740 his father died, his friends were in for Falstaff's surprise. There was to be nothing dilettante about Frederick's rule. He wished to be an enlightened autocrat and he longed for glory. His first action was to seize Silesia from Austria. The Hohenzollerns had some claim to this province, but Frederick's own explanation was, 'I was young, I had an army, I wanted to see my name in the newspapers'. His army won a battle after he had run away. Frederick neither explained, excused nor denied his cowardice, but he never ran away again. He was honest with nobody but himself, and with himself he was very honest. He emerged from this, his first war, with Silesia and a very bad reputation. The traditional enemies Austria and France, the new Russia that Peter had made, neighbours like Saxony, all saw the danger of so powerful an army and so unscrupulous a prince. Frederick's tongue added to his problems. His witticisms at the expense of three great ladies, Queen Maria Theresa of Austria (the Apostolic hag), the Empress Elizabeth of Russia (the tipsy tartar) and Madame de Pompadour (Mademoiselle Poisson) were all reported back and the ladies were very cross. Pious Maria Theresa wrote to her dear sister Madame de Pompadour. Russia, Sweden and Saxony were also approached and a secret 'squash Frederick league' was formed. Of this Frederick learned and in 1756 he attacked Saxony and conscripted the Saxon army, but he underrated the strength and coherence of his enemies. The Seven Years' War had started. Frederick's only friend was England, if friend be the right word. George II observed that 'the King of Prussia is a mischievous rascal, a bad friend, a bad ally, a bad relation and a bad neighbour, in fact the most dangerous and ill-disposed Prince in Europe'. All this was true, but England needed a second front in Europe, while she fought in Canada and India, and so she financed Frederick and lent him Hanoverian troops. This proved a good investment, for Frederick survived and won. He was saved by his military genius, by his unquenchable courage, by his leadership that shared every hardship with the humblest soldier, by the fighting quality of his Germans and by the death of the Empress Elizabeth of Russia.

Clive had won India and Wolfe Canada at a cost to be measured in hundreds rather than thousands of lives, but for Prussia the cost had been terrible. In Frederick's own words:

> Prussia's population had diminished by 500,000 during the 7 years war. On a population of 4,500,000 that decrease was considerable. The nobility and peasants had been pillaged and ransomed by so many armies that they had nothing save rags which covered their nudity. They had not credit enough to satisfy their daily needs. The towns had no police. Fairness and order had given way to anarchy and self interest. Judges and taxgatherers had given up work. The spirit of recklessness and of rapacity arose. All classes seemed intent on ruining each other by their exaction. The appearances of the provinces resembled that of Brandenburg after the end of the thirty years war.*

But for all this Prussia was now a nation, linked by a new national will.

Frederick was an autocrat, the Prussian system was autocratic but it was an autocracy in which all felt they had a share. The Prussians had been the well-tended, protected and prosperous cattle of Frederick William I. They were the citizens, often cruelly suffering citizens, but still the citizens of *Der Alte Fritze*, and they had shared his glory. Frederick had joined the very select company of men who have made a nation. It is odd, for he both disliked the Germans and despised their culture. His language was French and so was his thinking. His marginal notes on German state papers gibe

---

* Quoted in H. A. L. Fisher, *A History of Europe*, p. 854.

at the barbarity of the German language. He played French airs on his flute and thought ill of all German composers. To him Goethe seemed to be a follower of 'that barbarian Shakespeare'. In Germany he felt a foreigner. It may be noted that most nation makers have been foreigners.

Among Frederick's subjects was Immanuel Kant. He and his followers Fichte and Hegels, three respectable Berlin professors, founded German philosophy. Kant was a genius of the widest interests who was brought to philosophy by Hume and Rousseau. Hume's empiricism he sought, (according to Bertrand Russell, unsuccessfully) to refute and Rousseau's romance he endeavoured to systematise. The result was German idealism and the rationalisation of that new idea of nationalism that had come to Frederick's Prussia.

Hegel wrote 'For truth is the unity of the universal and subjective will and the universal is to be found in the State, in its laws, in its universal and rational arrangements. The state is the divine side as it exists on earth . . . The state is the idea of the spirit in the external manifestations of human will and its freedom.'

Frederick would have found all this sort of stuff very great nonsense, barbarously expressed, but Frederick was no ordinary German. The ideas of Kant and Hegel were destined to fuel German nationalism to destruction.

It will be seen that during the Age of Enlightenment the replacement of the Catholic ethic had developed differently in the different states of Western Europe. In Spain it did not happen at all; in Italy it had happened during the Renaissance but its development had been checked by Spanish and then Austrian arms; Austria and France had been pushed into reaction, the first by the Counter-Reformation and the second by royal centralism; Prussia had become a nation in Germany but a German nation was yet to come. Only England had achieved full nationhood.

13

THE AGE OF

REVOLUTION

WHEN THE DEMANDS of a community come into conflict with the instincts of its members a frustration aggression psychosis develops. This is a phenomenon that has been observed in almost every society that has been studied; bees, termites, jackdaws, monkeys and men all have their social breakdowns.

In human societies a sequence is generally to be observed. People are on the move and new prospects are surfacing. Poverty is not a revolutionary cause and destitution is profoundly conservative. Revolutions happen in advancing societies when hopes are aroused and frustrated. Restraints lose their guise of inevitability. The intellectuals begin to turn against the government. This process has been called the 'Le trahison des clercs'. Mocking authority becomes the fashion.

Government begins to lose its self-confidence. Authority depends more and more on coercion and coercion makes martyrs. A revolutionary leadership emerges and with it an alternative government taking the form of clubs, parties or societies. Revolutionary programmes are weapons in the struggle and become irrelevant with victory. When government fails moderates succeed, but they fail too for the machinery of government has been destroyed and power has passed to the alternative government of the party or the clubs. The true revolutionary government is firm only when it has destroyed all alternative authority. This is the process known as the eating of the children. It is only after this that the new society is born. The new government takes over the machinery of coercion against which it rebelled, and uses it with new vigour.

Do leaders make revolutions or do revolutions make leaders? This will always be debatable but it is certain that revolution opens up opportunity for greatness and much depends on the character of the men who take the opportunity.

In classical and medieval times revolution was a very bad word. Plato rated it as a disaster worse than famine or pestilence and Aristotle (*Politics*, Book V) agreed. The unalterable rule of Plato's guardians was designed to avoid this evil. Cicero agreed too. For him the first duty of the statesman was to arm himself against all emergencies that unsettled the constitution. In the Age of Faith man's fate was to suffer and obey. Revolution was rebellion against God's order. It was not till the seventeenth century that with the idea of the Social Contract rebellion became in certain circumstances justifiable and revolution respectable.

The two English revolutions (1642–1688) do not fall within my definition of revolution. They did not aim to overturn the existing order of society. The Parliament in 1639 and the Whigs in 1688 claimed to maintain the laws of the land against the encroachments of the king. The Parliament tried to keep Charles as king and it was only when he proved impossible that Cromwell became a substitute king. In 1688 the Whigs replaced James II with his daughter. In neither case was the system changed.

The American revolution seems to have been the first in the modern sense of the word. The thirteen British colonies in North America enjoyed more liberty and prosperity than any other part of the new world. Each had its own charter or constitution and, save for certain reserved subjects such as defence and the regulation of trade, enjoyed self-government. Britain's Canadian victories in the Seven Years' War had eliminated an external threat which might have made the British connection seem worthwhile. Royal governors treated Americans as social inferiors and there was no obvious advantage to compensate for the irritation. The colonists were in America because they or their fathers had dissented over something. They were a prickly lot. They did not see why they should obey a parliament in London.

The idea of parliamentary sovereignty was a new one that had come with cabinet government. The older idea, the idea of men like the great Chief Justice Coke in the seventeenth century, had been that the law was sovereign and that the rights of king and people were enshrined unalterably in Magna Carta. The laws of the English parliament were for the English. The colonists had their own parliaments operating under their own charters. They took the attitude which was much later to be enshrined in the Statute of Westminster (1932) that they were independent states who shared a king. The English Parliament had become a frustration, a 'reason why not'. Taxation was a peg to hang a quarrel on. Britain's case was reasonable; the colonies required a defence force to protect them from the Indian nations, and Britain felt that they should contribute to the cost of their own defence, but reason never answers emotion. The cry of 'no taxation without representation' became the cry of liberty.

The colonies were by no means united. There were many who remained loyal to the British connection, but the men of energy were with the rebels. Puritan Massachusetts took the lead. In Adams they found an organiser of genius. His invention, the correspondence club, was to provide the framework not only of the American Revolution but of all future revolutions. These clubs, or cells as we would now call them, were formed in all colonies, as co-ordinated centres of agitation. They became the alternative rebel government. It was through them that the Continental Congresses were organised. They provided a nucleus of zealots that kept, but only just kept, the fire burning during the hard years to come.

In England government dithered. There were loyalists in America and Americans in Britain. Chatham, Burke and Fox, the three best brains in British politics, were opposed to coercion. The Americans seemed to stand for liberty and liberty was the fashion. The Stamp Act, which was the government's first attempt at colonial taxation, had to be withdrawn. This triumph brazened the clubs. Indirect taxation was tried. A duty was imposed on tea. Boston braves disguised as Mohawks, threw the tea overboard. The British closed the port of Boston.

The Committees of Correspondence rallied to Boston's support. The first Continental Congress met at Philadelphia and agreed to organise a Continental Association to cut off all economic intercourse with Britain. By January 1775 bodies based on the Committees of Correspondence were acting as governments in ten states and by April fighting had started around Boston.

The second Congress met in May and spent a year seeking compromise, a year in which King George and his ministers did all in their power to consolidate colonial opinion behind the extremists. They employed German mercenaries and Indian irregulars. Both, according to their custom, behaved deplorably. Loyalists and rebels were scalped and pillaged without discrimination. Opinion became inflamed. The clubmen were able to drive 100,000 loyalists into exile. On 4 July, 1776, the die was cast—the Declaration of Independence was signed but war had only just begun.

The British had a regular army of 15,000 British and 30,000 Germans which could beat any continental army that it could bring to battle. But this was the difficulty. The Colonies had no heart that could be stopped beating. There was no centre that was vital to them. America was a big continent for an army of 45,000.

The British had a very incompetent government but the Continentals did not have a government at all. The Congress was only a coordinating committee. The states were allergic to taxation. The Congress tried to use paper money. 'Not worth a continental' is still an American expression. There were powerful inter-state antagonisms. All were dissenters but they did not dissent from the same things. There were the Puritans, Presbyterians, Baptists and Quakers; there were the Catholics; there were the Royalists, who had emigrated during the Commonwealth and the Roundheads who had come with the Restoration, there were the slave owners of the plantations and the working farmers, the ship owners and the merchants. Unity did not come easily. The tradition was individualistic and selfish. Enthusiasm was not evenly spread. The Congress was never able to put 20,000 men on a battlefield, but the Continentals had one asset without price His name was George Washington He was not a great soldier, for he lost nearly all his battles, and he was not a great thinker, he was just a great man He possessed a courage, an integrity and a constancy that united when all else divided. He alone kept the Continental army in being. But he still needed luck. It came in the form of two connected follies.

England's Secretary of State for War, who earlier in his career had been cashiered for cowardice. forgot to post a letter with the result that 'Gentleman Johnny' Burgoyne advancing from Canada was left unsupported and compelled to surrender at Saratoga with 5,000 men. This encouraged Louis XVI to recognise the Congress and join the war. France was smarting from her defeats in the Seven Years' War and Louis saw an opportunity for revenge. Not only was it an extravagance that he could not afford, but the spectacle of triumphant republicanism and the return of heroes of the American republic such as Lafayette lit an emotion that was to prove irresistible. Spain and Holland followed France and Britain found that a colonial war in which she had little heart, had become a European war in which she was without allies. The royal government of George III broke down, the Whigs returned to power and peace was made with America. Against all the odds the first revolution had succeeded and the job was now to make a state.

It was no easy task. The conflicts of interests and of temperament were great. The states had found it hard enough to unite in war, how could they be expected to do so in peace?

The Congress was a single chamber whose members were the delegates of state legislatures. Most important decisions required nine state votes and amendment of the Articles of Confederation required unanimity. It was a body incapable of rule. The ex-colonies carried on virtually without central government, but by 1786 it had become clear that Congress lacked the authority to conduct a credible foreign policy. Demand for the revision of the Articles of Confederation grew.

Everything depended on George Washington. He had been great in war, he was to prove even greater in peace. His trustworthiness was the constant which men hung on to. It transcended their jealousies.

The Congress was persuaded to authorise a convention of state representatives with Washington in the chair, to amend the Articles of Confederation. They met, decided to draft a new constitution, and to submit that constitution not to the legislatures but to the people of the states. This was a vital decision. It meant that the Federal Government would draw its authority directly from the people. It meant that the United States would be a democracy. There was still conflict of opinion between the advocates of strong government and those who stood for state rights, but this was really of secondary importance and under Washington's guidance a draft was hammered out. It was to come into operation when the voters of nine states had ratified. The popular debate was worthy of the occasion, and from it Alexander Hamilton emerged. He had served Washington as his Aide-de-Camp. He came from the West Indies and was of illegitimate birth. Talleyrand was later to describe him as the cleverest man he ever knew. He was twenty-six. The Federalist Papers for which he was largely responsible are still a classic. They did much to win the ratification of a constitution which in its essentials is still in force.

Washington was elected unopposed as President for two terms, and refused a third. Hamilton, who stood broadly for strong government and the industrial interest was Secretary of the Treasury. Jefferson, the chief author of the Declaration of Independence, stood for the landed interests and state rights. Washington steered a course between them. Hamilton took one very interesting decision. He accepted Federal responsibility for the near worthless state bonds, thereby creating a class of bond holders with a vested interest in the Federal Government. He also created a central bank with the same object in view. When Washington retired to his charming little estate on the Potomac, the United States of America was established.

It is hard to overestimate the influence of this uncomplicated country gentleman who respected his fellow Americans and did his duty as he saw it. The Americans were not conditioned to central authority. Without Washington there would probably never have been a United State of America, certainly not one in anything like the form which was acceptable only because he was there to be its President.

Within the American revolution one can trace the sequence in revolutionary events. Society was in motion and the middle classes at any rate were conscious of the prospect of improved fortune; government was out of touch, uncertain of itself and was seen as a frustration by the most vigorous classes in the colonies; the ideas of the age of enlightenment justified the rebels and sapped the will of the rulers. This was very important; for if you are to rule others you must believe in yourself. The leaders of discontent succeeded in forming an alternative government in the form of Committees of Correspondence. This cellular organisation originally invented by the early Church, has proved basic to revolutionary organisation. The rebel authority destroyed the loyalists and forced them into exile. Government had no alternative to force and the Revolutionary War broke out. So far the story is typical, but with the emergence of Washington the sequence changed. There was no devouring of the children. The rebel leaders did not kill each other. The war stopped with the internal conflict still unfought. There was just the great shade of Washington, but he did not rule for he was no Napoleon. The state legislatures ruled and the centre was inert. When the time came for power to pass to the federal democrats, who were the extremists of this revolution, it passed peaceably under the shadow of Washington and the best young brains were free to work out America's great destiny.

The ideology of the revolution came from Locke and remained remarkably constant. The laissez-faire ideas of Adam Smith influenced Jefferson and led to the defeat of Hamilton's proposals to protect emergent American industries. The wisdom of this decision is debatable.

There remains the question, on what was the American idea based, what was it that bound the states into a nation? There was common language and common national origin. There was common glory won in war but the continuing pressure of an external enemy, generally so necessary, was absent. There was a powerful class of bond holders whose bonds were underwritten by the Federal Government and there was an even wider class that had participated in robbing the loyalists. This meant that there was a vested interest in federal authority possessed by the richer citizens in all the states. There was the fact that new territories were vested in the federation. Eventually unity was to cost a bloody war, but judging by other federal experiences, it is surprising that a unity so lightly bonded lasted peacefully as long as it did.

The French revolution was influenced by the American but it developed on different lines. The autocracy built by the two Cardinals and conducted by Louis XIV (1661–1715) had run out of steam. It had been an unhappy era, a narrow cruel bureacracy extorting from the people of France the means to distress her neighbours.

The nobility, untaxed absentee landlords, became the courtiers of Versailles; their independence was lost; their local influence broken, their employment servility and their business intrigue. They were not merely the drones but the leeches of a society that looked ever more inwards upon itself. On the periphery of the court, but not of it, were the salons and the brothels, offering irresponsible relaxation, the one intellectual and the other physical. It was this aspect of irresponsibility that distinguished the philosophers of France from their contemporaries in England and America, for the intellectuals were excluded from the French establishment. France was ruled by the king. The local government of the *intendants* was the government of the king's servants. The army and navy were professional. All authority was centralised and with the weaker, lazier kings that succeeded, civil and military rule drifted into obsolescence. The costs rose and the means diminished. Taxes had to be extracted from the common people. The *taille* was a form of poll tax: the salt tax was high; there were customs on each provincial frontier. Smuggling was a profession. All taxes were farmed. When in the reign of Louis XV collectors started to be tortured for inadequate collection, things had indeed come to a pretty pass.

Privilege, medieval and functionless, was the creeping paralysis of the French body politic; privilege of Church, of nobility, of provincial parliaments, of judicial corporations and of trade guilds, polluted justice, diverted taxation and denied careers, civil and military, to the ablest. France did not rebel against property or against wealth but against privilege. This was inevitable. The form which that rebellion would take depended on the chance of personality.

The fashion of the age was reforming autocracy. Had Louis XVI (1774) been a Catherine of Russia or a Frederick of Prussia, history would have been different. France was ready for an autocrat who would destroy the abuses. Louis was a good man. He is perhaps the outstanding example of virtue's inferiority to vice in the government of mankind. It is not always so. We have just been talking of Washington but when we consider our debt to the infamous Tudors, France's to her terrible cardinals and to Napoleon, whose moral superiority to Hitler can be assessed only by the fashion of the age; Germany's to Frederick and Bismarck; Russia's to Peter and Catherine and Stalin and Turkey's to Kemal Pasha, we must acknowledge that in the art of statesmanship vice has the edge. It was a quality Louis XVI lacked. The poor good man did everything wrong. His first trouble was financial.

Bankruptcy is the wrong word to use in this context. States do not go bankrupt. It was simply a case of the revenue being insufficient to meet the expenses. He might have cut expenditure, reduced pilfering from the public till or increased revenue, or a bit of all three. Instead he recalled the parliament of Paris and its provincial equivalents. These parliaments were medieval guilds of lawyers, reactionary by nature and temporarily popular only because they were not part of the all-pervasive royal authority. In practice they proved a barrier to reform.

In 1778 Calonne, the most intelligent of the many ministers whom Louis appointed and failed to support wrote:

> France is a kingdom composed of separate states and countries, with mixed administrations the provinces of which know nothing of each other, where certain districts are completely free from burden, the whole weight of which is borne by others, where the richest class is the most lightly taxed, where privilege has upset all equilibrium, where it is impossible to have any constant rule or common will; necessarily it is a most imperfect kingdom, very full of abuses, and in its present condition impossible to govern.

In 1788, as a last resort, Louis turned to another medieval institution, the States General, which Richelieu had disposed of a hundred years before. Its procedure and function had been forgotten. It emerged as an assembly of 1,200 men, 300 of whom had been elected by the aristocracy, 300 by the clergy and 600 (in theory, at any rate) by the people, but in practice by the middle and professional classes. The government hoped for money and had no reform programme to propose to the estates. It had not even decided whether they should sit separately or whether they should form a single chamber. Eventually, under the pressure of the Paris mob, the States General met as a single assembly, the Royal government had broken down and *faute de mieux* the assembly had to govern. It was quite unfit for the task. A National Guard, recruited not exclusively but extensively from the jails, was raised and placed under the command of Lafayette the hero of France's intervention in the American revolution. Lafayette was no Washington. He proved vain and incompetent.

The King at Versailles vacillated. Under the influence of the Right he started assembling troops. On 14 July, 1789, the Paris mob responded by storming the Bastille. This was not a notable feat of arms. The guns were useless, the guards surrendered on terms and were then murdered, and there were no prisoners to liberate, but the political effect was enormous. The revolutionary mob was the master of Paris and Paris the master of France. The King dispersed his troops, dismissed his ministers, accepted the Tricolour cockade from Lafayette and publicly blessed the taking of the Bastille, but even this was not enough. Paris determined to hold her prisoner. On 5 October the mob, led by Madame Roland, the Maud Goune of her day, and with Lafayette and the National Guard trailing behind, marched on Versailles and brought the King and Queen back to the Tuileries. Paris had passed into the control of the Jacobin clubs.

Meanwhile the National Assembly proceeded with its constitutional task. The shivering *Ancien Régime* offered no resistance. In a single night nobles and clergy, provinces, municipalities and guilds surrendered their privileges. They had nothing to surrender. The army and navy had mutinied. The peasants were burning the châteaux. The idea that France belonged to her people had caught light. Every bourgeois felt a sovereign. That mysterious residue, the public will, was enshrined in the National Assembly. In the depths a new people were moving, the starved, the brutalised predators, smugglers, thieves, pimps, footpads and their women. On the night the Bastille fell they had danced round the headless corpses of three gentlemen whose crime had been that their coats were too good.

The constitution that emerged (September 1791) was written in fear. The assembly that had failed to govern feared government. A powerless kingship was retained but authority was dispersed amongst 40,000 municipalities whose every official was to be elected. The Church was submitted to a similar fate. Curé and bishop were to be chosen by ordinary voters who might or might not be Catholic or, for that matter, Christian. The Curés as a class had backed the Revolution against the intolerable privilege of the higher clergy, but this new constitution drove every priest who retained any respect for his church into rebellion. The *prêtres insermontés* became the backbone of the Royalist resistance. Talleyrand, Bishop of Autun, consecrated the new electoral bishops. Of all his sins this was the one that took the most forgiving. The Assembly disqualified themselves from membership of the new parliament thus, handing over authority to new men lacking even their two years of experience.

The group that emerged came from the Gironde and are so known to history. Their leader, if they had one, was that beautiful Madame Roland who had led the march to Versailles. Their enthusiasm was huge, their eloquence splendid, their sense minimal and their experience nil. The *emigrée* aristocrats, the non-juring priests and the Queen's Austrian relations were the enemy. On 20 April, 1792 they went to war. At the sound of their bugles they expected all oppressed humanity to rise against the oppressors.

Oppressed humanity did not rise, it marched and the Girondins found that they did not have an army. A man of sterner stuff grasped the helm; Danton, the apostle of terror. He saw that a divided France could not survive and that she could not be led by a king whose heart was with the enemy. He roused the mob to storm the Tuileries and massacre the Swiss Guard. The Republic was proclaimed. In the prisons the September massacres commenced. Crime is a bond. The principle that if we do not hang together we hang separately, has revolutionary validity. The officers of the Revolutionary armies got the idea that they conquered or else. At Volnay (20 September, 1792) they no longer ran away. There was a cannonade and the Prussians retired. The Republic was on the march, but the fight for power within the Republic was still on.

The great majority of the Assembly, called the Plain, were middle-class Frenchmen who wanted a quiet life. Their inclination was to the Girondins. Liberals of charm and reputation who believed in Liberty, Equality and Fraternity, and failed to provide themselves or the Assembly with a praetorian guard. The minority, called the Mountain, was based on Paris and the Jacobin clubs. Their leader was Robespierre, an idealist who, unlike the Girondins, was prepared to will the means. He demanded the head of the King. Why not? The King was a traitor to the Republic in proved communication with the invaders of French soil. The Girondins were out-manoeuvred. Basically humane, they shrank from blood but were hoist upon their own logic. They consented and in so doing lost the centre. They were regicides and they were lost.

The Jacobin Committee of Public Safety consisted of men past forgiveness whom only victory could save. Their weapon was terror. Robespierre arrested the Girondin orators and hauled them before his people's court. The bravoes from the Jacobin clubs terrified the Assembly, which consented to the death of its leaders. Daily the enemies of the people passed to the guillotine. Danton cried 'enough', and was himself condemned.

For a year Robespierre ruled, and what a year it was. Carnot created the army that would one day serve Napoleon and Saint André rebuilt the navy. The Royalist rebellion at Lyons was smashed, Toulon was recaptured, Belgium was conquered and the Duke of York driven into the sea. The Austrians were defeated at Wattignies and Fleurus, Holland was invaded and no enemy was left with a foothold in France. The terror had cost some 2,500 lives, a loss which even a humane commander would find acceptable as the price of a small victory.

Everywhere the ruthless energy of the Jacobins had been triumphant, but Robespierre made one mistake. His contempt for the Assembly was so great that he neglected to protect himself on its floor, while he threatened the lives of its members. Barras and Tallien, spurred by terror, raised a mob, stormed the unguarded assembly and popped Robespierre's head through the window of the guillotine. The moderates, made newly brave by their late fears, destroyed the tiny Jacobin band that had achieved so much.

Had the King and Queen been alive there might well have been a Royalist reaction, for the moderates were bound to the revolution only by their regicide. They wanted a quiet life but their lives depended on the continuity of regicide government. They proposed a legislature elected as to two thirds from the Convention that had voted the death of King and Queen and an executive of five directors, two Jacobins, two Girondins and Barras. Robespierre had had a committee of public safety, Barras proposed one of personal survival. The Right was indignant. A movement was organised in Paris by the rich and conservative; 26,000 were said to be mustered for attack. Barras did the right thing. He sent for Napoleon and Napoleon sent Murat galloping for the artillery. The rebellion was dispersed. The grim glory of the terror was past. The new rich wanted some fun. The Directors invented a new high waisted, breast-displaying classical line and for themselves gorgeous uniforms in which they looked a little ashamed, except for Barras who was shameless. The new government in which humanising corruption replaced fanatic virtue survived four years. There was then another whiff of grapeshot, and Council and Directors were replaced by Napoleon's consulate, an enlightened autocracy that was soon to become an empire.

The French loved it. They went on loving Napoleon even in defeat. They acclaimed his return after his first exile in Elba and then forty years later, having rejected the prosperity of an English style limited monarchy, they elected as their first president another Napoleon who once again they acclaimed as Emperor. Even today, if there was a surviving Napoleon, Giscard D'Estaing would not feel safe.

What happened to the ideas that made the Revolution. Liberty, equality and fraternity were strictly for export. They went very well in Poland and had affects in Germany and Italy. In Spain they were disastrous. The Spanish peasant was far too primitive for such enlightened notions. There was no Spanish nation for any government to take over. For some years the French controlled Madrid and the principal road systems, but away from the roads illiterate peasants, priests and monks killed any straying Frenchman.

The Sovereign People and the Common Will lived on as emotions. The Emperor was the people's executive and they shared his glory, for he expressed the Common Will. The Grand Army was the army of France. Sergeant Wilkins serving in Wellington's army of occupation after Waterloo, wrote in his diary: 'The French soldiers have medals. No wonder they love their Emperor.'

What then were the factors that made the Empire a successful society?

First there was faith. France was no longer the conglomeration of discordant provinces described by Calonne. France had acquired an emotional entity symbolised by the Eagles of the army, that was greater than all its units. For the first time France was national right through. Every man felt a citizen, equal at least in his Frenchness. The weight of privilege had been removed. Any man's son might one day be a Marshal of France. Property was free. The peasant, even when he did not own his land, could acquire it free from the old feudal burdens. France, like England, had become property owning.

Then there was the stimulus of glory. There had been no feeling other than dislike for the armies of the *Ancien Régime*, but the *Grande Armée* was the nation in arms. The cost was heavy. The fact that the average Frenchman tends to be smaller than his neighbours, has been ascribed to the fact that the *Grande Armée* took too many of the strongest sires before they could found families, but the ordinary man found the price worth paying. No Frenchman recalls with pleasure the English style monarchies that provided an interlude between the Napoleons, nor have her various republics proved emotionally satisfying. She has never responded to any republic as she did to Napoleon or, for a time, to de Gaulle.

Revolutions begin with an idea that will close the gap between men as they are and men as they would like to be. This idea may come from God, or nature or science, but it is essentially a religious idea, a faith. It is held by a small group of dedicated puritans. Nearly all revolutionary leaders have been ascetics. Danton was an exception, and he died largely because Robespierre did not like his morals. The puritans seize power when the moderates fail. They save the revolution at the cost of its principles. Liberty, equality and fraternity will not run an army. The faith that was universal becomes national. "All men" becomes all white Americans, the brotherhood of man becomes the brotherhood of Frenchmen; the workers of the world become the workers of Russia. The puritans become too great a strain and there is a reversion to 'normalcy', moral and political, but it is a different 'normalcy', that depends on the social evolution of each particular society, in America individualistic and republican; in France statist and by inclination imperial; in Russia autocratic. As far as one can judge revolution does not make all that difference to the end result. American society is not very different from Canadian, nor French from Belgian, and Breshnev's Russia is very reminiscent of the interregnums that followed Ivan and Peter. Equality is rejected, for civilised society is of its nature unequal. The gap between the pay of a general and the private and between the bench worker and the manager is proportionately larger in Russia than in England or America. Property is a different matter, but this is not the consequence of revolution. In Pharaoh's Egypt and in Shan China, all belonged to the Emperor. So it does in Russia.

Revolution or no revolution, human society seems to move along a path directed by the nature of its people and by the form of social evolution that has written its history.

14

THE RISE OF

CAPITALISM

Britain

IN 1776 Adam Smith wrote *The Wealth of Nations* in which he forecast the enormous riches that would accrue to a people who adopted the principles of laissez-faire industrialism and free trade. The Glasgow professor had found the Philosophers' Stone, but mankind had a price to pay. As Marx was later to point out, Smith's ideas would make the rich enormously richer and drive the poor down to sordid subsistence levels.

The discovery of winter fodder crops and of their rotation with cereals more than doubled the productivity of medieval village strip farming and reduced the labour requirement. Village labourers moved into the new industrial towns. James Watt developed the steam engine; Kay invented the Flying Shuttle; Hargreaves the Spinning Jenny; Brindley built the Bridgewater Canal; Arkwright founded the cotton factory system. Between 1760 and 1820 Britain's population almost doubled (6½ million to 12 million).

The Napoleonic Wars were a godsend, for they pushed up consumption until it nearly kept pace with production. With peace came deflation and misery. Statesmen had no understanding of what had happened, and no idea other than to repress the new and dangerous forces with which they were confronted. The Black Country, the Clyde, the conurbations of Lancashire and Yorkshire grew unplanned to deface our countryside. A window tax put a premium on dark rooms.

Competition in a falling market demanded cheaper and cheaper labour. Children from the age of six worked over twelve hours a day. Women, on hands and knees, hauled coal in the mines. Average life expectancy in the industrial population was twenty-six years.

And yet it was a society that worked. Man is an odd creature and sociologists can make no greater mistake than to equate comfort with happiness or indeed with contentment. I do not think any Black Country shanty town could ever have been as uncomfortable or have smelt as bad as a trawler on patrol in northern waters, but for me it was still a happy time.

These early industrial slums were savage places in which no policeman walked alone. Each street and court had its pecking order. Each man had his place. Factory workers were not meek; the employer or foreman who went too far did so at his peril. There was a powerful sense of identity, of territory and of local patriotism. The slum had dignity. Above all it was never dull. Others might be sorry for the slum dwellers but they were not sorry for themselves. Unlike the *canaille* of Paris, they were not in the least revolutionary. When eventually they got the vote most of them voted Conservative. Very gradually, as a result of reformist measures, the lot of the British working class improved.

The first Prime Minister to take a real interest in the question was Robert Peel in 1841. He ordered a number of reports which were available when Karl Marx, a Rhineland Jew then aged twenty-five, arrived in England as the guest of Frederick Engels. Marx's knowledge of the working class was based on his English experience in the main on reports ordered by Peel. Engels was a factory manager in Manchester. His joy was foxhunting. When Marx chided him for frivolity he replied that foxhunting was essential training for one who aspired to lead the cavalry of the Proletariat.

Marx claimed to be purely scientific in his approach. He evolved a theory of historical inevitability largely derived from Hegel. Put in admittedly over-simplified form, he believed that society was in constant flux by reason of the war of the classes; that every apparently stable settlement holds within it contradictions which will eventually destroy it and out of the destruction a new system will emerge that contains something of the old and something of the struggle. To me this seems a matter of political observation that is at least generally true. Then he goes on to argue that capitalism is the penultimate stage in human society, that it will be concluded by the victory of the Proletariat, at which point the class struggle will be concluded for there will be no other class to fight and the state can wither away. This I find no more convincing than any other religious dogma that asserts the ultimate victory of God and his saints. Russia does not look like a society in which the state is withering away, and I see no evidence that in the absence of firm compulsion Proletarians are more likely to live at peace than are other human groups. I believe that human society is ultimately instinctive and like all other societies, a response to emotion rather than to reason. The fact that it is faced with continually altering economic circumstances does not reduce but rather increases its tendency to disintegrate in the absence of powerful emotional and physical restraints. I believe that Marx was a generous human being who was outraged by the suffering which he saw in the British working class at its worst moment, and that he dedicated himself to the destruction of a cruel system. All pretence of objectivity was abandoned when he wrote the *Communist Manifesto* (1848), a magnificent piece of emotional writing. I find his economics, which owe much to Ricardo, far more convincing than his philosophy. He observed in his law of increasing misery the tendency of the system to reduce labour's share to bare subsistence and that of free trade to impose a similar fate on the producers of raw materials.

John Strachey has pointed out that had the free trade laissez-faire school had its way this would certainly have happened, but that the advance of the working class political power reversed the process. Redistributive taxation and welfare legislation has enabled labour to retain and marginally to increase its share of an ever-growing product.

Marx lived mainly in London, ill and poor. He saw his beloved daughter die. He was buried in Highgate Cemetery. He was a man of huge faith, but even he can hardly have realised that he was perhaps the most influential man who ever lived and that he had founded by far the most important of contemporary religions.

Marx supplied continental Socialism with its theory and in the Communist world *Das Kapital* has become Holy Writ. It is a very long and often obscure book. In a work of revelation this is an advantage, for it can be interpreted to support almost any chosen conclusion. There have been occasions when I think that Marx would have been scarcely less shocked than Jesus at the work to which his words have been put. In England Marx has had little influence. British Socialism has been Methodist rather than Marxist.

I have no liking for Christianity, but I cannot withhold my tribute to the Chapel in the English slums or even to such offbeat sects as the Salvation Army. The slums were a tribal society. The men went to work as they had once gone to hunt. The unemployed suffered the humiliation once experienced by males who could not find a place in a hunting group. The women ruled the home and coped as well as they could with their drunken husbands. The Chapel was the woman's organisation. If she could get her husband to belong he would join a society that did not centre on pub and gin palace. Dedicated men worked for salvation. Respectability acquired a status. The Chapel inspired much of the trade union movement and even today we find many unions organised into chapels. It led working men into politics and the idea of Christian Socialism emerged. British society was not rigid. There was little social division between workmen and small employers, many of whom had begun at the bench, and often attended the same Chapel. Robert Owen, factory owner, was the pioneer of English Socialism. The reformism, which Marx so despised, worked. A series of Factory Acts, Public Health Acts and Housing Acts were passed.

The slum dwellers were not revolutionary but they were highly political, far more so than their descendants today. There was less alternative entertainment. Political meetings were frequent and well attended. They were part of the life. Audience participation could be fierce. Anti-slavery fired a passion. During the American Civil War, Lancashire working men preferred to starve rather than to spin slave-grown cotton. When an Austrian general who was reputed to have played a brutal part in the suppression of Hungarian rebels, visited Whitbread's Brewery in East London, he was chased and whipped by the draymen. Vote or no vote, the working man participated.

The progress was very slow but it was sufficient to support the nineteenth century idea of the inevitability of progress. The Army, the colonies and America were safety valves for those who found conditions intolerable. Nineteenth century England was a self-confident society. What was its philosophy? It is very hard to say. The Liberals believed in free trade, the Conservatives had their doubts. Jeremy Bentham and the Utilitarians were influential. So was Darwin with his idea as to the survival of the fittest, and Herbert Spencer with his enlarged idea of an evolution working through all orders of existence. The Fabians came later with their ideas as to the inevitability of gradualness or, as some put it, creeping Socialism. There was a general feeling that the lot of the poor ought to be improved and that people who went to neither church nor chapel were not quite reliable. Conformity was enough. One must not take things too far. The nineteenth century British were a pragmatic people suspicious of all 'isms', but they were not in the least suspicious of themselves. Their self-confidence was imperial, for the sun never set upon their empire.

Nineteenth century England was still a society that fitted the instincts of its people, but not perhaps to the same extent that it had done in the eighteenth century. There was still the great feeling of English identity, the faith that united every Englishman against every foreigner, the certainty of superiority, but the rich had got rather too rich. Disraeli had seen two nations, the rich and the poor. Country and town were also becoming separate nations that no longer knew each other. The division had grown. In the eighteenth century most townsmen (Londoners possibly excepted), had rural links and were involved in rural sports. By the end of the nineteenth century much of the countryside had been absorbed by great estates that excluded the town. When vast parades celebrated the Diamond Jubilee of Victoria in 1897 many of the rural well-to-do saw the urban poor for the first time. They were a smaller people. Indeed to some they looked too small to bear their huge burden. Intellectuals were just beginning to doubt the validity of the system. The Boers were to shock our huge superiority complex.

France

France, which Napoleon had made into a nation, did not hold together. She had been humiliated in 1870. Communards of Paris had fought on and been repressed and persecuted by the Right. The Left was pagan, anti-clerical and radical, and the Right was Gallican, reactionary and militarist. There was no chapel to fill the gap. Right and left hated each other. Captain Dreyfus became the symbol. This unlucky Jewish artillery officer was charged with treason, convicted and sentenced to transportation. He was perfectly innocent. A genuine mistake had been made, but that mistake was discovered quite soon. The establishment would not confess it had been wrong. Documents were forged to support a conviction then known to be wrong. The Left made the persecution of this Jew their cause. In France one was Dreyfusard or anti-Dreyfusard. Families were divided. Dreyfus was convicted in 1894. It was not till 1903 that he was rehabilitated.

Governments were frequent and weak. Gradually the Left gained control. Briand in 1910 became the first Socialist to be a prime minister and to break a strike. Gradually France began to regain her self confidence a little, that faith in herself that alone makes a nation. Between 1914 and 1918 the Germans did much to heal her divisions, but with victory they began to reappear. By 1940 the will to defend herself had died. The war of 1939–45 did not bring Frenchmen together. It divided them.

Germany

It was in the nineteenth century that Germany became a nation. When the nationalism of Napoleon flooded over Germany, only in Prussia did it collide with national resistance. Goethe (1749–1832), who welcomed Napoleon and mourned his defeat, was by far the greatest literary figure in Europe. He despised Germany and the German writers but he venerated and, in a sense, recreated the German language. He drew on Shakespeare, on the poets of Italy and Spain, and on the Greeks. He studied Persian. He was fascinated by science and medicine. He was uninterested in nationalism and in the wars of liberation. He was neither a Christian nor a patriot. There were other great literary figures: Herder, Lessing, Schiller and Heine. Of these Schiller alone was attracted by the idea of Germanism.

While the French were looking for the laws and institutions that would make men good the Germans thought of the hero who cultivated his own soul. The great age of German literature was the age of her political impotence. German culture was Francophile and the average German preferred France to Austria and probably to Prussia. Napoleon changed all this.

He reorganised Germany to suit his convenience. He formed a Confederation of the Rhine under his Presidency, consisting of Bavaria and Würtemburg, old members of the Reich; Westphalia, a new conglomerate with Jerome Bonaparte as its king; the Grand Duchy of Baden and some lesser principalities. He encountered little opposition from the German rulers who competed for his favour. They did not mourn the demise of the Holy Roman Empire nor the expulsion of Prussia from Westphalia and Poland. It took Napoleon's continental system to turn favour into bitter hatred. Germany found herself supporting armies of occupation with a taste for pillage; her trade was cut off by the English blockade; she was denied access to French markets; she was taxed and her manpower conscripted. She learned to long for a nationhood that could expel the French. For this she had to look to Prussia. Defeat had not destroyed Prussian nationhood. In Stien Prussia had a statesman who saw that resurgent nationalism meant concessions in terms of freedom to peasant and burgher on a scale that was new in Germany.

When Napoleon was defeated, the Congress of Vienna rejected any liberal nonsense about self-determination and plumped for legitimacy. Germany was to be treated as a group of royal estates to be returned to their legitimate owners; but the idea of nationalism survived. Prussia, not Austria, was the magnet.

The liberals had a try in 1848. They felt that German unity must come from a German parliament so they summoned one to meet at Frankfurt. It was full of fine minds. Its debates were on a high level. Its trouble was that it represented nobody. There were plenty of professors but the princes, the nobles, the wage earners, big business and the bankers were not there. A rising young politician from Prussia, Otto von Bismarck, watched the proceedings with a contempt which he made no effort to conceal. This was not the way to make a nation.

Bismarck got his chance in 1862. Prussia had dallied with democracy and got herself a parliament that claimed to control supplies. William I was an old soldier and his interests were military. He and his War Minister, von Roon, worked out a plan that called for a larger army. Parliament refused supplies. There was an election and an even more radical majority was elected. William I prepared his abdication. Roon advised 'send for Bismarck'. Bismarck spent the money. Armies, he told parliament, were too important for them to interfere with. They could grant taxes and discuss laws, but they must not touch on policy or the army. Least of all was it their business to make or unmake governments. When he had beaten the Austrians and made Prussia supreme in Germany he asked for and received from the Diet an indemnity for the costs of a war that he had paid for without their vote or consent.

Bismarck had seen that German unity involved a war with Austria. It was a price he was prepared to pay. The fact that nobody else wanted this war worried him not at all. Over years he plotted. He isolated Austria. He bribed Italy. Then suddenly he offered to Germany a parliament elected by universal suffrage. Like Disraeli, he had perceived that universal suffrage was the way to dish the Liberals. Faced with the choice, the working man prefers Conservatives. The Austrians, still ox-drawn, were attacked and destroyed by Prussians who arrived by train with unexpected speed. Having won Bismarck made peace without indemnity or annexation. He would need Austrian co-operation in the war he now proposed to have with France. The German states could be left to join his North German Confederation in their own good time. Bismarck designed its constitution. The Reichstag could not make or unmake governments or interfere in military or foreign affairs. The majority was conservative, as he had foreseen. The Federal Council was the real governing body. It deliberated in secret under Bismarck's presidency and there was a built-in Prussian majority.

According to plan France was tricked into war and defeated by rail-assembled concentrations. In the Hall of Mirrors at Versailles the new German Empire was proclaimed. It was a very formidable nation indeed. For the first time all Germany north of the Austrian frontier had a common will. Frederick had made Prussia, but it was Bismarck who made Germany.

Prussia, and indeed Germany had been largely agrarian. They gained the advantage of a slow start. This Germany was to repeat in 1922 and 1947. Her working class was the best educated in Europe. She equipped and re-equipped herself on the research of her competitors and she made them obsolete. In ten years from 1880 she doubled her coal and steel output. She took the lead in the new industries of chemicals and electrics. German shipbuilding revived the tradition of the Hanseatic ports. Bismarck saw both the advantages and disadvantages of free trade. He opened markets but protected his developing industries. He saw too the dangers of laissez-faire. He pioneered sickness, accident and old age insurance. He was too cynical to accept the idea that private appetite would bring about the greatest happiness for the greatest number. He believed in Prussian paternalism. Expansion was planned. The family was protected. German education and public service kept pace with industrialism. By the turn of the century Germany had caught up with British industrial power.

What made this successful state?

We start with Napoleon. He gave to the Germans a necessary injection of xenophobia. Napoleonic arrogance implanted the will to be a nation. Germany fought for her nationhood. The Liberal attempts of the parliament of Frankfurt were treated by Bismarck with the contempt they deserved. Nationhood is not something that can be given or received. It has to be taken. German nationhood had to grow out of war and glory. Without it the German national spirit would never have gained the power to bind the German tribes. I am merely observing that a national faith or spirit, call it what you will, is necessary to nation building. It may be the world would have been better without a German nation, but that is another question.

The energy that was made available by German nationalism was constructively directed.

A human state is a combination of families rather than individuals. Bismarck protected the family. Female emancipation was discouraged. Industry from an early date was prevented from taking women away from their children. The home was the woman's sphere.

In the process of industrial development government sought to protect the countryside and the labour force from the appetite of the entrepreneurs. It was not wholly successful. Germany did not escape the wounds of industrialisation but they were better controlled than elsewhere.

Through the process of universal suffrage the German male was involved in his nation, but he was all the time made to feel the nation was something greater than its parts and that there were questions of national interest that belonged to the mystique of his state. When there was no longer a Bismarck in charge this became very dangerous. A national will of this potency needed to be entrusted to someone less vain and flighty than the Emperor William II.

The question as to whether philosophy forms or conforms to the spirit of the age must remain open, but the philosophies of the Bismarckian age, of which Hegel's was the most influential, certainly contributed to the idea of state divinity. Whether any idea less heady would have been potent enough to make a Germany must also remain open.

Italy

The Italian Risorgimento was not really Italian and did not create a real nation. It was rather an exercise in dynastic statecraft. It arose from Austrian weakness. Italians have always hated Germans and whenever the Germans have weakened, Italians have turned on them.

In 1848 revolution was in the air. In Vienna, Metternich had fallen and the Liberals were for the moment in control. Austrian garrisons were expelled from Lombard cities by popular risings. Charles Albert of Piedmont and Sardinia intervened with a real army. Austria recovered her balance and Charles Albert was defeated at Costazza, and the rebellions were suppressed. The King abdicated but he had done enough to make of his dynasty a credible nucleus for a united Italy. This was exploited by his son Victor Emmanuel and by his most able minister, Cavour.

A Venetian republic had been set up under Manin, a Jewish Liberal. This too fell before Austrian bayonets. In Rome the mob had chased the Pope out of the city and established a republic under Mazzini, a Liberal demagogue. Louis Napoleon, the Prince President, wanted Catholic votes and sent a French army. Rome was defended by Garibaldi, a great blond-bearded guerrilla leader who had learned much in South American revolutions, but had no chance against French regulars. For a time he came to England as a refugee where he visited my great-grandfather at the Boltons in London. My aunts used to tell me stories of this marvellously romantic figure.

Republicanism was discredited and Cavour took the opportunity to persuade Mazzini, Manin and Garibaldi to accept the leadership of Piedmont and of Victor Emmanuel. It was not an easy task.

Cavour then turned to Napoleon. At Plombières he made a secret deal. A North Italian kingdom was to be made out of Piedmont, Austrian Lombardy and Venetia, another monarchy of sorts under a Bonaparte prince was to be set up in Central Italy, and a Murat was to have Naples. Nice and Savoy were to be France's honorarium. Cavour then provoked a war with Austria and France marched to his assistance. Napoleon III was no general, but the Austrians were even worse. At Solferino he won a bloody victory and was so horrified that he made peace behind his allies' back. Lombardy went to Piedmont but Venetia was left to Austria. In the circumstances he did not ask for Nice and Savoy. Cavour was furious, and

throughout Italy Napoleon was the traitor. The rulers of central Italy who had been supported by France, were expelled
and the rebels chose Piedmont. Cavour now used Savoy,
which was French in language and clerical in sentiment, to
compensate France and obtain Napoleon's consent.

In the south King Bomba's rule, which was of the Dark
rather than of the Middle Ages, was already collapsing when
Garibaldi landed in Sicily, accompanied by a few hundred
red-shirted volunteers, and what was perhaps more important,
the uniform of a Piedmontese general. At the sound of his
bugles royal resistance collapsed. Under the benevolent eye
of the British Navy he crossed the straits and marched on
Naples. Bomba fled. From Cavour's point of view Garibaldi
had been almost too successful. The toppling of government
in the south might involve Austrian intervention. A Gari-
baldian advance on Rome might come into conflict with
French troops defending the Pope. Cavour decided that the
time had come for Victor Emmanuel to appear in Central
Italy. At Castelfidardo on 18 September, 1860, the Papal forces
surrendered. The Pope remained in Rome with his French
protectors. All this Cavour had arranged with Napoleon. In
1866 the new Italy received Venetia as a *pour-boire* for her
services to Bismarck in his Austrian war, and in 1870 Victor
Emmanuel moved into Rome when the French garrison was
withdrawn to fight the Prussians. The temporal powers of the
Papacy had ended and Italy was united.

It was then that Cavour said 'We have made Italy, now we
must make Italians.' In this he was not successful. The Italians
have never identified themselves with Italy or felt themselves
involved on the same side as government. Any fugitive, political or criminal, can rely on the protection, often the very
gallant protection, of the ordinary Italian. Why is this? Why
are the national feelings of Italy so different to those of
Germany?

One must remember that the emotion that outweighs man's
natural inclination to disunity must be a very powerful one.
The struggle that made Italy was inadequately Italian. Lombardy was won by France, Venetia by Prussia, the Romagna
by intrigue. The House of Savoy won no victories. Glory was
confined to Naples and this was the republican glory of Gari-

baldi. To Naples Savoy was just another dynasty, a frustration rather than a fulfilment of their moment of freedom.

Victor Emmanuel incarnated no myths of ancient renown, no victories, no glory; he was supported by no deep-rooted aristocracy; he was hedged by no divinity; the prisoner in the Vatican was his enemy. He won no loyalty from his new subjects, who had nothing else to be loyal to. Italy lacked an Italian ideal.

She participated in two European wars. She joined both dishonourably for booty. In 1915 the Northern Italians were lifted a little by their deep-rooted hatred of Germans and fought reasonably well in spite of the lamentable quality of their officer class. In 1940 the Italian soldier was not on his government's side and there was still no officer class with a tradition of service to lead him. The Italian state had failed to provide its citizens with that sense of identity that is the foundation of a sucessful nation. Today one Italian in three votes Communist.

The Balkans

By the nineteenth century Turkey was moribund and freedom the fashion. The Christians of the Balkans ardently awaited a new nation conceived in freedom and dedicated to the brotherhood of man. It was not to be. They had had the wrong sort of history, the wrong sort of geography and they were the wrong sort of people.

The Balkan peninsula has an open coastline, long accessible river valleys and inaccessible mountain ranges. Invaders travel the valleys and natives climb the mountains where they live hard lives till the people in the valleys weaken. There are few areas in which man has indulged more sparingly in peace.

We hear first of the Pelasgians and Thracians who may have been the fathers of the Aryan language group. Herodotus says of them:

> The Thracians are, after the Indians, the most numerous of all peoples. And if they had a leader, or were truly united, they could be unconquerable and by far the most powerful of all peoples. That is my opinion, but since it is by no means possible that this could ever be, they are correspondingly weak.

The Thracians were beaten by the Macedonians in the fifth
century BC. The Romans beat the Macedonians in the second
century BC, but it was not till the reign of Augustus that
Rome decided to intervene on a permanent scale.

For nearly 500 years the Balkans were a Roman province.
Then the frontier weakened and Slavs started to infiltrate.
They occupied the valleys of the interior. The natives, now
Latin speaking, were pushed up the mountains and into the
enclaves of the coastal towns. By AD 600 the Byzantine Empire had lost its grip on the Balkans. The nomadic horsemen
of the steppes were moving in. The Bulgars, a Hunnish tribe,
may have come by Byzantine invitation. They inter-married
with the Slavs. Behind them came Avars, Pecheneks and
Magyars. In the tenth century Byzantium returned and Venice
appeared on the Adriatic coast. The Slavs were harried and
the Romans came down from the hils. They were now known
as the Wallachian shepherds and eventually established themselves in Rumania. In the twelfth century Bulgarian and Serbian states appeared as did Frankish crusaders who set up
various principalities. Then, in the fifteenth century, the
whole peninsula once again had a master but it did not have
a ruler, for the Turks were not interested in government.
They required very moderate taxes, some male children for
training as janissaries, and obedience. They cut the heads off
the tallest poppies. No aristocracy survived Turkish conquest.
The Church was their chosen instrument of indirect rule. The
priests collected the taxes and the bishops administered. If
they got seriously out of line they were flayed alive and their
skins nailed to their church doors. Religious, cultural and
economic life was left alone. It was not a progressive form
of rule but it was very economical. Before the 1914 war the
Turks ran Palestine with fourteen policemen, but it was well
known that when the policemen turned up someone would be
hanged.

In the late eighteenth and early nineteenth century the
Turk's grip weakened. In Hungary and Croatia they were
pushed back and Slav communities came under Austrian rule
and joined the Roman Church. Bulgarian, Serbian, Rumanian
and Greek principalities each under the patronage of one or
other of the Great Powers, won autonomy which the Turks

feared to repress by their traditional methods. A new nation was generally expected but local hatreds were older than the Turks. There was a great moment. In 1912 the principalities formed a league and defeated the Turks. Bulgaria, who had won the principal glory and had in consequence become too cocky for the taste of her allies, was then set upon by Serbia, Greece and Rumania. Macedonia, whose population was an inextricable mix, was shared by Greece and Serbia. Not unnaturally Bulgaria sought revenge in 1915 by joining Austria against Serbia and for a second time she was a loser. Hungary too had been on the wrong side and found herself deprived of Slovenia, Transylvania and part of Croatia. In 1941 Hungary and Bulgaria again not unnaturally picked the wrong side. In 1945 they were absorbed by another Empire, the Russian, within which, again with Great Power patronage, Tito formed an autonomous principality. Greece with Anglo-American support remained independent.

What are the Balkan lessons? The first is that areas of traditional antagonism can only be held together by an Imperial power strong enough to enforce unity, and the second is that states who have not achieved the differentiation that is expressed by the presence of a substantial middle class will not work as democracies. Greece is possibly an exception. She has a tremendous feeling of Greekness and of the glories of an antiquity to which she feels the immediate heir. She has developed mostly abroad, a substantial middle class much of which has returned to Greece. She lacks an officer class and a class of administrators dedicated to public service. Under the Turks cheating the government was a patriotic duty. This is a difficult habit to drop, but there has, since the collapse of the Colonels, been an element of restraint and, dare one say it, maturity in the Greek behaviour that is very encouraging.

Austria

The Hapsburg Empire was the land of the Counter-Reformation, the Jesuits and the Church Triumphant. Slavs, Poles, Magyars, Croats were autocratically ruled by Germans in

Vienna. The Liberal moves of 1848 were successfully and brutally repressed. Change was successfully resisted. Italy apart, the frontiers settled by the Great Congress of 1815 were substantially maintained. Central Europe enjoyed its most peaceful century disturbed, only by Bismarck's one-battle war. Progress was not at the English or German rate but advance, both in population and in standards of living within the Austrian provinces was nonetheless considerable.

The crack came in 1867 with the formation of the dual monarchy, whereby the Empire was divided into two halves, one ruled by Germans and the other by Magyars. Now the dislike felt by Poles and Slavs for Germans was pale compared to the loathing felt by Croats, Slavs and Transylvanians for the Magyar aristocracy. Pan-Slavism made its bow and was backed by Russia. Poles were outraged. They had defended Christian Europe from the ravages of Magyar savages from Asia. By 1914 the strains had become intolerable and the Chief of Staff advised his Emperor:

'If we go to war I cannot tell you what will happen, but if you do not go to war Your Empire will dissolve.' So started the First World War.

America

The age of capitalism was also the age of liberalism. America was the land of liberalism. She had been born to assert the rights of the subject against the power of the king. Her Declaration of Independence had been an act of treason and a justification of treason; it had exalted private freedom and denied public authority; it had proclaimed the right to pursue private happiness and to rebel against any state that frustrates this quest. It had been no mere oratorical flourish. On occasions her Supreme Court was to come near to upholding the proposition that the individual is free to pursue his private interest without regard to the public interest and that the State has no right to interfere with his business. A charter of human rights attached to her constitution enshrines in its first clause the right to bear arms. This is and was intended to be a revolutionary right. The Founding Fathers feared that a president who had a monopoly of arms might play the tyrant, and they preserved in private hands the means to resist him.

The cult of the individual was conventional wisdom. It had found expression in Adam Smith's theory that society was but a conglomeration of individuals and was best served by each serving himself. It was an idea that was influential in Europe, particularly during the Industrial Revolution, but it never won the whole-hearted acceptance that it received in America, for it conflicted with European ideas as to the need for government. Medieval ideas on a fair price and a just reward lingered on. Goods were not generally held for highest price nor sold at the lowest, for custom played a part. Wages were not settled exclusively by the laws of supply and demand. Entrepreneurs were often reluctant to use their competitive power to destroy rivals and preferred to come to arrangements with their colleagues in the trade. Big Charter companies acquired a mystical entity more important than the particular interests of shareholders and sometimes rated profits relatively low amongst their priorities. Capitalists pursued their personal gain with less than theoretical ruthlessness, and Bismarck accepted social responsibility for industrial welfare. Europe still recognised that if governments are to hold states together they must have great powers; that the chief executive, whether he be emperor, king, president or prime minister, must rule; that he must be able to legislate and that if the consent of parliament is required he must in a general way control parliament; that he must make civic force his own, for it is only in primitive societies that enforcement can be left to clans or barons; that he must establish his authority over church and noble, city boss and corporation presidents for he cannot tolerate fiefs that lie beyond his control, and over judges who may interpret but must not deny his laws.

America took her liberalism far more literally and her citizens pursued their happiness with much less restraint. She denied to her President the powers that older states deemed necessary. He cannot legislate without the consent of Congress and Congress can impose laws over his veto; he must share force with any citizen who chooses to pack a gun; he can only intervene in the big cities when requested to do so by the state governor; his laws can be declared unconstitutional by the Supreme Court that does not happen to agree with them; and his foreign policy can be reversed by the Senate.

Jefferson (1800), who had defeated Hamilton and the old Federalists, believed that the role of the executive was to carry out the will of the legislature. This theory worked after a fashion so long as Jefferson's fame and magic guided the legislature. His successors, Monroe, Madison and John Quincey Adams were not Jeffersons. Congress ruled and Congress was incompetent to rule; its members were concerned primarily with their local interests and legislation was forwarded by a system of log rolling. The congressman bought support for bills in which he had an interest by promising support for bills in which he had no interest. Bills of national importance rarely passed at all, for procedural obstruction was all too easy. The states were moving apart; the South with its staple exports favoured low tariffs and low taxes; the North-East wanted high tariffs to protect growing industries and high prices for new lands to check the westward migration of cheap labour; the West called for cheap land and high taxes to support new Federal communications. It was lucky for the Americans that Europe was engaged in the Revolutionary and Napoleonic Wars while (apart from a little trouble in 1812) America enjoyed the prosperity of neutrality.

Andrew Jackson (1828), a rough, direct-minded Indian fighter from the frontier, re-asserted the authority of the Presidency. He had created a party, the New Democrats, as his base and he linked the office of President directly with the people through the primaries system, whereby the rank and file chose the candidate. Once elected the President spoke with the authority of a majority of the people and with a national organisation pledged to his support. He introduced the spoils system too, whereby a new government appointed its own civil servants. For the period of his term a Jacksonian president was a very strong king indeed. The ordinary American felt that Jackson was his President and America his country.

A new and strident American patriotism was shouted in the songs of the day. But the division of interest remained. The South felt itself left behind; the industrial North and food-raising West were expanding so much faster. The Southern economy was believed to depend on slave labour and the morality of slave-owning was challenged. This was bitterly resented. Civilised man had always used slaves. Revered generations had built a refined and beautiful civilisation. The common upstart Yankees not only threatened their interests but insulted their dead. The slaves were far safer and better off than their fellows in Africa (true), they were well treated and fond of their masters (sometimes true), they liked being slaves (very seldom true). Strongest of all was a fear. There were 3½ million slaves. What would they do if they were free? There were 22 million Northerners and 5½ million Southern whites. The Southern States felt they could no longer live their chosen life within the Union.

In the North the idea of Unity had achieved sanctity. There were not many Yankees who fought to free slaves; there were even fewer who fought because they felt that the retention of reluctant Southerners was to their advantage; the many defended unity because it formed part of their national faith. Largely as a result of Jacksonian Democracy this national faith had become strong enough to withstand disruption.

Civil War (1861 - 1865)

After the Civil War (1861–1865) the problem of the freed slave had to be faced. No Northern state gave black men the vote. Almost nobody in those days regarded the black man as equal to the white. Slavery was wrong but equality was quite another matter.

President Lincoln favoured apartheid or separate development. He was murdered. His successor was weak and ineffective. Power passed to an evil little demagogue in the Congress who was bent on revenge. This man was Stevens and his policy was integration. The black must be treated as an equal and since the rebels were disfranchised must enjoy the power due to a majority. White Northern 'carpet-baggers' moved

South to exploit negro power. Reconstruction was bitter and it failed. The Southern whites reasserted themselves. Their secret army, the Ku Klux Klan was born. The carpet-baggers were chased **away.**

The negro was disfranchised by a poll tax he could not pay and an education test he could not pass. Jim Crow ruled. The negro was segregated. It was a form of apartheid which laid more emphasis on the separation than on the development.

Gradually the South resumed its place in the Union. War is a great domestic healer. It was the patriotic fervour resulting from America's aggression against Spain that made the Confederates feel American once more.

America is now having its second dose of integration. In a later chapter we will consider how it is working out.

In North and West a different form of integration was taking place. In the Hudson River as one approaches the great battery of New York there stands a singularly hideous statue with a wonderful inscription:

> Give me your tired, your poor
> Your huddled masses yearning to breathe free,
> The wretched refuse of your teeming shore
> Send these homeless, tempest tossed, to me
> I lift my lamp beside the golden door.

The oppressed people of Europe were moving in. Between 1850 and 1914 nearly 30 million new Americans arrived.

During the middle years of the century potato famine drove not far off half the population of Ireland across the Atlantic. They spoke the language. They were tired of agriculture. Most were urbanised in the Eastern cities. They were on the whole welcome for they did the jobs nobody else wanted to do. They manned the municipal services. They laboured in expanding industry as more skilled Americans moved up the scale. They joined the police. They also joined the Democratic party. It was the day of the political machines and of professional politicians who lived by, and had their being in, politics. In the Eastern cities the Irish took over. The new immigrant was met at the docks, found lodging, helped with furniture, introduced to a job and to the Democratic party.

256

From the start he felt wanted. Early loyalties often lasted a lifetime.

Machine politics may have been corrupt but they were friendly and they did much to make the newcomers feel American. Later came Poles, Balts, Swedes and Germans who tended to move on to the Middle West. Some took farm work but it was industry that was really expanding. Chicago grew from nothing to 1,700,000 in little more than a generation. The local ward leader helped the immigrant to language classes so that he could qualify as a citizen and vote for the party. The Southern Europeans and the Jews came a little later. New York became the world's greatest Jewish city. No country catered for more or odder religions but the real religion was Americanism and it was acquired with astonishing speed and fervour. When war came trouble with the German population was negligible and German Americans were amongst the best soldiers in the US Army. It was a two-way traffic. The supply of immigrant labour made the growth and the growth absorbed the immigrants. Space and resources were virtually unlimited.

Locke's ideas on property and Adam Smith's ideas on laissez-faire were accepted with little modification. Herbert Spencer's version of Social Darwinianism proclaimed the survival of the fittest in society as well as in nature. Chief Justice Field construed the Fourteenth Amendment of the Constitution—'nor shall any State deprive any person of life, liberty or property without due process of law,' as precluding the intervention of government in economic affairs. Labour accepted the theory and joined the fight. In 1892 the steel workers fought a pitched battle with a force of strike breakers sent in by the Pinkerton Detective Agency. Strikes were frequent, violent and unpolitical. Marx had little influence on the American labour movement. Unions were strictly industrial. There were slumps but the booms galloped past the slumps. Standards of living advanced. Labour was never against the system. Employers were fought as buyers were fought. It was part of a hard played game. As the nation rolled West there was a sense of conquest, of glory, of victory over the forces of nature.

The problems of government were unsolved. Lincoln posed

the question, 'Is there in all republics this inherent and fatal weakness? Must a government of necessity be too strong for the liberties of its own people or too weak to maintain its own existence?'

In practice strong presidents have made the presidency far more powerful than the founders intended. Jackson's party system has meant that the President has usually, but not always, a majority in Congress and the Senate and the spoils system has given him a mighty patronage. Party discipline is not strong for the President lacks the threat of dissolution; but in general presidents have got most of their way although on occasion they have been defied. For all its liberalism there is something medieval about the American Constitution, for just as the order of feudal society depended on the strength and cunning of the king, so America depends on the will and wiliness of her President.

By our standards the USA has always been a violent society with a murder rate at least ten times as great as our own, but the main force of her aggression went to her expanding frontier, to her Indian and Mexican wars, to the gun law which for a few decades dominated the cattle country of the Middle West, to her exploding industrial cities and to the wars of capital and labour fought by the great corporations. It was a rough process. Everything had been expendable as the USA swept across her continent. The erosion and the dust bowls could wait. 'Conservation' had not been invented. The immigrants had moved in behind. The great cities had formed. A rural population had become overwhelmingly urban. The cities became baronies run by local bosses with political machines, corrupt, violent and popular. The federal writ rarely ran in the cities, but they, like the country were expanding and their growth absorbed their violence. Great interstate corporations controlling railways, steel, oil and banking grew up and became baronies of another sort against which Federal government fought with little success. By the turn of the century the tensions in American society had become critical. They were released by war. The Cubans were rebelling against Spain. A mysterious explosion on the battleship *Maine* provided an excuse. The Spanish war was short, easy and very, very popular. War is a great unifier. It brought the American people, including the South, together as Americans. The USA acquired Puerto Rico, Guam and the Philippines. She accepted her 'manifest destiny' as an imperial power. By good fortune rather than design, she found a great President.

Theodore Roosevelt, Teddy as he was universally called, had raised and commanded volunteer cavalry in the Cuban revolution and was adopted as Vice-Presidential candidate to cheer up the Republican ticket. Then in 1901 dull, rich, respectable President McKinley was shot and Teddy the rumbustious buccaneer was president. He believed in force and in 'manifest destiny'. He determined to dig the Panama Canal. When Columbia proved awkward he arranged a revolution and got his new terms from the new republic of Panama. He added a corollary to the Monroe doctrine 'Chronic wrongdoing may in America as elsewhere, ultimately require intervention by some civilised nation and in the Western hemisphere the Monroe doctrine may force the United States however reluctantly in flagrant cases of such wrongdoing or impotence, to the exercise of an international Police Power'. He described his methods. 'I never take a step in foreign policy unless I am assured that I will eventually be able to carry out my will by force.' At home he made war on the barons. In 1902 he intervened in the great anthracite strike and backed the workers. He denounced 'the malefactors of great wealth'. He launched a number of trust busting suits. He was not all that successful, but he inspired. There was a wave of American patriotism and of American self-confidence.

The past century had been a period of astonishing growth and of much peril. In 1800 her population had been about 5 million, in 1850 it was 23 million, in 1914 nearly 100 million. Wealth had grown faster still; national income had risen from 4 billion dollars in 1860 to over 60 billion in 1910. When 1914 came the USA was very much a nation. State and city governments were important but local. The Federal Government was the Government of America and the focus of American loyalty. The American idea was a national faith. Americans from the old colonials to the latest immigrants had a place and were a part of this most stimulating society. The negroes and the Indians were odd men out, but their problems had been put away for another day.

By 1914 Britain, America and Germany had become highly successful nation states. They had followed different philosophies; the British Utilitarian and Benthamite; the American Individualistic and Lockeian; the German Romantic and Hegelian. Their forms of government differed. The British were a constitutional monarchy, their society was highly class-conscious, power was divided but was moving leftwards. America was a republican democracy, within which giant corporations operating across state boundaries were beginning to acquire baronial status and to control political machines. Germany was an autocracy. The Emperor and his Chancellor exercised effective power. All three were the objects of their people's faith and within all three people of all classes identified with their nations and were stimulated by the forward and hopeful movement of their society. They were shaped by the circumstances of their age and the needs of an Industrial Society. France was falling back weakened by her internal divisions, Italy had not acquired a unity of faith, Austria was dying and Spain had never lived.

15

THE AGE OF

OCEANIC EMPIRE

In ancient and classical times, empires were political masses that grew by accretion. The emperor was the link, the more he conquered the larger his empire. Victors and vanquished were alike his subjects. At a certain point growth became defensive. Frontiers were protected by pushing enemies further back. Xerxes attacked Greece primarily to defend Anatolia. Marcus Aurelius pushed towards the Sudeten and Dolomite Mountains to protect his Dacian provinces. Rome invaded Britain because British druids were causing trouble in Gaul. Each move forward meant a new province and a new frontier.

At some point the imperial mass became too big to govern and started to crack. Civil war replaced foreign war. When empire finally collapsed the fragments did not become new states; they either acquired a new imperial master or they dissolved into the anarchy of a dark age. The process of evolving new states out of the rubble of empire has always been a slow one.

For the purpose of this book I am concerned with imperialism as the creator of new societies. This happens when vacant or near vacant territories are settled with the intention that they will be ruled by the mother country, or when a conqueror imposes his rule on a conquered people. The Greek city states formed colonies of the first sort but the link with the founding city never lasted long. Greeks were involved in their cities and they knew no wider patriotism. Once a new city lived, loyalty to the old one died. The founding city was remembered in religious festivals but the political link was completely broken.

England's American colonists knew a loyalty to England even though many of them had dissented. It was a loyalty that in many cases survived even the follies of George III's government. We have discussed the stresses and struggles of America's birth pangs. The Dutch settlers in Cape Colony were dissenters only more so. They went to Africa to be a separate people and to commune with their very peculiar God. When the British came their links with Holland were already broken and they trekked grimly north across the desert. These were the birth pangs of their nation. After the South African war their puissance absorbed their conquerors and the Republic of South Africa for all its colour problem, is a very real nation.

Brazil is another settler state. Her indigenous population was too backward to be of use as slaves and was treated as fauna to be cleared as space was required. Negro slaves were imported on a large scale. Brazil is huge. She includes all climates. The Matto Grosso is rain forest, Bahia plantation country, Grund di Sol ranching savanna. Spanish America disintegrated but Portuguese Brazil held together. The primary reason was a decision by the King of Portugal to go to Rio when Napoleon invaded. The court in Rio became a focus for the local magnates. It was their Paris. When Napoleon fell the Regent decided to stay and Brazil declared her independence. She was under pressure from the Portuguese, the Dutch and the Spaniards. She made common cause against her invaders. Portuguese, negroes and even Germans inter-married and bred a Brazilian people. A Brazilian culture developed and was much encouraged by King Pedro II. There was a common church administered from the centre. There was a common language. Brazil became a nation with a common sense of nationality. It may be a long time before she becomes a democratic nation but to become a nation at all is, as we have seen, no slight achievement.

Canada, Australia and New Zealand have a different story, for they did not take their statehood. Canada was the refuge and lodgement of the loyalists from the American colonies and the English speaking Canadians considered themselves English. So did the Australians and New Zealanders. Until very recently all spoke of England as home. They were autonomous but the Queen's government was their government and when the Queen went to war so did they, even though it meant crossing the globe to a quarrel that was not theirs. These old dominions have only very recently ceased to be English and it has not been by their choice. They have becomes states without a struggle for freedom and with no obvious foreign threat to hold them together. There is no precedent. No successful state has had so easy a birth. It is early yet to say whether they will hold together, when they meet the stress they have yet to experience. The increasing bitterness of Australian politics is ominous. So is the separatist movement in Canada.

The empires of the west have not covered contiguous land masses. They have consisted of overseas colonies. With the passing exception of Algiers, they have been too far off to become provinces for they have been oceans away from their conquerors. The 'natives' have not merely been the subjects of an alien emperor, but of an alien people.

How did this state of affairs come about? How is one people subjected by another? It begins with a contest of wills.

Mexico was the first trans-oceanic empire. Cortes (1518–1522) invaded an old style military empire of some 11 million inhabitants with a force of 450 men. It is true that he was helped initially by Aztec superstitions. There was a prophecy that their founder god Quetzalcoatl would return from the East and usher in a golden age. The Spaniards with their horses and guns and 'floating mountains' looked like supernatural visitors to a people whose technology was still of the stone age. The common people called them *Teotls*, which in their language meant 'gods'. The Emperor Montezuma was superstitious and irresolute.

The more sophisticated quickly concluded that Cortes was not Quetzalcoatl, but Montezuma dithered between a longing to rid himself of his terrifying visitors and a dread that even if they were not gods, they had been sent by the gods and must be obeyed. First he tried to keep them away from his capital.

Then he arranged to have them murdered on their march. Cortes outwitted and destroyed the imperial assassins. The Spaniards were then invited to visit Tenoctitlan, a city with perhaps a million inhabitants, double the size of contemporary London. Montezuma received them first as guests and then changed his mind and decided on massacre. Cortes struck first and made the emperor his prisoner. Then followed a phase during which Montezuma continued to govern his empire but did so as Cortes' obedient prisoner. A provincial governor who had, on the emperor's order, killed some Spaniards was summoned to Tenoctitlan and handed over to the Spaniards, who tried him for a war crime and burned him in public over a slow fire. It is a story that illuminates not only the sacred authority and the abjectness of the emperor but the will of the conqueror rooted in a self-righteousness as certain as it was crazy; a self-righteousness that was untinged by humour, that identified self-will with God's will and found expression in a 'war crimes' trial. It is the faith that founds empires. In the days before history it was probably this kind of faith that made gods of wandering marauders and civilisation possible.

The conquistadors certainly had need of faith. A rash band, genuinely shocked by the continuity and extent of human sacrifice, decided to cleanse the great pyramid in the central square of Tenoctitlan that carried the temple of the gods and the altar of sacrifice. The idols were hurled down the steps, the stinking coat of congealed human blood was chiselled off and the images of St Christopher and of the Virgin were raised.

The Aztecs, who had feared that to offend the Spaniards might offend the gods, were undeceived. From then on the Spaniards were men and enemies.

Cortes was in much the same position as Clive was to be in two centuries later when Fort William fell to the forces of Siraj-ad-Daula. Both were commanders of tiny forces of resolute men matching their wits, which were untrammelled by doubt or scruple, and their wills, which were certain, against empires that were vast, divided, irresolute and uncertain. In under two years Cortes extracted his forces from Tenoctitlan, survived a fighting retreat, roused all the subjects of the empire that were hostile to the Aztecs, formed and led an anti-Aztec alliance, beseiged and sacked Tenoctitlan and emerged as the undisputed ruler of the empire, his authority accepted as completely by his allies as by his defeated enemies. His only trouble came from the Spaniards.

The conquerors will is ill adapted to state building. It is a kind of anarchic will that can only be governed by extreme peril and impossible odds. Victory did not satiate the taste for violence. Discipline broke as the soldiers sought loot and the captains duchies. In one generation the population fell from about 11 million to less than 2 million. There were many causes. New diseases against which the natives lacked resistance; the paying off of old scores by subject tribes of the Aztec empire; the sadistic savagery of the Spaniards on the trail of gold, but to all these causes must be added another factor, despair, for a religious people had watched the fall of their gods. The idea, strange and terrible, that had made them into a nation was dead, and they lost the will to live.

Pizarro's conquest of Peru was even more astonishing and even more shocking, for the odds were even greater, the marches and the victories were even more prodigious, and the destruction even more complete. Cortes was in his way a gentleman. He respected himself and was capable of respecting others. He was not brutal without a purpose. Pizarro had no redeeming quality save courage. He was an illiterate, greedy, ruthless savage, a veritable scourge of God. The Aztecs deserved their fate. They were the Assyrians of central America and Tenoctitlan suffered the fate of Nineveh, for every hand was turned against it. The Incas had not incurred the hatred of their subjects and had not earned their disaster. After victory Cortes did his best to preserve what was left of Mexican society. No such idea occurred to Pizarro.

New Spain eventually broke up into settler republics. None have had a very happy or successful history. The process of integrating the Indian has been slow. The broadly speaking Marxist republic of Mexico may have been the most successful.

Britain has had three empires. All three were accidental, for no British government ever set out to win an empire.

Britain's American colonies were either dissenter settlements or grants to courtiers by kings who found land across the

Atlantic a cheap currency with which to reward service. This was Britain's first empire and she learned much in the losing of it.

India

India, the second, was won by the East India Company, a private trading association interested in profit. That it would rule India was an idea that one can safely say never occurred to its board of directors.

The critical moment came when the Company's trading post at Calcutta was taken by Siraj-ad-Daula, a young man who had recently become the virtually independent Satrap of Bengal. The British prisoners were crowded into their own guard room. Ventilation was inadequate and by morning 123 were dead. 'The Black Hole of Calcutta', a genuine if unintentional atrocity, was brilliantly exploited by the Company. The British government gave its assent to a forward policy in Bengal.

The 'Gentlemen at Madras' in Southern India had the will. They had at their disposal five warships which had been sent to defend them from the French at Pondicherry, and one regular battalion of infantry, together with some scratch units, mostly Indian, in all under 1,000 men commanded by Robert Clive, a clerk in their employ who had taken to soldiering, and they did not hesitate. They went to war with Bengal, a state with an army of 50,000 men in the field, backed by financial and military resources equal to those of a major European power.

It was a decision that could only have been taken by men infected by that high insanity which I have called conqueror's will. Fort William was recaptured. This was fairly easy for its guns did not match those of the fleet. Siraj-ad-Daula returned with his army. Clive with a few hundred men attacked at night. The Bengal army retired. Clive turned on the French at Chandernagore and destroyed them. His force was now about 3,000, for he had recruited some 2,000 Indians. He advanced on Daula's 50,000 entrenched at Plassey. When he attacked Daula bolted and his troops fled with him. Both armies were European trained. The Indians had the better artillery and the British the better musket. It was will and daring that overturned the odds.

Bengal was robbed as Mexico had been robbed. Clive ruled through a puppet Nabob, Mir Jaffier. When he left Mir Jaffier was got rid of and replaced by Mir Quasim whom, the Company believed, would prove even meeker. They were wrong. Mir Quasim rebelled and made his peace with the Mogul Emperor. Together they put some 60,000 men into the field. Both the Bengal and the Mogul armies were European trained and armed. Against them were sent nine battalions of sepoys commanded by a Major Monro.

A serious situation developed. First sepoys began deserting individually and then a battalion with its arms and accoutrements marched off to join the enemy. Monro's reaction was certain. He pursued them with another sepoy battalion that had not yet rebelled. Extraordinary things began to happen. Monro caught the rebel battalion. It surrendered, handed over the ring-leaders, and marched back to camp. The force was formed into hollow square and twenty-four rebels were condemned to be blown from guns, so that not only their bodies but their hope of immortality would be destroyed. They confessed their sin and asked only that they might die on the right of the line, which was the post of honour where they had been wont to serve. This request was granted and they were forthwith blown away. Monro then reported that his army 'was now in a state in which it might be trusted to meet the enemy'. He was right. Two days later at Buxar he led this force, numbering 7,000 sepoys with a hundred or so British officers, against the combined armies of Delhi and Bengal, and won a famous victory. He reported that his troops had fought with exceptional gallantry.

Buxar furnishes an example of the role of will in the formation of human societies. Men desert separately for private reasons, but when a battalion deserts with its arms, there is a collective purpose that has won a collective consent. The men were Bengali peasants. Bengal had been ruined by the rapacity of John Company. Peasants were starving. It may be that those sepoys had felt the first womb flutterings of nationalism or at least of hatred for the foreign rulers, but this was not strong enough to master for long their need to bow to the stronger will. We have become accustomed to confessions in public trials but there had been no opportunity to break the rebel sepoys down or to brainwash them in solitary confinement. They confessed freely and without hope of benefit. Monro's nerve had held. He had not doubted or hesitated. He had played the part of a god. The rebels were as the hosts of Satan. When they met God face to face they confessed their sins and submitted to a justice that seemed divine. The army approved. At Buxar it was in a mood to redeem its virtue.

Bengal was now at the mercy of these men of will. Horace Walpole was to write 'We have outdone the Spaniards in Peru. They were at least butchers on a religious principle, however diabolical their zeal. We have murdered, deposed, plundered and usurped—nay think you of the famine in Bengal, in which 3 millions perished, being caused by a monopoly of the provisions by the servants of the East India Company?'*

Warren Hastings' return in 1772 marked the beginning of the end of the rape of Bengal for from then onward order replaced plunder as the first objective of government. Hastings was amongst the greatest of Britain's servants. John Strachey said of him 'Brilliant, scholarly, brave, arbitrary, financially lax even to his own disadvantage, loving India, conquering India, enriching India, despoiling India, this strange man stands out as the first and perhaps the only, fascinating figure in the long stiff line of Governor Generals who came and went over the next 175 years.'† He learned Hindustani and Urdu. He wrote an introduction to the first translation of the *Gita*. He was fascinated by the art, culture and history of India. He was without racial prejudice. He loved not only India, he loved Indians. He is one of the few English conquerors who is even today remembered with affection by leading Indians. His own countrymen impeached him for tyranny. After a seven-year trial he was acquitted and ruined.

England was enjoying her age of reason. The ethical revolu-

---

* Quoted in John Strachey, *The End of Empire*, p. 42.
† *Ibid.*, p. 46.

tion was under way. Walpole was but one of many English-men who had come to recognise a humanist responsibility for people regardless of their colour or religion. The impeach-ment of Hastings was an ill-directed expression of moral indignation, but it served a useful purpose for it brought the East India Company under public scrutiny and made the government of India responsible to the British Parliament. Pitt's India Act 1784 subjected the Company to a Minister in London and a Governor-General in India whose directives included non-aggression, clean government and welfare. The first proved the most difficult in practice.

How should England rule? Hastings favoured the Mogul way. The English should rule as a caste. They were the guardians of an ancient civilisation. They should respect its customs and patronise its religions, culture and literature. They should be concerned with supervision rather than de-tailed administration. India should be ruled through Indians. Missionary activities, whether religious or social, should be firmly discouraged.

Cornwallis, the first Governor-General, was not an intellec-tual. He was a soldier and an aristocrat. He had the full support of Pitt and Dundas, and for seven years he ruled as an autocrat. He did not share Hastings' love for Indians nor his respect for their culture. All natives, Cornwallis wrote, were corrupt and their customs, in so far as he was aware of them, were deplorable. He proposed to rule Indians for their own good but strictly on English lines. First he cleaned up government. He separated the governing and trading activities of the Company. Those who opted for the political branch received generous salaries but could take no part in any trading activities. He purged the service. Many were sent home. The foundations of the world's most honest civil service were laid. It was British and Indians were excluded from all but subordinate posts. Cornwallis also introduced reforms in land tenure aimed at setting up an English landlord system under which the landlord would be responsible for the land tax, and he reformed the courts and introduced the rule of law. These were to be important later when an Indian middle class emerged, but at the time they were beyond Indian comprehension. To the ordinary Bengali the bad times had passed and Imperial rule had returned. The rulers had paler faces but still spoke a foreign language and collected taxes in much the same way. Order was restored and life, religious and customary, moved on. An uncomfortable but transitory roughness between rulers had passed, and things were as before.

Cornwallis and his successor, Shore, cleaned government, controlled famine, provided a modicum of welfare and let custom be. Bengal was being ruled in the Indian way by Englishmen. Non aggression was not so easy. India knew neither nationalism nor regionalism (save perhaps for a short period amongst the Mahrattas). Order meant the empire of the strongest. When the strongest refused its manifest destiny, anarchy prevailed. Petty rulers sought to found petty empires. Thugs and pindaris marauded for religion and plunder. Trade became impossible. A power vacuum sucked at the British. Napoleon moved into his oriental phase. A forward policy seemed a safer policy. The Governor-General, Lord Mornington, was thirty-seven, ambitious and a convinced imperialist. He had the authority and his brother Arthur Wellesley wielded the sword. Tipu, Sultan of Mysore, the strongest of the petty Caesars, was chosen and destroyed before instructions could come from London. The Carnatic was annexed for alleged correspondence with Tipu. The Nawab of Oudh offered half his state. Surat was annexed. A number of Rajput and Maratha states accepted protection. This meant a British resident in charge of external affairs and a force of Company troops maintained at the expense of the protected state. The ruler insured against Indian conquest; the premium was British conquest. Nobody was shocked for Indian patriotism did not exist even as an idea. By 1818 India was a British-ruled empire.

How did it come about that within a period of about eighty years a foreign trading company was able to master a subcontinent with some 200 million inhabitants, a rich and ancient civilisation and a well established imperial military tradition? It was not because India lacked resources. During the eighteenth century the wealth of India was at least equal to that of Britain. It was not because her weapons were inferior. It was the age of fire-power. Battles were no longer won by stronger men on better horses. European guns were at all times available to Indian rulers. So were military advisers. Sindhia's army under de Boigne was at least as good as any troops available to the Company. The Sikh army was probably better. Nor was it, as the Nationalists allege, because of the superior wickedness of the British. The Indian leaders were certainly no more inhibited by virtue than were our own.

The difference lay in will and unity. When the British suffered a reverse they closed ranks. The Indians fell apart. In diplomacy there were always Indian differences to exploit. British differences were strictly domestic. In battle, when a breach was blown in the line, junior British officers closed it. A breach in the Indian line meant that the line was broken, for without very special discipline and leadership it is in the nature of men to move away from danger. The power of a human society depends on its coherence, and this Indian society had not achieved. Success bred success. Like the Arabs in the days of the Prophet the British felt that destiny was theirs. No defeat seemed more than a temporary set-back, for God served in their ranks. The British of that age had the nation-making will. The Indians did not. All India had become a British responsibility. The age of reason had passed. The Evangelicals rediscovered sin and the Utilitarians accepted the revelations of Adam Smith as set out in *The Wealth of Nations*. Both were becoming powerful. The victory of the reformers in 1830 strengthened their hand.

The Evangelicals saw heathen sinfulness, idolatry, child marriage, sacred prostitution, the burning of widows and resolved that it must stop. The poor benighted Indians must be led into the Christian fold. The Utilitarians believed passionately in European superiority. In India they saw a closed traditional economy and determined that it should be thrown open to the cleansing winds of free competition. Lord William Bentinck, Governor-General 1828–1835, was both a Christian and a Benthamite.

India was no longer to be ruled the Indian way. She was to be reformed. Indians must be brought to accept the superiority of Western ideology. This was to prove a momentous decision.

The first reform was moral. *Suttee* (the burning of widows), and *thuggee* (ritual murder) were suppressed. The Indian was required to accept the European Ethic.

271

Government-supported schools and colleges would no longer teach the learning of the East. They would teach the language, the literature and the science of England. Persian, the official language of the Moguls, was dropped and English became the language of government and of higher courts.

The law was recast on English lines. The Common Law of England, based on English moral ideas, became and remains the law of India.

India was to be ruled in the English way by an ever increasing proportion of Indians, but there was no social coming together. Such intermarriage as took place was confined to the lowest orders. This had not always been so. In the eighteenth and nineteenth centuries English rulers married Indian wives, but not in sufficient numbers to establish a Eurasian caste. The tight colour bar came with the invention of the steamship. White women began to come in the cool weather and to return in the hot. They feared that social contact might result in romances during the hot season. The Rt Hon Julian Amery tells me that his grandfather, who was in the ICS, wrote that while the arrival of white women was a very pleasant change, he feared that they would create very rigid social barriers.

The Mutiny of 1857 was a fruit of the new policy. India had no objection to foreign rule on principle. She had accepted the Moguls and she was willing to accept the British. All she asked of government was that it should not interfere with religion, custom and a conservative way of life. The British were shaking the pillars. Boys who received Western education started to ask questions. Missionaries who insulted the gods and profaned the Gita were tolerated and even patronised. New laws upset traditional land tenures. Dalhousie's attempts to impose good government on princely states started tremors. A tension had built up and the issue of cartridges greased with the fat of cows (sacred to the Hindu) and of pigs (unclean to the Moslem) was taken as an attack on religion. This indeed was the spark, but the rebellion was not merely a sepoy mutiny. Nana Sahib brought out Maratha princes scared of reform; the old emperor in Delhi focused a Moslem reaction; agrarian grievances enlisted landlords in Oudh and Behar. Peasants obeyed reluctantly whoever was nearest and strongest. It was not a national rebellion. The Punjabis and the Sikhs remained loyal. The south on the whole took the British side and the Madras army did not mutiny. It was a rebellion of conservatives made anxious by change. Under stress the British came together and the rebels disintegrated. Atrocities were committed on both sides. Liberal opinion in Britain was shocked by our reprisals, but India took a different view. The British were demi-gods and occasional roughness was in character. Gods are notoriously vengeful.

British self-confidence, previously total, was shaken. We diagnosed the causes correctly. We had frightened the men of caste and the men of property. We determined to correct our errors. This meant going backwards and it was to prove a mistake, for the events of the Mutiny had destroyed the mystique of the leadership which we now sought to propitiate. We stopped social reform. We rewarded those princes who had shivered in uncertain neutrality and urged them to become enlightened despots We reassured the land-owning caste and hoped they would become improving landlords after the English fashion. We wound up John Company and put the Queen in its place. Rule became a direct government responsibility. Princes were brought into the Governor's Council. For the new Western-educated class that we had created and which had proved actively loyal throughout the Mutiny we did nothing. It was only at the military level that reform went forward and here it was radical. The army we then created served us loyally in two wars and serves the Governments of India and of Pakistan today.

The fifty years that followed the Mutiny were the heyday of the Raj. India was run at the top level by the Indian Civil Service, numbering about 1,000. They were a select body, the top echelon of the British Civil Service University entry. They were deeply conscious of their own superiority. They were too proud to be corrupt. They ruled great provinces and retired without fortune to villas at Cheltenham. They set new standards of integrity in public service. They formed the unmatched instrument of a static society. They were temperamentally unsuited to social change. The Raj was conservative. It was an age of public works. Railways were built, canals dug, agriculture irrigated and famines controlled. The development of native industry was handicapped by our

obsession with free trade and, apart from the Tata Parsee
steel mills, it was mostly British owned. The wealth of India
grew but it did not grow noticeably faster than population.
Western-style education was now accepted with enthusiasm
and schools and colleges assisted by government grants were
founded all over India. The new educated middle class was
still a tiny minority but it was spreading over the entire
sub-continent. It was Anglophile. It wanted to join the Raj. It
was rejected by the Raj. Indian nationalism was born.

India was used to conquerors. She was used to new religions.
She had lived with them and remained apart. She had accepted
John Company as she had accepted the Moguls. Her soldiers
had joined the Company's army and her financiers had
attached themselves to the merchants who raped Bengal. She
had withdrawn herself into what Percival Spear calls 'the socio-
religious chrysalis that sheltered her from the emotional pains
of foreign conquest'.* Now for the first time foreign ideas
began to break in. Why were the apparently godless British
so successful? Could humanism be superimposed on Hinduism?
Was the caste system consistent with human rights? Was
idolatry consistent with reason? Ram Mohan Roy (1772–
1833), a Brahman from Calcutta learned in Latin and Greek
as well as English, Arabic, Persian and Sanskrit, posed these
questions. He asserted that the ideas of reason and of individual human rights underlay both Hindu and Western
thought, and that upon the basis of their joint ethic Hindus
could claim equal rights with Europeans; that each could
borrow from the other and that in the process the Hindus
should reform their own society. He criticised *suttee*, the
debasement of women, idolatry and caste. He advocated the
adoption of English in place of Persian as the official language,
and the study of English science and literature.

Any religion can adopt any ethic. There was no reason
why Hinduism should not adopt Western humanism. The
new Westernised Indians did so. They did not reject their
religion but they grafted Western humanism on to it. They
were the rising new middle class, the subordinate executive,
the clerks in the ministries, the city officials, the lawyers,

---

* *A History of India*, p. 159.

the doctors who accepted Western medicine, technicians, engineers and merchants. The great Gandhi was of their number. He was a Western saint hunger-striking for humanist ends. He was not concerned as to how he could get off the wheel of life. He was in life working for the physical salvation of his fellows.

The new Indians had accepted their inferiority. They accepted the superiority of the English ethic, of the English education, of the English technology and of the English discipline. They accepted these things. They adapted them. They were Anglophile, but the English still rejected them.

The Indian National Congress of 1885 was an expression of the new class's identity. The Congress was not anti-British. It expressed its loyalty to the Raj and its gratitude for the blessings of British rule. It included British members several of whom were elected to the annual presidency. But if the Congress was to mean anything it had to fight for its members. This brought it up against the bureaucracy of the Raj which was principally occupied in rural administration, and was far too conservative to get on with the new men. Congressmen were treated with a formality flavoured with contempt. They were made to feel inferior as Indians. The relationship began to turn sour. The new class did not abandon its quest for Westernism but it sought to build up an Indian ego. European works that romanticised Indian history became popular. Tod's *Annals of Rajasthan* (1816) was rediscovered and became a best-seller. The author had given Rajput anarchy an Arthurian slant of high Western chivalry. By 1900 the Congress had become the loyal opposition.

In 1906 the Liberals won the British election on a landslide. The new men were Morley and Minto. They recognised at last the Indians with whom they would have to deal. The Morley-Minto reforms provided for legislative councils with elected unofficial minorities and separate Moslem representation. Gokhale, the leader of the Congress moderates, made excellent use of the Councils. He agitated not only on sectarian issues but on such Western concepts as universal education. He co-operated in the new King's great Durbar. Self-government, it was felt, would advance with measured tread as Indians became Englishmen and fit to govern. When war came in 1914, Indian enthusiasm rivalled our own. She provided over a million men to fight in our cause and a 100 million in money. She took over her own defence. Our troops in India were reduced to a mere 15,000.

Africa

This brings us to Africa and Britain's third empire, which came mainly in the last quarter of the nineteenth century. Empire was still being won more or less accidentally, but moral considerations rather than interests had begun to play a dominant role in imperial decision.

Now what were these principles? I would put first the duty of rulers to govern in the interests of the governed. The British Colonial Service regarded themselves as guardians of a native population, which must be protected against the settler and the trader. The slogan which one finds being repeated time after time by Colonial Secretaries was 'The interests of the natives must come first'. Adherence to principle is never perfect and nationalists can always find instances in which interests other than those of the inhabitants were obviously preferred, but they are relatively rare. My grandfather was a colonial governor and my childhood impression was that the settler and the trader were the natural enemies of mankind.

The second was the evangelical concept of conferring the blessings of civilisation. The Christian denominations became highly competitive in the missionary field and missionary societies were a popular charity. This led to some conflict with the Colonial Service, who ranked missionaries amongst those from whom the natives needed protection. The Service believed that the native should not be prised prematurely from his tribal beliefs and disciplines. Traditional religions should only be discouraged when they included human sacrifice, infanticide and certain forms of witchcraft which flagrantly offended the Western ethic. Colonial powers should concentrate on law and order, medical and agricultural services plus a little education. Third came the principle that colonial rule should prepare a people for self-rule. In this the

British were unique. The French, Belgians and Portuguese sought to make their colonials into Frenchmen, Belgians and Portuguese *asimilados*; Britain aimed to make them independent.

Finally, free trade became a moral principle. British colonies must be open to the trade of all the world and it was our duty to see that they were. The fact that as the leading industrial power, free trade served our interest, was coincidental.

Egypt

Egypt had not been a nation since the Persians came in the fifth century BC. She had been ruled by Greeks, Romans, Byzantines. Arabs, Turks and, after 1880, by the British. The British made them into a nation. As Sir Evelyn Baring (later Lord Cromer) states in the opening sentence of *Modern Egypt*, 'the origin of the Egyptian question was financial'. Egypt, like Bengal, was a province of a derelict empire ruled by Turkish nobles of whom the chief was the Khedive. She had got into debt. The creditors were English and French bankers. It was in the days of the Concert of Europe. The great powers accepted responsibility for public order, and order in a trading world depended on international debts being paid, so Britain and France put in a receiver to take charge of Egyptian finances. Baring was the receiver. The Egyptian treasury was reorganised and payment of coupons resumed. There then occurred a military rebellion. The leader was Colonel Arabi and he forced the Khedive to appoint him Minister of War. The revolt was narrow based within the army but it was not a mere mutiny, for Arabi was inspired by a nationalist desire to get rid of the Turkish pashas and their European masters. Under pressure from France, Britain agreed to a joint note stating that they found Colonel Arabi unacceptable. Then the French government changed and Britain was left carrying the baby, or rather the debt and the canal. Alexandria was bombarded, an expeditionary force routed the Egyptian army, Arabi was sent to an island, and Baring returned as 'British Agent and Consul General'. For the next twenty-six years he was the absolute ruler of Egypt, now in effect a province of the British Empire. It was not a result that Mr Gladstone had desired. We had been sucked into a vacuum. Arabi could not have ruled Egypt for there was no Egypt to rule. The infrastructure of a nation did not exist. There was no Egyptian middle class. The Turks had proved incompetent but without the Turks there was no administration at all. If government was to function Britain had to guide. Of course we could have washed our hands of the whole business but this would have meant writing off our investment and the canal. It would also have meant abandoning something which had become more and more evidently our responsibility. Baring had no doubt as to what that responsibility was. It was to create a free Egypt capable of governing herself.

His task was not easy. In the Sudan he was faced with the Mahdist rebellion, the loss of an Egyptian army under General Hicks and of General Gordon in Khartoum. He cut his losses and waited fourteen years. He created a civil service and employed Sir Herbert (later Lord) Kitchener to forge an army. In 1898 Kitchener advanced building a railway as he marched and at Omdurman the Dervish host was smashed and young Winston Churchill rode in the last cavalry charge. We need shed no tears for the Mahdists. They were fundamentalist Muslim zealots, fabulously cruel. They had scourged the Sudan much as Chaka had scourged Natal. They were replaced by Condominion or the joint rule of Britain and Egypt, an invention of Baring's whereby the amour propre of Egypt could be preserved while Britain did the actual ruling. The Sudan civil service was created on the model of the ICS. It became a corporation of dedicated rulers, administrators and magistrates, selected men of the highest quality and integrity. For the first time in all history the Sudanese cockpit knew peace and order.

When Baring left Egypt in 1907 taxation had been halved and the revenue doubled. The irrigation system and the canals had been salvaged. Forced labour had been abolished. Conscientious administrators and honest judges had been appointed. A competent army was in being. A middle class was weaned and thriving. The peasants were enjoying a relative prosperity that enabled them to breed more children. This was the rub. Since 1880 the population has risen from 6 million to 37 million.

Negro Africa

Until the mid-nineteenth century black Africa, south of the Sahara, had been unknown. Many had wondered but none knew where the Nile, the Congo and the Zambesi rose. No Arab or European had ever heard of Mounts Kenya and Kilimanjaro or of the great lakes. Somewhere in this vast area the negro race that was to inherit Africa was emerging. The earliest Egyption paintings depict black men from the south but they do not have negro features or, as far as one can see, negro hair. Where the sun burns, black protects. Ethiopia shows us black Caucasoids; very beautiful some of them are, coal-black with thin lips and noses, very delicate features, very slender bones, beautiful hands and feet and long slender, graceful necks. The sun has selected those best able to survive his rays, and it is men like this that appear in early Egyptian pictures. It is not till the New Kingdom (circa 1400 BC) that we find our first picture of a negro.

The negroids can perhaps be split into four sub-races. On the west coast they are at their purest, black, short legged, long bodied, with spread noses and very thick lips. The Ibos are perhaps typical. Further north the Sudanids display their Caucasoid genes. They are taller, more slender and less thick featured. The Nilotids in the upper reaches of the Nile and around its head-waters are even taller and even more slender, with a Semitic look about them that comes from Ethiopia, and further south the Bantu-speaking tribes show a mixture both of Nilotic and Capoid genes.

If we wish to find the indigenous culture of Africa we have to look south of the Sahara, and primarily at the Bantu-speaking people for they, until recently, developed without foreign influence. Africa of late has become a cult and left-wing writers have been providing us with an African history. Their theme is that Africa had a series of native civilisations which dissolved some time before the mid-nineteenth century, into a period of chaos that resulted, perhaps indirectly, from

279

the pressures created by the white man's exploitation of the slave trade, and that it was as a result of this temporary chaos that Africa fell into the servitude of colonialism from which she has recently liberated herself.

This is not a scenario that fits the known facts. The truth is nearer the 'blank, uninteresting, brutal barbarism' described by Professor Egerton in the Oxford Colonial History, 1920.

We have found few traces of a negro Stone Age or Bronze Age. The negro seems to have entered history with iron. Negroes had iron while the Berbers were still neolithic. This did not make them the masters of the Berbers. On the contrary they became the Berbers' slave smiths. We do not know of the negro as a hunter or as a pastoralist although at a later date pastoral tribes such as the Masai appeared. The negro enters history as a farmer growing crops, some of which are of Asiatic origin. It was at this point that negro culture stopped.

The negroes have never domesticated an animal or bird, their cattle are Asiatic, their goats are Mediterranean, their chickens are Indian, and yet they had plenty of animals available for domestication. African Elephants marched with Hannibal and one left its bones in the Alps. The eland is a splendid meat producer and has been imported into Russia as a farm animal. The zebra has been trained as a draught and pack animal, the guinea fowl has been domesticated in Europe for 1,500 years, but never in negro Africa.

The negro was neither a builder nor a mechanic. He has never used the wheel for draught, nor for pottery, nor for raising water.

The negro has never had any form of written language. Negro tribesmen can often describe in detail any missing animal but can rarely tell you how many there were in the herd. Some African languages lack any words for figures. No negroid language has proved capable of expressing the ideas necessary to civilised government and every nationalist has found himself compelled to adopt the colonial language. Tanzania and Kenya are trying to make Swahili into an official language but Swahili is scarcely a negro language; it is a lingua franca composed of Arabic, Portuguese, English and African words that grew up on the east coast much as pidgin grew on the China coast. Swahili comes from an Arabic word meaning 'of the coast'. Language both expresses and controls thought. Primitive languages have many nouns but little means of collecting and relating them. In the Akkad language of the west coast, for instance, there are five unconnected words for different kinds of baskets but no general word for basket. There is an absence of words for concepts that cannot been seen or felt. There are, for instance, no words for 'time' or 'place', although there are words for 'sleeping time' and 'sleeping place'. The absence of words of classification and abstraction makes reasoning difficult. Negro Africa has little oral literature, nothing equivalent to the Homeric poems or the Norse sagas. Folk memory seems to be short. This is not because the African memory is bad, it is generally excellent, but because there seems to be a lack of interest in things gone by. The African lives in the present. He is more interested in custom and habit than in change.

Perhaps strangest of all, the Africans had no calendar and no means of measuring time. Nowhere have we found any form of sundial. '2.30 pm on Mid-summer's day' could not be translated into any Bantu language.

The Bantu built only one-storey buildings of wood and mud. Stone he used rarely and save for one site at Engaraka in Northern Tanzania, where stone appears to have been used in the construction of some hut walls, never for housing. Stone was used extensively in Rhodesia during several centuries to face terraces and build free-standing walls. This stone was granite which, as a result of the fierce changes of temperature between day and night, split off the face of great granite boulders much as an onion peels. These stone peelings formed rectangular slabs, which when matched gave the appearance of dressed stone blocks. No mortar and little bonding was used, the facing of the walls consisted of courses of selected rectangular stones and the core was filled with loose stones. Walls never carried roofs and were not used for fortification. No Bantu ever built a castle to protect himself from slavers.

The only notable building in black Africa is the oval at Great Zimbabwe. The outer wall is some 800 feet long and in places 17 feet thick and 34 feet high. It is an irregular ellipse with a maximum diameter of nearly 100 yards. The walls do not conform to any regular curve and seem to have been built up to their full height at one point and then extended horizontally so that the working face of the wall formed a ramp up which the labourers could carry their stones. More stone was used in this building than in all the other stone buildings in black Africa put together.

Ever since the rediscovery of Zimbabwe in the late nineteenth century, the questions asked have been When? By whom? and Why?

The first theory was that Zimbabwe had been built by some ancient people before the Bantu came south, perhaps by Prester John or even by King Solomon. Could Zimbabwe be Orphir?

Later it became possible to date the ruins from the trade goods which were found in all the layers of habitation. These goods existed in great quantities and linked Zimbabwe with the Arab towns which had existed on the coast since the seventh century and in particular with Kilwa. Zimbabwe was on the edge of the gold-bearing plateau and was the trade link with the coast. From Zimbabwe went the gold and the slaves, and to Zimbabwe came the beads, the jewellery, the china (some of it Ming) and much later the gin bottles from Holland. The remains of these trade goods are found in the layers of refuse, and from them the layers can be dated. The first walls went up about AD 1100 but the main building is early fifteenth century. In the second half of this century when Kilwa fell to the Portuguese Zimbabwe declined.

I do not think that there can be any real doubt that the Bantu were the builders because nobody else at that date could have built so badly. Kilwa, Sofala and the other Arab cities, older contemporaries of Zimbabwe, are sophisticated medieval towns with a number of multi-storeyed stone buildings. In 1332 Ibn Batuta, an Arab scholar, described Kilwa as one of the most beautiful and best constructed towns in the world. Had the builders of Zimbabwe had any Arab assistance they would surely have got some of their walls straight or regularly curved. The question 'Why?' remains a mystery. Zimbabwe is not a city or a temple or a fort or a palace. It seems to me that it is designed not to keep people out but to keep them in. I think it was a slave compound, put up probably at Arab suggestion to contain slaves awaiting convoy to the coast. If I were a Rhodesian it is not a place after which I would wish to name my country.

Nothing from Arab civilisation seems to have rubbed off onto the indigenous populations. Some chiefs in Zimbabwe were strong enough to make their people collect alluvial gold and to corral slaves. For this they received nothing but gewgaws. The Bantu continued to live as tribesmen in a subsistence economy.

There were a number of negro kingdoms but they left no heirs. We know of them only from coastal rumour reported by civilised navigators.

The Zimbabwe people are said to have been succeeded by the empire of Monotopo which stretched from Rhodesia to Angola; Loanga according to the Portuguese extended from Cape Lopez to the mouth of the Congo; the kingdom of Congo lay to the south of the river and reached the Kwanga and Kwanya valleys, while the kingdom of Lunda included most of Angola.

When travellers first entered negro Africa in the nineteenth century, they found a new generation of empires and kingdoms. Baker travelled up the Nile, passing first through naked Nilotid tribes, some of whom were cannibal and none of whom had acquired government, and reaching Bunyoro and Buganda where he found strong monarchies extending over great areas. The royal families he believed to be Ethiopian by descent, though the people were negroid. In Natal Fynn lived with Chaka the Zulu emperor, and in what is now Zambia Livingstone visited the Barotze kingdom. In the west there were kingdoms in Congo and Ashanti.

The Bantu kingdoms never achieved civilisation. The royal kraals were big villages that never became cities, and never achieved the common services, the inter-dependent, specialisation and the class division that goes to the making of an urban society. They never broke the inertia of the tribe.

Professor Max Gluckman, in *Politics, Law and Ritual in Tribal Society* wrote:

There is an apparent instability deep-rooted in these [African] states; though the unifying influence of the kingship may keep the segments united for many years, the state was likely in the end to break up. This has happened for various reasons to formerly great states, like the Karanga Empire in South Rhodesia, both from external attack and internal dissension. I suggest that if we knew enough of the history of Africa it would show the constant temporary emergence of states of this type out of pressure of population on the land, or the sudden arrival of a band of conquering migrants and the establishment of kingship which was acceptable to all subjects. Since the kingdom's segments were not dependent upon one another for specialised production of various goods, after periods whose limits I cannot fix, the state would fall apart, and there would be left many small chieftainships and tribes.

The negro empire of which we know most is the Zulu, because throughout the major part of Zulu history there were white men writing at the Royal Kraal. We know something too of how this kingship came into being.

Sometime after the Empire of Monotopo had dissolved itself into tribes, a Bantu language group known as the Nguni moved south. They were a pastoral people whose women grew some crops. They were organised on a clan basis. Their currency was cattle and it was in cattle that the bride price was paid. Inter-clan cattle raiding occurred and clan alliances, defensive and offensive, involved the appointment of leaders, whose authority over clans other than their own tended to become permanent. Cattle-raiding warfare became conventionalised with the wrong-doer normally backing down to a show of force, and the chieftaincies remained for a long period small, local and moving from clan to clan as strong personalities emerged.

This ended with Dingiswayo. He was the son of a clan chief who had been exiled in his youth. According to Henry Francis Fynn he met a white man, Dr Cowan, who had disappeared on a journey to Delagoa Bay, but the dates do not fit. Dingiswayo, however, certainly met new ideas. He reorganised his clansmen into disciplined regiments. He fought not merely for cattle but to enlarge his authority and to bring new clans and new tribes into his army. He spared the women and children and left the conquered their cows so that they could rebuild their herds. He claimed no divine authority. He won his power and maintained it by force autocratically administered. Among the tribes he conquered were the Zulu and serving in his army was a Zulu called Chaka.

Chaka was the unwanted child of a Zulu chief. Sex play between warriors and unmarried girls was customary but the man was expected to keep his semen out of the woman. To get her in a family way was by tribal custom deplorable. Nandy the mother belonged to the Longeni clan and she met, returning from a raid, a young Zulu chief. When Nandy started to swell her clan demanded that the Zulu should marry the girl and pay the bride price. The Zulu denied responsibility and said, 'It must be *ishaka*', a beetle that interferes with menstruation. Such was the humiliating origin of the great name of Chaka. Nandy's people insisted and so by the Zulu equivalent of a shot-gun marriage, Nandy became the unwanted third wife of the Zulu chief. She was a passionate, violent lady and was soon sent back to her father's kraal. Here too her life was a humiliation. She fled with her son and after some adventures arrived at the Mthethwa, Dingiswayo's people. Here Chaka joined the army.

He was now a very dangerous young man. Physically he was superb, a veritable Mohammed Ali. He had a sex problem, probably homosexual, a mother fixation and a maniacal will to power fuelled by the humiliations suffered by himself and by his beloved mother. As a warrior he had the idea of using the assegai as a short stabbing spear instead of as a missile. This, backed by the fury of the charge, proved irresistible. In his early twenties, Chaka's feats as a warrior had won him command of a regiment. In 1816 Chaka's father died and the Zulu chieftaincy was vacant. Chaka asked Dingiswayo's permission to take his regiment to back his claim. There was no resistance. Chaka descended on the Zulu kraal where he seized everyone against whom either he or his mother had a childhood grudge and executed them by driving a stake up the anus. He then moved on to his mother's kraal and did the same thing. His conduct does not seem to have attracted any adverse comment. The fact that he ordered the grass under some of his victims to be lit so as to shorten their slaying was rated as mercy.

A year or two later, probably about 1819, Dingiswayo was killed. Fynn says he was betrayed by Chaka. Be this as it may,

Chaka certainly disposed of the Mthethwa heir and established the Zulu as head of the confederacy or empire.

It is to be noted that Chaka claimed no divine mandate. He was not a priest and never acted as one. He employed witch doctors to protect him against the spirits and to smell out his enemies. He ruled by terror, but it was an earthy terror. Henry Francis Fynn resided with Chaka for months on end. Here is an account from his diary:

> He would by a movement of his finger, point out one of the gathering sitting around him, upon which to the surprise of strangers, the man would be carried off and killed. This was a daily occurrence. On one occasion I witnessed 60 boys under 12 years of age dispatched before he had breakfasted. No sooner is the signal given than those sitting around him scramble to kill him . . . No sooner is the condemned individual taken hold of, than one, while the others are dragging him away, seizes the head and by a sudden twist and jerk, dislocates the neck joint, the others meanwhile beating him with knob sticks. As soon as they arrive at the Golgotha about a mile from the Kraal, where all those executed are placed, they thrust a stake through the bodies. There the vultures, sit, flocks waiting for their daily prey.

There were rougher days than this. When Nandy died 7,000 people were killed, and this was not a sacrifice. The King ordered some to be executed because they were not weeping sufficiently and the idea caught on till the whole kraal was engaged in self destruction. The count was 7,000.

When the armies came home, regimental leaders were required to designate all who had failed to show courage, and they were executed. Return for an unsuccessful army was a dangerous operation. Some just marched off rather than face their king. Some of the Matabele were once such an army.

Chaka's wars depopulated most of Northern Natal. He was eventually murdered by two half brothers, one of whom, Dingaan, after murdering his confederate, succeeded to Chaka's office and methods, if not to his skill as a commander.

Eventually Chaka's successors were defeated by Boer and Briton and Southern Africa was freed from the pest of Zulu impis.

There was nothing constructive in Zulu rule. The Royal

Kraal was simply a collection of huts. There was no city. Tribal society remained undifferentiated. The kraal lived on the booty of its marauding impis, and yet Chaka is not condemned by African opinion. As recently as 1972 the Zulu people erected a memorial to his honour and the Zulu territorial authority nominated Chaka's day as national day for the newly formed Kwa Zulu.

There is reason to believe that Zulu history is not untypical of those other Bantu-speaking kingdoms of which we know less. A clan chief or the chief of a migrant group displays military talents that enable him to impose his authority on his neighbours. His rule is purely military. His instrument of government is terror. His authority does not replace the tribal system; it is imposed upon it. Eventually the military power is defeated either by an outside enemy or as a result of internal dissension and the kingdom breaks up into the independent tribes upon which it was imposed.

There would seem to have been certain constants in the history of these negro empires. The first we have touched on is 'Instability'. The pre-exploration ones simply disappeared, leaving nothing but a vague note in an alien history. Of Monotopo, Loango, Congo and Lunda there remains not so much as a folk memory, not a ruin, not an artefact, not a geographical expression. The nineteenth century empires were taken over by the colonialists and preserved as protectorates or as instruments of indirect rule, but they too are rapidly disappearing in the hands of nationalists.

The second constant seems to have been the absence of anything that can properly be called a religion. Negro religion never got beyond the 'Ghoulies and ghosties and long-legged beasties and things that go bump in the night' stage. The spirits of ancestors were appeased rather than worshipped. If they were neglected they might get up to mischief. The spirits of the game and of other animals also needed appeasement. There were fetishes and taboos. Some tribes believed in a creator who gave the land to mythical tribal ancestors. This creator was always a nature god. Ngai, the Kikuyu god, was the thunder demon. The claps were the cracking of his joints and the lightning was his sword. If anyone looked up they ran the risk of seeing Ngai and dying. Ngai was also a rain

god and it was to him that the rain sacrifices were made. The
Murle god was similar save that he had a special link with
pythons. The Masai sacrificed to Ngai, who to them was
linked with the spirit of the lion. Negro Africa never developed an organised priesthood. Witch doctors operated as
individuals, not as members of a priestly caste. They were
members of the tribe who performed an occasional function.
It is only in West Africa that one begins to find priests linked
with a godhead by some special experience. Bantu kings were
neither gods nor priests. Chaka was no more a god than
Hitler. Both were leaders who imposed themselves by
violence. Negro kings did not embody the kind of idea that
in other continents lifted man out of his family tribal pool
and made him a citizen. Negro monarchy was never more
than an excrescence on tribal society. Africa never found the
kind of faith that could lift her out of tribal society or hold
a greater society together.

The third constant was an astonishing lack of respect for
human life. As we have seen the vultures never went hungry
on the execution hill outside Chaka's kraal. When Speke presented a musket to Mutesa II, King of Buganda, the king
asked him to demonstrate by shooting a courtier. When Speke
refused, the king was amused by his squeamishness and
handed the gun to a small boy. A courtier was shot, the
musket was praised and nobody was surprised. Samuel Baker
found the King of Bunjoro equally casual about ordering
executions. A mere royal gesture was sufficient condemnation. Livingstone describes how the King of Buganda organised
expeditions to pounce on villages in his own dominions, to
kill the head man, to sell all that were saleable to a slave
dealer and to kill the rest lest they resort to witchcraft to
avenge their village. On the west coast European visitors were
astonished both by the extent and by the casualness of government killing. It is true that these western kingdoms and
those on the savannas of the southern Sahara were not
primarily Negro. Ghana was founded about AD 400 by Jews
and Berbers, and Songhai, Nupe, Sasso, Mali and Benin and Ife
were all traditionally founded by migrants from the north.
In the eleventh century Moslems from the north took over
and, such as it was, the civilisation of this area became Mos-

lem. This does not seem to have raised the value of human life, if we take Sultan Moulay Ismael of Morocco, 1672–1727, as an example. Some of our contemporaries keep a game book in which they record the number of pheasants they shoot. Sultan Moulay kept a man book in which he recorded the numbers he killed personally. It added up to 36,000. He had one trick of which he was particularly proud: he could cut off the head of a slave with a single stroke of his scimitar as he mounted his horse. It required a lot of slaves to keep in practice, but slaves were cheap. They were caught for him by his neighbouring monarchs.

The final common factor was slave dealing. All civilisations have used slaves. Africa lacked the civilisation to use slaves. She provided slaves for the use of others. If there ever was an African king who opposed slaving we do not know of him. The negro kings whom the white man and the brown man met were all prepared to sell their prisoners and often their subjects. The anti-slavery campaign received no support in Africa and after the slavers had been cleared from the seas, slavery had to be checked by the intervention of British troops.

I am the great-grandson of William Rathbone, who with Wilberforce and Clarkson led the anti-slavery agitation. I have a number of his letters. The campaign to rouse the Nonconformist conscience of England makes fascinating reading. Anti-slavery became a national crusade. Britain's colonies in West and East Africa were by-products of this campaign.

In the old slaving days nobody had needed African territory. All that was required was a trading post. White men did not catch slaves, for local kings could do it far cheaper. Slaves were brought to market on the coast and bartered for trinkets. It was a most profitable trade. After Waterloo Britain dedicated herself to its suppression. Experience proved that it required far more territory to suppress the trade than to conduct it. Where were we to put the slaves whom we released from the slave ships? We found a place for them at Freetown, Sierra Leone. It was not long before they started slaving for themselves. We had to govern. The west coast of Africa is a long coast to blockade. It soon became clear that if slaving was to be stopped we would have to go to the

source. We were horrified by what we saw. The local kingdoms were the remains of Africa's first colonial experience
when, towards the end of the first Christian millennium,
'white men from the North' founded urban states on the
southern borders of the Sahara. They had probably brought
from Egypt the idea of funeral sacrifices. Now that slaves
were more difficult to dispose of on the coast many more
were used for sacrifice to attend dead chiefs in another world.
Winwood Reade (*The Martyrdom, of Man* 1872) describes
the terror in which the West African lived. Missionaries penetrated and agitated. Traders penetrated but with the elmina-
tion of Africa's principal export there was very little to
trade. Gradually, reluctantly and bit by bit Britain assumed
responsibility. Very little force was necessary. West Africa
was in tribal anarchy, and only the Ashanti had to be conquered. They would raid the Fanta on the coast and we were
protecting the Fanta. The capture of Kumasi, the Ashanti
capital, was a revelation not unlike the relief of Belsen. The
troops were horrified by what they saw. The West Coast
before the British came was a terrible place. Of course trade
improved with order but trade in the early days was trivial.
Britain ruled indirectly through tribal authorities and initially
confined herself to a peace-keeping and communications role.

The East Coast was less thickly inhabited. The slave trade
was in Arab hands passing through Zanzibar. Britain first
assumed a protectorate over the Sultanate on the coast in
order to suppress the trade. Inland was explorer and missionary country. Buganda was the only organised kingdom.
Slavers' tracks were the only system of communication. When
Britain decided to open up the country and to build a railway to the lakes the negro population was too primitive to
use as labour and we had to import coolies from India. They
became the ancestors of the present Indian population of
East Africa. Nairobi was a railway camp. Zambia, Malawi,
Zanzibar, Kenya and Uganda had all been brought under the
protection of the Colonial Office by 1890.

Why did we acquire these vast blocks of territory in West,
Central and Eastern Africa? It was not for commercial
reasons. The staple export had always been slaves, and when
the trade stopped there was some palm oil and cocoa in the

west, some ivory in the east, and not much else. Commercially these parts of Africa have always been deficit areas and we never expected them to be anything else. Nor was it, as Hobson and Lenin suggested, because our capitalists wanted more profitable fields of investment. The export of British capital to Central Africa was trivial when compared with export to America, Europe, India or Southern Africa. Capital exports on any scale only started with the finding of copper in Zambia and oil in Nigeria. Our motives were not material. They were emotional. Imperialism was fashionable. We liked to see the map coloured red. An imperial Cape to Cairo railway was an idea that inspired and excited. At a rather deeper level was the feeling that there was a job to be done. Travellers and missionaries had looked inside the Dark Continent and seen how dark it was. It was an age of optimism. We believed in our civilisation. We believed in its blessings. We believed in ourselves. Our public school system was producing young, idealistic administrators. They felt an urge to a task for which they knew they were fitted. Africa must be saved. This was the white man's burden and we felt we ought to pick it up. It was an emotion that was backed by a fear that if we did not do it someone else would. We distrusted foreigners. We doubted whether they could be trusted with natives and in any event once they got there they might threaten British interests. We were not quite clear what interests, but you could never trust a foreigner. Romance, philanthropy and xenophobia came together and produced a mood. Reluctantly, step by step, government was nudged forward, protesting that it must not cost too much. Captain Johnston was given a £10,000 grant in aid with which to found a colonial administration in Nyasaland, a country rather larger than Britain; Colville in Uganda started with £50,000, while Lugard in Northern Nigeria had £100,000 with which to govern 10 million people. There were certainly a dozen emirates far stronger than he was. Success depended on the nerve of solitary white men.

The first residents were generally officers seconded from one of the Services. They usually followed missionaries who had learned the local languages and something of local politics. Later the Colonial Service took over. It acquired many of the characteristics of a religious order. Its members eschewed all opportunity of enrichment and, so far as the governed were concerned, remained celibate. It was a racialist service. A strict colour bar was maintained. The black man was not the white man's equal. It was for this reason that he needed protection.

The idea was that colonies and protectorates should become self-supporting. They rarely did so, and grants in aid continually had to be increased. Taxation depended on a cash economy, and this came slowly. We ruled through tribal authorities when we could find them. Where the Africans had not reached the chief stage of tribal evolution, we appointed chiefs for them. District officers covered huge areas, listening, persuading and chiding. Small African police forces were selected and trained. Peace was maintained. The people came out of fear and multiplied. As everywhere this was the problem.

West Africa was not considered suitable for European settlement, but the highlands of East Africa had a wonderful climate, warm sun by day, cold clear nights and adequate rain that kept regular hours. Areas of vacant land were allocated for white settlement. The most important area was called the White Highlands in Kenya. It had been used for occasional seasonal grazing by the Masai, but when trouble came it was not the Masai who objected but the Kikuyu who had been a forestry people in mortal fear of the Masai, who raided them for wives. Under British rule the Kikuyu kept their women, multiplied and protested that they had been robbed of land on which in the old days they would never have dared to trespass. The settlers were an asset to the protectorates, for they brought wealth and agricultural investment. They paid taxes which made services, roads, schools and hospitals available on a scale that would not otherwise have been possible. In colonial areas HMG always made it clear that the interests of the native would be preferred.

Southern Africa was a different proposition. It was territory we took from the Dutch in the Napoleonic wars. It was always conceived as white man's country in which native rights were subordinate. The protectorates of Bechuanaland, Basutoland and Swaziland were excepted. Here we were trustees for the native interests but, the protectorates apart, Southern Africa was white man's country. It had been Bushman country. White man and negro had arrived at much the same time. The negro had bred faster. When after the war we granted independence to the defeated Boers, everyone considered that we had acted with liberal generosity.

Southern Rhodesia belonged to a chartered company. It was hoped that occupation would show a profit. It was an area in which the Mashona majority were treated as game by a Zulu Matabele minority. Cecil Rhodes' pioneers established law, order and safety. It would have been better if the Colonial Office had been present to guard native interests, but for the majority of the population British rule was certainly preferred to Matabele rule. As elsewhere native problems grew with numbers. In the Union and in Rhodesia industrialisation developed and with it a black proletariat of urbanised and de-tribalised negroes. This is one of the problems with which apartheid, or separate development, is trying to deal. An urban society cannot be run on tribal lines.

The French idea was to make their colonies into provinces and their colonials into Frenchmen. They too had a Treasury that wanted to see colonies self-supporting. Their method was to grant monopoly rights to chartered companies, hoping thereby to generate a taxable income. It was not very successful, for the companies tended to go bankrupt.

The Congo Company of the King of the Belgians exemplified the evils of this system. Slave trading was suppressed and replaced by a form of peonage whereby black peasants were submitted to shocking brutality in order to make them collect rubber.

German colonial rule was, by our standards, astonishingly brutal. Von Trotha wrote from German East Africa 'I know these African tribes. They respect nothing but force. I wipe out rebellious tribes'. He was probably right in his estimate of African respect for force. At any rate the Germans received astonishing loyalty from their African subjects. Cut off from Europe, Paul von Lettow-Vorbeck, the German commander in Tanganyika maintained his African army in being throughout the whole of the 1914–18 War, in spite of several expeditionary forces sent to destroy him, one of which was commanded by General Smuts in person. On the conclusion of the Armistice, in obedience to the orders of his Emperor, he marched his army into Dar-es-Salaam and offered his surrender in good order. When as a tourist he returned to Tanganyika, which had then enjoyed twenty years of British administration, he was received on the quay by 20,000 Africans who had assembled from the bush to greet him. When I was in Tanganyika some twenty years ago I had a talk with one of von Lettow's old soldiers. He was a courteous old man who did not want to say anything against the English, but when I asked him about the Germans his face lit up and he said 'Ah, with the Germans one always knew where one was'.

The Portuguese had no racial feelings and were not in such a hurry as the other colonial powers. Their rule was inefficient and relaxed. It seemed to suit the African temperament.

When European colonists came to Africa south of the Sahara they found tribes punished spasmodically by marauding warlords and, on the west coast a few cities whose bloodiness horrified. None had achieved civilisation. Civilisation has come to Africa through colonialism. If civilisation was right for Africa then colonialism deserves the praise.

It was Britain's declared policy that her dominions and colonies would become independent nations, but the time was not yet. The trauma of the South African war passed and the wound healed. The Empire was not forever but in 1914 it looked durable.

16

THE FIRST PEOPLE'S
WAR AND PEACE

BEFORE 1914 European wars had been the business of kings and of governments. In the words of Clausewitz they had been the continuation of diplomacy by other means. There had been a political aim and a political solution.

People's wars proved different. Mass education, mass communications and mass parties involved the common man in his nation and in its quarrels as never before. He is an animal that needs to hate. He is also a highly suggestible animal. Everything he saw and read directed his hatred against the enemy. His hatred inspired his neighbour and his neighbour's hatred inspired him. When war was declared the streets of London, Paris, Berlin and Vienna filled with cheering, happy people being nice to each other. Only Russia went glumly to war. She was not a nation state.

The Social Democrats were the second largest party in the Reichstag. They were a Marxist party dedicated to the proposition that the workers of the world should unite for they had nothing to lose but their chains. They voted for war. So did their French colleagues in the Second Socialist International. So with, the rarest exceptions, did the British Pacifists.

There can seldom have been a war as unnecessary as that which wrecked the European system in 1914. Austria felt she needed a popular war to heal the cracks in her society. Russia felt her position as patron of the Slavs had been challenged and could think of no alternative to mobilisation. William II failed to see the danger, indulged in theatricals and then found that his staff had no plans for countering Russia that did not involve hitting France through Belgium. Belgian neutrality was guaranteed by England and there had been Anglo-French staff talks. So it was that the Great Powers, enmeshed by the rigidity of their mobilisation plans, blundered into war. By winter the Germans had got a bloody nose on the Marne, Russia had been turned at Tannenberg and Serbia had been punished. There were no pressing territorial claims. It was time for peace, but nation states cannot make peace. Once public opinion has been worked up to war it is almost impossible to put it into reverse.

The American civil war should have given us notice, for that had been a people's war; a war that was not just fought by armies but by the people and against the people. Sherman's march through Georgia had been designed to wreck the living and break the will of the Confederate people. The war that had been provoked by Southern mass hysteria had to grind on to unconditional surrender. The eventual compromise on the negro problem that was worked out after ten miserable years of war and reconstruction could have been negotiated at any time after Gettysburg if either government had dared to be sane. So it was in Europe. When the powers had fought themselves to a standstill America intervened and after 18 more months of suffering Germany surrendered unconditionally. Some twenty-five million had died.

By the time the victors met at Versailles they had learned something else about the wars of democracy. Once the fighting stops reaction sets in and armies bent on demobilisation are unusable. The great men could do little but acquiesce in that which had already happened for they could no longer use their armies. Wilson had the most power. America had only come in at the end. The war that had impoverished the allies had left her vastly rich. From being a debtor nation she had become everybody's creditor; but Wilson could not use a single American soldier to impose his will. Nor could Lloyd George or, save on France's frontiers, Clemenceau. The Allies measured their impotence when they tried to intervene in Russia.

My concern is not with the insane economics of the peace but with the process of state building.

Austria had disintegrated and the subject races had turned on their masters. The Czechs had seized Slovakia from the Magyars and the Sudeten from the Germans. The Poles had the corridor part of Silesia and much of Russia, the Rumanians had taken Transylvania from Hungary and the Serbs had occupied Croatia. Nobody was in a position to interfere, even if they had wanted to. None of these states had a real prospect of stability.

When an empire collapses the fragments do not become independent states. One province may capture the empire. This happened successively in Assyria, Media and Persia. It was simply a change of master. When strangers wreck an empire they may stay as emperors as the Greeks did in Persia or they may go away leaving anarchy behind them as the Mongols usually did. They do not leave independent sovereign states behind them, for nation making is a long and painful process.

Successful states emerge from struggle; they are hammered together by their foes and linked in mutual dependence by their fears. The nation forms on the army that won the struggle. Its success depends largely on the extent to which it can carry into its civil organisation the discipline, the sense of duty and the acceptance of authority that went to make the army, and into the army respect for and obedience to the civil authority. No two nations have achieved this in the same way, for institutions cannot be imported ready-made. Authority is the business of the state and it must be strong to contain its internal antagonisms. Liberal ideas are a luxury which only strong states can indulge in. With the astonishing exception of Switzerland, multi-tribal and multi-lingual republics do not work. Voters divide on tribal or linguistic lines and the authority of a majority is not accepted by a racial minority. It must be imposed as in Russia.

The Versailles nations did not fit. They had not come into being as a result of their own efforts. The Czech army had been raised in Russia from Czech prisoners of war and had made a famous march across Siberia. It was small, inexperienced and exclusively Czech. Masarik won recognition from

Wilson largely by adopting American ideas of democracy. The institutions he imported imposed permanent minority impotence on Sudeten and Slovak, for democracy lacks a king's power to bring minorities into his government. When the stress came the minorities preferred their race to their new found nationality. Poland never had a chance. Her minorities were too big and her divisions religious, racial and cultural, were too bitter. Rumanians had been serfs too long. They lacked the professional and middle class necessary for nation building. The moneyed Rumanian tended to be a Levantine businessman. The kingdom of Yugoslavia looked the best prospect. She had certainly struggled for her statehood. Serbs were divided from Croats by religion and culture but Austria had become too weak to be a counter-attraction and the Croats disliked the Italians a good deal more than they disliked the Serbs. Austria was reduced to six millions and in those days was judged to be an unviable state. She was forbidden to join Germany by a prohibition lacking means of enforcement. Hungary was sure to seek revenge.

The states created by Versailles neither looked nor proved stable. The new countries lacked the strength to hold together. With the exception of Austria and perhaps Yugoslavia they now enjoy varying degrees of autonomy within the Russian Empire. It is an arrangement that looks more stable, for they are people who have been conditioned to an imperial order.

Britain secured her interest; the German fleet and the lion's share of the German and Turkish colonial empires. France wanted to hold Germany down. She wanted the Rhineland. She was fobbed off with the League of Nations, an idea that President Wilson had fallen in love with. It was idealistic. It provided false security. Reluctantly France accepted the substitute and America ratted on her President's commitment. The French marched into the Rhineland but without conviction. They came out again on a promise of de-militarisation.

The People's Peace

Nations can work together as allies so long as the external pressure is strong enough to hold them together. Attempts to continue alliances after their purpose has been achieved fail when divergent interests start to outweigh the common interest. Czar Alexander's Holy Alliance, the League of Nations and the United Nations all fall into this category.

In practice, sovereignty has proved to be indivisible and states that have ceased to be sovereign have ceased to be nations.

Within a state the sovereign power can be controlled by balancing institutions, such as the Presidency, Legislature and High Court of the USA, but it cannot be successfully pooled with other sovereignties. Dynastic unions result either in one state becoming a province of the other (England and Scotland) or in the dissolution of the union (Norway and Sweden). Federations travel the same road. Either the states lose their identity and survive only as local government administrative areas, or the federation collapses. Sovereign power does not go on being shared.

Supra-national organisations that attempt something less than government do not have a good record.

The Church lasted longest. It had some success. It mitigated the severity of medieval war but it failed to keep the Christian princes at peace. It was faced with a dilemma that still lacks a solution. If the disputes of nations are not to be settled by war they must be settled by judgement, and a judge needs a policeman. An authority with judicial and police powers is a government, and its subjects are no longer independent nations. An authority without these powers must rely on power which others can grant or withhold, and will very soon find itself a contestant rather than a judge in the power struggle.

In the eleventh century Pope Gregory VII proclaimed that all Christian princes were his vassals and could be removed at his will, but excommunication and papal interdict, though formidable, proved inadequate. He had to call on other princes to enforce his authority. In so doing he became a partisan and lost judicial credibility. Popes struggling for power promoted far more wars than they arrested.

The Holy Alliance that followed the defeat of Napoleon was primarily a league of emperors and kings against their own subjects. They had a common interest in the suppression of Liberalism but it did not prove an overriding interest. The signatories soon fell out.

The League of Nations had no powers of its own and had to rely on its members to enforce its decisions. Only the USA ever looked like having both judicial credibility and power. When the Senate repudiated Wilson the key-stone was removed from the arch. No other nation had any intention of making war in any cause other than its own, and economic sanctions proved futile. The League was successfully defied by Japan in Manchuria and by Italy in Abyssinia. When the Spanish war (1936) came it had already sunk into futility. It must bear a measure of responsibility for the outbreak of Hitler's war, because it provided decadent democracies with an excuse for neglecting their military and diplomatic defences. The League's interference in colonial quarrels that affected no European interest had pushed Japan and Italy into Hitler's arms.

Italy adopted Fascism as a device to create a national spirit. She was manifestly disintegrating when Mussolini, a revolutionary socialist who had been intimate with many of the Russian leaders during their exile, conceived the idea of a party that would inspire Italy with ideas of ancient glory. The forms and insignia of the Roman Republic were aped. Empire was pursued. Libya, which Italy had collected from the dissolving Turk in 1912 was built up into a show province. Abyssinia was invaded and the League of Nations defied. It was all very splendid but it did not work. Dressing up as Imperial Romans did not make Italians like each other. The whole performance was essentially bogus. Italians might join in victory parades, but they felt no deep involvement. When real war came they were not on their government's side and had nothing to fight for. They were brave only when they had Germans to fight against.

Fascism in Germany was a horse of a very different colour. The Germans had fought with courage and stamina in the 1914–18 War. They did not feel that they had been beaten by better men, nor by a juster cause. They felt they had been beaten by American materials and cheated by American terms. They had been starved by a blockade which had been maintained for eight months after the armistice, in order to

deprive them of any alternative to immediate and unconditional acceptance of the diktat prepared by the Allies at
Versailles.

'Faites entrer les Allemands.' Clemenceau had spat the
words, and the Germans had been marched up the Hall of
Mirrors to sign.

The new Democratic government and the new Socialist
president were given no chance. There was no Marshall Aid.
Impossible reparations were demanded. U-boat commanders
who had fought the blockade were indicted as war criminals.
The Americans failed to ratify the peace and the French
marched into the Rhineland. Inflation wiped out all money
wealth. Then when the French had at last left the Rhineland
and the economy was beginning to work, came the Wall
Street crash, the great slump and for Germany six million
unemployed.

But the Germans had not lost faith in themselves. They
needed a leader and they found one.

Adolf Hitler was the child of the rage and grief of a mighty
empire and race which had suffered overwhelming defeat in war.
He it was who exorcised the spirit of despair from the German
mind by substituting for it the not less baleful but far less morbid
spirit of revenge. When the terrible German armies, which had
held half Europe in their grip, recoiled on every front and
sought armistice from nations upon whose land they even then
stood as invaders; when the pride and willpower of the Prussian
race broke into surrender and revolution behind the fighting
lines . . . then it was that one corporal, a former Austrian
housepainter, set out to regain all . . .

In the fifteen years that have followed this resolve he has
succeeded in restoring Germany to the most powerful position
in Europe, and not only has he restored the position of his
country, but he has even to a very great extent reversed the
results of the Great War.*

Our minds are so fixed on the squalid end of the Nazis,
that we forget their great beginnings.

Hitler's revolution was a masterpiece. Within the party he
created, department by department, an alternative govern-

---

* Winston S. Churchill, *Great Contemporaries* (1935).

ment; he gained authority with little bloodshed; he had the machinery to enforce his will within the bureaucracy and through the bureaucracy; he ate his children in a single night. Roehm and the roughnecks, good street fighters but a liability in government (together with a few personal enemies), were murdered on the Night of the Long Knives. The army was reassured and obliged, for Roehm's Brown Shirts had been the Party army, and the generals regarded them as a threat. In gratitude they accepted into the army the Fuehrer's personal bodyguard, the Himmler-led SS. On Hindenburg's death, Hitler became the Commander-in-Chief and received from the Prussian soldiers the military oath. It was not given unwillingly.

In the economic field Dr Schacht's monetary policy reassured and refinanced German industry. Money was created to activate a capacity that monetary deficiency had stopped. It was a novel and brilliantly successful device. Rearmament provided a market but not the only market; a vast road system, only partly strategic, was built; housing, construction, health service, consumer industry all leapt forward. Within three years a defeated, bankrupt, destitute nation had become the envy and terror of all Europe.

How was it done?

Like Marxism, Nazism was a religion. A faith was created. Faith is two-faced. Faith needs a god and a devil. It may be that the devil is the more important, for man is a hating animal. If he is to love his comrade he must hate his enemy. The foreigner was the devil of the Nazi myth and the handiest foreigner was the Jew. The goodies and baddies required differentiation. Race was the test. The racially pure German felt tremendous. Nothing seemed beyond his will. Nazism was a 'chosen people' theology. It catered for man's basic social needs, a sense of identity, a place within the pack, the stimulus of an enemy and the security of corporate strength: for it millions worked and died willingly.

What went wrong?

Hitler had a Napoleonic will but he lacked a Napoleonic intelligence. Unlike Napoleon he became intoxicated with his own nonsense. Faith is for followers. The leader needs to use his brains. The Germans are an idealistic people with a tendency to chase the ideal to its logical conclusion. Ideals must not be treated in this way. Ideals must never be pressed too hard for it is then that the burnings start. The Church in the Counter-Reformation, the Calvinists in Geneva, in Scotland and in Salem, the Communists in the purge, and the Nazis in the concentration camps all pressed their ideals too hard. Ideals are like stars, they guide from a distance and the wise man is careful where and on whom he puts his feet. Hitler lacked this wisdom of moderation. He was in too great a hurry. He believed that he needed a war to consolidate Germany's New Reich, a Reich that was to endure for 1,000 years. Bismarck had thought the same but he had been willing to wait for the right moment. Hitler wanted his war before he was fifty. I remember a drawing in *Punch* of a lady with a mop, and the caption 'I do wish this 'ere 'Itler would marry and settle down.' She may have had the answer. Dynasts tended to take a longer view than modern dictators.

Czechoslovakia was Hitler's Schleswig-Holstein. As Bismarck had done before him he regained an essentially German province. He had correctly assessed the decadence of the French people and of the British Government. He had been disappointed to succeed without war. Success went to his head. The war he wanted would be short and victorious, culminating in a triumphal march up the Wilhelmstrasse as he greeted his legions. Instead he bumped into a people's war, that ground the West to destruction.

Of the winners in 1918, America lost her momentum. She was geared to a growth large enough to absorb her uncontrolled capitalist expansion. She needed expanding markets and a growing labour force. Immigration was a condition of her full employment. There can be no choice of jobs unless there be new people to take the jobs that the natives do not choose. In 1924 America reduced immigration and increased tariffs. The consequences of this folly were delayed by a huge speculative boom. Six million automobiles became twenty-seven million; 27,000 fridges became 775,000; national income rose from $60 billion in 1918 to $89 billion in 1928.

Increased expenditure was not financed by earnings, for in this free enterprise gallop wages and farm earnings tended downwards, and organised labour lost power and membership. Spending was financed by credit based on ever-mounting stock values. Prices rose from an average of ten times earnings to fifty times earnings.

In October 1928 the turn came. It went on for three years. The Industrial Average price on the New York Stock Market sank from 350 to 58. US Steel and General Motors dropped from 262 and 73 respectively to 22 and 8, 3,500 banks failed, industrial production halved, wages halved. Shop girls in New York worked for $3 a week, unemployment hit thirteen million, America's slump crossed the Atlantic, Britain's Labour Government and German democracy were among the casualties.

It was all foreseeable. Marx had foreseen it. Maynard Keynes had been writing. *The Treatise on Money* and *The General Theory* had yet to come, but the warning had been given in a series of articles and pamphlets so beautifully written that they should have been compulsory reading even if they had been wrong. 5 per cent of Americans had 33 per cent of the national income, which was far more than they could spend. Income was therefore diverted from consumer demand to industrial development. This meant more goods and less purchasing power. It also led to ever more inflated stock prices. All was exacerbated by dishonesty. Banks had leapt in to the speculation with other people's money. So had the New York Stock Exchange. Private enterprise had been uncontrolled, order was falling apart, prohibition had handed the drink trade to bootleggers, crime was incorporated and private gangster armies fought bloody battles. America had not only been hit in her pocket. Her cherished American free enterprise faith had crashed.

Recovery may have been the most remarkable achievement in America's history. It came with Franklin Roosevelt. He had been Assistant Secretary to the Navy in 1917 and had run for Vice-President on the Wilson ticket in 1920 with the idea of encouraging conservative democrats. Crippled by poliomyelitis, he was a very brave man: his ambition was without limit, his industry was tireless and his charm great; his intelligence was receptive rather than creative; he was entirely pragmatic; he was not bothered by scruples, principles or respect for the truth; his disloyalty to those who served him was right royal. He was just the leader that America needed.

He went to war with the depression as he was later to go to war with the Germans. In his inaugural address he warned Congress that if necessary he would ask them for 'broad executive power to wage war against the emergency, as great as the power that would be given me if we were in fact invaded by a foreign foe'.

All thoughts of leaving capitalism to solve its own problems were abandoned. A huge public works programme was inaugurated and State leadership was introduced into industry at all levels. Roosevelt thought in terms of the powers Wilson had used in the First World War; the civil service grew to wartime proportions; the farmers were given fixed prices on controlled acreages; 250,000 young men were put to work on environment projects; the water power of the Tennessee Valley was harnessed and became a public yardstick by which could be measured the efficiency of private utility companies. He talked to the people and told them what he was doing. He was the first public figure to realise that on the radio one does not talk to x million but to two or three people sitting in a parlour. His fireside chats became part of the pre-television American way of life.

In 1934 he devalued the dollar, effectively ending the gold standard. His methods were characteristically devious. Cordell Hull, his Secretary of State, was negotiating at the London Economic Conference to re-establish confidence in the gold standard, sound money and low tariffs when Roosevelt torpedoed him with a message, conveyed by a Presidential adviser, in which he denounced 'the elderly fetishes of international bankers' and announced his intention to raise American prices by currency manipulation. In the words of Keynes, he was magnificently right.

America was moving back to work and prosperity and in 1936 Roosevelt was re-elected by a record majority. The New Deal had been effective but it had been a rushed job. New problems were emerging. In 1937 unemployment climbed back to the ten million mark and stuck there. Deficit spending proved to be only a palliative. New investment never reached a quarter of the 1924–1929 level. As in 1914, it needed war to stir the as yet unfathomed depths of America's economic capacity.

France did not recover the blood she had lost in her trenches. She was too experienced to believe in the League of Nations and too decadent to reject it. She sought security behind a Maginot Line which she lacked the will to complete. Weak and corrupt governments followed one another with bewildering speed. The faith that holds a nation together had gone, for Communism divided national loyalty. When Russia made her pact with Nazi Germany a fatal sufficiency of Frenchmen changed sides.

Britain did not fare as badly as France. For this she could thank her working class. They did not go Communist. They stuck to the Labour Party, a coalition of Trade Unionists, Nonconformists and Progressive Liberals, woolly, incoherent and sentimental, but deeply British.

The performance of her governing classes was deplorable. Lloyd George went to the country with a coalition coupon and proposals to hang the Kaiser and squeeze the Germans. Keynes described the new Commons as hard-faced men who looked as though they had done well out of the war. The best of the new generation had died in the trenches. The same deflationary policy that had followed the Napoleonic War was pursued. We returned to the gold standard largely from pride. Wages were forced down. A General Strike failed in 1926. The war children of the middle class, frequently growing up without fathers, felt something was wrong and became rebels without a cause. This is brilliantly described by Jessica Mitford in *Hons and Rebels*. Hooliganism was upper class and was dealt with sympathetically by class-orientated police. A minority Labour Government (1929–31) fell through sheer incompetence. One of its ex-cabinet ministers was heard to say afterwards, 'Nobody told us we could go off the gold standard'. A 'National' Government of almost equal incompetence followed. Ramsay Macdonald (Labour) stayed on as Prime Minister but by then he was a senile figurehead. Stanley Baldwin (Conservative) was the real leader. He was a decent, humane man who took no interest in foreign affairs. The rise of Nazi Germany almost literally passed his notice. Neville Chamberlain followed. Lloyd George, who had sacked him during the war, described him as a good Mayor of Birmingham in a lean year. Chamberlain's experience and his temperament were municipal; he tried to treat Hitler as a recalcitrant official at the Ministry whom patience would persuade.

The British people were more sensitive. It is unfashionable to talk about national characteristics, but it is still true that the reaction of nations, even of neighbours within a common culture, differ. The national ethos derives from national history and philosophy. Models differ. The British ideal was the gentleman, the German the masterman: when news came through of concentration camps, beatings up of elderly people, the star of David, insult and persecution in the street, the British people were shocked.

They were shocked too by Nazi arrogance. In England we like to see the underdog get up and win. The Germans like to see him dead. This is odd, because the English have enjoyed more than their share of upperdoggishness and the Germans less. The German Olympics of 1936 had a formidable effect. Nazi sympathies were confined to a very small group of very nasty people. The vast majority of the British felt that what was happening in Germany was devil's work. At a slightly more intellectual and perhaps imperial level the Spanish war was important. A legitimate democratic government was being invaded by militarists with coloured alien troops. This was a little simplistic. Democracy is an alien word in Spain. If the Government represented the majority it did so only so long as the minority fought them. Had they won the war their factions would almost certainly have fought each other, indeed even in wartime they were only too liable to do so; but the policy of non-intervention as Italian and German troops arrived seemed a humiliation. The hearts of the British people were with the British Battalion of the International Brigade. Emotion mounted. The rebel youth had found a cause. The Fascists must be stopped.

Towards de-colonisation

By the end of the Kaiser's war the British Empire had become by far the biggest the world had ever seen, but for all that it had passed its zenith.

Britain had long accepted that it was her duty to advance the natives to the point at which they would become capable of ruling themselves. It was an aspiration that was becoming more urgent. The Royal Navy had lost its overwhelming pre-eminence. The justification of empire was being questioned. Faith in the white man's divine mission was weakening. The USA, although she had herself become a colonial power, remembered the anti-colonial sentiments of her revolution. When the ex-enemy colonies were distributed amongst the victors, the recipients accepted a mandate to prepare them for self-government. This was of itself a recognition that there was something wrong about owning somebody else's country.

Britain's response to India's effort in the Kaiser's war had been inadequate. Smuts, the South African, had been made a field-marshal and had served in the War Cabinet. No Indian had been given comparable authority. As the war had gone on British prestige had suffered. We had ceased to be invincible demi-gods. We had fought for our lives with indifferent success. We had suffered defeats. A British army consisting mainly of Indian troops had surrendered at Kut. The younger members of the ICS had foolishly been permitted to join the forces, with the result that British administration was under-staffed and over-aged.

In 1917 Her Majesty's Government felt that something must be done. Edwin Montague, the Liberal Secretary of State for India pledged increasing association of Indians in every branch of administration and 'the development of self-governing institutions with a view to the progressive realisation of responsible government in India as an integral part of the Empire'. These intentions were imaginatively applied in what came to be known as the Mountford reforms, and seemed to be acceptable to the political classes.

But in 1915 there had arrived from South Africa a forty-nine-year-old lawyer who had earned a reputation as a leader of the Natal Indians. His name was Gandhi and Indian politics would never be the same again. He was a westerner, who had been called to the bar at the Inner Temple. He was an ugly, shy little man and he had gone to South Africa because he could not earn a living in India. There he had matched his meekness against the white man's boorishness. He had ignored racial legislation and defied arrest. He had filled the jails and got away with it. In the Boer War he had raised a Red Cross regiment for the British. On his return to India he displayed formidable talents as a labour and agrarian agitator. He was still strongly pro-British, and with his usual dedication threw himself into our recruiting campaign. He wrote at the time, 'Indians have a double duty to perform. If they are to preach a mission of peace they must first prove their ability in war . . . A nation that is unfit to fight cannot from experience prove the virtue of not fighting.' (A letter to Esther Faering.) It was not a success. The people loved Gandhi but they did not like his new role. He was unhappy. He lost some of his love for Britain and determined to fight Western rule, but to do so with Western ethics applied in an entirely Indian way.

His opportunity came when the British introduced some Special Powers legislation designed primarily to deal with disturbances resulting from Moslem disapproval of the Allied dissolution of the Turkish Caliphate. Gandhi denounced the new powers as an infringement of the natural rights of man. This could hardly have been a more Western concept, but Gandhi sought to enforce it by organising religious strikes called *hartals* in the major cities. Token General Strikes, however non violent in principle, were apt to lead to rioting and these were no exception.

In Amritsar General Dyer lost his head and fired into a *hartaling* crowd. He was sacked. In England the House of Lords, with artless insensitivity, passed a resolution congratulating Dyer. Gandhi proclaimed that 'cooperation in any shape or form with this Satanic government is sinful', and in Congress he carried a motion to this effect. Satan, incidentally, is a purely Western conception. The motion came at an inconvenient moment. For a hundred years Westernised Indians had fought to join the Raj and now, with the implementation of the Mountford reforms, they were getting their chance. Congressmen were being elected to the new Central and Provincial legislatives and Indians were being accepted into the ICS and receiving King's Commissions in the Army. There were few resignations but the new Indians who had accepted responsibility in government lost their link with the Congress, which became opposition minded.

Gandhi went to jail. There was some civil disobedience and some riots, but things gradually came off the boil and the shared responsibility of the Mountford dispensation worked rather well. The Westernised Indians who were to provide free India with a civil service and an officer corps got their training. The Congress acted as an opposition demanding *Sawaraj* (total independence), and Gandhi forged his links with the people.

He had seen the poor of India and had determined to join them. He discarded his European clothes and adopted not the saffron of a teacher, but the white cotton *dhoti* of the peasant. He challenged Hindu ethics as a Hindu. He disavowed caste and lived with Untouchables, whom he named *Harijas* or sons of God. He ended the sufferings of a sacred cow. He rejected violence. He seems to have got the idea from the Quakers, for non-violence has no place in the Hindu ethic. He saw that power rested on violence and he rejected power. He idealised a peasant society of loosely federated village republics. He led from the background with sinuous dexterity. He held together the disparate interests and hostile religions (the Moslems were then in Congress). He became the indispensable link between the Westernised Indians, who had little sympathy with Gandhian primitiveness, and the peasants, who had little sympathy with Western progress. He put the British in the wrong, for he challenged them on the basis of their own ethic. He developed the non-violent resistance that provoked violence. He was awkward and unreasonable. He was the Charlie Chaplin figure matched against the establishment, and the Raj felt foolish and lost confidence. When he was crossed he started to starve unto death and nobody, friend or foe, dared take the responsibility of letting the Mahatma die.

When, in 1928, Lord Irwin invited the Congress to attend a round table conference on Dominion status, Gandhi decided to resist the salt tax. He set out to walk sixty miles to the sea, wearing his cotton *dhoti* and spectacles, there illegally to distil salt. When he arrived he had 2 million companions and the round table talks became impossible. He had to be jailed. He was released and had private conversations with Lord Irwin. The talks were on again.

What was Gandhi's real influence on modern India? His idea of non violent peasant republics was never a starter; during the Mountford period of joint rule his antics diverted the Congress from a real showdown and enabled a generation of Indians to get their training in government and administration; he enabled the Indian peasants to identify themselves with him and, for the first time in Indian history, to feel themselves involved in Indian government; he prevented the young left wing leadership of Congress from breaking away and becoming a revolutionary Marxist party, and he did so by becoming their leader; of the two leading young radicals Nehru and Bose he chose Nehru to be his successor. It was an odd choice. Nehru was an enlightened English gentleman, a progressive Socialist public school boy educated at Harrow (where he shared a room with my brother-in-law) and Cambridge, a Secularist who sought a lay society, a Brahman who had rejected Hinduism. But Gandhi recognised his quality and he recognised Gandhi's. He became in turn Gandhi's disciple, his son and his lieutenant. He wore the Gandhi peasant cap, but unlike the Mahatma he never quite looked the part.

The Government of India Act 1935, was designed to grant independence to a conservative India. The structure was to be federal. I do not think it could ever have worked. India needs strong government, but the Act gave India a sense of moving forward. When Hitler's war came the majority of Indians were firmly on Britain's side.

By 1918 Egypt had the beginnings of a capacity for self-rule. The infrastructure of a state was in being and was Egyptian. The peasants had at least begun to feel that they were Egyptians and that to be Egyptian was not wholly contemptible. They had had some sense of participation in victory over the hated Turk. There were germs of the pride so necessary to nationalism.

Britain, always sensitive to imperial communications retained control over defence and external relations but the Khedive became a king and Egypt enjoyed full autonomy.

She was not fortunate in her leaders. The king was very poor quality and the nationalists were corrupt, but on balance (and with considerable assistance from Britain) consumption did keep ahead of population and the Fellaheen, though still among the poorest of mankind, felt better off. In 1936 the Protectorate was brought to an end, Egypt became a member of the League of Nations and a treaty was made under which Britain undertook to defend Egypt and, in the event of war, was granted the right to use Egyptian territory.

Britain tried to make states out of the provinces which she had inherited from the Turkish Empire. In this she was not successful. One cannot make states for people. The process of social evolution cannot be skipped. States have to evolve. Monarchy was tried. Hashemite princes were given kingdoms in Syria and Iraq which they had neither ruled nor conquered. Their authority lacked a base. There was no external pressure sufficient to make them acceptable. The only people with experience of government were discredited Turkish nobles. Party politics became a game for small intellectual groups capable of laying on a riot in the capital. There was no officer class and no civil service. Armies, useless against a foreign foe, operated as political parties. When after the Hitler war, these states became fully independent, their only national faith was hatred of Israel. Oil riches have done little beyond enriching the very rich. They have lacked the coherence of nationhood. Only the Palestine Mandate sired a real nation, and that unintentionally. Israel was born in the fiercest struggle and bonded by her faith.

Metropolitan Turkey has been far more interesting. Kemal Pasha defied the victorious Allies, who were busy arranging for the partition of Anatolia. The Greeks received a bloody nose. The troops of the Allies were no longer usable. Kemal set up a new lay state. He determined with savage ruthlessness to impose democracy on a people whose social evolution had been conditioned by theocratic despotism. Kemal, who took the title Ataturk, father of the Turks, was an Albanian. Fathers of new nations have generally been foreigners. One cannot describe Turkey as a very successful democracy, but her social experiment has been sincere and unique. It is probably still too early to say whether she has acquired a new form of nationhood strong enough to hold her people together, or whether she will revert to some form of autocracy.

Australia, New Zealand, Canada and South Africa became formally independent under a common Crown. Rhodesia too became effectively independent, save that at her request we handled her foreign affairs, but all were as British as the home country and without hesitation declared war when we did. The rest of the empire in Africa and in the Pacific seemed a long way from independence.

In the bad period between the wars, when France lost her self-respect, our empire did much to sustain our own. It still carried the smell of success and power. We felt we could beat the Germans. The French did not.

17

THE SECOND PEOPLE'S WAR

THERE WERE NO CHEERS for the second people's war. France after abandoning her ally Czechoslovakia, fought lest she be left to face Hitler all alone. She encouraged herself with the slogan 'We are the strongest', followed by statistics. It was not very inspiring. She attempted nothing while the German army was in Poland. She hoped to sit in the Maginot Line until it was all over.

To the ordinary Englishman war came as a relief. A year before Chamberlain had returned from Munich waving a bit of paper, and talking of peace with honour. The ordinary Englishman had cheered. Then through radio and press he had participated in the martyrdom of the Czechs and had felt shame. Hitler was clearly a cheat. The English knew that there had been no honour and had accepted that there could be no peace. Now the decision was taken and the worry was past. There was no rush to recruiting booths, just a mounting resolve. It was going to be a long war.

Poland, invaded from east and west was partitioned in a matter of weeks. There followed the phoney war, the invasion of Norway and Winston Churchill. Hitler had rightly rated the decadence of the British Government, but he had under-rated the stubborn will of the British Empire. When the English people forced Chamberlain into war Hitler was sur-prised and hurt, for he was Anglophile. To him the English were not foreigners, they were the sea Aryans and the Germans the land Aryans. World order required an Anglo-German alliance. All this he had set out in *Mein Kampf* in 1923 and he never departed from the *Mein Kampf* programme. Having agreed with the Russians on a partition of Poland he did not believe that Britain and France would interfere. After his Polish victory he proposed peace, but by then people's war had acquired its unstoppable momentum. After the passing of the Maginot Line he tried again. The British Army was in full retreat to Dunkirk and the German spearhead, sweeping round our flank was in a position to cut off our line of retreat. A direct Fuehrer order to General von Kleist, the German Panzer commander, commanded the withdrawal of this spearhead, and the British army was permitted to make its escape. Later Hitler visited Von Rundstedt's headquarters. Field-Marshal Manstein, whom I defended at his war crimes trial, told me the story. When von Rundstedt had grumbled at the order that enabled the British to get away Hitler had replied, 'I propose to make peace with the British. I do not wish to impose on them the humiliation of a lost army. I have no wish to destroy the British Empire and see America pick up the bits.' Operation Sea Lion, the invasion of Britain which Manstein was to have commanded, was not prosecuted with the usual Fuehrer drive and was cancelled at the first opportunity.

Churchill's authority was strengthened rather than weakened as disaster followed disaster. The English people had abandoned reason and surrendered to faith. Winston was their prophet. I can remember what it felt like to be a man of faith. I was then in Hayling Island, training our first landing-craft flotilla. I can remember joining the cheer that greeted the news of France's surrender. Now that we had got rid of them nothing would stop us licking the Krauts. I remember telling my sailors how next year we would have the honour to land our blitzkreig, and believing it. I was responsible for the defence of the island. I had 380 ratings, 260 South African War Ross Rifles with eleven rounds of ammunition per rifle, and two water-cooled Zulu War belt-fed machine-guns. We made our own bombs with bottles, petrol and phosphorus and we were confident that they would be most effective against tanks. Looking back I feel like a discharged patient recalling his delusions, but at the time they were real and a part of the grand delusion of the British people that became reality. Winston rightly described this bout of communal insanity as our finest hour. It was only after we had experienced in Crete the power of airborne invasion that we realised how lucky we had been. Hitler's determination to achieve the *Mein Kampf* programme—Aryan dominion of the West with the Ukraine as a German colony and Aryan dominion of the sea through the British Empire—proved his undoing. The English people had taken the bit in their teeth and nothing would stop them. They were now far too dangerous to leave unconquered.

On the whole Britain enjoyed her war. The humiliations of unemployment were over. Every one was wanted. Class barriers seemed to drop. People were extraordinarily nice to each other. Everywhere, on the farm, on the road, in the wrecked cities, people welcomed the chance to help other people. Air attack sometimes became a strain but on balance people enjoyed the blitz. There was a great sense of community. It was good to feel that the boys in the forces were not having all the glory. Many people found that love-making during an air raid had a special quality. There were new opportunities. Those who had failed in one line were offered a second chance. Rationing made one appreciate one's food, but no one starved. Casualty lists never approached those of the First World War.

The RAF and the Royal Navy equalled and probably surpassed the achievements of their ancestors. The army was not quite so good. For 300 years the British infantry had known no equal. This was no longer so. They needed the dice, in the form of air power, heavily weighted in their favour to fight the Germans or the Japanese on equal terms. This may have been because the RAF and the Navy tended to be the first of choice, but I think that one must admit that the gentling effect of improved living resulted in a softer soldier.

In the summer of 1940 after the fall of France, the RAF successfullly denied the Luftwaffe total air superiority over the invasion area. In the winter O'Connor won sensational victories over the Italians in Libya and Cunningham liberated Abyssinia. The Italians had entered the war as jackals and had found the victim not only alive but kicking.

In the spring of 1941, Hitler turned east and attacked Greece, Yugoslavia and on 22 June, Russia. Stalin had concentrated his best troops on the threatened frontier and they suffered an unexampled disaster. The Germans swept on to Moscow, but the Balkans had delayed their campaign, and like Napoleon Hitler arrived too late in the year. General Frost took control. In the south the Ukrainians, Tartars and Cossacks had welcomed the Germans, but in the north the will of the Communist Empire held and the people fought the Germans with grim resolve. Nobody enjoyed this war. Russian losses were enormous, but their numbers seemed to be without limit.

From 1935, as the war clouds gathered over Europe, the American people's determination to keep out was matched by the President's secret determination to get in. A number of neutrality acts forbidding the supply of arms to belligerents were passed. Roosevelt assented rather than show his hand. When war started he persuaded Congress to exempt arms paid for in cash and carried by the buyer. In 1940 he was re-elected for a third term on a 'Keep America Out' ticket. Then he let us have fifty over-age American destroyers in exchange for bases on British territory. These three-funnel contraptions were not of much value but Churchill accepted them gladly as a symbol of American involvement. In May 1941 came lend-lease, which successfully side-stepped all neutrality legislation. American volunteers were arriving in Britain. Meanwhile the President was putting the squeeze on Japan by denying her vital imports. At Pearl Harbour the Japanese struck. The blow was harder than expected but to the President not unwelcome. Then Germany declared war on America. That Hitler should have thought that Japan as an ally was worth America as an enemy is a measure of his ignorance of abroad. Roosevelt and Churchill had arranged to give the defeat of Germany priority over the defeat of Japan in early 1940. The fate of Hitler was sealed.

Roosevelt was a secret man without confidants. We shall probably never know quite why he willed America to war. Hitler's motivation was relatively simple. War was a part of his vision of his own and Germany's glory. Roosevelt operated within a different ethic and his mind was more subtle. We shall never know the part that was played in his resolve by a recognition that America needed a war, and a feeling that she must have the experience, practical and emotional, of participation when events and her power thrust upon her the leadership of the post-war world.

In the autumn of 1941 the Japanese attacked Britain's Asian empire and demonstrated that British troops could be beaten, something which Asia had not previously believed.

In Europe we bombed Germany and our Navy fought the U-boats while America out-built their sinkings. The Germans accepted our bombs as heroically as we had accepted theirs, but they had far more to accept. A policy of de-housing the German working class was pursued. The damage was spectacular but the effect on the German war effort was small. Blockade mattered much more. Germany was getting short of fuel and of some vital metals, and this became the more acute as she was steadily being driven out of Russia and denied the use of Russian resources.

By the summer of 1944 Germany's position had become hopeless. She had had enough of the Nazis and of their war. Field-Marshal Rommel, Commander-in-Chief of the German armies defending France from invasion, was willing to turn his armies against Hitler. So were most of his fellow generals in the west. All that was needed was an allied indication that a reasonable peace would be available to a German government that toppled Hitler and an intimation that our forces would consider informal co-operation with German commands that rebelled. Any terms would have been acceptable that did not include admitting the Russian hordes into Germany.

No terms were offered. Churchill and Roosevelt had committed themselves at Casablanca in the autumn of 1943 to 'unconditional surrender'. There would be no negotiation. So war ground on for another year and in that year far more people died than in all the rest of the war, and central Europe was taken by armies at least as cruel, and submitted to a regime at least as brutal, as that of the Germans.

Years afterwards, during Attlee's government, when I was a Member of Parliament, I was the first to state the necessity of German re-armament. In doing so I turned on Winston

Churchill and said, 'This is a grim choice. That we are faced with it is your fault for it is the consequence of unconditional surrender. The belly of Europe cannot be left empty.' Immediately afterwards he came up to me in the lobby. I think I remember his words exactly. 'What you said—it was not only me—Roosevelt produced it one night—it meant something in American history. I telegraphed the cabinet. They agreed—your Attlee—your Bevin agreed—it was not only me.' Winston was a great man and in his heart he knew the folly, but he was right in saying 'it was not only me'. It was a people's folly.

The Americans were as reluctant to get out of the war as they had been to get in. They regarded war as a crusade—General Eisenhower was to call his book *Crusade in Europe*. The enemy were criminals and had to be treated as such. You do not deal with criminals. They have to surrender. The British attitude was a little different. We had a Russian fixation. It was partly because we had felt a huge and, to some extent, guilt-laden sympathy with Russia as she took the full weight of the German blow, while we, as it seemed, were impotent spectators; and partly because we suspected our government of treating these heroes as class enemies. The British people were deeply suspicious of any reluctance to comply with Russian requests, however unreasonable. The consequence was that we were condemned to go on fighting for another year to achieve that which we had fought many wars to prevent, the domination of Europe by a single power.

When the time came for unconditional surrender the Russian armies occupied all middle Europe and half Germany. My brother had been a prisoner of the Luftwaffe in Poland and was released by the advancing Russians. He made his way back with a stolen lorry and a letter from Harrod's with a splendid heading which, when produced with a flourish, served as a passport, for the Russians never confessed that they could not read. He witnessed the full horror of the Mongol advance, the looting, the rape, the feckless, frivolous killing. He told me of an old German refugee, sitting on the pavement with his legs across the curb, nodding in exhausted sleep, and of a Russian tank driver who had swerved to cut off the old man's legs and how the Russians had laughed to see such fun. He returned just before the Blackpool Conference and in perhaps the most unpopular speech ever delivered at a Labour Party Conference I warned that identification with the Russians might involve a backlash. Afterwards Ernest Bevin said to me, 'You are a foolish young man. You will have to learn when the truth is untimely'.

Japan was now out on a limb and the atom bomb was ready. Ironically the principal contributors had been German Jews expelled by Hitler. The first bomb was dropped on Hiroshima and killed over 100,000 people. I thought then and I think now that if there be such a concept as an international crime, this was it. If a demonstration of power to save life was the purpose, why not pick a mountain or a forest? Why pick a crowded city? The second bomb on Nagasaki was a different matter. Its purpose was purely scientific. The Americans wanted to see whether a plutonium bomb worked as well as a fission bomb. The real trouble was the American philosophy of war. The enemy are criminals and outlaws. They have no rights. The results of these American crimes would appear (victims apart) to have been almost wholly beneficial and to have resulted in admirable American-Japanese relations.

The war was over.

Germany and Japan had gone to war joyously, had fought brilliantly, had endured greatly and been defeated utterly. Their men had been decimated, their homelands had been wrecked and their faith shattered. In victory they had shown little mercy and they expected little mercy.

Italy had once again been a field for other people's wars and Spain had again enjoyed a neutrality that she had been too backward to exploit.

France was humiliated. There is a Chinese proverb: 'If rape is inevitable lie back and enjoy it.' France had lain back but she had not enjoyed it. She had collaborated. The vast majority of Frenchmen had backed Pétain and Vichy. They had felt the shame but they had offered no resistance. Very, very few escaped to join de Gaulle. Some helped our airmen but again they were very few. *La Resistance* of subsequent fame started when the Germans began to demand the conscription of French labour for German war industry. Unwilling conscripts took to the *maquis* but they only started to fight on any scale when the Germans were clearly beaten. Throughout most of the war German troops had been free to use French hotels, shops and restaurants and had needed no special protection. Nations that have been knocked down get up. It is more difficult for nations that have lain down. It is a question of self-respect. Frances post-war record has been one of aggressive self-assertion that has failed to carry conviction.

Britain had spent the whole of her foreign investments and was heavily in debt. She was faced with the demobilisation of some 5 million men, and the conversion of a near-total war economy to peace. She had won, but it did not feel like victory. There was none of the wild jubilation that greeted the Armistice in 1918. The Americans, overpaid, over-sexed and over here as it was said, behaved extremely well but they felt a bit like a victorious army of occupation.

Russia had suffered hugely. Her western armies had been destroyed. Half her country had been wrecked. Her casualties, military and civilian, could not be counted but probably exceeded a score of millions. Her Asiatic levies had met the Allies across Central Europe. She was united as never before. The Germans had taught her dissident minorities to be Russian. Stalin was her autocrat and Czar. Of the victors he alone had armies he could still use.

America alone had had a lovely war. Her troops had seen the world and tasted its wine and its women. There had been some very rough spots but for most of them the risk had not been substantially greater than that which sportsmen accept for their favourite thrill. Her war casualties had rarely exceeded those occasioned by her motor cars. Indeed even in war the greatest risk run by American troops generally came from their drivers. They postered their roads 'Careful! Death is so final'. It frequently was. America had suffered no war damage. Her slump economy had been put to rights. Her industrial and agricultural wealth had expanded. She enjoyed 40 per cent of the world's income, and was five times richer than her nearest rival. She had one-sixteenth of the world's population, one third of the world's wealth and half of the world's manufactured goods. She had atomic monopoly. She seemed all powerful. Never in the history of the world had a single nation possessed comparable power.

18

THE END OF EMPIRE

EMPIRE WAS FOUNDED by will. During the war Britain lost that will. It was not because we were exhausted or impoverished. We recovered with remarkable rapidity. Within two years our wealth, our productivity and our trade were greater than they had ever been. So was the technological gap that separated us from those we governed. It was simply because we had lost the will to govern. We had lost our faith that God was an Englishman. We doubted the morality of our authority. We left our task half done.

The Congress had muffed its chance to unite India. The Viceroy had declared war without consulting the Congress provincial governments. It was a tactless action, but the resignation of the Congress governments that followed, was ill-judged for it had little effect on India's war effort and served only to weaken Congress's authority to speak for India.

The Indian Army expanded from 175,000 to 2,000,000 men, fought well and gave very little trouble. It was supported and maintained by Indian industrial expansion. The Moslem League, led by Jinnah, denied Congress' claim to represent all India and co-operated in the war effort. In 1942 after the entry of the USA and Japan, Stafford Cripps came with a renewed offer of dominion status and immediate seats on the Viceroy's Council for the Congress leaders. Gandhi held back, hoping for an immediate control that would enable him to dispose of the Moslem League. He missed his opportunity, for

Britain's need receded and the lodging of the Congress leaders in jail caused little trouble. Bose went to raise an Indian legion on the Japanese side which proved more embarrassing to the Congress than to ourselves.

Attlee's government was even more determined to get rid of India than India was to get rid of Britain. Indian nationalism had been born but it was not yet as strong as religion or probably as caste. The Moslems were determined not to be ruled by Hindus, and the Untouchables or scheduled classes were very doubtful as to whether they wanted to be either. More time was needed but the British were resolved to go. They gave a deadline. Communal fighting broke out.

The religions divided and their frontiers were settled by force. Hundreds of thousands died and about 7 million people became refugees. In Delhi the Moslem minority awaited a pogrom. At this point Gandhi, whose intransigence had been a major cause of the trouble, came to Delhi. He came with total courage to defend the Moslems. Alone he quelled the riots. Then he demanded that the agreed assets of central government be handed over to Pakistan and that the mosques be evacuated and he went on hunger strike till this was done. It was his finest hour. Twelve days later he was murdered by a Hindu fanatic. Both sides were too shocked for further hostilities.

Pakistan was divided into two parts, separated by about 1,000 miles of Indian territory. The west had the smaller but by far the more virile population. It descended from invaders. The east, with the majority, came from low or no caste Hindus who had adopted the conqueror's religion. The minority ruled the majority until the break came. Bangladesh is too young to judge, but she seems to have slipped back into the old Indian tradition, a weak and corrupt centre ignored as far as possible by village communities. India and West Pakistan, on the other hand are (or have been until recently) ruled by the Westerners in the English tradition, and in accordance with the Western ethic. This has been England's legacy to India.

Lord Cornwallis in the eighteenth century said 'All natives are corrupt', and by Western standards this was true. A powerful man was expected to enrich his family. Akbar's attempt to create an honest civil service was short lived. Salaries were seldom paid. Men were left to make what they could out of their jobs.

India today has a civil service and a judiciary that accepts British standards of integrity. Of course she has her backsliders, but then so do we. She is not numbered amongst the countries in which the saleman's first enquiry is 'Who do I bribe here and how much?' Standards are not very different from those we meet at home and a lot better than those we meet in America. The armies of both India and Pakistan have been brought up in the Sandhurst tradition and an Indian mess is very much an English mess, perhaps rather more so. The Pakistani army's entry into politics was reluctant and government under a military President was mainly civilian. There was a reversion to civilian rule but this, unhappily has proved short lived.

India has been ruled by the Congress, the party of the Westernised middle class, and has adopted a Social Democratic ethic. With a 75 per cent illiterate franchise democracy has had its limitations but India has moved from a caste to a class society. Nehru ruled the Congress. His iron hand had little occasion to emerge from his velvet glove. His aspirations were sensible and his authority generally acceptable. After a short interval he was succeeded by his daughter, Mrs Gandhi, and times became more difficult.

The achievements of the Nehrus were remarkable. Indian women, in defiance of Hindu custom and religion, were granted the right to inherit property and receive alimony. India's greatest ill, fecundity, was tackled and the birth rate reduced. English was retained as the effective language. Foreign-owned businesses were Indianised on terms that were not so onerous as to inhibit foreign investment. International aid was sought and obtained. The rise in India's product began to outstrip the increase in her population. Her gross national income went up by over half and her income per head by nearly a quarter. Uniquely amongst developing countries, the gap between rich and poor, although still enormous, started to contract. Wonderful above all, India began to exist.

Throughout history India alone amongst advanced cultures had failed to achieve a coherent society. She had failed to resist her conquerors in the field, but had always succeeded in evading their endeavours to involve her in their empires or to imbue her with a common will. The Congress ruling class was small but it was spread over India and her people had begun to react and to feel as Indians.

Congress has fallen as a result of social reform, particularly sterilisation, being pushed too hard and has been replaced by a senile rag-bag of discordant interests. It is not a government that can last long. India, if she is to go on existing, must have strong centralised government. Either Congress will come back or the military will govern. For India democracy is a wrong priority. India needs the stability of a dynasty.

Hitler's war brought much material benefit to Egypt. Great armies spent money and provided employment. But it also brought humiliation. We did not treat Egypt as a partner. She had a new young king who was personally popular. Later he was to prove a worthless debauchee, but that side of his character was not then revealed. We bullied him. We ordered him to dismiss and appoint ministers and our ambassador arrived at the palace in a tank to see he did it. In 1918 Egypt had shared in victory. In 1945 she had no such sense of participation. British insensitivity was to blame. Egypt sought to salve her pride by adopting Arab racialism. In 1948 she received a drubbing from the underground army Israel had created. For this she blamed Britain. The British Army in the Canal Zone was an irritant. India had parted with the Raj on terms of real affection, but in Egypt we were becoming the enemy. In 1952 a Colonel Nasser organised a junior officers' rebellion and a parliamentary government which, for all its corruption, had acquired considerable experience, was replaced by a military dictatorship manned by brash young officers who launched their country on a policy of Arabist aggression which she could not afford. Nasser involved Egypt in three wars, two in Sinai and one in the Yemen. In all three he was badly beaten. He suffered even greater humiliation in his attempts to take the Sudan. He turned his back on the West and found himself in pawn to the Russians. The Fellaheen got poorer. In 1970 he died to be replaced by an unknown politician named Sadat. Egypt had at last found her great man.

In seven years he has got rid of the Russians (in itself no mean achievement), rebuilt his bridges with the West, won a victory at Suez, regained and reopened the canal and recovered the oil wells of Sinai. The victory was perhaps only half a victory and he would have been in real trouble if America had not imposed a cease-fire, but Egypt's last success had been in about 1,000 BC and national morale needed the smell of victory. In the economic field in spite of world recession he has got growth going again. Under Sadat Egypt has acquired a sense of coherence and responsibility that ranks her as a nation. This would not have been possible without the infrastructure provided by colonialism. It is just this infrastructure that Syria, Iraq and Jordan have lacked.

In India and in Egypt the foundations of a new society had been laid. In Indo-China, Burma and Malaya there is the remains of an ancient civilisation. In Africa there were no real foundations and no indigenous civilisation on which to build.

Britain tried to prepare a succession but the constitutions she devised broke down. France under de Gaulle left hurriedly but tried to retain influence through economic patronage. Belgium, after her fashion, simply bolted.

Portugal was the last to go. I regretted it. Of all the colonial powers I think she understood Africa best. She had been a coastal power since the age of the navigators. Negro kings collected gold and slaves and passed them to the Portuguese through Arab middlemen. Only in this century did she start to govern the interior. I think she avoided Africa's three cardinal errors, Racialism, Democracy and Efficiency.

There was no racialism in Portuguese Africa. Both in the army and in the civil service white men often served under blacks. The Portuguese conscript was accusomed to a standard of living not substantially superior to that of the African. Democracy is a device whereby strong government can alternate between parties. Subtract the alternative and democracy becomes party tyranny. Africans subtract the alternative. African governments do not lose elections. Efficiency is something Africa hates. The African Inferno would not be staffed by devils but by time-and-motion men. The job that took one man in the Union of South Africa and one and a half in Rhodesia took five in Mozambique, but the five were much happier. Frelimo came from outside and from tribes divided by artificial boundaries.

I felt that given the chance, the Portuguese might have evolved a genuine multi-racial society that might have upgraded the African to the point at which he might have managed civilisation but it was not to be. The strain was more than the Portuguese economy could bear, and her colonies have reverted to barbarism.

Portugal was not the only power that lost money in Africa, but she was the one that could least afford to. The Marxist theory that imperialists lived by exploiting colonial peoples is untrue. King Leopold apart, no African colonial power ran a favourable balance with its colonies. Empire in Africa was heavily subsidised by the imperialists and the infrastructure of African civilisation was provided by the colonial powers for little return.

The dissolution of colonialism came too soon for the good of Africa, but it has come. The spirit of the age has blown it away. What is the result? The nationalists have sought to step into the shoes of the colonialists. Their leaders were mission boys whose intelligence had taken them to foreign universities. Almost without exception they had become aliens within their tribes. They have adopted the colonial language as the official language of their new countries, for no native tongue could express their ideas. In so far as they were able, they adopted the governmental methods of the colonial power, both at the parliamentary and at the administrative level. The new rulers are as alien as their predecessors, but they lack their competence and in general their integrity. Of the Independence constitutions little survives. Some of the new states have become one-party regimes seeking to perpetuate the power of a new class but the majority have become military dictatorships since this has been the surviving power instrument.

I think we would be hard put to it to describe any of the new African nations as successful.

The senior is Liberia. It was the fruit of American philanthropy, a settlement in their homeland for freed slaves. It did not take long for the freed slaves to become slavers, and they maintained slavery long after colonial Africa had abolished it. The *Report* of the International Commission of Enquiry into the Existence of Slavery in the Republic of Liberia 1931, makes grim reading. The President, the Vice-President and almost the whole government were involved. Liberian natives were being conscripted and sold to Spanish cocoa planters in Fernando Po for £16 a head, plus a bonus for groups of over 1,500 boys. A system of pawning existed whereby debtors pawned children or other relations into slavery pending the repayment of a debt. Masters were free to flog their slaves. Later the Firestone Company came to Liberia, receiving great tracts of territory from the government at 6 cents an acre. Charter companies of this sort are hardly within the spirit of our present age but Firestone proved a blessing to Liberia; so did the war and the arrival of an American base; but for all this Liberia is still probably the poorest of all the poor countries in Africa, and the one in which the class division between the black colonialists and the native population is widest. At the other end of the scale Kenya has probably done the best. The Kikuyu have in effect stepped into the British shoes as an imperial race in much the same way as the Persians stepped into the shoes of the Medes in ancient Babylon. The empire has continued much as before under new masters. Kenyatta like Cyrus has proved himself a man of wisdom, magnanimity and tolerance. Kenya faces the oldest imperial problem—succession. Will the subject tribes go on submitting to Kikuyu rule when the old man has gone? The greed and corruption of the Kikuyu rulers has not made them popular.

A generous desire to place the best interpretation on all black governments has confused political definition. I will therefore define my terms. Democracy is a system whereby an elected government rules and an opposition is free to criticise, to organise and to replace government peacefully in free elections. Fascism is a system whereby a dictator rules and no opposition is permitted to criticise, to organise or too contest elections.

Of the thirty-four Bantu and Sudanic states twenty-eight are fascist and six roughly democratic. These latter are rather

THE END OF EMPIRE

special cases. In Botswana, Gambia and Mauritania the forms continue since they do not impede the rule of Sir Seretse Khama, Sir Dawda Jawara and Mokkah Daddah. In Lesotho Leabua Jonathan will probably have dispensed with the opposition before this book is printed, in Senegal President Senghor permits opposition and promises elections. In Sierra Leone Dr Siaka Stevens, after three military coups, conducts a parliamentary system under military supervision. No black government has ever lost an election, although Dr Milton Margai looked like doing so in 1967. He had to be restored by the army. Further military coups installed Dr Stevens. The twenty-eight fascist states may be divided into civil and military. In the civilian states a dictator rules through a party of which he is the leader. In Kenya and Tanzania Presidents Kenyatta and Nyerere permit fairly free elections within their parties so that members of their parliament and indeed ministers have to retain a measure of personal popularity in their constituencies; in Zambia some forms of election are allowed within the ruling party but the success of unofficial candidates is rare; in Cameroon, Chad, Malawi, Swaziland, Gabon, Ivory Coast, the Guineas and Liberia personal dictatorship is not limited by any form of internal party democracy. The military dictatorships Burundi, Central African Republic, both Congos, Dahomey, Ghana, Madagascar, Mali, Niger, Nigeria, Rwanda, Somalia, Togo, Uganda, and Upper Volta vary in their sophistication. General Idi Amin rules Uganda in the Chaka tradition.

In the economy only Nigeria (oil) is solvent; neither aid nor science's green revolution have prevented agricultural production per head from declining; public expenditure on government and administrative salaries is outstripping rises in production, and the gap between the governing elite and the people is widening.

The tendencies that have been present in all the black states of which we have knowledge are present now. Governments become more autocratic and less careful of human life, the court moves further from the subject and the town from the countryside.

Why has the history of the negroids been so different to that of the caucasoids and mongoloids? I cannot escape the obvious but unfashionable answer. It is because they are different. It would be surprising if this were not so. They have evolved more recently, in different conditions within which different survival factors operated. In the course of their evolution, physical and social, they have developed qualities and aptitudes that fitted them for their tribal life as subsistence farmers. The qualities and aptitudes needed by Western technological society are different.

A friend of mine who is a great lover of Africa and the Africans and who was principal of Ghana University, has told me that he is opposed to the whole concept of a multi-racial society, because such a society can only result in the African being the hewer of wood and the drawer of water for the other races. His experienced opinion is that the African can never survive in anything like equal competition with Europeans, Asians or Chinese because he lacks the intellectual equipment to do so. He believes that an African society can only protect itself by excluding the foreigner.

I have discussed the problem of black and white pupils with many teachers both in Europe and Africa. None have told me that the black pupils are on average competitive with the white, although all have spoken of some very bright black children. I have attended schools in Africa. The children are attentive and long to learn. They are convinced that education is the key to the white man's magic and from this magic flow all the good things of life; but for all their keenness, on average they find the work arduous. Many of my teacher friends, while acknowledging the difference, ascribe it to environment and in Africa to diet. These may well be contributory factors—but I do not believe that one can eliminate a hereditary factor. There has been a great deal of research into negro intelligence and learning capacity, mostly in America. This is not a book in which to discuss this problem in detail, but the evidence in favour of the proposition that races differ is overwhelming. Immanuel Kant wrote 200 years ago :

Hume asserts that among the hundreds of thousands of blacks who have been seduced away from their own countries although many of them have been set free, yet not a single one has ever been found that has performed anything great either in art or science; but among the whites people constantly rise up from their superior gifts. The difference between these two races of man is thus a substantial one: it appears to be just as great in respect of the faculties of mind as in colour.

What are the names with which today we would refute the philosophers? Who are the negroes who have performed 'anything great in art or science'?

In literature Hanson Baldwin, Leopold Senghor, Chinua Achebe in Nigeria. Readers will certainly be able to think of other names but I am afraid the list will still be on the short side.

In science, mathematics and medicine I cannot think of a name. No negro has won a Nobel prize in science, medicine or literature. Jews, with less than 1 per cent of the world's population, have won more than sixty. It is difficult to escape from the proposition that the negroid and Jewish races are differently equipped. An intellectual upbringing probably helped Albert Einstein, but he still needed the quite extraordinary brain which only his heredity could provide.

African art is different. It was admired by Picasso. Unlike the bushmen, whose drawings are wonderfully natural, negro art is not representational. It appears to be based on the distortion of witch-doctor masks. To this the Ife bronzes are an exception. They are portrait heads of great beauty and can be dated at some time before the fifteenth century. I have little doubt that they are the work of a single master. As an art form in Africa they are without ancestry and without progeny. I do not believe that they are African. Some of the sitters are European in feature. We know from other sources that the medieval Sudanic cities owed their foundation to the North. I believe the artist was a Greek. The whole style is Greek. The technique of bronze casting was inherited by Benin from Ife, but not the art form. Benin bronzes are much admired but their form is grotesque. It is not for us to make value judgements as to whether African art is superior or inferior to the art of other races, it is sufficient to say that it is wholly different. The same may be said of negro music. The evidence of the negro performance both in Africa and America seems to me to establish that the black and white races have different capacities and different talents, and that the assumption that institutions that suit one will suit the other is without foundation.

Civilisation involves the balancing of interdependent specialist groups and interests within a dynamic association that can both hold together and change. It is something that has evolved through centuries during which the customs of urban and of rural groups have linked themselves within a system of accepted rights and duties. I do not think that civilisation can be imposed. In Negro Africa it can only be imposed, for there is nothing to build on. In Africa civilisation is an alien system, which an alien trained group using an alien language seek to impose. I do not think they will be successful. I do not believe that the negro people have evolved socially or probably biologically, to the point at which so complex a social arrangement is within their capacities. I think that the present batch of negro states will follow the path trodden by all their predecessors. They will revert to those forms of tribal society that are best suited to the evolutionary status of their members.

Let us consider the Imperial balance sheet. How has it served human society? The old American civilisations were destroyed, and the replacements were inadequate. It is hard to believe that left to themselves they would not have achieved a better society than they have now got. Equally I do not think that we can deny injuring the society of Bengal. In the settlement areas primitive societies have suffered. The Tasmanians have gone. The Australian aborigines are disappearing, as have many of the forest Indians of the Amazon. The Red Indians are exhibits in reserves. The Maoris of New Zealand are an exception. They have prospered and intermarried.

Settler populations, American, Canadian, Australian, New Zealand, in their initial phases benefited from Imperial support.

India, after many thousand years of social failure, has been provided with a new model, a new ethic and a new anglicised ruling class that is now in its fourth or fifth generation. If the Raj could have gone on a little longer, nationalism might have overtaken religion and the Indian sub-continent been saved the trauma of division.

Burma, after only fifty years of British rule, has reverted to the power vacuum which originally pulled us in, and she awaits another conqueror.

Malaysia and Singapore moved from under the Imperial umbrella before their racial and religious differences had come into balance. Their future is precarious.

To Java and Sumatra the Dutch have bequeathed a unifying xenophobia. 'Who-hates-who most' societies tend to shed a lot of blood in their formative period, but they do have a certain coherence.

Egypt, after twenty-five centuries of slavery, has received identity. Under British rule she developed a middle and officer class that was Egyptian. Sadat has used it for balance and authority.

The West Indies have exterminated the Caribs and replaced them with a mulatto society which will stay until the ethical weathercock shifts from self-government to good government. They show no signs of developing a coherence that will enable them to take this decision for themselves.

Negro Africa is the saddest case. Such civilisation as she has she owes to the colonialist. She is ruled by a small governing class that has adopted a colonial language and a colonial ethic. Only General Amin has an African background. In India it took four or five generations to develop an anglicised governing class. In Africa it is in its first generation. The Indians started with a civilised culture behind them, the Africans from the tribal level of social evolution. In spite of generous aid and assistance African society moves backwards. The need for integrity in public service is a lesson that has not been learned. Office is the opportunity to serve one's friends and enrich one's family. Opposition is intolerable. Law and order is breaking down. Government is a primitive form of fascism. Tragedy looms. Population and urbanisation require a scale of government that Africa is incapable of providing. The old negro empires could and did divert to tribalism. To a dense urban society tribalism is not available. The city states of the Southern Sahara provide a horrid example of what happened when colonial rule broke down and power over urban communities passed into negro hands.

What has been the effect on the colonial powers?

In Spanish America and in India there was initial plunder. Individual fortunes were made but the benefit to the Imperial State is doubtful. Spain got treasure, which probably did her more harm than good. Her position was not unlike that of the oil states. Her currency was inflated at a time when her industry was too undeveloped to benefit from increased purchasing power. Her enlarged capacity to import depressed her home production, and we find the Spanish Government forbidding the export of bullion without providing any scope for internal investment. Spain became and has remained Europe's depressed area. Britain did not get any treasure. John Company did its best to reduce 'the investment' and obtain its imports for nothing, but it was never quite successful. We always had to pay something for our Indian plunder, and consisting as it did for the most part of luxury goods and textiles, it contributed more to the gracious living of the rich than to the process of capital formation that was launching the Industrial Revolution. It has been argued that any reduction in the price of consumer goods increases the margin available for investment. In my observation it is more likely to increase consumption and set off that display competition that we call 'keeping up with the Joneses'. The personal fortunes of the Nabobs, as the robbers of Bengal were called, were invested in country estates, thereby inflating land values. But some of their money must have become available in one way or another for industrial investment. We are dealing with the days before statistics, and it is difficult to quantify the benefit, but it is probably true to say that the industrialisation of Britain owed something, but not very much, to Indian plunder.

With Pitt's India Act (1784) and the appointment of Cornwallis as Governor-General, the days of the Nabobs were over and the rulers of India no longer had fortunes to invest. From then onwards empire became an economic liability. In no single year since 1792, when relevant statistics first began to become available, has Britain had a favourable balance of payments with her colonies. We have not found our colonial empire a particularly profitable field of investment. During the heyday of imperialism in the thirty years before 1914, when we were investing over half our savings abroad, far more went to the Americas and to Europe than ever went to the Empire. We never bought cheaper or sold dearer in our colonies. The terms of trade, that is the relationship of the prices we pay for our imports to the prices we receive for our exports, have been far more favourable to us since we lost our Empire. The Lenin-Hobson theory that imperialists grow rich by exploiting their subjects has always been the opposite to the truth. Empires, like racing stables, are luxuries. They are rather fine things to have; one sometimes gets a winner but on balance they cost a lot more than they bring in. Britain paid for her Empire out of the profits which she earned in those parts of the world where she could trade without having to bear the cost of government. Of this she has always in a general way been aware, and her Empire grew in spite of the reluctance of her Government and over the protests of her Treasury. Europe has experienced the age of decolonisation, and all the ex-colonial powers have seen their standards of living rise much faster than at any period in their colonialist history. This has even been true of Holland, where the exploitation of Java looked profitable. Trade without the defence costs of empire has proved much more profitable. Only Portugal hung on, with disastrous consequences to her economy.

The benefits of Empire were spiritual rather than material. Britain was the first industrial nation. We became embarrassingly rich. The imperial will held us together and postponed our decadence for perhaps 150 years. It buttressed our sense of identity as Englishmen. The poet of the age, Rudyard Kipling, spoke of 'lesser breeds without the Law'. We were not as they were. We knew no equals. Our will was not merely the conqueror's will, although it included that high contempt for odds, it was nearer to that which the Greeks called *Arete*, a self-confidence rooted in the pride of conscious excellence. It involved not only the awareness that God was an Englishman but the recognition that he was a just servant of mankind. The Victorians knew that the duty to serve marched with their high destiny. Doctor Arnold's public school system mass-produced the subalterns of empire. Small boys were sent to boarding establishments where they were submitted to the mental disciplines of dead languages and to the physical disciplines imposed by older boys. Life was Spartan, government was arbitrary and punishment was corporal. I went to Eton in 1920. I was twelve. The process had softened, but there was still no central heating; the coal allowance was half a scuttle every other day; sanitation was outdoor; there was one bathroom, reserved for prefects; fags ran whenever the call 'boy' was heard; flogging was at the discretion of the Captain of the House and of the Captain of the Games. There was no appeal. The apprentice ruler learned what it was like to be on the receiving end of arbitrary government. He learned to accept injustice without undue resentment, and to trust nobody but himself. Above all, he was inoculated against unhappiness. Never again would he be so lonely, so helpless and so frightened. But there was joy too and, if one survived, *Arete*, the sense of eliteness. The system continues, but its purpose has gone. We no longer have a world to rule. The superiority, so expensively produced, is a snobbish embarrassment. As that great man Dean Acheson put it, we have lost an empire and failed to find a role. We need the qualities necessary to a small country, Swiss qualities, Norwegian qualities. They are not public schools qualities. We have lost an imperial will and we have found no substitute.

19

THE DECLINE OF THE

WEST

BEFORE THE Hitler's war had finished, the Allies had consulted as to world settlement. The League of Nations was not to be revived. The new world authority was to be more realistic. The victorious Allies would stay together and the United Nations would serve as the secretariat of a great power concert. It would be permanently domiciled in the USA. Power would be in the Security Council. America would have four permanent votes (Britain, France, Nationalist China and her own) and Russia one. A veto would confine the UN's activities to subjects upon which there was Great Power agreement. The General Assembly would be a debating forum without power, a sounding board for the little nations. The great power concert would keep the little nations in line and the agencies of the UN would confer on them benefits that would keep them happy.

It did not work. As in all previous associations of this sort, the interests that held the Allies together soon became weaker than those that divided them. Stalin preferred the expansion of his empire in Central Europe to the acceptance of American aid ond co-operation. America believed that she had an interest in Western European independence. The issue was settled by power and nerve. The Russians got Czechoslovakia but abandoned Austria and Greece. Germany was divided. So, after a fierce confrontation that at one point looked like war, was Berlin. Russia's army faced America's superior industrial power. When Russia blockaded Western-occupied Berlin, America demonstrated that she could supply this great urban population by air. Russia was impressed. Division was accepted and Russia built a wall to keep her Germans in. The UN played no part in this diplomatic battle for Europe. Peace depended on America and Russia judging each other's will and capacity correctly. In Asia America's friend Chiang Kai-shek was beaten by the Communists. Russia had advised against the Communist attack and contributed little to the victory. The UN again was irrelevant.

In Korea the position was a little different. Korea had been a Japanese colony and after Japan's surrender, it was occupied by Russia and America. The zones of occupation were divided by the 38th Parallel. America decided to terminate her occupation and withdrew her troops. Russia assumed that the US were no longer interested and their puppets in the North moved into the South. America reacted violently. Russia had withdrawn from the UN in protest at the continued presence of Chiang's representatives after Chiang had been chased out of China. This enabled America to use the UN as a front. Her allies, including Britain, sent token contributions. Had Russia attended the Security Council and said 'no', the UN flag would probably not have been displayed but it would have made no other difference. Korea was an American war, an assertion of American interest in the sanctity of the frontiers of her friends.

America used her power with generosity and restraint. Western Europe came to depend on American strength rather than upon her own. It was an insidious process. The A-bomb had a good deal to do with it. In the end the war did not seem to have been won by man but by a new power so enormous that man could not resist. Why then should man try? Why not trust the bomb and our great friend to whom the bomb belonged, to outlaw war? American generosity made European recovery surprisingly easy, firstly by cheap credit provided under the Bretton Woods Monetary Agreement and then by direct grant under the Marshall Aid scheme. We were fully employed building new riches and enjoying standards of living of which most Europeans had only dreamed.

The moment of truth came in 1952. Russia had exploded her first A-bomb and her H-bomb was nearly ready. War had broken out in Korea. In Europe confrontation was the order of the day. The North Atlantic Treaty Organisation (NATO) had been formed. The chiefs of staff of the member nations met at Lisbon to assess Europe's defence requirements and to advise. Their answer was fifty divisions at the ready, 120 divisions at so many days' notice, and air force of 4,000 combat planes. Most important of all, they advised that the main force must be held behind the Rhine so that it could be launched when the axis of enemy advance was disclosed.

This advice was turned down. The Allies were unwilling to provide the divisions and Germany was unwilling to provide the battlefield. The will to defend ourselves had gone. Instead we have made do with pretence.

Twenty-two divisions are stationed on the German frontier. They are not only hopelessly outnumbered but, the British apart, their quality is deplorable. American peacetime troops are not interested. The Germans have been successfully democratised and are heavily infiltrated from the East. The Dutch and Belgians are not serious troops, and the French have gone home. NATO lives where barracks happen to be. The British are farther from their deployment positions than are the Russians whom they face. German democratisation and the priority given to civil rights over military requirements makes any form of fortification or mining in the line of enemy advance impossible. If the Russians moved NATO would not last a week. In the unlikely event of anyone using tactical nuclears most strategic analysts believe that they would advantage the attacker rather than the defender. Europe is defenceless and in England we now have a generation that has never pulled a trigger. This assessment is based on a report I wrote some ten years ago when I was spokesman on military matters for the Labour Party then in opposition. At that time I had access to defence documents and opportunities to discuss the situation with officials and generals. My report was discussed with the late Sir Basil Liddell-Hart and its contents had his agreement. I have no reason to believe that our defence posture as compared to the offensive posture of the Warsaw Pact has improved during the decade which has passed since I wrote my report. On the contrary I am certain that it has deteriorated.

Britain and France have built nuclears of their own, but this has not contributed either to their security or to their independence.

The question as to whether nuclears could ever be used in war has been much debated by strategic analysts, but I think all are agreed that it could only be very small ones. As has been pointed out in earlier chapters war is an affair of Kings or governments, it involves capacities to command and control. This is a mutual requirement. There is little point in winning unless there is someone with the authority to surrender. If you destroy authority you acquire nought but anarchy. Nuclears used on any scale would do just this. The warring nations would cease to exist as nations, because the channels of command that go to make a nation would have been destroyed. The function of nuclears is not to fight but to deter. Their value depends on their not being used.

Now how does this game of deterrence work? It has its rules. If you propose to deter you have got to recognise that you can be deterred.

Nuclears have not been very successful in deterring non-nuclear powers. Suez occurred just when our nuclears had become operational. They had no effect on Nasser or anyone else. We became involved in warlike operations with Indonesia. Our nuclear capacity was irrelevant. The only instance I know of in which nuclear deterrents worked against a non-nuclear power was when the Israelis painted 'Nuclear Cannon' in Arabic on a tarpaulin and a Syrian brigadier, reading it through his binoculars, bolted with his brigade.

But once one has got nuclears one can no longer ignore them; one is committed to their credibility; one has joined the game, and it is a game the lesser power must lose.

The Rand Institute of Strategic Research in California made a study of Britain's vulnerability. Their assessment was that it would take eleven medium nuclears to destroy Britain as a political unit capable of acting as a nation. We are within range and totally defenceless against at least 500 Soviet medium nuclear rockets. Supposing that we found ourselves in confrontation with the Russians on an issue which they considered vital and as an act of coercion they put a nuclear on, say, Northampton, saying at the same time submit or London, Birmingham and Glasgow go tomorrow. What would we do? Would we launch a Polaris at one of their cities and die? Of course not, unless we had a lunatic in charge. We would have no alternative to submission. Our nuclear defence is a busted flush and our cards are transparent. The same is true of France. Western population is concentrated in easy target areas. In 1940 France surrendered Paris rather than submit the city to conventional bombardment.

American protection has involved acceptance of American foreign policy. This indeed is the traditional price.

The Suez incident brought home our satellite status. Britain had, since the Disraeli purchase in the middle of the nineteenth century, been the leading shareholder in the international company that owned and administered the Suez Canal. The canal had traditionally been rated as a vital British interest, as our link with India and with our oil in the Gulf. Nasser, the new Egyptian nationalist leader, had nationalised this item of international property. His action had certainly involved breach of several treaty obligations. He was also entertaining a rebel government of Algiers, then a French colony, and terrorist forces who were raiding Israel. Britain, France and Israel determined to take independent military action to enforce their rights. Foster Dulles, the US Secretary of State, whose ineptitude had been the principal cause of the trouble, was furious and imposed a most humiliating withdrawal. Harold Macmillan, then Chancellor of the Exchequer, declared that failure to comply with America's wishes would endanger the pound. Nothing could better have expressed our loss of independence and of will. Without even noticing it Britain had ceased to be a power.

France tried to regain her self-respect by turning to General de Gaulle, the wartime leader of the Free French. The first thing he had to do was to accept defeat in Algiers. This followed on defeat in Indo-China. De Gaulle wished to escape from American dependence. He developed a nuclear force. It proved no more credible than the British. He left NATO. This made little difference, for NATO was but a pretence. He made anti-American noises. He aspired to create a Europe under French leadership that would be a super power, a third force that would balance the world. We heard much of Europe's manpower and of her productivity potential. It was reminiscent of France's, 'We are the strongest' wartime propaganda. It forgot that the will was no longer there. De Gaulle died, but Gaullism had died first. There was no stamina in France's short-lived bout of self-respect. Neither the Federalist aspirations of the Common Marketeers nor de Gaulle's Charlemagne romance have discovered any European will. The military impotence of NATO is irrelevant. Europe has no will to defend itself.

Germany is divided; Nazism, with its glory, its guilt and its disaster is old history. War, hunger, defeat and humiliation is remembered experience. Germany is no longer romantic. On both sides of her divide are pragmatic German nations dedicated to getting the best out of things as they are. Anything is better than war. Leon Trotsky called this process Belgianisation; the renunciation of all national vision, dreams and ideals in favour of the universal pursuit of individual wealth and comfort. The West is rich, comfortable and successful. It wishes without belief, that things could always be this way, but few West Germans have failed to consider their personal role within the alternative Eastern dispensation if and when it comes. Fewer still are in any doubt that it is better to be Red than Dead. A NATO report published in March 1976 stated that there are 16,000 Russian agents working in Western Germany. I do not know how the count was made save on the basis that being a Russian agent is today an accepted West German profession, and that they are the people with whom one arranges one's personal insurance should the Russians come. Of one thing, however, I am confident, West Germany will not resist an Eastern advance should one come.

The Italian Communists are on the way to becoming a part of the Italian Government. They have proclaimed themselves nationalists and supporters of NATO. Those who like comforting beliefs may believe. In France too, the principal working class movement is Communist and the Communist-Socialist alliance looks very like winning power. The French Communists certainly possess the power to prevent French participation in a war against Russia. Russia would not have to invade. She has only to blow her trumpets for the walls to come tumbling down.

Initially Europe was guarded by American nuclear threats. Today, as a result of the SALT agreements between Russia and USA these threats have gone for each has bared his breast and knows that nuclear assault means death to the attacker as surely as to the attacked. Our safety depends on the strongly conservative instincts of the gerontocracy in Moscow, old tired men who feel their Empire cannot manage any more people and hope that the present dispensation will see them out. When a new young Czar comes to power, believing perhaps in World Revolution as a policy rather than as an incantation, then we will know that the end of our world is nigh.

Of the major European powers, Britain alone has retained some faith in herself. This may in part be due to her traditional stupidity and in part to her experience. To Britain war has been something that happened in other people's countries and ended in victory. Many Britons died, but they won. After all, we won the Second World War. We did not repeat our mistakes of 1918. We elected a new parliament of young men, many of them very able. We chose a new, forward-looking government. In Attlee, Bevin and Cripps we found some remarkable leaders. The task of demobilisation and reconstruction went through smoothly and without social bitterness, but during the fifties we began to lose our grip.

We had lost our imperial role and there was no other role for us. We had ceased to be a power and become a small country. We needed to escape from the vanities of our former greatness. We needed to believe in ourselves within our new limits. The new Commonwealth was no substitute for old empire. It is a phoney association within which Britain accepts responsibilities and receives no loyalties. Still less is Europe a substitute. Europe can offer no more than an alliance with allies of proven worthlessness.

Britain needs to learn the Swedish lesson, which is that there is no substitute for empire and that when empire goes, one must settle down to be oneself. This Britain has so far been unable to accept. By continuing to pretend to a position which is no longer hers she has been losing faith in herself. We think far too much of the individual and far too little of the state. We think of ourselves as trade unionists or as employers or as shop-keepers or as farmers, as anything except Englishmen. Our nationalised industries have become corporations devoted to serving miners, railwaymen or postmen. The idea of serving the public is lost. We are losing respect for our public institutions. Never have Parliament and its Members been held in such contempt. Our laws are respected less. Our children are rejecting the authority of parent, teacher and state. Crime mounts every year and juvenile crime mounts fastest. There may yet be time for Britain to recover but we shall have to do it by our own efforts. Europe is not going to be our salvation. We will not escape decadence by joining greater decadence. We shall not acquire a will to defend our liberties from nations who have abandoned all will to defend their own. We will not survive indefinitely under American protection, because it is becoming more and more evident America is losing both the will and the means to protect us. We shall have to protect our own independence.

I think that the prospects of the neutrals, small powers like Sweden and Switzerland who are prepared to mind their own business is good. Resistance and guerrilla tactics have been developed. Great powers no longer voluntarily take on the job of ruling small states within which they can expect to find an organised and resolute resistance. We ourselves have got out of Eire and only wish we could get out of Ulster. Finland and Greece enjoy reasonable security. I do not think that Russia is interested in occupying states within which there is no Communist Party capable of becoming an effective government. The real deterrent is not nuclear weapons that cannot be used, but a population trained and determined to resist. If we care for national survival we should get out of NATO, get rid of our nuclears, give our young men a period of national training, and organise them into local resistance units. Citizens need the experience of discipline. Undisciplined societies do not survive long.

America

America had supreme power, but she lacked the self-confidence to use it. The rot had started in the Twenties. Her sense of 'manifest destiny' had gone. It was partly a case of *trahison des clercs*. Europe was in shock as a result of her appalling First War casualties. Pacifism had become the fashion and America had always tended to follow the European fashion in ideas. She became infected with that irresponsibility of which pacifism is a symptom. She withdrew into isolation and reneged on her great power responsibilities. Having rejected 'manifest destiny' herself, she resented the assumption of the civilising responsibility by others. She became anti-colonial. Prohibition too played a part in this creeping irresponsibility, for it made of crime both an industry and a political force. Respect for authority was damaged. The boom years concentrated minds on the pursuit if not of happiness, at least of individual prosperity, and the great slump shook faith in a society that had enriched men so quickly and impoverished them so suddenly. War came again to mend the system. America has been lucky with her wars, for they have always come when her constitution has needed refreshment, but this time victory did not restore the confidence of Teddy Roosevelt's decade.

A people who are to lead the world cannot afford to doubt themselves, or to question the righteousness of their authority. The Americans had been brought up to question all authority including especially that of their own government. They now doubted America's right to impose her leadership. America wanted to be loved. She was generous. She was permissive. She was irresponsible. She had the wrong sort of faith for the destiny that was now hers.

The test of will came soon. Russia started to build an atom bomb. Should she be permitted to do so? America was in a position to adopt the words of the Great Khan of the Mongols, 'Stop and if thou stoppest not the Great Khan knoweth not what will happen for God alone knows what will happen', or more specifically, she could have said 'Stop and deliver your nuclears either to us or the United Nations if you find that easier, and if you do not we will put an A-bomb on your nuclear complex while we have the power to do so and you lack the power to retaliate.' Only Bertrand Russell, the pacifist, urged her to do so. Of course any US demand of this sort would have been quite illegal. In the life of nations law is for calm water. President Kennedy's prohibition of atomic deployment on Cuba was illegal. Britain has sunk two neutral fleets, rather than risk her security. The great must be tough. The world today would be a far safer place had America possessed an imperial will.

In Korea the American army was humiliated by the Chinese Communists who did not believe she had the will to use her ultimate weapon, and eventually she had to accept a compromise peace. In Vietnam a much larger American army was defeated and disgraced. America has not been able to manage the 'little Tory wars' that were the price of Pax Britannica. Neither Korea nor Vietnam were formally-declared wars and the executive did not receive the same accretion of powers that had so greatly benefited America's polity in earlier wars.

The results were all bad. America has now lost her primacy in military power. Her nuclear capacity has in effect been neutralised as a result of the SALT negotiations and the effective power of her army and navy have fallen behind the Russian. She can no longer control her allies because she can no longer protect them. This was the real casualty of the Vietnam war. At the very beginning of that war I had a conversation with Mr Rusk, then Kennedy's Secretary of State, and asked him what America's stake in Indo-China was. He replied, 'It is the worth of our guarantee everywhere.'

America and the world have lost what Teddy Roosevelt referred to as 'the international police authority'. At San Francisco in the last years of the war she had agreed that the United Nations should have this international police power believing that she and her friends the Russians would have a common interest in world order and that through the Security Council they would be able to use the UN as their instrument. Largely as a result of her adventures into anti-colonialism the USA has lost control of the UN, where the majority is now controlled by gentlemen whose titles rest on the victory of lawless violence in their country's latest coup. American intervention at Suez ended the traditional right of great powers to enforce their treaty and property rights. We have found no substitute. World order has receded some centuries. Small, weak, semi-civilised states do not hesitate to nationalise without compensation the property of other nationals; or to refuse compensation to foreigners whom they have failed to protect from the lawless violence of their mobs; or to permit the formation of guerrilla training camps within their borders or to give asylum to the hi-jackers of other people's aircraft. If the matter is taken to UNO it will be the victims who are censured.

The root trouble has been lack of American self-confidence. At home American government is failing. The office of President is weak. General Eisenhower was a conciliator. When he became Commander in Chief in Europe he had never commanded a formation in war. His job was to keep happy the various Allied generals serving in his command. He did it very well. I got to know him when he had the NATO command. Nobody could have been more welcoming and charming to visiting Allied politicians. He always said the right thing. He made no enemies. He believed he could run the Presidency in the same way, but the Presidency is a very different job. It requires a tough, mean, power-hungry ruler. Under Eisenhower the Presidency lost authority. Nobody ruled. Kennedy died too soon, Johnson did something to restore authority and then came Nixon and disgrace. All that the Roosevelts had done to give America the government a great state needs, has been dissipated.

Order is breaking down. During the four years of war in Europe and in the Pacific America averaged 220 fatal casualties per day. Today, in peace-time, more than twice as many die daily, by violence. Murders have increased from 8,000 in 1960 to nearly 25,000 in 1975. (For comparison England and Scotland with rather more than a quarter of America's population, averages about 200 murders a year.) Violent crime (murder, rape, robbery, felonious wounding) has increased from 287,000 in 1960 to over a million in 1975.

The great conurbations are out of control. Traditionally cities have been corrupt. They have been ruled by politicians who have organised new arrivals from the countryside and from Europe and in time the new arrivals were absorbed. Since the war European immigration has been greatly reduced and the new arrivals have been black. The massive war and post war boom attracted Southern negro labour to the North and West. Over a million negroes have been demobilised from the US forces. The great majority have moved into the towns. They have not been absorbed. The result has been anarchy. The violent crime rate for negroes runs at between ten and eighteen times that for whites. The city crime rate is six times that of the rural crime rate. In America's capital city during 1974 to 1975 natural causes account for less than half the recorded deaths. Negroes and Puerto Ricans have taken over many city centres and whites have moved to the suburbs. Anyone who has lived in a large American city for twenty years without being the victim of a violent crime can rate his luck as better than average for the urban victim rate is one in nineteen every year. It is far safer to live in Belfast. How long can it go on?

International corporations are another field within which government control seems to be diminishing. Corporations like Standard Oil, Ford, General Motors, Lockheed, Gulf Oil, ITC and IBM have more money and produce more wealth than most countries. Their position is analogous to that of religious orders in medieval society. They are international states within national states.

Americans of first-rate ability tend to prefer corporation service to government service. In their dealings with the US government it is generally the government official who pulls up the chair. Within their world-wide interests they maintain intelligence services which are often better than the CIA and they run private foreign policies. Their movements of funds can and do affect the stability of national currencies. The siting of their factories becomes a major factor in the economies of host countries. In many countries corruption is what greases the wheels. Experience of recent years has demonstrated that the US Government is not all that incorruptible. It was widely rumoured that ITT settled a trust-breaking suit by paying for the Democratic Convention at San Diego. It is certain that ITT did much to promote rebellion in Chile, as did the International Fruit Company in other Central Ameri-

can republics. If the foreign policy of the corporations co-
incides with that of the USA it is indeed purely coincidental.

Discipline has been less than automatic in the army, in the
universities, in the schools and in the home. When the army
was withdrawn from Vietnam much of it was in a state of
near mutiny, in which officers dared not give orders for fear
of their men's weapons. D. H. Lawrence once said 'The
essential American soul is hard, isolate, stoic and a killer'. He
might have had this army in mind. The stories that have
come back have done much to undermine American confidence both in her army and in her government.

Breakdown of discipline in the home must in some measure
be ascribed to the failures of the American male to assert
himself. Man has from hunting days been the provider. He
has left home to hunt, work or fight. Woman has run the
home and governed the children but when father came back
he was master. In a measure this suited the wife. Her
authority was backed by the threat 'You see what happens
to you when I tell your father'. The American male has
tended to be too tired when he gets home. America spends
on advertising rather more than she spends on liquor and
tobacco and three times as much as she spends on her social
services. That advertising is directed to convince the poor
American that he always needs something else and that he
is a poor thing if he does not get it, and to convince his wife
that she will be socially degraded if he does not. Employer
and wife are on the same lines. They are driving the poor
fellow to exhaustion. The same advertising pushes the wife
into social competition with her neighbours. Labour-saving
devices relieve her of home drudgery. She joins women's
clubs. She finds herself recruited to good works where she will
meet nice people or to bad works where she will have fun.
Either way she finds herself too busy to look after the
children and her husband. The divorce rate is high. The television looks after the children. Violence maximises the
audience assembled for commercials. Neglected children form
gangs where 'rep' depends on violence.

When the child goes to school he does not go to a very
good school. America spends on education less than half as

much as she spends on motor cars and about the same as on advertising. School teachers are paid on average less than industrial workers. Some hold on, but many have gone over to industry where they earn a lot more money. The size of forms has become unwieldly. Schools in rich suburbs have been subsidised by subscription and local taxation. Funds of this sort become more difficult to raise when the authorities start 'busing' in negro children, so as to promote integration. It is not a policy that works well, either educationally or socially. When 'Project Talent' examined 450,000 students they found that only 1 per cent could write a five-minute essay without grammatical mistakes. The Military Selective Service test has proved to be beyond nearly a third of the school leavers. It is a very simple test that goes little beyond the three 'Rs'.

By our standards American schools are permissive. Some indeed are jungles in which pupils and teachers are terrorised by child gangs. In New York an average of about a dozen children a year die in school gang warfare. Dope too is a problem. According to a report by Nelson Rockefeller's Council on Drug Addiction in New York, the child that leaves school without having tried drugs is an exception. Some are using narcotics at the age of eight.

School leavers rarely have sufficient education to warrant specialisation, but they go to university where they are offered an extraordinary variety of specialist courses. many of which we would consider more appropriate for a technical high school. One can, for instance, get a degree in embalming. This tends to discredit degrees. When American graduates come to our universities they seem to be about level or a little behind the entry from our schools. During the Vietnam war most universities were at one time or another paralysed by anti-war campus riots. Student bodies assumed, and in many instances retain, power to review the disciplinary decisions of the authority and the authority submits rather than face student violence.

In Europe we have similar symptoms; the loss of pride, of discipline and of faith in our nations; the breakdown of family life; criminal violence, juvenile delinquency and the young who contract out of the system and live on doles in much the same way as the medieval beggar lived on alms, but the American disease is far more advanced than ours.

Western civilisation is very sick indeed. What has gone wrong? Firstly the family.

The family is the woman's. She bears, suckles, protects and rules the children. The home is hers. When Mum is not there, there is no home. The enlarged family is the domain of Grandmamma. I believe it is to this matriarchy of the home that the Jewish people owe their durability. It is not merely coincidence that links female emancipation with the decadence of every civilisation we have looked at. There are many different forms of emancipation. Rich women have always wished to get rid of their chores and have employed nurses, nursemaids and governesses. All aristocracies have neglected their children, but there has been discipline in the nursery; servants have sometimes proved effective substitute parents and in England there has been the public school system. In America there is affluence without servants and the boarding school system is almost non-existent. The emancipated American mother tends to leave the home empty. The child has a key and knows how to switch on the television. Generally available housing has in most places abolished the enlarged family, for Grandmamma is apt to live on a caravan site in Florida.

In Europe affluence takes more earning. It generally needs two pay packets. Our latch-key children usually have mothers who go out to work, but the result is much the same, a generation of insecure delinquents. Of course this is not universal and it is not nearly as bad in Europe as it is in America. Housing shortage still leaves us with some extended families, but they are not very successful for we have created an atmosphere in which they feel deprived and in which every wife feels that society and her husband owes her a home of her own.

I spent thirty years involved as an MP in Northampton's housing problems. I remember an old friend, Albert Hope, of the Boot and Shoe Union, telling me about the Northampton of his youth sixty or seventy years ago. It had about one-third of the houses that it has now for seven tenths of its present population. There were 'To Let' notices in every street. Landlords were offering houses with a month rent free. At the end of the month there were secret midnight flits to get the furniture out. People could not afford homes of their own. When the children came home they might find much that was deplorable, but they did not find the home empty. Juvenile delinquency is not easy to measure but in so far as one can judge from police returns, it was then at about one twentieth of its present level.

America has lost faith in herself. Faith involves a capacity for dichotomy. The founding fathers had no difficulty in believing in slavery and liberty. They had faith in both. America today has no such faith. She doubts herself and all she does. She suffers from a guilt complex with regard to her blacks. This may or may not be well founded, but its results are unfortunate, for she seeks to impose on them and on the community an equality of opportunity of which they are incapable of taking advantage. Men accept caste, class and status within a traditional system. It is not one's fault if one is born an Untouchable or a peasant, one can still retain one's self-respect, but if one is given all the opportunities and still finds oneself hewing wood and drawing water, then life is unbearable and one can only compensate for ones inadequacy by violence. This is the unhappy situation of the American negro. He is not on average competitive within a civilised society. Other immigrants started at the bottom and worked their way up. The negro stays at the bottom. The white man begins to resent the opportunities the negro wastes, the deterioration of the schools to which he is bussed, and when unemployment is a problem, the jobs which he holds as a result of anti-discrimination legislation merely because he is black.

Negro frustration mounts particularly in the North and West, where there is no traditional framework. The great negro riots have been in northern and western cities in which there has been no tradition of segregation. They have not been directed against the white man. The wrecking, looting and burning has been in the negro quarters and has involved an element of self-destruction. The authorities refrain from taking the steps necessary to maintain order because they feel it would be discriminatory to do so, with the result that the negro quarters have become jungles. This disorder is infectious.

In American civil government there is a general lack of faith in the state. Gambling and dope are what gin was in prohibition days, the stock-in-trade of crime, and crime is big business with its own lawyers and a stake in politics. The civil rights of the criminal are well understood and skilfully exploited. The police get little or no co-operation from the public. When hold-ups and muggings occur on crowded streets nobody sees anything and the victim is left lying on the pavement.

In Europe we have mounting crime rates and deteriorating order, but on nothing like the same scale. Kidnapping is a relatively new crime. It results from weak government and will continue as long as kidnappers get the ransom. There is a general slackening of respect for the law. Nobody believes in anything much.

All political ideas work themselves out long before they reach their logical conclusions. This has been the fate of liberalism. It broke a system of authority and privilege that had outlived its purpose; it released great energies that had long been frustrated; it was a faith that conquered, but now it has swung past its apogee, for it no longer inspires the self-confidence that was identity, the belief in progress that was stimulation and the unity that was security. The old authorities—parent, school master, employer, priest and magistrate —have lost their power and no adequate system of self-discipline has emerged to replace them. The parliamentary system first in France, then in Britain and now in America has lost respect. The West's need for order has become at least as great as the East's need for liberty. I do not think the West can retrace its steps. It may recover its greatness, as Rome did under the Dacian emperors, but as in Rome a new faith must be found. States need a divinity with which the citizen can identify himself, for they do not live long without adoration.

Whether we like it or not we may have to do with less liberty and accept more authority. I doubt whether family formation can be left much longer to private whim. The pill, safe abortion and the control of infant and child mortality have radically altered the problems of reproduction. I think that sex's emancipation from the Christian doctrine of sin is likely to continue. Sexual sensuality is an especially human characteristic in which our species ought to take pride. It is about tenderness. It is only incidentally and occasionally concerned with reproduction. Adolescent pairing is likely to become even more acceptable than it is today, but the production of illegitimate children is another matter. It is one with which the state must be concerned. Wives should receive a good wage from public funds but this should not be payable to wives who engage in employment outside the home. Child allowances will probably be generous, but divorce while there are children at home should be very difficult indeed. If we are to have secure families within the sort of society that we in the West have evolved motherhood will have to be a career.

We may find we have to do with less equality. Equality is for the tribe, inequality is the basis of civilisation. Men are not created equal, they are created different. Man's genius lies in his variety, but he is still a pack animal needing leaders, a great variety of leaders. An elite has always been necessary to his advancement. The purpose of education is to promote inequality, to provide every pupil with the opportunities to develop every unequal talent which he may possess. An advancing society needs an elite to lead at all the levels of its varied activities. The greater the variety the better. Ideally everyone should have the chance of leading at something. Education may become more selective.

Equality of opportunity neither can nor should be complete. It cannot be complete because the child of superior parents has on balance a better heredity and a better environment; it should not be because society needs an element of stability and feels in a very general way that it is right and proper for children to acquire the same kind of status as their fathers. Career must be open to the talents but we do not all want to be conscripted for a universal rat-race. The farm-worker's son who becomes a farm worker should be able to respect himself and need not resent the farmer's son who becomes a farmer. If equality of opportunity is pushed too far it involves a race in which there are too many losers.

The rights of owners are decreasing and are likely to decrease further. In the liberal revolution the men of privilege were overturned by the men of property. The rights and privileges of property were set high. Over the years they have been eroded. In industry the managerial revolution has transferred power from the owner to the manager. Agriculture is controlled by farmers with security of tenure. The state exercises more and more authority over use and management. Whether we like it or not the means of production, distribution and exchange are likely to pass more and more into public control. Ownership is losing its functions and its rewards are likely to diminish. The role of the state as a shareholder and landowner is increasing and is likely to increase further.

The 'bigger the better' principle may be reversed. The movement towards what in a general way we now call socialism seems to be inevitable and in small countries socialism is a lot pleasanter to live with than it is in big ones. In an age when big wars have become unmanageable small countries are more defensible than they used to be. Big corporations are developing bureaucracies that we are finding more and more difficult to live with. The next age may see them breaking into smaller units. The performance of the United Nations and of the Common Market have disillusioned many who treasured internationalist ideals and thought in terms of world government.

The rewards and prestige of status are likely to go up. This is of course the Russian system. Country houses, town flats, servants, cars, special schools, special shops, dower houses for widows, pensions paid in privilege, all go with the top jobs. Industry has been inclined to follow this example. Top managers have Rolls-Royces, chauffeurs and entertain at the Ritz, one below come Rovers, lady chauffeurs and Grosvenor house, and so on down the line. Special pensions and education schemes for the children often go with the job.

The state already uses honours to pay for a lot of valuable services, and there are still men who will do more for a knighthood than a pay rise. Life peerages have replaced hereditary peerages. Status privilege is replacing and will continue to replace property privilege. We are moving from a society rewarded by, and in general ranked in accordance with, wealth, into one where prestige depends more on a man's job than on his riches and is expressed in his privileges rather than in his cash.

Japan has been remarkably successful in linking private enterprise and social cohesion.

When, in the mid-nineteenth century, Western civilisation broke into Japan's chosen seclusion, she determined to beat the West at its own game. She did so. She garnered and applied the knowledge of the West but she did it in a Japanese way.

The liberal faith proclaims that all men (and women) are very much the same. Observation says otherwise. Species and societies that evolve separately evolve differently. Social habits, relationships and mores evolve as society evolves. National personality, like private personality, is a social adjustment. The more I have studied comparative sociology, the more I have been impressed by the homogeneity of re-actions within a social unit and the variety as between societies.

Like the British, the Japanese are a group of tribes that have, through feudalism, evolved a balance of duty, obliga-tion and mutual respect that has resulted in a society based on compromise rather than upon submission, but here the resemblance ends. The Japanese system of social relationship is different to that of the West, and Japanese personality is different because it is adjusted to a different society. The West has developed the cult of the individual and Western society is an association of individuals concerned primarily with their rights. The Japanese think of themselves as mem-bers of a group, the family, the business, the team, and they are primarily concerned with the duties they owe to the groups to which they belong, and gain their satisfaction from group success and from their standing within the group. This group feeling provides a social coherence which the West lacks.

The Japanese extended family is a hierarchy built on a structure of mutual obligations. Almost any Japanese to whom one talks will tell you that as an institution the family is in decay, but all things are relative. What he really means is that the modern young man and, to a lesser extent, young woman, demands some say in such questions as to whom he or she will be married, that the Japanese wife may sometimes go to tea with a friend without asking her husband's permission, and that students sometimes become rebellious. There has been an increase in juvenile crime, but by our standards it is from almost nil to very little. There have been riots in universities, but the rebel students generally slip back into their social niches. The Japanese have a word for it—*tenko*. It expresses the Japanese fear of social loneliness, and the need to creep back into conformity.

Japanese businesses are tribes. The employee is not just taken on, he is initiated and he stays for his working life. He becomes a business tribesman. He identifies his own success and that of his nation with the success of the firm for which he works. Defence Secretary Wilson's famous *faux pas*, 'What is good for General Motors is good for the United States', would have been totally acceptable in Japan.

The Japanese man is far more concerned with harmony within his group than with the assertion of his own personality. In decision-making the search is for consensus rather than authority. Everybody concerned is consulted, and the process often starts at the bottom and works its way up. Decisions are often long delayed while the search for consensus continues, but once the decision is taken implementation is whole-hearted. Those who have given way are not humiliated. On the contrary, they have placed the majority under an obligation and can expect additional weight to be given to their wishes next time. Promotion, at any rate up to board level, is strictly by seniority. The tribe does not want jealousy or anything much in the way of internal competition within the organisation. Junior staff tend to be under-paid, but find this acceptable because they know they will become senior in their turn. Unions are company unions primarily concerned with the good of the company.

Personal ethics play very little part. Japanese ethics are group ethics. Good is that which tends towards the harmony of the group, and evil that which disrupts. The trouble-maker is on the lowest rung of the ethical ladder. The Japanese have little sense of guilt but much concern with shame, for they are very sensitive to the opinion of others. They are haunted by the fear of bringing shame on their family, their business or their nation. They have little concern with conventional religion, for their god is Japan and it is Japan that inspires their most potent faith.

The Japanese appear to have devised a system within which the groupings that are natural to man are harnessed to success in a competitive world. Herman Kahn, the author of *The Emerging Japanese Super State,* has prophesied that the twenty-first century will be the Japanese century. He may well be right.

For us Westerners the great unsolved problem of the future is faith. This is the one thing that all the civilisations that we have looked at have had in common, they have all believed and served something greater than themselves. Our grandfathers believed in God, king and empire, our fathers believed in the great liberal commonweealth. For these faiths they were willing to live and to sacrifice and to die. We believe in the individual and the individual is a lonely creature. Authority is breaking down because we have lost faith in the purpose of authority. Nothing matters much any more so long as Jack, the individual, is all right. How do we create that faith which alone can bind our society together now that war has become too dangerous to do its traditional job?

It may be that the era of *Homo sapiens* is nearing its end.

Evolutionary advance demands heavy culling. This the ice ages provided. Living was terribly hard. Only the fit and the foresighted survived. It was then that man developed the big head that distinguishes *Homo sapiens* from *Homo erectus.* When the weather improved thirty or forty thousand years ago, man's evolutionary progress seems to have stopped. Some people believe that it has receded and point out that modern man's cranium is on average no larger than that of Neanderthal man and smaller than that of Cromagnon man. As against this it may be said that whilst in a general way there seems to be a correlation amongst the anthropoids between cranium capacity and intelligence, it is an over simplification to assume that a larger brain is necessarily a more intelligent one. It depends on which bits are larger. Let it suffice us to say that there is no evidence that man's ability today is greater than that of the men who, with no cultural heritage behind them, created the great cave paintings; still less can modern man claim to be superior to the inventors of civilisation or to the Greeks of the fourth and fifth centuries BC.

Homo sapiens has been successful. He has increased, but until recently war, famine and pestilence have kept that increase within reasonable bounds. As a species he did not, until recently, outrun the resources available to him but during the last century this has changed. Population growth has become a geometrical progression. The dead are no longer the great majority. Probably less than a million survived the ice ages. By the time the first cities began to appear eight or nine thousand years ago, the population may have reached five million. By 1,500 BC (the Cretan Palaces, the Achaeans, Stonehenge, the Shepherd kings, the Indus cities and early Babylon) the population may have numbered 70 million, by the year 1 perhaps 150 million, by AD 1,600 500, by AD 1,800 900, by AD 1900 1,500 million. Then the acceleration really took off. By AD 1950 the population had doubled to 3,000 million, by 1990 it will have doubled again to 6,000 million. More than half the men who have ever lived have lived in my life time. Nearly two thirds of the built up area in the world was open land when I was born; 350,000 years ago man was using fire. Of the fire man has used for heat, transport, power and war, four fifths has been used during my life time. I am 70. This population explosion has not resulted from larger families, on the contrary almost everywhere couples have been having fewer children. The trouble has been that public health has checked nature's cull. Too few babies have died. More and more unfit babies are surviving to puberty and passing on their inferior genes. Anybody who has been concerned with the breeding of a pack of hounds or of a herd of cattle knows that when the cull is inadequate the pack or herd deteriorates. This is not a process that can just go on. Something has to cut the population back.

Civilised man has pinned his hopes on family planning. Mrs Gandhi who faced the severest problem, found to her cost that effective family planning needed a very authoritarian government indeed. If the multiplication and deterioration of our species is to be checked by birth control governments will have to intervene in a big way. That they will do so is unlikely.

The answer is far more likely to be catastrophe because catastrophe is far more available. At least a dozen nations have the means to make nuclear weapons. Tens of thousands of nuclear warheads, hundreds or thousands of times more powerful than that which wrecked Nagasaki, exist. Surely it is only a question of time before somebody lets some of these off.

As in the ice ages, man will be faced with an environment within which living will be very difficult. Survival will be for the Dr Strangeloves, the ablest, the most disciplined and the most foresighted. In evolutionary terms a radioactive atmosphere has major advantages for it promotes genetic mutations. The world will be full of freaks; few will survive but some favourable mutations will appear and assert their superiority by surviving. The transition from *Homo sapiens* to *Homo the next* may be quicker and larger than that from *Homo erectus* to *Homo sapiens*.

INDEX